T0191604

UNDERGRADUATE TEXTS IN COMPUTER SCIENCE

Editors
David Gries
Fred B. Schneider

Springer
New York
Berlin
Heidelberg
Barcelona
Hong Kong
London
Milan
Paris
Singapore
Tokyo

UNDERGRADUATE TEXTS IN COMPUTER SCIENCE

David R. Brooks

C Programming:
The Essentials for
Engineers and Scientists

With 39 Illustrations

 Springer

David R. Brooks
Department of Mathematics
   and Computer Science
Drexel University
Philadelphia, PA 19104
USA

Series Editors
David Gries
Fred B. Schneider
Department of Computer Science
Cornell University
Upson Hall
Ithaca, NY 14853-7501
USA

Library of Congress Cataloging-in-Publication Data
Brooks, David R., 1941–
      C programming : the essentials for engineers and scientists /
   David R. Brooks.
         p.   cm. — (Undergraduate texts in computer science)
      Includes bibliographical references and index.
      ISBN 0-387-98632-4 (alk. paper)
      1. C (Computer program language). I. Title. II. Series.
   QA76.73.C15B755   1998
   500'.285'5133—dc21   98-31041

Printed on acid-free paper.

Production coordinated by Robert Wexler and managed by Steven Pisano; manufacturing supervised by
Jacqui Ashri.
Photocomposed copy prepared from the author's Word Perfect files.

9 8 7 6 5 4 3 2 1

ISBN 0-387-98632-4 Springer-Verlag New York Berlin Heidelberg SPIN 10693889

Preface

1 The Purpose of This Text

This text has been written in response to two trends that have gained considerable momentum over the past few years. The first is the decision by many undergraduate engineering and science departments to abandon the traditional programming course based on the aging Fortran 77 standard. This decision is not surprising, considering the more modern features found in languages such as Pascal and C. However, Pascal never developed a strong following in scientific computing, and its use is in decline. The new Fortran 90 standard defines a powerful, modern language, but this long-overdue redesign of Fortran has come too late to prevent many colleges and universities from switching to C. The acceptance of C by scientists and engineers is based perhaps as much on their perceptions of C as an important language, which it certainly is, and on C programming experience as a highly marketable skill, as it is on the suitability of C for scientific computation. For whatever reason, C or its derivative C++ is now widely taught as the first and often only programming language for undergraduates in science and engineering.

The second trend is the evolving nature of the undergraduate engineering curriculum. At a growing number of institutions, the traditional approach of stressing theory and mathematics fundamentals in the early undergraduate years, and postponing real engineering applications until later in the curriculum, has been turned upside down. The result is a lab-intensive, tightly structured curriculum with little time for elective courses such as programming in the early years. The advantage of this approach is that, from the very beginning of their undergraduate studies, engineering students spend a great deal of time participating in the hands-on experiences that define the essential nature of engineering.

Nonetheless, many faculty and potential employers continue to believe that learning a programming language is an important part of an engineering or science education. Even if students never need to rely solely on their own programming skills for solving computational problems, learning to program effectively provides a unique opportunity to learn essential problem-solving strategies that are easily transferable to other endeavors.

As a result of the restructuring of some engineering curricula, formal programming courses may be delayed until after the freshman or sophomore years. For example, students taking a course based on this text at Drexel University are typically pre-juniors, as they are designated in Drexel's five-year curriculum. They have had work experiences through Drexel's mandatory co-op program, and they are expected to have had some significant exposure to computers, including experience with specialized applications such as spreadsheets, statistical packages, virtual laboratory software, or symbolic algebra software. Thus even though this text does not assume a formal programming background, it moves quickly through introductory material by taking advantage of the fact that the intended audience is no longer intimidated by the mechanics of using computers.

2 Decisions About Content

Even as the value of a formal programming course continues to be recognized, it is widely conceded that, due to the pervasive availability of specialized computing tools, such a course will no longer occupy the central position it once did in undergraduate science and engineering curriculums. In recognition of this reality, this text presents a problem-driven and somewhat abridged introduction to the C programming language which will be useful to engineering and science students, and which can be presented in a one-quarter or one-semester course.

C is a complex and sometimes obscure language that can be used for a variety of purposes. Hence a short course aimed at a specific audience must have limited and well-defined objectives. Within a problem-driven context, how should these objectives be defined? I believe there are two essential considerations:

1. Engineering and science problems should be used to introduce programming concepts based on the requirements of those problems, rather than the other way around. As a result, even though C plays a major role as the fundamental language underlying some operating systems and graphical interface applications, for example, such uses of C are ignored in this text.

2. C's interface with external sources of data should be emphasized. It is my experience that students generally are reluctant to use a programming language outside a course in which they are required to learn that language. If a short course in C is to have a lasting impact as one of several tools science and engineering students can and will use to meet their computational needs, a great deal of practice with processing external data is necessary in order to develop the skills required to write useful programs. Early exposure to using data in the form of ASCII text files is especially important because C is less convenient for manipulating text data than languages such as Fortran. Thus, more practice is required to reach what I consider to be a useful level of proficiency.

During the one-quarter course I teach at Drexel University, I cover Chapters 1 through 7 so that students learn these basic skills:

1. How to solve problems using top-down design and modularized code
2. How to implement the basic sequential, selection, and repetition control structures of a procedural programming language
3. How to use C's basic I/O functions
4. How to represent and manipulate data using arrays and structures

This coverage leaves a little time at the end of the quarter for a brief look at one or two applications from later chapters. A one-semester or longer course could, of course, spend more time examining discipline-specific applications and general-purpose numerical analysis algorithms taken from this text or elsewhere. It would also be worthwhile to spend more time discussing pointers and their application to dynamic memory allocation and linked structures.

3 Pedagogical Issues

In the interest of presenting an abridged course in C for science and engineering students, I have minimized detailed discussions of programming concepts that would be appropriate for a more intensive course taught to computer science majors, for example. Therefore, this text attempts to teach largely through example, by providing many complete programs. To put it another way, the text emphasizes the how over the why of programming. At the same time, it strives to present a general approach to solving problems and a programming style that can be applied to other languages and also to other computing applications.

In order to gain maximum benefit from this text and its learning-by-doing approach, students should spend as much time as possible studying the programming examples. It is insufficient simply to read the code. Instead, students should enter the code into their own computers (my own preference is for students to manually type code rather than downloading it), run the programs, and try various modifications. This is simply the only way I know to become comfortable with the mechanical process of creating and debugging source code.

I have tried to present many of the code examples in the text as templates for solving a particular kind of problem. It is especially important for students to focus on recycling code from such examples into other programs. This is a skill that requires practice because it is not always obvious which parts of a program are specific to a particular problem and which parts can easily be transferred to a different problem. Weekly computing labs, if offered as part of a course, are the ideal place to practice working with code in this way.

With the advent of C++ and other object-oriented languages, it is certainly possible to argue that a process-oriented approach to programming is old-fashioned and needs to be replaced with a more modern object-oriented, problem-solving model. However, I continue to believe that engineering and scientific problem solving is inherently procedural; that is, it remains centered around processes rather than properties. Hence, the procedural programming language model will never be irrelevant for solving these kinds of problems.

In view of the fact that C and its derivatives are widely used for commercial applications, it is worth commenting on the nature of the programming examples given in this text and, by implication, the programs students are expected to write. Commercial software applications should be exceedingly robust in the sense that they should keep running no matter what, and they should be as "idiot proof" as possible with respect to user input. It should be obvious that no software developer can afford to market programs that crash, although any user of commercial applications knows that this is apparently not as obvious as it should be. Commercial programs should provide extensive testing of the input supplied by the program user, and just this component of a program can take a great deal of code. Consequently, a large percentage of the code for commercial programs is devoted to the user interface, which is almost always graphics-based.

In contrast, the programs in this text will be written exclusively in text mode, mostly by the single user of that program. If such a program expects as input a number in a specific range, it is reasonable in this context to assume that the user will do that. If not, the program will crash or produce meaningless results. If that happens, nothing is lost and the user simply starts over. To put it another way, even though the design of an appropriate and robust user interface for computer applications is an important topic in its own right, it is relatively unimportant for a course based on this text. What *is* important is for students to develop a working understanding of basic programming concepts, their implementation in C, and their relationship to a particular class of computational problems. In terms of user interface issues, it is sufficient for engineering and science students in a first programming course to become proficient at choosing appropriate representations for data and at prompting a program user to provide just the information required to solve a problem—no more and no less—while maintaining consistent physical units across the user-program interface.

4 The Programming Environment Used for This Text

I have used two different compilers to develop the programs in this text: an ancient MS-DOS compiler—Microsoft QuickC—and Sun Microsystem's cc compiler for UNIX systems. The cc compiler resides on the computer that provides e-mail accounts for all Drexel University students, so it has the advantage of being widely available to students from every discipline. There are always some students who prefer to use a different compiler, but because this text uses ANSI-standard C and stresses straightforward rather than clever programming style, there should be no compatibility problems. For an introductory programming course, I can find no justification for asking students to overcome the additional learning curve required to become proficient in the use of visual programming environments for graphics-based operating systems such as Windows. The extensive capabilities such environments provide for professional programmers who develop large and complex applications is inconsistent with the goals of an introductory course that requires writing many small standalone programs.

Nonetheless, it is certainly possible for students to use such programming environments if they wish.[1]

5 Succeeding at Learning a Programming Language

Finally, here is some advice to students about how to succeed in a programming course. The first thing you need to know is what this text assumes about your background. As noted above, you are expected to be computer literate in the sense that you know how to use computers for word processing, e-mail, surfing the Web, and perhaps solving some kinds of problems using applications such as spreadsheets and database programs. Consequently, this text does not offer the hand-holding introduction to computing that would be appropriate for neophytes; this is an audience that has essentially disappeared from the colleges and universities where this text is likely to be used.

If you have had some programming experience in another language, you may find the material at the beginning of the text very simple. However, C is sufficiently different from other languages that you will likely have a few questions about implementation even with the early material. If you have never done any computer programming, you may find the early material too terse and insufficiently detailed. If so, you should ask your instructor for additional help as soon as possible so you do not fall behind. You may also wish to study other introductory programming texts that present material in a different way; my experience is that good students rarely depend only on the assigned text.

My students often tell me that programming courses take more hours per week, per credit hour, than any other course. This may simply be because it is more obvious how to determine whether you have mastered the material; either your program works properly or it doesn't! One way to minimize the work load is to learn how to manage your time effectively. The basic rule is *never* to get behind on programming assignments. Nothing is more frustrating than getting stuck on a minor programming detail in the middle of the night before an assignment is due. You can avoid this situation by starting early, finding out where the difficulties are, and getting help as soon as possible. If your instructor allows it, you should discuss programming problems with your peers; my opinion is that it is unfair to ask students to learn a programming language on their own without extensive interaction with their peers.

The first and best place to look for help on programming assignments should be in your instructor's office. Many students, especially those who have

---

[1]One programming environment used in my department at Drexel requires nearly a minute to recompile and execute even a very short program. As beginning programmers need to write many short programs and tend to make many mistakes, this environment is *not* an efficient teaching or learning tool.

been very successful in high school, apparently believe that asking for help is a sign of weakness, to be done only as a last resort. However, in my courses, I *expect* some, if not most, students to need help to complete at least some of the programming assignments. The sooner you accept this fact and learn to view it as a part of the learning process, as essential as going to class and taking tests, the more successful you will be.

Finally, you must understand that it is as impossible to learn how to write programs just by reading *about* programming as it is to learn to speak Russian by reading about Russia. Although careful study of this or any other text is obviously a good idea, the only way to succeed at programming is to write code—lots of code. Only in this way can you develop your skills, determine what parts of the language you don't yet understand, and become proficient at finding and correcting the inevitable errors that creep into your programs.

For most of you, it will not be enough just to write the programs that are required for homework. In this text, I have tried to make homework exercises interesting by dealing with real computational problems. As a result, the problems themselves may require at least as much thought as the source code. In order to solve such problems as efficiently as possible, you need to devote some time to writing many short programs just to make sure you understand details of implementation and syntax. If you don't do that during the regular study hours you devote to a course based on this text, writing homework programs may be a very difficult and discouraging task, and you will never develop the proficiency you need to concentrate on solving problems rather than on language implementation details.

6 Contacting the Author

I look forward to hearing about your experiences with this text. You can contact me at dbrooks@mcs.drexel.edu. You can find source code and data files for all complete programs included in the text, and data files required for the exercises, at http://www.springer-ny.com/supplements/dbrooks. Instructors can contact me directly to obtain source code for my solutions to the programming exercises. The names of the source code files are given in brackets at the end of each exercise.

7 Suggested Supplementary Material

I have presented in this text only what I consider to be the most relevant elements of the C language for students of science and engineering. However, it is inevitable that students and instructors will have questions about C that are not addressed in this text; neither I nor any other textbook author can possibly anticipate all those questions. At least part of the solution is to supplement this text with a language reference manual. The one I require for my courses is:

Herbert Schildt, *C/C++ Programmer's Reference*, Osborne McGraw-Hill, 1997, ISBN 0-07-882367-6.

8 Acknowledgments

I would like to thank my students, who collectively have lived through several preliminary versions of this manuscript, and especially my partner, Susan Caughlan, for her editorial oversight and for her many allowances for the time required to complete this project.

David R. Brooks
Drexel University

Contents

Programming Preliminaries

1.1 A Five-Step Problem-Solving Process

There are two basic skills you must develop while learning to write programs in C. Obviously, you must learn details of the C programming language. However, it is equally important to develop a consistent strategy for solving computational problems that is *independent* of the language in which the solutions are implemented. Thus a course based on this text is as much about learning how to solve typical science and engineering problems with computers as it is about C per se. The skills you develop will be applicable when you learn other languages, or even when you use other kinds of problem-solving applications such as spreadsheets and symbolic algebra software.

For the purpose of developing a consistent problem-solving strategy, this text will follow this five-step procedure:

1   *Define the problem.*

2   *Outline a solution.*

3   *Design an algorithm.*

4   *Convert the algorithm into a program.*

5   *Verify the operation of the program.*

1.1.1 Step 1: Define the Problem

In the real world, it is often difficult to formulate problems in a useful way in the context of the range of available problem-solving tools. In fact, defining a problem appropriately is often a large part of the solution to that problem.

In an introductory course, you can assume that problems have been formulated correctly. However, instructors can explain problems poorly or make mistakes! Thus the first step is to make sure you understand the problem and can restate it in your own words. It's not possible to solve a problem you don't understand. Common mistakes that students make include solving only part of a problem or providing a solution that doesn't address the problem as stated. These kinds of mistakes have nothing to do with programming per se.

1.1.2 Step 2: Outline a Solution

The second step is very informal, but important. You should focus on obtaining information needed to solve the problem and especially on the nature of the required input and output. Assignments in this course should provide you with most of this information. This is so you can concentrate more on the programming parts of the solution. However, you should be aware that many students have difficulty thinking about solving problems in programming terms; that is, in terms of specifying input to a procedure that processes information and returns output.

1.1.3 Step 3: Design an Algorithm

The third step is critical to writing successful programs. In a programming context, an *algorithm*[1] consists of specific steps to be followed in sequence to attain a clearly defined goal. This

| *algorithm* |

may seem obvious, but a common problem students encounter when they begin to write programs is that the algorithm on which the program is based, either as explicitly written or implicitly assumed, makes no sense.

To the extent possible, algorithms should be language independent. In some cases, the problem may be simpler to solve in one language than another, so the algorithm may depend

| *procedural language* |
| *procedural programming* |

somewhat on the capabilities of the language that will eventually be used to write the program. More typically, however, problems in this course can be solved with equal ease using any *procedural language*—C just happens to be the language of choice. The purpose of learning to write algorithms is not only to help you organize your thoughts about a particular problem, but also to introduce you to the concepts of *procedural programming*, with the understanding that these concepts apply to all procedural languages, not just to C.

---

[1]Words appearing in the text in **bold italics** are defined in the glossary (Appendix 3).

1.1.4 Step 4: Convert the Algorithm Into a Program

The fourth step in the process is the only language-specific step, in which you will translate your algorithm into a C program. We will discuss this step in great detail in subsequent chapters.

1.1.5 Step 5: Verify the Operation of the Program

The fifth step—verifying your program's operation—is often overlooked. Beginning programmers can be so overjoyed at writing a program without syntax errors that they assume the answers the program produces must be right. This is a dangerous assumption! It is wiser to assume that programs produce incorrect answers unless proven otherwise. If you are lucky, incorrect errors will look obviously wrong. However, it is common for incorrect answers to look as reasonable as correct answers.

You can often verify a program's operation by checking representative calculations by hand, and you should do this whenever possible. However, if it were easy to check answers by hand, you probably wouldn't have needed to write a computer program in the first place. In any case, devising a strategy for verifying your solutions is an essential part of solving computational problems.

In the earlier days of computer science, computer programming was considered a worthwhile skill on its own. In the extreme, the science and art of writing elegantly constructed computer programs overshadowed the nature of the problems being solved. Now, however, students from many disciplines must learn to write computer programs, and correct answers presumably matter in all those disciplines. If you overlook this fact, you will eventually be sorry, if not in one of your courses, then in your first on-the-job programming assignment!

1.2 Defining a Pseudocode Language for Algorithm Development

The algorithm development step, Step 3 in the problem-solving process, can best be undertaken using what is often called *pseudocode* because the resulting step-by-step instructions look something

> *pseudocode*
> *pseudocode command*

like the instructions you write in a high-level programming language.[2] However, the instructions in the pseudocode don't have to, and generally won't, look exactly like commands in a specific language. *Pseudocode commands* should specify an

---

[2]An alternate approach, traditionally favored by Fortran programmers but largely abandoned in modern programming style, is to use flowcharts consisting of standardized symbols, lines, and arrows to illustrate the steps in a program.

action to be taken without being restricted by the syntax details of a particular language. Basically, your algorithm will consist of a series of action commands which, when translated into a real programming language, will tell your computer what to do. With this in mind, an informal language is useful to express these commands. There aren't any syntax rules for this language. However, it is important to define a set of actions that are common to all procedural programming languages. C is one such language, but certainly not the only one to which this pseudocode language could apply.

The list of such action commands is short because the list of basic actions that can be taken within a program written in a high-level procedural language is short. If you keep a description of this command language nearby when you start to solve problems and write programs, you should be able to focus on the logical design of the program without worrying about the syntax details.

Carefully written pseudocode should be relatively simple to convert to a working program. This process emphasizes the fact that C, even with its seemingly endless implementation details, is not an arbitrary or inherently complicated language. In fact, it provides a simple and efficient mechanism for transforming an algorithm—a problem solution—into a working program. Remember that the problem solution comes first, then the program. Here is a list of pseudocode action commands, in alphabetical order. Some of the terminology may be unfamiliar now, but new terms will be explained as we need them later in the text.

ASSIGN

Set a variable equal to a value, another variable, or an expression. See also the *INCREMENT* and *INITIALIZE* commands.

CALL

Invoke a subprogram. (See *SUBPROGRAM*.) Your use of this command should describe information flow between a subprogram and the point in your pseudocode from which the *CALL* is invoked. It is especially important to differentiate between input to and output from the subprogram. The ability to modularize a program by creating subprograms is an essential element of modern programming languages.

CHOOSE

This implies that a choice of actions can be taken based on a restricted list of possibilities—responses to a menu of choices, for example. Often, each response may be no more than a *CALL* to a *SUBPROGRAM* that takes action appropriate to a particular choice.

CLOSE

Close an open file.

DEFINE

Define variables and user-defined data types. In this section of your pseudocode, you should think about the kinds of variables and data objects, such as arrays, your program will need. It is especially important in scientific and engineering work to give physical definitions and units when you define variables.

IF...THEN...ELSE...

If something is true, then take a specified action. If it is false, then take some other action. The **ELSE...** branch is optional, as there may not be an "else" when the "if" isn't true. In many languages, the sequence of actions can be extended:

IF...THEN...ELSE IF...ELSE IF...ELSE...

In any case, implementation is based on the existence of relational operators, as discussed later in this chapter.

INCREMENT

This is a special type of assignment command used to indicate operations such as $x = x + 1$. (We'll discuss later the significance of this expression, which has a clearly defined meaning in programming even though it makes no sense as an algebraic expression.) It is often used inside loops to count the number of times actions inside the loop have been taken.

INITIALIZE

This is a special kind of assignment command used to indicate that a variable must be given an initial value before it can be **INCREMENT**ed. This is often required before a loop is started.

LOOP (conditions)...END LOOP

Execute instructions inside the loop repeatedly until (or as long as) certain conditions are met. Loops may be pre-test, post-test, or count-controlled. With pre-test loops, a condition is tested *before* the instructions inside the loop are executed. Depending on conditions in the program, the instructions inside the loop may never be executed. With post-test loops, a condition is tested *after* instructions inside the loop are executed. As a result, instructions inside the loop will always be executed at least once. Count-controlled loops are appropriate when your program knows prior to starting a loop how many times to repeat the instructions inside that loop. Under some conditions, the instructions inside a count-controlled loop may never be executed.

OPEN

Open an external file for reading or writing.

READ

This is the basic command for passing information to a program. The source of information is typically either the keyboard or an external data file.

SUBPROGRAM

This command marks the start of a subprogram module. Use it to specify the flow of information between parts of a program. (See **CALL**.)

WRITE

This is the basic command for displaying or saving output from a program. The destination is typically either the monitor screen or an external data file.

To what do these action commands apply? Often, they define actions performed on values stored in your program. At the machine level, many of these commands result in changes to the contents of specific memory locations. At the programming level, these memory locations are
referred to symbolically by names. These names are called *variable names* or *variables*. In *strongly typed languages* such as C, variables are always associated with specific *data types*. High-level languages typically support several different kinds of data, as shown in Table 1.1.

variable name
variable
strongly typed language
data type

Table 1.1. Data types supported by high-level languages

Data Type	Examples
integer numbers	-30000, 17
real numbers	6.5×10^{-10}, -0.002
characters	a, A, &, _
strings of characters	This is a character string.
logical (boolean) variables	true, false

When you design algorithms to solve problems, you must think carefully about the kinds of information your program will require, and you should choose appropriate names and data types for this information. Beginning programmers often overuse the integer data type when real numbers would be more appropriate;

this is an easy mistake to make when physical values are expressed as whole numbers. For example, temperature is often expressed as a whole number, such as 70° Fahrenheit, even though it is more appropriate to represent temperatures as real numbers rather than integers. On the other hand, integers typically require less memory space and allow faster and more accurate arithmetic operations than real numbers, so their appropriate use can result in faster program execution times and more efficient use of your computer's resources.

In addition to action commands, various *operators* need to be part of a pseudocode language; without them you couldn't perform the mathematical operations that are at the heart of many calculations. Table 1.2 shows some basic mathematical operators that are supported by high-level programming languages.

operator

Table 1.2. Mathematical operators supported by high-level languages

Operation	Mathematical Symbol
addition	+
subtraction	−
multiplication	•, ×, or implied
division	/ or ÷

The operations +, −, •, or ×, and / or ÷ are familiar. Multiplication is often implied; in the algebraic expression $y = ax + b$, ax implies "a times x." As we will see, C supports all these mathematics operators as well as several others. Note, however, that C does not support an exponentiation operator. That is, the operation x^y cannot be implemented directly with operator notation.[3]

Finally, relational and logical operators are needed to construct *IF... THEN...ELSE...* statements. These are given in Table 1.3. We will discuss the C implementation of all these operators later.

---

[3]In contrast, x^y can be represented in Fortran by the expression x**y.

Table 1.3. Relational and logical operators

Mathematical Operator	Meaning
=	equal to
≠	not equal to
≤	less than or equal to
≥	greater than or equal to
<	less than
>	greater than
"and"	logical "and"
"not"	logical "not"
"or"	logical "or"

Finally, keep in mind that any high-level language will include some built-in functions, called *intrinsic functions*, that allow you to perform common *intrinsic function* calculations without having to reinvent the code every time you write a program. Some functions—for example, trigonometric functions such as sin(x)—are common to many procedural languages. Computers don't have any inherent ability to evaluate these functions. When a programming language supports a function such as sin(x), it means that the language can call upon a predefined algorithm to evaluate the function in terms of basic mathematical operations. This is done automatically and the programmer usually doesn't even have to be aware of how the calculations are performed.

The advantage of intrinsic functions as part of a programming language standard is that you can depend on the availability of these functions no matter which version of the language you use. When you convert an algorithm into a working program, it's important to be aware of the functions a language supports as part of its standard. C has a relatively limited set of intrinsic mathematical functions compared to Fortran, for example, but more than Pascal. A list of C intrinsic functions will be given in Chapter 3.

Specific implementations of C and other languages usually include many nonstandard *language extensions*, including *nonstandard functions*. For example, implementations of C and its derivatives, such as C++ for Macintosh or Windows-based computers, may include extensions that deal with the graphical

language extension
nonstandard function
ANSI-standard C

user interface presented by the operating system. These can be important for some programming applications, but this course will concentrate on *ANSI-standard C*, a language with a text-based interface.

1.3 Organizing Pseudocode Into a Program

Once you understand the elements of a pseudocode language for developing algorithms, you must organize these elements in an appropriate way. Specifically, you have to think about how to get from the beginning of 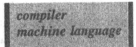 your algorithm to the end; this may seem obvious, but it is often a problem for beginning programmers. Steps in an algorithm are executed one at a time. When you transform your algorithm into a program, the steps in that program are also executed one at a time. For all practical purposes, the *compiler* that converts your program into *machine language* is restricted in the sense that it can never look ahead. When you tell it to do something, it must have all the information it needs to execute that instruction.

Does this mean that every statement in a program must necessarily be executed one step at a time in sequence? To put it another way, is it impossible to write code that deals with the programming equivalent of coming to a fork in the road? No. However, the alternatives are limited and very specific. There are only three basic ways to control the order in which steps in an algorithm or program are executed:

1. *Sequence*

    Steps are performed one after the other in sequence. Each step is performed once and only once. See the *ASSIGN*, *INITIALIZE*, and *INCREMENT* pseudocode commands.

2. *Selection*

    One of several alternative sequences of actions is selected and executed, bypassing the other alternatives. See the *IF...THEN...ELSE* and *CHOOSE* pseudocode commands.

3. *Repetition*

    One or more steps are performed repeatedly until a terminating condition is met. See the *LOOP...END LOOP* pseudocode command.

It is a basic programming principle that any algorithm can be implemented using a combination of these three *control structures*. Sequence structures are implemented simply by writing consecutive statements. As we will see, languages such as C have specific syntax for implementing selection and repetition structures.

1.4 Examples

Once you understand pseudocode commands, operators, functions, and control structures, you are ready to combine these pieces into an algorithm. In this section, we will develop algorithms for some simple problems, using the formal five-step problem-solving procedure outlined above. For now, we will skip the fourth step—the writing of an actual program—since it will be the topic of the rest of the text. These problems, except for the last one, may appear to be very simple, but it's important to practice applying a formal step-by-step approach that will work even when the problems aren't so easy.

Pseudocode Problem #1

1 Define the problem.

Find the largest and smallest score in a list of scores. Calculate the range of the scores.

2 Outline a solution.

1. Assume that the first number in the list is both the largest and the smallest score.
2. As you read each subsequent score in the list, reassign the largest and smallest score as required.
3. The range is the largest score minus the smallest.

This approach for finding the largest and smallest scores may not be intuitive. Consider this list of five numbers:

15 11 8 21 17

You can easily find the largest and smallest numbers in this list just by inspection. An amazing characteristic of the human brain is that it can formulate and implement an algorithm for solving this problem at an unconscious level. However, computers can't do that. Instead, you must provide a specific algorithm.

What would you do if the above list contained 5,000 numbers instead of five? You would probably have to be more precise in your thinking. You might, for example, write down the largest and smallest values in as much of the list as your eyes could scan at once. Then you could scan another section of the list and replace the largest and smallest values if required. The algorithm suggested here is a simplified and formalized interpretation of this approach which can easily be implemented in a step-by-step fashion.

3   *Design an algorithm.*

DEFINE *largest, smallest, range, and score as real numbers*
ASSIGN *largest score = smallest score = first score in list*
LOOP *(until no more scores)*
    READ *(score)*
    IF *score > largest* **THEN ASSIGN** *largest = score*
    IF *score < smallest* **THEN ASSIGN** *smallest = score*
END LOOP
ASSIGN *range = largest - smallest*
WRITE *(largest, smallest, range)*

4   *Convert the algorithm into a program.*

Defer this step for now.

5   *Verify the operation of the program.*

Be sure to check the calculations with a set of scores for which the smallest and largest values are known. Never assume that calculations done within a computer program are correct until you have checked them by hand or verified the operation of the program in some other way. (This isn't always easy!)

Pseudocode Problem #2

1 *Define the problem.*

Air quality is given as a numerical index value. If the index is less than 35, the air quality is rated as "pleasant." If it is between 35 and 60, the quality is "unpleasant." If the index is greater than 60, the quality is "hazardous."

2 *Outline a solution.*

1. Read each index value.
2. Decide which message to print, based on the value of the index.

3 *Design an algorithm.*

DEFINE *index as real number*
LOOP *(until no more input)*
    READ *(index)*
    IF *index<35* **THEN WRITE** *("pleasant")*
    IF *index ≥ 35 and ≤ 60* **THEN**
        WRITE *("unpleasant")*
    IF *index > 60* **THEN WRITE** *("hazardous")*
END LOOP

Here's an alternate way to implement the **IF...** command:

IF *index < 35* **THEN WRITE** *("pleasant")*
ELSE IF *index ≤ 60* **THEN WRITE** *("unpleasant")*
ELSE WRITE *("hazardous")*

The second implementation is a little less obvious than the first because you have to be convinced that, within the **IF...** command structure, only one branch will be taken. Suppose the index is 20. This value is less than 35, so the **WRITE** *("pleasant")* branch will be executed. This value is also less than 60, but the second branch won't be executed because another branch has already been executed. As you will see in Chapter 4, programming language implementations of **IF...** structures really do work this way.

4 *Convert the algorithm into a program.*

Defer this step for now.

5 *Verify the operation of the program.*

For this problem, it's important to implement the relational operators correctly. The phrase "between 35 and 60" must be interpreted properly; you need to check values at the break points to be certain your algorithm reflects the problem statement. Exactly where the break points lie may be vague in the problem statement, but you must be specific about them in your algorithm definition.

Pseudocode Problem #3

1 *Define the problem.*

Your supervisor hands you a diskette with a file containing student names, IDs, and GPAs and says, "Please create two new files. One should be the dean's list file of students whose GPA is at least 3.0. The other should be a probation file of students whose GPA is below 2.0."

2 *Outline a solution.*

1. Open the file containing student records.
2. Create two new files, one for the dean's list and the other for the probation list.
3. Read each record and compare the GPA with the criteria for the dean's and probation lists. If it doesn't belong in one of the files, go on to the next record. Otherwise, write the data into the appropriate file.
4. Close all the files when you're done with them.

The file opening and closing parts of the solution, steps 1 and 4, may not be part of your initial thinking because these steps are not really part of the solution. However, as noted previously, it is important in this step to consider the sources of information required to solve the problem. The file-related steps remind you to make sure that you understand the structure of the file containing the input data and that you give some thought to the form of the output file.

3 Design an algorithm.

DEFINE student name and ID as character strings
GPA as a real number
OPEN (original file)
OPEN (dean's list file)
OPEN (probation file)
LOOP (until there aren't any more names in original file)
    READ (from original file, name, ID, GPA)
    IF (GPA ≥ 3) **THEN WRITE** (to dean's list file: name, ID, GPA)
    IF (GPA < 2) **THEN WRITE** (to probation file: name, ID, GPA)
END LOOP
CLOSE (all files)

4 Convert the algorithm into a program.

Defer this step for now.

5 Verify the operation of the program.

You can verify the operation of this program by inspection, perhaps with only a subset of the student data.

Pseudocode Problem # 4

1 Define the problem.

A data file contains many two-line records. Each pair of lines contains a date and 24 hourly temperatures:

```
01/01/94
20,22,21,19,18,...,17,18
```

Read the data for each day. Display the date and the maximum and minimum temperature for the day, plus the hour, from 1 to 24, at which each of these values occurred.

2 *Outline a solution.*

In this case, the problem itself contains an explanation of what you must do. For a simple solution, you would like to be able to assume that there are no missing data in the file. In the real world, this will not always be a good assumption!

3 *Design an algorithm.*

DEFINE *max, min, max_hour, min_hour, current_hour*
         (all integer variables); date (character string)
OPEN *(data file)*
LOOP *(until you get to the end of the file)*
        READ *(from data file, date)*
        READ *(from data file, 1st temperature)*
        ASSIGN *max = 1st temperature*
                min = 1st temperature
                min_hour = 1, max_hour = 1
        INITIALIZE *current_hour = 1*
        LOOP *(for current hour from 2 to 24)*
                READ *(from data file: temperature)*
                IF *temperature > max* **THEN**
                        ASSIGN *max = temperature*
                                max_hour = current_hour
                (end IF...)
                IF *temperature < min* **THEN**
                        ASSIGN *min = temperature*
                                min_hour = current_hour
                (end IF...)
        END LOOP
        WRITE *(date, max, max_hour, min, min_hour)*
END LOOP
CLOSE *(data file)*

Note that this algorithm uses an approach identical to the one discussed in Pseudocode Problem #1 to find the maximum and minimum values.

4 *Convert the algorithm into a program.*

Defer this step for now.

5 *Verify the operation of the program.*

You can verify the operation of this program by inspection. If your program works for one day, there is no reason to think it won't work for all days. However, because of the way this algorithm is written, you should check examples where the minimum or maximum temperature actually occurs at hour 1 to be sure these initial values are not changed.

Pseudocode Problem #5

1 *Define the problem.*

Write a program that reads and stores a list of student names and grades. The program should then be able to perform the following user-selected tasks:

1. Search for any student name.
2. Sort the list by name or grade.
3. Add a new name.
4. Delete an existing name.
5. Print a list of all students whose grades are above or below a specified value.

2 *Outline a solution.*

The structure of this problem lends itself to a modularized solution. The main program will contain a menu of the indicated choices. Each choice will invoke a subprogram that will perform one of the specific tasks listed. Assume that the list is contained in a data file and that the data file can be entirely contained in the amount of memory available to your computer program. (In programming terms, this means that the data will be stored in a data structure called an array, which we will discuss in Chapter 6.)

This is a more complex problem than the ones we have discussed so far. You should solve it in steps, one menu choice at a time. The first task is to write a subprogram to read the list and store it in your computer's memory. This needs to be done before you present the user of your program with the menu options. It will be helpful to display the contents of the list, too. Until you can read the list correctly and display its contents, there is no point worrying about the rest of the program. Within the menu of choices, probably the easiest subprogram to write is the one that looks for a specified name or grade; we will develop pseudocode for this subprogram, but not the rest.

3 *Design an algorithm.*

Pseudocode for main program:
DEFINE *(variables to hold the names and grades,*
        number of students, response to menu selection)
CALL Read_List *(store list of names and grades in memory)*
LOOP *(until user wants to stop)*
    WRITE *(display menu)*
    WRITE *(What do you want to do?)*
    READ *(response)*
    CHOOSE *(based on response)*
        SEARCH: **CALL** *Search (by name or grade)*
        SORT: **CALL** *Sort (by name or grade)*
        ADD: **CALL** *Add (a new name)*
        DELETE: **CALL** *Delete (an existing name)*
        OUTPUT: **CALL** *Output (list of students who meet specified*
                          criterion)
        QUIT: (end program)
        OTHER: (print input error message)
    (end **CHOOSE***)*
END LOOP

Note how the **CHOOSE** statement attempts to trap an inappropriate response by giving an "other" option.

    Now, develop subprograms one at a time. The first step is to read the list of names and grades:

SUBPROGRAM Read_List *(IN: name of data file;*
                          OUT: name_array, grade_array, number
                                    of names and grades (n))
    OPEN *(data file)*
    INITIALIZE *n = 0*

```
        LOOP (as long as there are more records)
            INCREMENT n = n + 1
                READ (name_array(n), grade_array(n))
                WRITE (name_array(n), grade_array(n))
        END LOOP
        CLOSE (data file)
(end Read_List)
```

Note how the index value n is used to notate parallel lists of names and grades. That is, the n^(th) name will always correspond to the n^(th) grade. When the loop is terminated, the value of n will be equal to the total number of students. The **WRITE** statement can be removed when you're sure you can read the list correctly.

Here's an algorithm to control a search of the lists.

```
SUBPROGRAM Search (IN: name_list,grade_list,n_students)
        READ (search choice: name or grade?)
        CHOOSE (based on search choice)
        for name:
          READ (which_name)
          CALL SearchByName (IN:name_list,grade_list,
                                    n_students,which_name)
        for grade:
          READ (which_grade)
          CALL SearchByGrade (IN:name_list,grade_list,
                                    n_students,which_grade)
(end Search)
```

Note that this algorithm uses the **CHOOSE** pseudocode command rather than an **IF...THEN...ELSE...** approach. Either will work, but the former is easier to extend to other choices. Here's an algorithm to search for a name. Because more than one student may have the same name, the algorithm searches through the entire list.

```
SUBPROGRAM SearchByName (IN:name_list,grade_list,
                                    n_students,which_name)
        DEFINE counter
        LOOP (for counter = 1 to n_students)
                IF name_list(counter)=which_name THEN
                        WRITE (name_list(counter), grade_list(counter))
        END LOOP
```

A subprogram to search for a specified grade will be nearly identical to **SUBPROGRAM** *SearchByName*. Although you could combine these functions into a single subprogram at the pseudocode level, the actual code will need to be different because names and grades are represented by different data types.

Suppose you decide to maintain a list of student IDs rather than names. Presumably, IDs are unique. Therefore, the search should stop when the specified ID is found, rather than searching through the entire list. Can you modify the algorithm so that the loop terminates when it either gets to the end of the list or finds the specified name?

Note that the names list and grades list must both be made available as input to these subprograms. They are parallel lists in which, for example, the third name in the names list is associated with the third grade in the grades list. This has some important implications for writing the rest of this program. Suppose the names list is originally sorted by name. If you decide to sort the lists by grade, you must sort both lists at the same time to make sure that the relationship between each name and grade is maintained. In C, as we will see later in the text, it is possible to overcome this inconvenience by defining a new kind of data structure that combines the names and grades into a single list.

4   *Convert the algorithm into a program.*

Defer this step for now.

5   *Verify the operation of the program.*

As noted, a large program such as this needs to developed one subprogram at a time. You should check the operation of the program each time you add a new subprogram.

1.5 What Is the Point of Programming?

Here's a reasonable question: Does the world really need more computer programmers? After all, there are lots of software applications for solving a wide range of computational problems. And it's a little discouraging to realize that even the most straightforward application (such as Pseudocode Problem #5, above) requires the accumulation of considerable programming skills.

Of course, there are many reasons to write your own programs. Some people do it for fun (yes, that's really true), others need programming skills to do research, and others need a thorough understanding of programming to continue their studies in computer or information science. Almost any research organization in any field will require programming skills for solving specialized research problems. Graduate programs in any technical discipline you can name will expect their students to have some programming skills.

However, the best reason for learning how to program a computer is to teach yourself how to think logically. Even if you never have to write programs for a living, as a necessary evil in the course of your work, or just for your own use and amusement, the programming process is a good way to teach yourself how to solve problems. A language like C is especially useful because it encourages you to approach difficult problems in a step-by-step, top-down fashion that separates each problem into a series of smaller and hopefully more manageable tasks.

Even though this kind of thinking may not always be the best way to solve problems, we will treat programming as an inherently linear process, so the kinds of problems we will solve in this course will lend themselves to this kind of solution.[4]

By the way, since we have decided that learning how to program is a good idea, you are allowed to ask this follow-up question: Why learn to program in C? A good answer is that C is the **| UNIX |** basic language of choice for many commercial computer applications, and it is fundamental to understanding the widely used *UNIX* computer operating system. As I will point out from time to time in this text, C has some characteristics that pose implementation problems in scientific and engineering programming. However, this has not prevented C from gaining a prominent role in these disciplines. Once you have become proficient in C, it is relatively easy to learn languages such as Fortran, which is still widely used in science and engineering, as well as more modern languages such as C++ and Java.

1.6 Your First C Program

You are now ready to create your first C program. This will be a "cookbook" exercise that emphasizes the mechanics of writing and executing a program. You are not yet expected to understand all the details of the code. The exercise assumes you will be writing programs on a UNIX computer that supports Sun Microsystem's cc compiler or its equivalent.

If you are a complete UNIX novice, you will need some help learning how to use a UNIX-based system. Your institution or department probably provides training courses on using UNIX systems. If such training isn't part of a programming course, you will need to learn the fundamentals on your own.

Assuming you are successfully logged on to your UNIX account:

---

[4]Author's note: This problem-solving approach generally does not work with people.

1. Create a new *source code file* by typing `pico test.c`. This invokes a simple text editor and creates a new and currently empty file called `test.c`. The source code file will contain instructions for solving a particular problem. These instructions must be written according to the *syntax rules* of C. To create the source code file, which you will then *compile* and *link* to create an *executable program file*, enter the following lines exactly as shown:

source code file
syntax rule
compile
link
executable program file

```
/* My first C Program. */
#include <stdio.h>
int main(void)
{
        printf("Hello, world.\n");
        return 0;
}
```

When you're done typing, you need to make sure your work is saved. Enter ^x by holding down the `control` (or `Ctrl`) key on your keyboard while pressing the (unshifted) x key. This two-key combination is sometimes notated as `control-x` or `Ctrl-x`. In this context, the ^ symbol has nothing to do with the carat symbol in the uppercase position over the 6 key on your keyboard. Do not press `Shift-6` followed by x or `Ctrl-Shift-X`. Pressing ^x exits the `pico` editor. You will be asked if you want to "save modified buffer." Press y (for "yes") and then the `Return` key. You can also save your work at any time from within the `pico` editor by pressing the ^o key combination

IMPORTANT NOTE: Whenever you type a command on a UNIX system, you *must* use the specified combination of lowercase and uppercase letters because UNIX commands are case-sensitive. This is different from computers using a Windows/DOS-based operating system, for example, which is case-insensitive. Also, the C language itself is case-sensitive. This means that when you create the above code file above, you must preserve the use of uppercase and lowercase letters. For example, `printf` is *not* the same thing as `PRINTF` or `PrintF`, or any other combination.

You can also create source code with the more flexible but more complicated UNIX `vi` text editor instead of `pico`. Refer to the documentation for your system.

2. Once you have created a source code file, you must compile and link it to create an executable file. The compiler/linker we will use is `cc` (for "C compiler"). Type

```
cc test.c -otest.exe
```

This invokes the cc compiler, which tries to compile the source code file named test.c. If the compilation is successful, cc translates your source code into machine language instructions and creates an executable file named test.exe. (If you do not include the -o option, cc creates a file named a.out by default.) If you get error messages, edit the file so that it looks exactly like the one above. Then try again. When you no longer get any error messages,

3. Type

```
test.exe
```

to execute your C program. If you have done everything correctly, the text

```
Hello, world.
```

should appear on your screen. You have now created and executed your first C program.

Note that although we will often speak of source code as a program, it is actually the executable *binary file* that contains machine-level instructions that the computer understands and follows. In this example, we have given the binary file a .exe extension (for "executable").[5] The cc compiler generates, by default, a file with a .out extension. In common with other high-level languages, the source code file you create with a text editor generally is portable to any computer that supports a C compiler, as long as the source code does not include implementation-specific features that are not part of the C language standard. However, the executable program file is not portable to a different kind of computer. (Commercial programs generally are not portable among various kinds of computers even at the source code level, specifically because they take advantage of features of a particular operating system and computer hardware architecture.)

4. Depending on how heavily you use your UNIX account, and for what, you may wish to create a separate directory just for C programs. For example, typing

```
mkdir c_stuff
```

will create a new directory called c_stuff. You can move to this directory by typing

```
cd c_stuff
```

From this directory, you can return to your "home" directory by typing cd.

---

[5]The convention of using a .exe extension will be familiar to MS-DOS users.

The Basics of C Programming

2.1 C Program Layout

The source code for a C program contains at least the following elements:

1. Preprocessor directives, including:
   - (a) standard header files
   - (b) constant definitions
2. Main function header and body
3. Reserved words and identifiers
4. Comments (optional, but required as a matter of style)

Program P-2.1 illustrates each of these elements. The program prints the message Hello, world! and the numbers 3.14159 and 6.28318 on your monitor screen.

P-2.1 [hello.c]

```c
/* "Hello, world." */
/* preprocessor directives */
#include <stdio.h>  /* standard I/O header file */
#define PI 3.14159  /* defines PI as a "constant" */

int main(void) /* main function header */
{ /* start of main body */

  /* variable declaration */
     double two_pi;
  /* printf is the usual way to produce output on a monitor. */
     printf("Hello, world!\n");
  /* assign value to two_pi */
     two_pi=2.0*PI;
  /* "%lf" is a format specifier for displaying real numbers */
  /* Note that "l" is a lowercase letter L, and not the numeral 1 */
     printf("%lf %lf\n",PI,two_pi);
  /* return value from main function */
     return 0;

} /* end of main body */
```

Running P-2.1

```
Hello, world!
3.141590 6.283180
```

Every C program must have one and only one *function* named main, the body of which is included inside braces {...}. (In other programming languages, this would be called the *main program*.)

| *function* |
| *main program* |

For our purposes, every C source code file must include the *preprocessor directive*

```
#include <stdio.h>
```

so it can access the *standard input/output (I/O) functions* through the stdio.h *header file*. You can think of a header file as a source of information your program

| *preprocessor directive* |
| *standard input/output (I/O) functions* |
| *header file* |

needs in order to interpret certain kinds of instructions. There are many header files that are part of the C standard that you can #include only as required, but because every program needs to execute some I/O instructions in order to process input and produce usable output, the stdio.h header file is needed for every program. The angle brackets around stdio.h tell C to look in a particular system-dependent directory for the header file. As a programmer, you usually don't have to worry about where these files are stored.[1]

Although it might seem unnecessary for the main function in P-2.1 to return a value when it's done, it's a good idea to give the main function a data type of int and have it return a value of 0 when it executes successfully. This is because some operating systems can use this value to determine whether the program has executed successfully. The alternative is to define the main function as having data type void, which means that it doesn't return a value.

```
void main(void)
{
    ...
}
```

The void word inside parentheses following main means that this program does not require any user input from the keyboard in order to execute. The void is optional, and either int main() or void main() is also acceptable syntax.

In this text, we will usually assume that the main function will return a 0 when it executes, so the shell of a main function will usually look like this:

---

[1]Because stdio.h is required for every program, it might seem reasonable for C to "include" this file automatically. However, C simply doesn't work this way. It is even possible to conceive of programs that don't use C's standard I/O library, in which case stdio.h would not be needed.

```
int main(void)
{
/* Program statements go here. */
  return 0;
}
```

The #define preprocessor directive in P-2.1 performs a word-processor-like search-and-replace operation when your program is compiled. In P-2.1, the directive

```
#define PI 3.14159
```

causes a C compiler to replace every occurrence of the name PI with the characters 3.14159. (There is only one such occurrence in P-2.1). Then the programming 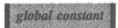 environment will interpret the characters 3.14159 as a number, just as if you had typed that number directly into the source code. It is common C programming practice to use uppercase letters for the names of *global constants* defined in this way, to distinguish them from variable names. Although you don't *have* to follow this convention, it is so widely accepted that it is almost a style requirement.

The statement printf("Hello, world!\n"); displays the message Hello, world! on your monitor screen.

Finally, P-2.1 calculates the value of the variable two_pi and displays both PI and  two_pi. Before the program can use the variable name two_pi, it must first be given an appropriate data type. The *data declaration statement*

```
double two_pi;
```

associates two_pi with a real number. The significance of the data type description double will be discussed in Chapter 3, along with other data types.

The *assignment statement*

```
two_pi=2.0*PI;
```

results in the variable two_pi having the value of 2π, or approximately 6.2831852. In an assignment statement, the value of an expression on the right side of the = sign is assigned to a variable name on the left side of the = sign. It looks like an algebraic equation, but it is not, as we will discuss further in Chapter 3.

With these brief explanations, you should be able to make sense of the source code in P-2.1, even though you may not understand the details. We will, of course, discuss at length the details of performing calculations and displaying results in programs.

2.2 Basic Input and Output

Especially for scientific and engineering calculations, it is necessary to develop a working knowledge of how a programming language interfaces with external data. We will consider two situations:

1. The input required for a program to do its job is supplied by a user typing values at the keyboard while the program is running. This is known as an *interactive program*, or *interactive mode*.

interactive program
interactive mode

2. The input required for a program to do its job comes from an *external data file* that is accessed while the program is running. This is known as a *batch program*, or *batch mode*. A user's intervention is not needed while the program is running.

external data file
batch program
batch mode

2.2.1 Keyboard Input and Monitor Output

In this section we will discuss how a C program communicates with two basic devices: a keyboard for input and a monitor for output.

Reading and Displaying Numbers

Consider the following simple problem, which we will solve in accordance with the five-step process outlined in Chapter 1.

1 Define the problem.

For a user-supplied value of the radius, calculate the area and circumference of a circle.

2 Outline a solution.

The calculations are straightforward:

$$area = \pi r^2$$
$$circumference = 2\pi r$$

If the radius must be given in some particular physical units, let the program user know that. Be sure to label the output.

3 Design an algorithm.

This algorithm contains all the elements of simple programming problems: defining variables, prompting the user for input from the keyboard, doing the required calculations, and displaying the output on the monitor screen.

DEFINE radius, area, circumference as real numbers; π as a real constant
WRITE ("Give the radius of a circle (units?)")
READ (radius)
ASSIGN area = π•radius²
       circumference = 2π•radius
WRITE (area and circumference, with identifying labels)

4 Convert the algorithm into a program.

Program P-2.2 implements this algorithm.

P-2.2 [circle.c]

```c
/* Calculate area and circumference of a circle. */
#include <stdio.h>
#define PI 3.14159

int main(void)
{
    /* Declare data types. */
    double radius,         /* input - radius of a circle, cm        */
           area,           /* output - area of a circle, cm^2       */
           circumference;  /* output - circumference of a circle, cm */
    /* Get the radius. */
    printf("Enter the radius in cm: ");
    scanf("%lf",&radius);
    /* Calculate the area and circumference. */
    area = PI*radius*radius;
    circumference = 2.0*PI*radius;
    /* Display the output. */

    printf("The area is %lf cm^2.\n",area);
    printf("The circumference is %lf cm.\n",circumference);
    return 0;
}
```

Running P-2.2

```
Enter the radius in cm: 5
The area is 78.539750 cm^2.
The circumference is 31.415900 cm.
```

5 *Verify the operation of the program.*

Check your results with a hand calculator. Note that r = 1 is *not* a good value with which to test the program. (Why not?)

In terms of the user interface for P-2.2, the essential code is contained in the statements

```
printf("Enter the radius in cm: ");
scanf("%lf",&radius);
```

The basic output-processing function for C is printf ("print formatted"). In this context, a function provides predefined code that enables a program to perform certain common tasks, such as displaying output. We will return to the topic of functions in Chapter 4. The general syntax of the printf function is

```
type int variable =
            printf(character string describing output format
                    and/or other characters
                        ⟨,one or more variables or constants⟩)
or
            (void)printf(...
```

The large angle brackets ⟨...⟩ indicate an optional parameter. In this case, the brackets indicate that the printf function doesn't have to display the values of variables or constants. An example is the first printf statement in P-2.2, which simply displays the text enclosed in quotation marks.

When variables or constants are displayed, each must be matched with an appropriate *format specifier* in the output string. These specifiers, which tell C how to convert a number into its exernal representation and display that value, always begin with the % symbol. Some examples are %lf for type double variables and %i for integers. A detailed list of format specifiers for a variety of data types is given in Table 3.2 in Chapter 3.

As an example of how to use format specifiers, return to the final task in P-2.2, which is to display the results of the calculations. The statements

```
printf("The area is %lf cm^2.\n",area);
printf("The circumference is %lf cm.\n",circumference);
```

display the values of the variables `area` and `circumference` along with an explanatory message. The text messages, if there are any, and the format specifiers for the values to be displayed are given as a character string surrounded by quotation marks. Because `area` and `circumference` are type `double` variables, a `%lf` format specifier is used. The control character `\n` causes C to print a new-line character at the end of the line. Otherwise, the output from the second `printf` statement would start on the same line as the end of the first `printf` statement.

It is possible to display multiple values with a single `printf` statement:

```
printf("The area and circumference are %lf cm^2 and %lf cm.\n",
       area,circumference);
```

Each variable must have its own format specifier.

Most C functions return a value. The `printf` function returns an integer value equal to the number of characters printed. In nearly all cases, this return value can be ignored. Strictly speaking, the `printf` function should be preceded by `(void)`, as shown in the syntax box. This tells the compiler, "I know that `printf` returns a value, but I'm choosing to ignore that value." However, as a practical matter, it is also okay simply to use `printf` without assigning its output to a variable and without the `(void)`, as has been done in P-2.2. Some C compilers may flag this use of a function with a warning message.

In P-2.2, the first `printf` statement provides a user prompt in the form of a message displayed on the user's monitor screen. This prompt describes what the program expects the user to do. Depending on the circumstances, this message can be brief or very detailed. In scientific and engineering problems, the prompt message will often specify the units for the physical quantities the user is expected to provide. In P-2.2, the prompt message tells the user that the radius should be provided in centimeters.

The basic C function for getting input from the keyboard is `scanf`. Its general syntax is

```
type int variable =
            scanf(character string describing input format,
                  one or more variable addresses)
or
            (void)scanf(...
```

The input format string contains **conversion specifiers**, which tell C how to interpret values entered at the keyboard. These specifiers must match the data types of the variables whose addresses are supplied in the list.

When a scanf function is encountered, the program suspends further execution and waits for the user to enter an appropriate response. When the

floating-point number

user presses the Enter (or Return) key, program execution resumes. Then the scanf function reads (scans) the keyboard buffer and attempts to interpret what it finds according to the conversion specifiers provided. In P-2.2, scanf is instructed by the specifier "%lf" to look for a single real number (*floating-point number*) of type double. (The character preceding the f in the format specifier, which stands for "long" in "long float," is a lowercase L, not the numeral 1.) Conversion specifiers use the same vocabulary of symbols as format specifiers. Inside a scanf function, they tell C how to interpret characters typed on the keyboard rather than how to display values.

The & in front of the variable name radius in the scanf statement is the "address-of" operator. It means, "Place the value found by scanf into the memory location (address) associated with the variable named radius." In many other high-level programming languages, the association of a variable name with a memory location is implemented transparently, without extra syntax requirements. So, especially if you have done any programming in other languages, it is easy to forget the & in the scanf argument list. If you do forget it, your program may crash. As a minimum, your program will *not* have access to the value you provided at the keyboard.

The calculations in P-2.2 are straightforward. Remember to spell the symbol for π as PI because that's how it is spelled in the #define directive, and C is

control character

always case-sensitive in its interpretation of words and characters. In the printf statements, text is intermixed with output format specifications. The characters \n add new-line characters to the output. If you neglect to include them, all the output will appear on the same line. The new-line symbol is one of several *control characters* used for formatting output. These characters are always preceded by a backslash. A list of control characters is given in Table 3.2 in Chapter 3.

In P-2.2, radius, area, and circumference are the variable names used by the program. These are the symbolic names that the C programming environment uses to assign and access memory locations. Indeed, a major advantage of high-level programming languages is the ability to provide this kind of symbolic access. The ANSI-standard C rules for assigning identifiers, of which variable names are one type, are:

1. An identifier name consists only of letters, digits, and the underscore character.
2. An identifier name may not start with a digit.
3. A C reserved word cannot be used as an identifier name.

There are, in addition, two restrictions that should be followed even though they are not syntax rules:

> 1. An identifier name should not be the same as any identifier name in the standard C library because this will prevent access to the standard C library functions in that library.
> 2. An identifier name should contain no more than 31 characters because some systems distinguish names based on only the first 31 characters.

Finally, remember that C implementations always consider case to be significant. Thus `radius` and `Radius` are interpreted as two *different* variable names. A widely accepted programming style is that variable names use lowercase letters and, as previously noted, constants appearing in a `define` directive use uppercase letters. In general, you should avoid using variable names that differ only in their use of uppercase and lowercase letters; ignoring this style convention makes your programs hard to interpret and prone to errors.

Reading and Displaying Characters and Strings of Characters

Up to now, I/O has been restricted to string constants (as prompts to the program user) and numerical values. However, it is also important to be able to read and display text values. At a basic level, this is easy to do in C, but the nature of the language imposes some significant restrictions that can be troublesome to overcome. This section presents just the basics.

First, consider the problem of reading and displaying a single character. This is simple, and it works just like numerical I/O:

```
char grade;
...
printf("What grade do you expect in this course? ");
scanf("%c",&grade);
printf("Well, I hope you get a %c.\n",grade);
```

The data type `char` is used to declare a character variable. Use the `%c` specifier for I/O. The `&` operator is required just as it is for numerical values.

Now suppose you wish a program to request a student ID in the form of a social security number. This isn't actually a number because it is usually given in the format nnn-nn-nnnn. The presence of the dashes means that this ID value must be treated as a string of characters.

There is no separate data type for strings of characters in C. Instead, use the `char` data type with additional information about how many characters you wish to represent. Here is the code to read a social security number:

```
char ID[12];
...
printf("Give your student ID in the format nnn-nn-nnnn: ");
scanf("%s",ID);
printf("You told me that your student ID is %s.\n",ID);
```

First, the data declaration statement defines the variable ID as a character string that can hold up to 12 characters. You might notice that a social security number contains 11 characters rather than 12. In C, strings include a special terminating character, so it is usual practice to declare strings that hold at least one more than the maximum number of characters you wish to store.

In the scanf statement, the conversion specifier %s tells C to interpret what you type as a string of characters. To display a string, use %s as a format specifier. Note that the variable ID is *not* preceded by the address-of operator & in the scanf statement. The reason for this won't become clear until we study arrays in Chapter 6. (Basically, C treats a string of characters as an array of characters.) The variable name associated with a character string is actually the address of the first character in the string. Because it is *already* an address, the address of operator & is not required.

A problem occurs with C's handling of character strings when these strings include embedded blanks. For example, suppose a program asks you to enter your name:

```
printf("Enter your full name: ");
scanf("%s",name);
```

You might reply by typing Laura Brooks. This will *not* work. The reason is that C's "scan" of what you type starts at the first nonblank character and stops at the first blank character. Thus, the variable name will contain just Laura and not Laura Brooks. Even worse, the characters ƀBrooks remain in the keyboard buffer. (The ƀ represents a blank space.) This will cause problems if your program contains another scanf statement.

The simple way around this difficulty is to store the first and last names in separate variables:

```
printf("Enter your first and last name: ");
scanf("%s %s",first_name,last_name);
```

However, suppose you use this code:

```
printf("Enter your name in the format last, first: ");
scanf("%s %s",last_name,first_name);
```

This won't work. If you enter your name as Brooks, Laura, first_name will have the value Laura, but last_name will have the value Brooks, (including the comma as part of the name), rather than just Brooks. As you can see, reading strings in C can be tricky. The text will discuss solutions to specific problems as they occur.

Reading Values With Leading Zeros and Nonblank Separators

Up to now, we have assumed that numerical values entered at the keyboard will be separated by one or more blanks. This is not always a good assumption. A good example involves reading a date in the American format mm/dd/yyyy, with slashes separating the values. Another potential problem with the date format arises when leading zeros are used with single-digit months and days; for example, 01/09/1998 instead of 1/9/1998.

Special care is required to read such values correctly. First of all, we will assume that the / in a date always follows *directly* after the number with no intervening blank space. In that case, we can include the / character as part of the conversion string. Second, we will treat the date values as integers. There are two conversion specifiers that are available for reading integers, %i and %d. If there is a possibility that an integer value might include a leading zero, we must use a %d specifier to read the values. Here is some sample code:

```
printf("Give date in mm/dd/yyyy format: ");
scanf("%d/%d/%d",&m,&d,&y);
```

Why is the %d specifier required? Generally, we will consider %i and %d to be equivalent. (See Table 3.2 in Chapter 3.) However, this is not always true. Consider program P-2.3.

P-2.3 [oct.c]

```
#include <stdio.h>

int main(void)
{
  int i;

  printf("Give integer: ");
  scanf("%i",&i);
  printf("%i %d\n",i,i);
  printf("Give integer: ");
  scanf("%d",&i);
  printf("%i %d\n",i,i);

  return 0;
}
```

Running P-2.3 (three times)

```
(first execution)
Give integer: 12
12 12
Give integer: 12
12 12

(second execution)
Give integer: 012
10 10
Give integer: 012
12 12

(third execution)
Give integer: 09
0 0
Give integer: 09
9 9
```

The first execution of the program is straightforward, as either conversion specifier interprets the digits 12 correctly. In the second execution, the 12 is preceded by a leading 0. If you expect C to ignore the leading 0, you will be in for a surprise! When a %i specifier is used, the resulting value is 10, whereas a %d specifier returns the expected value of 12. In the third execution, reading the digits 09 with a %i specifier gives a value of 0, and the %d specifier returns the expected value. You might encounter a similar situation if your program tries to interpret a date in mm/dd/yyyy format as three integers. If the date 09/08/2001 is encountered, for example, the conversion string "%i/%i/%i" will not work properly, but the conversion string "%d/%d/%d" will.

How can we explain this behavior? The answer lies in the fact that C inteprets leading 0s as indicating that the following digits are to be interpreted as an octal (base 8) number rather than a decimal (base 10) number. We won't provide a complete explanation of non-base-10 number systems, but it is sufficient for this discussion to note that the octal number 12 (or 012 in C notation) is equivalent to $1\times8^1 + 2\times8^0$, or decimal 10. The digits 09 make no sense as an octal number because the digit 9 doesn't exist in the base 8 number system.

P-2.3 demonstrates that the %i conversion specifier can be used to interpret numbers expressed in base 10 (decimal) or octal notation. Thus the digits 012 are processed on input as the octal number 12, equivalent to decimal 10. In the third execution, the digit 9 is treated as a terminating character when the program tries to interpret the characters 09 as an octal number, producing a result of 0. In contrast, the %d conversion specifier always tries to interpret digits as base-10 integers, which is why it produces the expected result in P-2.3. Note that because integers are always output as decimal (base 10) integers, %d and %i specifiers work equivalently as format specifiers for output.

Exercises 10 and 11 at the end of this chapter involve problems in which it is important to use a %d conversion specifier for input, for the reasons discussed here.

2.2.2 File I/O

In order for a programming language to be useful for solving practical problems, it must support interfaces with external sources. The simplest such source is information typed on your computer's keyboard, as in P-2.2. However, keyboard input is impractical for large amounts of data.

We will now consider a different version of P-2.2. The purpose of P-2.4 is the same as that of P-2.2, but the value for the radius will come from an external data file rather than from the keyboard. Also, the output from P-2.4 will be written to an external data file in addition to being displayed on the monitor screen.

P-2.4 [circle_f.c]

```c
/* Calculate the area and circumference of a circle
   of specified radius, using an external data file. */

#include <stdio.h>
#define PI 3.14159

int main(void)
{
   double radius,          /* input - radius of a circle        */
          area,            /* output - area of a circle         */
          circumference;   /* output - circumference of a circle */
   FILE   *inp, *outp;     /* pointers to input and output files */

   /* Open the input and output files. */

   inp  = fopen("circle.dat","r");
   outp = fopen("circle.out","w");

   /* Read the radius. */

   fscanf(inp,"%lf",&radius);
   fprintf(outp,"The radius is %.2f\n",radius);
   printf("The radius is %.2f\n",radius);
   fclose(inp); /* Close the input file. */

   /* Calculate the area and circumference. */

   area = PI*radius*radius;
   circumference = 2*PI*radius;

   /* Store the output. */

   fprintf(outp,"The area is %.2f\n",area);
   fprintf(outp,"The circumference is %.2f\n",circumference);
```

```
printf(       "The area is %.2f\n",area);
printf(       "The circumference is %.2f\n",circumference);

fclose(outp); /* Close the output file. */

return 0;
}
```

P-2.4 requires two files—one for input and one for output. The identifier FILE is used to declare two **pointers** to the files, *inp, and *outp:

```
FILE *inp, *outp;        /* pointers to input and output files */
```

(The asterisk in front of the variable names inp and outp is what identifies them as pointers rather than variables. We will have more to say about pointers in Chapter 5.) In order to access the files, they must first be opened. The general syntax for the fopen function is

```
type FILE * variable = fopen(file name, "status")
```

For now, we will specify either read-only ("r") or write-only ("w") status for a file. We will always need the return value from fopen, so we will not include the (void)fopen(...) option in the syntax description.

In P-2.4, the statements

```
inp  = fopen("circle.dat","r");
outp = fopen("circle.out","w");
```

open the two files needed for the program. The pointers inp and outp, which have previously been declared as type FILE * variables, are assigned by the calls to fopen. (These pointers can be given any convenient name.) In the first statement, inp is associated with the data file circle.dat, and because this is the input file, it is specified as an "r" (read-only) file. Similarly, the second statement associates outp with a "w" (write-only) file, circle.out, to hold the output from the program. The name of the input file to be read by the program is specified by the character string "circle.dat". The lack of any other directory or folder reference in the file name implies that the file resides in the same directory or folder in which the program is being created and is going to be executed. If this is not true, then more information about the location of the file must be given. In a Windows/MS-DOS environment, for example, a full path name could be specified as "c:\\c_stuff\\data\\circle.dat". The double backslashes are necessary because C uses a single backslash character to indicate that a control character follows, as in \n for the "new line" character in a printf function.

In order to read one or more values from a file, use the fscanf function. Its general syntax is

```
        type int variable = fscanf(type FILE * variable,
             format string, one or more variable addresses)
  or
                        (void)fscanf(...
```

The syntax for fscanf is identical to that for scanf except that the input device—the name of a file in this case—must be specified.

It's important to close a file when your program is finished with it. The general syntax for fclose is

```
        type int variable = fclose(type FILE * variable)
  or
                        (void)fclose(...
```

You should not normally need the value returned from fclose; this value is equal to 0 if the file is closed successfully and to the predefined value EOF if it's not.

2.2.3 I/O Redirection

There is another way to get input from a data file that may not be so obvious. Recall program P-2.2, which is designed for keyboard input and monitor output. Assuming an executable version of circle.c exists, it is possible to replace keyboard input with input from an external file by using input redirection. On MS-DOS or UNIX systems, the redirection statement

```
circle.exe < circle.dat
```

will produce the same results as the original program, except that the data will come from the file circle.dat. As a practical matter, it would be better to modify P-2.2 so that the radius value is echoed in the output, just as it was in P-2.4.

Likewise, output redirection can be used to send the output from a program to an external file. The statement

```
circle > circle.out
```

sends the output from `circle` (P-2.2) to the file `circle.out`. However, the prompt for the user to supply an input radius is also sent to the output file and will not appear on the monitor screen. You can type the value even though you don't see the prompt, and the program will then execute and send output to the file, but this isn't very practical! Output redirection makes sense only for a batch mode program that doesn't require user input or that gets its input from an external data file.

2.3 Reading External Text Files of Unknown Length

The contents of files required as input to programs are usually more complicated than those discussed in Section 2.2.2. Typically, these are text files prepared by the programmer or obtained from some other source. Assuming you understand the contents and structure of a file, how do you read it in C?

The fact is that C is a relatively inconvenient language for this task, compared to Fortran or Pascal. Our approach will be to find some workable solutions and stick with them. The purpose of presenting this kind of "cookbook" approach early in the text is to help you develop a basic working knowledge of how to access data for use in a program. We will return to some of the details later in the text.

Consider the file `structur.dat`:

```
 1   2   3  66.6
 4   3  16  17.7
11  12  56  3.3
12   0   1  4.4
12  15  33  5.5
12  59  58  13.3
14   2  13  12.2
```

This short file contains three integers (they could be interpreted as hours, minutes, and seconds, for example) and one real number in each record, or line, of the file. We will assume that the program does *not* know ahead of time how many records there will be in the file. This is a typical situation with external files and has important implications for how a file is processed.

In order to develop a strategy for reading text files, you need to know that every text file has two important characteristics: it includes an *end-of-line mark* at the end of every line and an *end-of-file mark* at the end of the file. When you create a text file with a text editor, the end-of-line (eol) mark is put in the file whenever you press the Enter or Return key. When a program creates a text file, the eol mark is put in the file whenever you include the \n control character as part of an `fprintf` format string. The end-of-file (eof) mark is put in the file without any additional action

end-of-line (eol) mark
end-of-file (eof) mark

on your part whenever you save a file from within a text editor or `fclose` it in a program.

The goal in writing code to read a text file is to read one record at a time inside a *loop structure* that terminates when the end of the file is detected. We haven't discussed C's implementation of loop structures yet, but we described them in Chapter 1 in the context of the **LOOP... END LOOP** pseudocode command. For now, we will provide code for some loop structures to perform the specific task of reading a file of unknown length. P-2.5 shows one way to read `structur.dat`.

| loop structure |

P-2.5 [`filetest.c`]

```c
#include <stdio.h>
#define FILE_NAME "structur.dat"

int main()
{
    FILE *Infile;
    int count=0;
    int hr,min,sec;
    float x;
    int status;

    Infile=fopen(FILE_NAME,"r");
    while (1)
    {
        status=fscanf(Infile,"%i %i %i %f",&hr,&min,&sec,&x);
        if (status == EOF) break;
        printf("%2i %2i %2i %6.2f\n",hr,min,sec,x);
        count=count+1;
    }
    fclose(Infile);
    printf("Lines in file = %i",count);
    return 0;
}
```

Running P-2.5

```
 1  2  3  66.60
 4  3 16  17.70
11 12 56   3.30
12  0  1   4.40
12 15 33   5.50
12 59 58  13.30
14  2 13  12.20
Lines in file = 7
```

The `fscanf` function is used to read the file in the same way that `scanf` reads input from the keyboard. This function returns an integer value, and the basic strategy of P-2.5 is to use this value to control the execution and termination of the loop. Loop syntax will be discussed in more detail in Chapter 4, but the intent of this code should be clear in context. The loop

```
while (1) {
    ...
}
```

causes statements inside the loop to execute indefinitely until something happens inside the loop to terminate it. The C language includes a predefined value called EOF, which is returned by fscanf through variable status, whenever fscanf is unable to find *any* of the values whose addresses are given in the list following the format string. As long as status isn't equal to EOF, the loop continues to execute. In this example, as long as the file contains valid data that can be read by the fscanf statement, the program displays the data and increments the counter. The if... statement is also an element of C we haven't discussed yet, but its intent should be clear if you recall the *IF... THEN...* pseudocode command from Chapter 1. (In C, the *THEN* part of the pseudocode command is implied.) This statement examines the current value of variable status and terminates the loop with a break; when status has a value of EOF.

The data declarations in P-2.5 illustrate another feature of C: variables can be initialized at the same time they are declared. The initialization for count is required in P-2.5 because count will later be incremented inside the while... loop; it is very poor programming practice to assume that any variable will automatically be initialized to 0. In P-2.5, count is initialized to 0 because of how it is used, but any appropriate value is allowed. It is also always okay to initialize a variable with an assignment statement rather than as part of its declaration.

A different approach to reading files is shown in P-2.6.

P-2.6 [filetes2.c]

```
#include <stdio.h>
#include <string.h>
#define FILE_NAME "structur.dat"

int main()
{
    FILE *Infile;
    char one_line[100];
    int count=0;
    int hr,min,sec;
    float x;
    char *line_ptr;
    Infile=fopen(FILE_NAME,"r");
```

```
while (1) {
    /* First read the line into a string. */
    line_ptr=fgets(one_line,sizeof(one_line),Infile);

    /* Quit if at end-of-file. */
    if (line_ptr == NULL) break;

    /* Replace "new line" with null character (optional).*/
    one_line[strlen(one_line)-1]='\0';

    /* Print the string just as a test (optional). */
    printf("%s\n",one_line);

    /* Then scan the line to get numerical data. */
    (void) sscanf(one_line,"%d %d %d %f",&hr,&min,&sec,&x);
    printf("%2i %2i %2i %6.2f\n",hr,min,sec,x);

    /* Keep track of number of lines (optional). */
    count++;
}
fclose(Infile);
printf("Lines in file = %i",count);
return 0;
}
```

Instead of reading values directly from the file, P-2.6 reads each line into string one_line using the fgets ("get string") function and then performs an *internal read* on that string to extract the numerical information. The general syntax for the fgets function is

```
type char * variable = fgets(character string,
                             integer equal to size of character string,
                             type FILE * variable)
or
                    (void)fgets(...
```

The file-handling loop in P-2.6 shows another way to detect the end of a file and exit the loop:

```
char *line_ptr;
    ...
    while (1) {
        ...
        line_ptr=fgets(one_line,sizeof(one_line),Infile);
        if (line_ptr == NULL) break;
        ...
    }
```

As was the case in P-2.5, this is an infinite loop that will continue until a break; statement is executed, because the value 1 is interpreted by C as "true."

The fgets function reports the presence of an end-of-file mark in its return value, which is a pointer to the first character in the character string one_line. When an end-of-file is encountered, the pointer returned by fgets has a value of NULL. We can test for this:

```
if (line_ptr == NULL) break;
```

and exit the loop using a break;.

When fgets reads a string, it adds a new-line character to the end of the string. This is the same control character, \n, that is used in a printf statement to start a new line. If we want to use the string itself for anything (we don't in this program), we can get rid of the new-line character by replacing it with a null character. If we are curious about the contents of one_line, we can print it.

```
one_line[strlen(one_line)-1]='\0';
printf("%s\n",one_line);
```

In C, characters are always enclosed in single quote marks. The '\0' is treated like a single character because of the backslash. The strlen function returns the length of its string argument, including the new line character. According to the ANSI C standard, programs that use strlen require access to the string.h header file, even though not all compilers (including the cc compiler) require that this header file be #included.

All that remains is to scan the line to extract the numerical data. Use the sscanf ("string scan") function. This works just like scanf except that it gets its input from a character string rather than from the keyboard buffer. Its general syntax is

```
type int variable = sscanf(input string, conversion specifier,
                           list of variable addresses)
or
                    (void)sscanf(...
```

In P-2.6, the sscanf function is used to read the four numerical values on each line:

```
(void) sscanf(one_line,"%i %i %i %f",&hr,&min,&sec,&x);
printf("%2i %2i %2i %6.2f\n",hr,min,sec,x);
```

In many cases, your program will want to know how many lines the file contained, so increment a counter with the statement count++;. After the termination of the while... loop, close the file and print the results:

```
fclose(Infile);
printf("Lines in file = %i",count);
```

An important difference between fscanf and fgets is that fgets always reads an entire line from a text file; the end of the line is detected by looking for an end-of-line mark.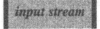
On the other hand, fscanf reads one or more values as specified by a format string. It treats the text file as an *input stream* of characters, and it treats end-of-line marks simply as "white space" separating the requested values. (That is, it basically ignores the end-of-line marks.) This works well for reading numerical values, but it can sometimes cause problems when characters, character strings, and numerical values are mixed in the same file.

Here is a modified data file that contains some text information, in the form of one character string at the beginning of each line of the file, in addition to numerical values:

```
Jan  1  2  3 66.6
Apr  4  3 16 17.7
Nov 11 12 96  3.3
```

Program P-2.7 illustrates the minor modification of P-2.5 required to read this file and display its contents. In this case, it is still possible to use scanf, rather than fgets.

P-2.7 [filetes3.c]

```c
#include <stdio.h>
#define FILE_NAME "structr2.dat"

int main()
{
    FILE *Infile;
    char month[10];
    int count=0;
    int hr,min,sec;
    float x;
    int status;
    Infile=fopen(FILE_NAME,"r");
    while (1)
    {
       status=fscanf(Infile,"%s %i %i %i %f",
                   month,&hr,&min,&sec,&x);
       if (status == EOF) break;
       printf("%3s %2i %2i %2i %6.2f\n",month,hr,min,sec,x);
       count++;
    }
    fclose(Infile);
    printf("Lines in file = %i",count);
    return 0;
}
```

An important point about P-2.7 is that the & operator is *not* used in front of a variable name associated with a character string. Such a variable name is actually a memory location; specifically, it is the address in memory of the first character in that string.

Although programs P-2.5, P-2.6, and P-2.7 may seem somewhat repetitious, each provides an example of code that solves a specific programming problem. The choice of which approach to use depends on the task at hand. Some programmers prefer fgets for accessing files, as they believe that fscanf is sometimes unreliable. However, when you know ahead of time how many values a line will hold, you should be able to use fscanf without problems. The code in P-2.6, using fgets and sscanf, may be appropriate when you are not sure ahead of time how many values are included in a specific record, or when you have some other reason to hold a line from a file temporarily in a string variable.

In any event, it is important not to stray far from the code models in P-2.5, P-2.6, and P-2.7 when you write your own programs to read external text files. In all programs that use input files, it is important to concentrate on reading and displaying the contents *before* tackling the rest of the program. By the time you have finished Chapter 4, which presents a general discussion of loop structures, you will have developed a much better understanding of the code presented in this section. Then if you need to develop different file processing strategies, you will be in a better position to do so.

As a final example, consider this typical problem:

> A data collection system consists of several measurement stations, each with its own ID, which is expressed as an integer. When a station reports measurements, it sends its ID along with one or more measurements in the form of real numbers, but it never sends more than eight measurements in a single report. These station reports have been collected and compiled into a text file for processing. Write a program that reads this file and calculates the total number of reports and the total number of measurements reported by all stations.

The data file used for this program, stations.dat, can be found on the Web site mentioned in Section 6 of the Preface.[2] It looks like this:

```
1001 14 17.7 13.3 12.9 19.9 11 9 20
1002 17.7
1003 14 15 16 17 18 19 20
1001 4.4 5.5 6.6
1004 14 15 17.1 18.1
1004 11.1 12.1 13.3 4.4 8.8
1005 39 38 37 36 35 34 33 32
```

---

[2]All data files required for programs in the text as well as for the exercises can be found on this Web site.

The required calculations are remarkably easy to do in C if you take proper advantage of the return values from the appropriate I/O functions, as demonstrated in P-2.8.

P-2.8 [stations.c]

```
#include <stdio.h>

int main(void)
{
  FILE *in;
  int ID,status,n_reports=0,n_measurements=0;
  char *line_ptr;
  char one_line[80];
  float x;

  in=fopen("stations.dat","r");
  while (1) {
    line_ptr=fgets(one_line,sizeof(one_line),in);
    if (line_ptr == NULL) break;
    status=sscanf(one_line,"%i %f %f %f %f %f %f %f %f",
            &ID,&x,&x,&x,&x,&x,&x,&x,&x);
    n_reports=n_reports+1;
    n_measurements=n_measurements+(status-1);
  }
  fclose(in);
  printf("There are %i records and %i measurements.\n",
          n_reports,n_measurements);
  return 0;
}
```

Running P-2.8

There are 7 records and 36 measurements.

For this problem, the data cannot be read directly with fscanf, as it is not clear ahead of time how many measurements (the floating-point numbers) follow each station ID (the integer). Asking your program to read an ID and eight data values will work for the first line but not for the second line. When your program tries to read the second line, fscanf will try to find the requested values by looking ahead to the third line. This will soon cause problems! However, if each *line* of the file is first read separately into a string, sscanf can then be used to read the ID and up to eight data values. It won't matter if sscanf runs out of values in that string; it will simply "give up" and return the total number of values successfully read. The total number of reports is obtained by incrementing a counter after each successful fgets. The total number of measurements reported by all stations is obtained by incrementing a counter by status-1 after each sscanf. (The number of measurements is one less than the value returned in status because the ID isn't counted as a measurement.)

Note that in the sscanf statement, all the measurements are read into the same variable address, &x. This isn't a very useful approach in general, but it is okay for this simple problem.

2.4 Reading a File One Character at a Time

Occasionally, it is useful to read a file one character at a time and this section describes how to do that. One application of this technique might be to deal with the transfer of text files created on an MS-DOS system to some other system. In order to understand what is required, we must mention briefly the *ASCII character collating sequence*. This is a widely used standard for encoding characters. The sequence contains 256 characters, the first 128 of which are identical for all computer systems using this standard.[3] The second 128 characters are system-dependent. Appendix 1 gives a table of ASCII characters for Windows/MS-DOS-based computers.

When text files are created on a Windows/DOS computer, they have an end-of-line mark that actually consists of two characters—a new-line character (decimal value 10 in the ASCII character collating sequence) and a carriage return character (decimal value 13). On Macintosh or UNIX systems, the end-of-line character consists just of the new-line character. The default strategy of utilities that convert MS-DOS text files to Macintosh is to remove the carriage return character from the end of every line. However, it is certainly possible that an MS-DOS file could be downloaded or copied onto a Macintosh or UNIX platform, or vice versa, without this translation having been made. Depending on how the file will be read by a program, it might be necessary to remove or add the carriage return character.

Program P-2.9 examines a text file and displays the integer equivalent of every character in the file except ASCII character 13, the carriage return character. When the program encounters ASCII character 10, it prints a new-line character.

P-2.9 [fileview.c]

```
/* Displays contents of a text file character by character. */
#include <stdio.h>

int main(void)
{
    FILE *in;
    char name[20];
    int ch;
```

---

[3]Some IBM mainframe computers use EBCDIC encoding, which is significantly different from ASCII encoding. IBM and IBM-compatible personal computers use ASCII encoding.

```
printf("Give file to fix: ");
scanf("%s",name);

in=fopen(name,"r");
if (in == NULL) {
  printf("Can't find file.  Abort program.");
  exit();
}
while (!feof(in)) {
  ch=fgetc(in);
  if (ch != 13) printf("%3i",ch);
  if (ch == 10) printf("\n");
}
fclose(in);

return 0;
}
```

P-2.9 contains some new syntax and three new functions. The syntax involves the use of an if... statement. You can interpret its meaning based on the *IF... THEN... ELSE* pseudocode command. (The *THEN...* is implied in C.) We will discuss this syntax in Chapter 4. The new functions are feof, fgetc, and exit. The first of these returns a nonzero value when the file pointer is at the eof mark and 0 otherwise. The second reads a single character from the file and returns its integer value in the ASCII collating sequence—not its character value, as you might expect. (That is why the variable ch is declared as type int rather than as type char.) Actually, characters and integers are interchangeable in the sense that you can easily switch back and forth between the two representations. All that is required to display characters rather than integers is to change the format specifier in the printf statement from %3i to

```
printf("%c",ch);
```

or

```
printf("c",(char)ch);
```

In the latter case, the (char) makes clear that you wish the variable ch to be treated as a character rather than as an integer.[4]

The exit function terminates the program immediately. By convention, exit(0) indicates normal program termination and a nonzero value indicates a problem. Using the function without a value inside the parentheses is also okay. In this text, we will not bother to write code that specifies exit values.

---

[4]This kind of operation is called type casting, and we will have more to say about it later in the text.

2.5 Applications

In this section, and in similar sections in later chapters, we will develop programs that use and sometimes extend the material discussed in the chapter. The purpose of presenting detailed solutions even when the problems seem simple is to help you develop a consistent problem-solving approach that you can use in programming as well as in your other science, engineering, and mathematics courses. It will always be helpful for you to read the problem statement and then try to design the algorithm and write the program on your own.

2.5.1 Maximum Deflection of a Beam Under Load

1 *Define the problem.*

Consider a beam of length L supported at each end and subject to a downward force of F pounds concentrated at the middle of the beam. The maximum downward deflection of the beam (at its middle) is $-FL^3/(48EI)$, where F is the downward force in pounds, L is the beam length in inches, E is the elasticity in units of lb/in^2, and I is the moment of inertia in units of in^4. Write a program to calculate the maximum deflection for specified values of L, F, E, and I. For a particular steel I-beam (a beam with an I-shaped cross-section), $E = 30 \times 10^6$ lb/in^2 and $I = 797$ in^4. The deflection of such a beam as a function of length (in feet) is shown in Figure 2.1.

2 *Outline a solution.*

1. Create a data file containing the desired values of L, F, E, and I. Let your program convert length from feet to inches, if required.
2. Calculate deflection according to the above formula. The sign of the deflection can be either positive or negative as long as it's understood that the deflection is in the downward direction.
3. Display the output.

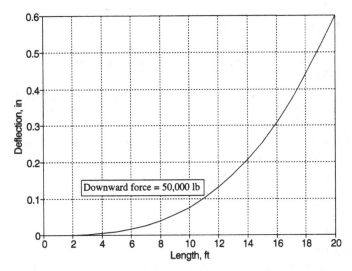

*Figure 2.1. Deflection of a steel **I**-beam under a central load.*

3 *Design an algorithm.*

DEFINE *(L = length, ft; F = central force, lb; E = elasticity, lb/in^2;*
  I = moment of inertia, in^4; deflection, in)

OPEN *(file containing input data)*
READ *(L,F,E,I)*
CLOSE *(file containing input data)*
ASSIGN *L = L•12.0 (convert to inches)*
  deflection = -F•L^3/(48EI)
WRITE *(deflection)*

4 *Convert the algorithm into a program.*

P-2.10 [beam.c]

```
#include <stdio.h>
#define FILENAME "beam.dat"

int main(void)
{
```

```
double length,force,elasticity,mom_of_inertia;
FILE *infile;

infile=fopen(FILENAME,"r");

fscanf(infile,"%lf %lf",&length,&force);
fscanf(infile,"%lf %lf",&elasticity,&mom_of_inertia);
fclose(infile);
printf(
   "Length of beam (feet) and central force (lb): %.1lf %.1lf\n",
   length,force);
length=length*12.0;
printf(
   "Elasticity (lb/in^2) and moment of inertia (in^4): %e %.1lf\n",
   elasticity,mom_of_inertia);
printf("deflection = %lf in\n",
      -force*length*length*length/48.0/elasticity/mom_of_inertia);

return 0;
}
```

Running P-2.10

```
Length of beam (feet) and central force (lb): 20.0 50000.0
Elasticity (lb/in^2) and moment of inertia (in^4):
3.000000e-007 800.0
deflection = -0.600000 in
```

5 *Verify the operation of the program.*

You probably don't have an intuitive feel for what the answer should be for a beam having the values of elasticity and moment of inertia specified in the problem statement. According to Figure 2.1, the maximum deflection of a 20-foot beam with the indicated properties is about 0.6 inches when subjected to a load of 50,000 pounds concentrated in the middle of the beam. What would you think about using this formula if it returned an answer of 0.001 inches? How about 10 inches?

Problem Discussion

P-2.10 is a straightforward program using a simple external text file for input, but there are some important details. First, it is important that the creator of the data file (beam.dat) be aware of which units to use for input. In particular, the elasticity and moment of inertia are given in units that use inches, but the problem statement indicates that the beam length should be given in feet. It is probably best to retain this unit for input and let your program do the conversion to inches. Regardless of the solution you choose, it is essential that your program account for the fact that, for example, an input of 20 for the length means 20 feet and not 20 inches! The value for elasticity of 30×10^6 can be written in scientific notation as `30e6`.

Second, note that L^3 is coded as `length*length*length`, as there is no exponentiation operator in C. In Chapter 3, we will see that there is another way to do this calculation using an intrinsic function.

Up to now, the `%lf` conversion/format specifier has been used for I/O of type `double` variables. However, the C language has several different specifiers that control the appearance of displayed output. In P-2.10, one of those alternatives, `%e`, is used to display the elasticity and moment of inertia. This specifier is useful for displaying very large or very small real numbers in scientific notation. (See Table 3.2 in Chapter 3 for a list of conversion/format specifiers.)

Finally, it may be helpful to know that for a simple file such as the one needed by P-2.10, C doesn't care about the line-by-line arrangement of the values in the file. The order in which the input values are given in the data file is important, of course, but these values can be given either on the same line or on two or more lines. For example:

```
20 50000 30e6 800
```

and

```
20
50000
30e6
800
```

are equivalent and equally acceptable ways to provide one set of input values.

2.5.2 Relativistic Mass and Speed of an Electron

This particular problem has been chosen specifically because the quantities involved may be unfamiliar. Hopefully, this unfamiliarity will encourage you to be careful when you translate this and every other problem statement into a program, and also to be diligent when you verify that program's operation.

1 Define the problem.

An electron accelerated by a voltage V in an electron gun acquires an energy of $Ve = mc^2 - m_0c^2$, where $e = 1.602 \times 10^{-19}$ coulomb is the charge on an electron, $m_0 = 9.109 \times 10^{-31}$ kg is the rest mass, m is the relativistic mass in kg, and c = 2.9979×10^8 m/s is the speed of light. The speed v of an electron of relativistic mass m is obtained from $m/m_o = [1 - (v/c)^2]^{-1/2}$. Write a program that reads several voltages from an external file and calculates the relativistic mass and speed of an electron accelerated by that voltage. (Sample answer: For a voltage of 1.5×10^6 V, m = 3.58×10^{-30} kg and v = 2.9×10^8 m/s. See Figure 2.2 for more information.)

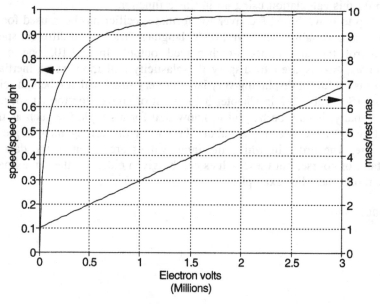

Figure 2.2. Relativistic mass and speed of an electron.

2 Outline a solution.

The terminology of this problem may be unfamiliar, but the required algebraic manipulations are not difficult. The relativistic mass is a consequence of relativity theory, which predicts that mass is not a constant property of matter, but increases with speed with respect to a stationary observer. The solution is straightforward:

1. Read the voltage of the electron gun.
2. Calculate the mass first, then the speed, using the equations given in Step 1.
3. Display the output.

3 *Design an algorithm.*

DEFINE *(All variables are real numbers. The rest_mass,*
charge e, and speed of light c are constants.)
OPEN *(file containing voltages)*
LOOP *(as long as there are voltages to read)*
    READ *(voltage)*
    WRITE *(echo voltage from file)*
    ASSIGN *mass = (voltage•e + rest_mass*c^2)/c^2*
            velocity = c•[1 − (rest_mass/mass)^2]$^{1/2}$
    WRITE *(mass and velocity)*
END LOOP
CLOSE *(file containing voltages)*

4 *Convert the algorithm into a program.*

P-2.11 [rel_mass.c]

```
#include <stdio.h>
#include <math.h>

#define E 1.602e-19          /* Coulomb */
#define C 2.9979e8           /* m/s */
#define REST_MASS 9.109e-31 /* kg */
#define FILENAME "rel_mass.dat"

int main(void)
{
  double voltage,speed,rel_mass;
  FILE *infile;
  int status;

  infile=fopen(FILENAME, "r");
  while (1) {
    status=fscanf(infile,"%lf",&voltage);
    if (status == EOF) break;
    printf("for voltage of : %e V\n",voltage);
    rel_mass=(voltage*E+REST_MASS*C*C)/(C*C);
    speed=C*sqrt(1.0-(REST_MASS/rel_mass)*(REST_MASS/rel_mass));
    printf("relativistic mass and speed: %g %g\n",rel_mass,speed);
  }
  fclose(infile);

  return 0;
}
```

Running P-2.11

```
for voltage of : 1.500000e+006 V
relativistic mass and speed: 3.58464e-030 2.89949e+008
for voltage of : 1.500000e+007 V
relativistic mass and speed: 2.76483e-029 2.99627e+008
for voltage of : 1.500000e+005 V
relativistic mass and speed: 1.17827e-030 1.90159e+008
for voltage of : 0.000000e+000 V
relativistic mass and speed: 9.109e-031 0
```

5 *Verify the operation of the program.*

These calculations are easy to implement in C, but you must check them by hand, using a calculator to do the math. Be careful when you calculate the exponents on powers of 10. It is easy to make mistakes and accept wrong answers when the numbers are so large or small that it is difficult to develop a feel for them. If you have never had an introductory physics course, or even if you have, the numbers may be essentially meaningless, so a wrong answer will look as reasonable or unreasonable as the right one. As another test of the reasonableness of your answers, you could add to your code the calculations for the ratio of the electron's speed to the speed of light—it must be less than 1—and the ratio of its relativistic mass to its rest mass—it must be greater than 1; these are the values shown in Figure 2.2.

Problem Discussion

As implied in the problem statement, the code should treat the data file as a file of unknown length. Therefore, the voltages in the file are read with `fscanf` inside a conditional loop that terminates when the end-of-file is detected.

Program P-2.11 gets a little ahead of our discussion of C in one respect: it makes use of C's `sqrt` function to calculate the square root required to obtain the electron's speed. In Chapter 3, we will give more details about using such functions, which are essential for any language used to do scientific and engineering calculations. For now, the intent of this function should certainly be clear in the context of the program. It is necessary to include the `<math.h>` header file in order to use the `sqrt` function. If you are using the UNIX `cc` compiler, you will also have to include the option `-lm` (to link the math library) in the command line when you compile this program:

```
cc rel_mass.c -orel_mass.exe -lm.
```

Note the use of scientific notation to express the physical constants in the program. The voltage input can also be given in scientific notation, and it can still be read with a `%lf` specifier. In P-2.11, an alternative specifier, `%g`, is used for output. It displays real numbers in floating point or scientific notation, whichever is shorter. This is useful when you're not sure of the magnitude of the answers your program will produce.

2.6 Debugging Your Programs

There is no shortage of potential problems in even the simplest C programs. The first errors you will encounter are *compile-time errors*, or *syntax errors*, that your programming environment will detect when it tries to

> *compile-time error*
> *syntax error*

compile your program. Unfortunately, the messages that C compilers give about these errors are not always very helpful. One result of the free-format nature of C is that sometimes an error message will be reported far from its actual location, as your compiler defers reporting the error until it is forced to give up on determining how you wish your source code to be interpreted. The C language is this way by design; the penalty to be paid for having a very flexible language is that programmers must assume a great deal of responsibility for writing syntactically correct code. All syntax errors must be removed from a source code file before an executable program can be generated.

Even after your program is free of syntax errors, there is another class of errors that your programming environment can detect only after a program has begun

> *run-time errors*

executing. These *run-time errors* must be corrected by modifications to your source code to allow your program to execute properly or to produce correct answers.

The only way to become proficient at finding *bugs* and *debugging* your programs is to make errors (not a problem!), note the messages resulting from those errors, and learn how to

> *bug*
> *debugging*

respond to those messages. Each programming environment is a little different because the messages displayed in response to syntax or run-time errors are generated by the compiler you are using; the content of these messages isn't regulated by the C language standard. In the next sections, some common compile-time and run-time errors are described.

2.6.1 Compile-Time Errors

1. Misspelled keywords and function names

This includes using inappropriate combinations of uppercase and lowercase letters, such as `Printf` instead of `printf`. It is difficult for a C compiler to give a useful message about such errors because it has no way of determining what you actually meant. Your defense against this kind of error is to be careful when you type your source code in the first place.

2. Undefined variable names

This is a "good" error because it forces you to declare every variable appearing in your program. It is easy to make spelling errors when you type in source code, and the messages resulting from this error will show you where variable names have been misspelled.

3. Inappropriate use of semicolons on lines containing compiler directives

Compiler directives are not C statements, so they do not end with a semicolon. For example, `#include <stdio.h>;` will produce an error, but the message may not be very helpful and may appear to relate to an entirely different part of your source code. Again, your only defense is to be careful.

4. Missing semicolons

Because of the free-format nature of C, this error is usually reported on the line *after* the one on which the missing semicolon was expected. Remember that *every* C statement must end with a semicolon.

5. Unbalanced curly braces ({ . . . }) around statement blocks

This is another error that is difficult for a compiler to interpret because it "keeps hoping" that the missing brace will be found. Thus the error message often references a source code line, perhaps even the last line of the program, that is far from where the missing brace should have been. Your defense against this kind of error is to be consistent about indenting statement blocks so that it is easy to see the correspondence between the start of a code block and its closing brace; this has the added advantage of making your code much easier to read and understand.

6. Unbalanced parentheses

Every left parenthesis must be balanced by a right parenthesis in an assignment statement or a call to a function. You are encouraged to use extra parentheses whenever their presence makes calculations more clear, but many beginning programmers overuse parentheses in simple assignment statements. Code such as

```
x = a + (b/c);
```

is okay, but these parentheses are not needed because multiplication and division take precedence over addition and subtraction. The use of too many parentheses in more complicated arithmetic expressions makes mistakes more likely and should be avoided. A more detailed discussion of the precedence of operations will be found in Chapter 3.

7. Missing quote marks around conversion specifier strings in I/O statements

Quote marks around string constants (string literals) must always occur in pairs—an opening quote and a closing quote. Your compiler will try to find a missing quote mark and may report the error far from the line in which the error actually occurred.

2.6.2 Run-Time Errors

1. Inappropriate I/O conversion specifiers

This error can result in "garbage" values or program crashes. Such errors won't be detected as compile-time errors, but they can cause incorrect answers or odd errors when you try to run your program. If values print as 0 even though you know they have nonzero values, or if variables appear to have wildly inappropriate values, the most likely cause is an inappropriate conversion specifier.

Your defense against this kind of error is to check compatibility between variables and conversion specifiers in `printf` and `scanf` functions (and their corresponding file I/O functions). Although some inconsistencies are of little consequence—it is okay to use a `%f` format, rather than `%lf`, to display a type `double` variable, for example—it is better practice to be consistent about using an I/O conversion specifier that is properly associated with the data type of the quantity being read or written.

2. Omitting the address-of operator (`&`) for nonstring variables used as arguments in input functions

Variable names associated with characters, integers, and real numbers must always be preceded by the `&` character when your program reads their values using `scanf` or some other input function. Failure to do so asks C to consider the variable name as an address rather than as a symbolic name. When you read strings, the names of string variables are considered by C to be addresses—a detail which certainly isn't obvious, and which will be discussed later in more detail—so the `&` operator isn't used. This kind of error will be detected only when your program executes. The results range from variables having values of 0 to obscure messages such as `segmentation fault`.

3. Not finding a requested input file

Because nearly all C functions, including I/O functions, return values, the C language depends on these values to detect certain kinds of error conditions. You might want a program to crash if it can't find a file you asked it to read from, but it won't do that. Instead, the `fopen` function will return a value that can be interpreted as, "I couldn't find this file."

It is certainly possible, and even desirable, to write code that will respond appropriately to such a message, but we have avoided it in the examples presented in this chapter. Such code uses syntax we haven't discussed yet, and it makes programs longer, harder to read, and less clear in their basic purpose. For programs you write for your own use, it is not hard to keep track of where data files are stored, so you aren't likely to ask your program to open a file that doesn't exist.

4. Using inappropriate mixed-mode calculations
    Consider this code fragment:

```
int min,sec;
float decimal_minutes;
...
decimal_minutes = min + sec/60;
```

Even though decimal_minutes is declared as type float, the result is an integer always equal to the value of min. Why? Because sec/60 is an *integer* calculation and always produces a value of 0 unless sec equals exactly 60. The meaning imposed by C on the division operator depends on the data type of both its operands. If both operands are integers, as in this case, the division operator returns the integer quotient of dividing sec by 60. This is sometimes a desirable result, but not in this code fragment.

    To avoid this kind of error, always be aware of whether you are doing integer or real arithmetic, regardless of the *appearance* of the values involved. Physical quantities should almost always be associated with floating-point variables even when the quantities are expressed as whole numbers. In this example, you could get the correct answer by typing sec/60.0. The fact that one of the operands is now a real number forces C to perform real arithmetic and to generate a real number result. A better idea would be to declare all three quantities as real variables *and* use 60.0 rather than 60, even though 60 is a whole number.

2.7 Exercises

In these exercises, the input may come either from values typed at the keyboard or from an external data file, as specified by your instructor. When you use a data file, be sure to echo the contents of the file as part of your program's output. Your instructor also may ask you to write output to a file instead of or in addition to your computer monitor. Also, if you use a data file for input, you can try using your system's redirection operator to direct your program's output to another file rather than to your computer monitor.

    In this and subsequent chapters, data files mentioned in the exercises can be downloaded from the Web site mentioned in Section 6 of the Preface. Instructors can obtain source code for the exercise problems directly from the author, as noted in Section 6 of the Preface. The names of the source code files are given in brackets at the end of each exercise.

1. Write a program that calculates and displays the volume and surface area of a cylinder, given the radius and height in meters. The volume of such a cylinder is $\pi r^2 h$, and its surface area is $2\pi r^2 + 2\pi r h$. [cylinder.c]

Extra Credit:
1. Assuming that the cylinder is solid and the density (g/cm^3) of the material is specified as input, calculate the mass of the cylinder. (Use an engineering handbook to find densities for one or more materials and be sure to specify in your program output what those materials are.)
2. Assuming that the cylinder is an empty container made of thin sheets of material with a known mass per unit area (g/cm^2), calculate the mass of the cylinder for a specified wall thickness. Is it appropriate to assume that this value is just the surface area times the mass per unit area of the material?
3. Create a data file with several sets of material densities and dimensions and modify your program so that it will read input values from this file rather than from the keyboard. [cylindr2.c]

2. "Block and pulley" problems are a staple of introductory physics courses.
(a) Consider a block of mass m_a hanging from a massless string that passes over a frictionless pulley and is connected to another block of mass m_b resting upon a horizontal surface as shown in Figure 2.3(a). The coefficient of

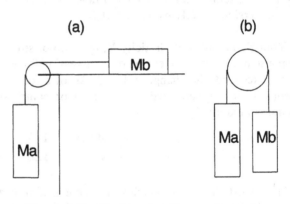

Figure 2.3. Block-and-pulley configurations.

friction between the second block and the horizontal surface is μ. Under the influence of gravity, the system of blocks undergoes an acceleration a, where the balance of forces is

$$F = (m_a - \mu m_b)g = (m_a + m_b)a$$

Write a program that calculates the acceleration of the block system for specified values of m_a, m_b, and μ. What is the maximum value of μ such that the hanging block will fall?

(b) Consider the masses from part (a) hanging from either side of a frictionless pulley, as shown in Figure 2.3(b). Now the balance of forces is

$$F = (m_a - m_b)g = (m_a + m_b)a$$

Add to your program the calculation for the acceleration of this block system.

3. The Carnot cycle describes a theoretical heat engine that absorbs heat at temperature T_1, converts some of the heat to work, and exhausts the rest at a lower temperature T_2. The efficiency of a Carnot engine, which is always less than 1, is determined by the ratio of output to input temperatures:

$$\text{efficiency} = 1 - T_2/T_1$$

where temperatures are expressed in Kelvins and $0°$ C equals 273 K. Write a program that accepts as input values of T_1 and T_2 and calculates the efficiency. Express the temperatures in units of degrees Centigrade and let your program do the conversion to Kelvins. [carnot.c]

4. Young's modulus of elasticity Y, the ratio of stress to strain, characterizes the response of materials to tension or compression forces. Assuming the elastic limit is not exceeded, the change in length ΔL of a rod of initial length L and cross-sectional area A subjected to a tension or compression force F is related to Young's modulus by

$$Y = \frac{\text{stress}}{\text{strain}} = \frac{F/A}{\Delta L/L}$$

Table 2.1 lists Young's modulus and the elastic limit for several materials.
    Write a program that determines, for each of the tabulated materials, the change in length ΔL for a 1-mm-diameter, 2-meter rod subjected to a specified force F that will not cause the elastic limit to be exceeded for any of the materials. For each material, calculate the minimum diameter a rod can have without its elastic limit being exceeded for a user-specified force. Use an external file to store all your input data. [young.c]

Table 2.1. Young's modulus and elastic limit for selected materials

Material	Young's Modulus, 10^{10} N/m^2	Elastic Limit, 108 N/m^2
aluminum	7.0	1.3
brass	9.1	3.8
copper	11.0	1.5
wrought iron	9.1	1.6
spring steel	10.0	4.1

5. Write a program that asks the user to supply the mass and velocity of an object and then calculates and displays the kinetic energy and momentum of that object. The kinetic energy is $mv^2/2$ and the momentum is mv. Use metric units (mass in kilograms, velocity in meters per second, energy in joules).

Extra Credit:
    Include source code that will convert the kinetic energy and momentum to their British system equivalents. The British unit of energy is ft-lb and the unit of momentum is slug-ft/s. 1 ft-lb = 1.356 joule; 1 slug = 14.59 kg; 1 ft/s = 0.3048 m/s. [kinetic.c]

6. Write a program that asks the user to supply the mass m, radius r , linear speed v, and rotational speed ω of a rolling solid spherical ball. The total kinetic energy of an object is the sum of its translational and rotational kinetic energies:

$$KE_{total} = I\omega^2/2 + mv^2/2$$

where I is the moment of inertia. For a solid sphere of radius r, the moment of inertia is $2mr^2/5$. Use metric units to calculate and display the linear, rotational, and total kinetic energy in joules. Rotational speed is measured in units of rad/s. [rolling.c]

7. The drag force F_D on a moving object is given by

$$F_D = (\rho/2)v^2 AC_d$$

where ρ is the density of the gas or fluid through which an object of projected (cross-sectional) area A m^2 moves at a speed v m/s. (For air, $\rho = 1.23$ kg/m^3.) The dimensionless drag coefficient C_d has a value in the range 0.2 to 0.5 for automobiles. The power required to overcome the drag is

$$P = F_D v$$

For force and speed in mks units, power is measured in watts. One horsepower is equivalent to 746 watts.

Write a program that asks the user to supply the speed in units of mph, cross-sectional area in units of square feet, and drag coefficient of a moving automobile and then calculates the drag force in newtons and the power in horsepower required to overcome this drag force. [dragforc.c]

8. Write a program that calculates and prints the total resistance of three resistors connected (a) in parallel and (b) in series, as illustrated in Figure 2.4. When they are connected in parallel, the total resistance of n resistors is $1/r_T = 1/r_1 + 1/r_2 + 1/r_3 + ... + 1/r_n$. When they are connected in series, the total resistance of n resistors is $r_T = r_1 + r_2 + r_3 + ... + r_n$. Prompt the user to enter values in ohms, the usual unit of resistance. [resistor.c]

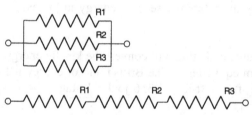

Figure 2.4. Resistors in parallel and in series.

9. Consider the reliability of a system consisting of three components connected in series or in parallel. If the reliability of the components is given as R_1, R_2, and R_3, where $0 \le R \le 1$, then the reliability of a system with the components wired in series is

$$R_{series} = R_1 R_2 R_3$$

If the same components are wired in parallel, and if the system remains functional as long as any one of the components is working, then the system reliability is

$$R_{parallel} = 1 - (1 - R_1)(1 - R_2)(1 - R_3)$$

Write a program to calculate the reliability of such systems for three user-specified values of reliability.

Systems using components in series are vulnerable to failure even if the individual components are very reliable. On the other hand, redundant systems, with components in parallel, are very reliable even if the components aren't very reliable individually. For example, if each component has a reliability of 0.900, a system with these components in series has a reliability of only 0.729. If the same components are in parallel, then the system reliability is 0.999. [reliable.c]

10. Write a program that requests as input the clock time in hours (0 to 24), minutes, and seconds in the format hh:mm:ss and displays the time in both seconds and fractions of a day. One day contains 86,400 seconds. For example, 12:00:00 is 43,200 seconds, or 0.5 days.
Hint: Be sure to read the discussion at the end of Section 2.2.1 before writing the code for this problem. [time.c]

11. Write a program that requests as input an angle expressed in degrees, minutes, and seconds in the format dd:mm:ss and converts it to whole and fractional degrees. There are 60 minutes in a degree and 60 seconds in a minute. For example, 30:15:04 equals 30.25111 degrees.
Hint: Be sure to read the discussion at the end of Section 2.2.1 before writing the code for this problem. [angles.c]

12. Write a program that requests as input the time in seconds required to run a distance of one mile and calculates the speed in units of feet per second, meters per second, and miles per hour. For example, a 4-minute (240-second) mile is run at an average speed of 22 feet per second, 6.71 meters per second, or 15 miles per hour. There are 5280 feet in one mile and 3.2808 feet in one meter. [speed.c]

13. Write a program that calculates and prints the energy of a photon whose wavelength λ is given in centimeters. The energy = hf joule, where $h = 6.626 \times 10^{-34}$ joule-s (Planck's constant), $f = c/\lambda$, where $c = 2.9979 \times 10^8$ m/s (the speed of light) and wavelength is given in meters. (See Figure 2.5.)
Hint: Use a defined constant and scientific notation to define the speed of light and Planck's constant. As an example of using scientific notation in C, the number 6.626×10^{-34} can be represented as 6.626e-34.

Extra Credit: A 1 eV (electron volt) photon has an energy of 1.602×10^{-19} joule. Modify your program so it will also calculate the wavelength of a photon with an energy of 1 eV. (Answer: about 1240×10^{-9} m. This is in the infrared part of the electromagnetic spectrum.) [photon.c]

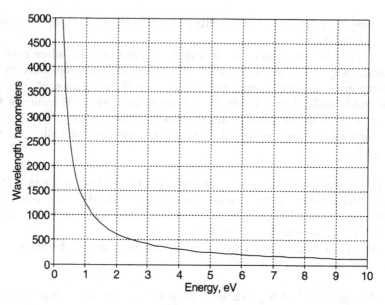

Figure 2.5. Wavelength of a photon as a function of energy.

14. Recalling programs P-2.2 and P-2.4, which calculated the area and circumference of a circle for a specified radius, write a version that performs these calculations for several radius values stored in an external data file. Your program should not assume ahead of time how many radius values there will be. [circl_f2.c]

15. (a) Write a program that asks for a student's name, ID (in the form of a social security number), cumulative grade point average (GPA), and total number of credit hours accumulated through the most recent grading period. Calculate the total number of grade points by multiplying the number of credit hours by the GPA. Now ask the user to supply information about a newly completed course. This information should include the number of credit hours for the course and the number of points for each credit hour—4 for an A, 3 for a B, 2 for a C, 1 for a D, and 0 for an F. Multiply the credit hours by the number of points corresponding to the grade earned in the new course and add it to the old number of total grade points. Add the new credit hours to the old credit hours. Divide the new grade point total by the new total credit hours to recalculate the GPA. Display this value. [gpa.c]

(b) Rewrite the program in part (a) so that data about several students are contained in a single data file. Create the file yourself, with whatever format you think will simplify your programming. The file should contain, for each student, the same information entered at the keyboard for the program in part (a). This new program should require no keyboard input to run and should display the data in the file as well as the new total credit hours and GPA. Do *not* assume that your program knows ahead of time how many students will be represented in the file. If you like, you can send output both to your monitor and to a new data file. [gpa2.c]

16. The ideal gas law describes the relationships among pressure (p), volume (V), and temperature (T) of an ideal gas:

$$pV = \mu RT$$

where μ is the number of kilomoles of gas and R is the universal gas constant. For volume in m³, temperature in kelvins, and pressure in newton/m² (pascal), R = 8314.3 joule/kilomole-K, and 1.0132×10^5 pascal = 1 standard atmosphere (atm). Write a program that calculates the volume occupied by a specified number of kilomoles of an ideal gas at temperature T (°C) and pressure p (atm). (Sample answer: under standard conditions of T = 273.15 K (0°C) and a pressure of 1 atm, 1 kilomole of an ideal gas occupies a volume of about 22.4 m³.) [gas_law.c]

Extra Credit:
1. If you were trying to determine the validity of the ideal gas law experimentally, it would make more sense to use the law to calculate pressure for a specified volume and temperature. Modify the program to do this calculation instead of the calculation specified in the original problem statement.

2. Because molecules occupy volume and exert intermolecular forces on each other, the ideal gas law becomes less accurate as density increases—that is, as more molecules occupy the same volume. The van der Waals modification to the ideal gas law attempts to take this into account with the following empirical formula:

$$(p + a/v^2)(v - b) = RT$$

where v is the specific volume (m³/kilomole, for example). The constants a and b are different for each gas and are experimentally derived. Table 2.2 contains data for several gases and Figure 2.6 shows pressure as a function of specific volume for nitrogen.

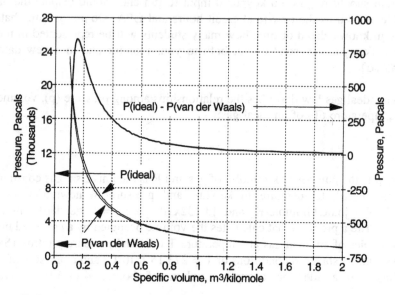

Figure 2.6. Pressure as a function of specific volume for nitrogen at
T = 273.15 K.

Table 2.2. Molar masses and van der Waals coefficients for selected gases

Gas	Molar mass, gm/mole	van der Waals coefficients			
		a, kPa-m^6/ kg^2	b, m^3/kg	a, l^2-atm/ mole^2	b, l/mole
air	28.97	0.1630	0.001270	1.350	0.0368
ammonia	17.03	1.4680	0.002200	4.202	0.0375
carbon dioxide	44.01	0.1883	0.000972	3.600	0.0428
helium	4.00	0.2140	0.005870	0.034	0.0235
hydrogen	2.02	6.0830	0.013200	0.245	0.0267
methane	16.04	0.8880	0.002660	2.255	0.0427
nitrogen	28.02	0.1747	0.001380	1.354	0.0387
oxygen	32.00	0.1344	0.000993	1.358	0.0318
propane	44.09	0.4810	0.002040	9.228	0.0899

Source: M. C. Potter and C. W. Somerton (1993), Schaum's Outline
Series: *Theory and Problems of Engineering Thermodynamics,*
Tables B-3, B-8.

Modify your program (the extra credit one, not the original one) to do calculations for both the ideal gas law and the van der Waals modified law.
Hint: Be careful with units! 1 liter/mole is numerically identical to 1 m^3/kilomole. If the pressure is calculated in pascals, then the tabulated value for a must be multiplied by 101320. [gas2.c]

17. In braking tests on automobiles, the initial speed v and stopping distance d are recorded. Write a program that reads several pairs of v and d values from an external file. Assume that the automobile decelerates at a constant rate while the brakes are applied. Calculate the time to stop t and the deceleration a for each pair of values. The relevant formulas are

$$d = at^2/2$$
$$v = at$$

The initial speed should be given in units of miles per hour and the stopping distance should be given in feet. Note that these units are inconsistent, so speed should be converted to units of feet per second before you do the calculations. [car_stop.c]

18. The Body Mass Index (BMI) provides a way to characterize normal weights for human adult bodies as a function of height. It is defined by

$$BMI = w/h^2$$

where w is mass in kilograms (2.2 kilograms mass per pound weight) and h is height in meters. A BMI in the range 20-25 is considered normal and a BMI over 30 is considered obese.

One problem with the BMI is that it doesn't distinguish between fat and muscle. Thus a professional football player might be considered obese because he has an abnormal amount of muscle weight relative to his height.

An alternative formula that takes into account the source of body weight is

$$BMI' = (a_F F + a_L L)/h^2$$

where F and L are fat and lean weights (F + L = w) and a_F and a_L are constants that give different weights (in the statistical sense) to muscle weight and fat weight. The constants are chosen to satisfy these constraints:

1. BMI = BMI' for average adults with a body fat content of 20 percent.
2. $a_F = 2a_L$

The second somewhat arbitrary constraint means that fat weight counts twice as much as lean weight in the calculation of BMI'. To look at it another way, an exercise program that replaced one pound of fat with two pounds of muscle would leave BMI' unchanged. Let p equal the fraction of total body weight associated with fat. Then

$$F = pw$$
$$L = (1 - p)w$$
$$a_F pw + a_L(1 - p)w = w$$
$$a_F = 2a_L$$
$$0.2(2a_L) + 0.8a_L = 1$$
$$a_L = 0.833$$
$$a_F = 1.667$$

Write a program that calculates both BMI and BMI'. Ask the user to enter her or his total weight in pounds, height in inches, and percent body fat.

19. An external data file (`weather.96`) contains weather data for Philadelphia, Pennsylvania, in the following format:

```
   Date  hi    time  lo    time   rec. hi  rec. lo  norm.
         bar.6a   noon    6p    mid.
    hum. hi  lo prec.   mon. year. norm.   AQ    cl   sun rise/set
01/01/96   43 12:45p  34   5:28a   62 1973    4 1881  39   24
         29.92r 29.96f 29.93r 29.90f
          85   64 TRACE TRACE TRACE   0.11 ---- --  100   7:22a   4:46p
01/02/96   37 12:01a  32   9:50p   67 1876    7 1968  39   24
         29.85f 29.83f 29.73s 29.57f
         100   75  0.56   0.56   0.56   0.22 g 43 pa 100   7:23a   4:47p
(and so forth)
```

Using this file, find and print the maximum temperature and date of all days during 1996 on which the maximum temperature was at least 90° F. You can assume that:

1. The three header lines appear only once, at the beginning of the file.
2. There are no missing days.
3. Every day in the year is represented by three lines in the file, consistently formatted as shown.
4. The maximum temperature, in contrast with some of the other parameters, is always present and is right-justified in columns 10–12. [`weather.c`]

20. Consider the file `track.dat`, which contains winning times for the 1500 meter and marathon races in the modern Olympics.

```
      Men                 Women
year 1500 m  marathon
1896 4:33.20 2:58:50.00
1900 4:06.20 2:59:45.00
1904 4:05.40 3:28:53.00
1908 4:03.40 2:55:18.40
1912 3:56.80 2:36:54.80
1916
1920 4:01.80 2:32:35.80
1924 3:53.60 2:41:22.60
1928 3:53.20 2:32:57.00
1932 3:51.20 2:31:36.00
1936 3:47.80 2:29:19.20
1940
1944
1948 3:49.80 2:34:51.60
1952 3:45.20 2:23:03.20
1956 3:41.20 2:25:00.00
1960 3:35.60 2:15:16.20
1964 3:38.10 2:12:11.20
1968 3:34.90 2:20:26.40
1972 3:36.30 2:12:19.70 4:01.40
1976 3:39.17 2:09:55.00 4:05.48
1980 3:38.40 2:11:03.00 3:56.60
1984 3:32.53 2:09:21.00 4:03.25 2:24:52.00
1988 3:35.96 2:10:32.00 3:53.96 2:25:40.00
1992 3:40.12 2:12:23.00 3:55.30 2:32:41.00
1996 3:35.78 2:12:36.00 4:00.83 2:26:05.00
```

In some years since 1896, there haven't been any Olympic games at all because of World Wars I and II. Also, the women's events were phased in at different years starting in 1972.

Write a program that will read this file and report the years for which there were no Olympic games. This programming problem can easily be solved in C by using `fgets` to read each line of the file and then acting on the value returned when the resulting string is interpreted with `sscanf`. You will need one statement that requires syntax we have not discussed yet. Suppose the value returned by `sscanf` is stored in `int` variable `status`. Then

```
if (status == 1) printf(...
```

will print an appropriate message for a year in which no Olympics were held.

Data Types, Operators, and Functions

3.1 Specifying and Using Data Types

C is a strongly typed language that demands a specific programmer-supplied data type for every variable name used in a program. We have already used several different data types in the programs presented in Chapter 2. In this section, we will give a more detailed description of data types. C supports basic data types for integers, real ("floating-point") numbers, and characters. For each of the numerical data types, there are choices that define the number of digits that can be represented as integers as well as the number of significant digits and the range of real numbers. Some data types have one or more alias names that can be used in a program. Table 3.1 lists these data types and gives ranges for one particular C implementation, Microsoft's MS-DOS-based Quick C. It is important to realize that these ranges are not fixed by the ANSI C standard and can differ among various C implementations.

The nature of C requires that I/O operations be associated with specific data types. This association is made with format and conversion specifiers. When used with input statements, conversion specifiers tell C what kind of variable is being read. To put it another way, specifiers tell C how to translate characters typed at the keyboard or read from a file. For example, the statement

```
scanf("%lf",&x);
```

tells C to interpret characters typed at the keyboard as a real number of type double. Each data type has its own conversion or format specifiers for reading values with scanf or displaying values with printf, as shown in Table 3.2.

Within the format specifiers used with output statements such as printf, it is possible to further control the appearance of the output by specifying the total number of characters allocated for the output and, for floating-point numbers, the number of digits appearing to the right of the decimal point. The general form is w for character, string, and integer output and $w.d$ for floating-point number output, inserted between the % symbol and the format specifier. The hard-coded value w is the total number of characters allocated for the output field. In the case of real numbers, d is the number of digits appearing to the right of the decimal point. Numbers are right-justified in their fields. For example, the value 17.7 displayed with format specifier "%10.3lf" will be displayed as ƀƀƀ17.700. If the number of characters is insufficient to display the output, the field will be expanded to allow the display. Thus the conversion specifier "%3.3lf" will display any numerical value, no matter how large, with three digits to the right of the decimal point. For example, 17.7 will be displayed as 17.700. Numbers are properly rounded when using the $w.d$ option to specify the number of digits to the right of the decimal point. Thus 17.766 will print as 17.77 with a "%5.21f" specifier and as 18 with a "%2.01f" specifier.

Characters and character strings are also right-justified when their field lengths are specified, and C will expand the field to display an entire character string, if necessary.

Table 3.1. Some C data types

Data Type	Alias(es)	Range of Values (for Microsoft Quick C)
short	short int, signed short signed short int	-32767 to 32767
int	signed int signed	-32767 to 32767
long	long int, signed long signed long int	-2147483647 to 2147483647
unsigned short	unsigned short int	0 to 65535
unsigned	unsigned int	0 to 65535
unsigned long	unsigned long int	0 to 4294967295
float	(none)	1.175494e-038 to 3.402823e+038
double	(none)	2.225074e-308 to 1.797693e+308
long double	(none)	3.362103e-4932 to 1.189731e+4932
char	(none)	'A' (example)
(character string)	(none)	char a[80]; (example) ... a="This is a string.";

The %f and %lf specifiers will *read* numbers in either decimal or scientific notation, but they *display* numbers in decimal notation, which can lead to a loss of information. For example, a %lf specifier will read the value 3e-9 correctly, but it will display this value as 0.000000. Use a %e or %g specifier to display very small values correctly.

Especially for scientific and engineering applications, you need to be aware of the limits on ranges for the various data types. These ranges are implementation dependent. The only requirement of the ANSI C standard is that when progressing from "smaller" to "larger" data types, the number of integers, the range, and the precision must be at least as large or precise as for the previous "smaller" data type.

Table 3.2. Conversion/format specifiers and control characters for I/O

Character(s)	Purpose
%	Begin conversion specification.
%%	Display the character %.
c	Read/display character.
d (i), ld (li)	Read/display signed integer.
e (E), le (1E), Le (LE)	Display type float, double, or long double floating point number in scientific notation. Read such data types expressed in either decimal or scientific notation.
f, lf, Lf	Display type float, double, or long double floating point number in decimal notation. Read such data types expressed in either decimal or scientific notation.
g (G), lg (1G), Lg (LG)	Display type float, double, or long double floating point number in scientific or decimal notation, depending on which is shorter. Read such data types expressed in either decimal or scientific notation.
s	Read/display string.
u, lu	Read/display unsigned short, unsigned, or unsigned long.
\	escape character: \b move cursor one character to the left \f "form feed" to top of next page \n go to beginning of next line \r go to beginning of current line \t go to next tab stop (eight character tabs) \" print the character " \\ print the character \

Program P-3.1 shows how to determine the ranges and, for floating-point numbers, the number of significant digits for your C implementation. This program requires the standard header files limits.h and float.h to access the built-in constants INT_MAX, INT_MIN, FLT_MAX, FLT_MIN, DBL_MAX, and DBL_MIN.

P-3.1 [ranges.c]

```c
/* Find ranges for numeric data. */
#include <stdio.h>
#include <limits.h>
#include <float.h>
#include <stdlib.h>
#include <math.h>

int main(void)
{
  printf("Range of short integer: %d %d\n",SHRT_MAX,SHRT_MIN);
  printf("Range of integer: %d %d\n",INT_MAX,INT_MIN);
  printf("Range of long integer: %ld %ld\n",LONG_MAX,LONG_MIN);
  printf("Max unsigned short integer: %u\n",USHRT_MAX);
  printf("Max unsigned integer: %u\n",UINT_MAX);
  printf("Max unsigned long integer: %lu\n",ULONG_MAX);
  printf("Range of float: %e %e\n",FLT_MAX,FLT_MIN);
  printf("Precision of float: %i\n",FLT_DIG);
  printf("Range of double: %e %e\n",DBL_MAX,DBL_MIN);
  printf("Precision of double: %i\n",DBL_DIG);
  printf("Range of long double: %Le %Le\n",LDBL_MAX,LDBL_MIN);
  printf("Precision of long double: %i\n",LDBL_DIG);
  printf("%e\n",HUGE_VAL);
  return 0;
}
```

Running P-3.1

```
Range of short integer: 32767 -32767
Range of integer: 32767 -32767
Range of long integer: 2147483647 -2147483647
Max unsigned short integer: 65535
Max unsigned integer: 65535
Max unsigned long integer: 4294967295
Range of float: 3.402823e+038 1.175494e-038
Precision of float: 7
Range of double: 1.797693E+308 2.225074E-308
Precision of double: 15
Range of long double: 1.18973E+4932 3.3621E-4932
Precision of long double: 19
1.797693e+308
```

Some programmers prefer to use type double variables for all numerical calculations, even though this data type requires more memory than float and may slow the performance of calculation-intensive programs. The justification for this choice is that the so-called intrinsic functions for mathematical calculations, which will be discussed later in this chapter, expect type double arguments and return type double results. Thus the use of type double variables eliminates the need for "downward" type casting, a topic we will deal with later. In ANSI-standard C, the minimum range for positive values of type double is from 10^{-37} to 10^{37}. However, you will likely find that even the float data type in your implementation supports numbers in this range, with seven or eight significant digits. This is enough range and precision for many calculations, so it will sometimes be acceptable to use type float rather than type double numerical variables.

3.2 Operators

C supports a great many operators. Some of these are straightforward, such as the +, -, *, and / operators for the basic mathematical operations of addition, subtraction, multiplication, and division. The * and / arithmetic

binary operator
unary operator

operators work only as *binary operators*. These require two operands, one to the left of the operator and the other to the right, as in a*b. The + and – operators work either as binary operators or as *unary operators*, in which a single operand appears to the right of the operator, as in -x. Other operators are unique to C and provide shortcuts for specifying certain common programming operations, such as incrementing and decrementing values. Table 3.3 lists these operators.

Of the math operators, only the / and % deserve special mention, as the operation of the others is straightforward. The % is the *modulus operator* that

modulus operator

returns the remainder from integer division. For example, 7%4 returns a value of 3. For two integer operands, or integer-valued expressions, the / operator returns the integer quotient. For example, 7/4 returns a value of 1. This perhaps unexpected result, briefly mentioned in Section 2.6 of Chapter 2, is due to the fact that, in C, the data type of the operands determines the data type of the result.

The real challenge in mastering C's operators lies in learning the rules that determine the order in which operations in an

operator precedence rules

expression are evaluated. These *operator precedence rules* are given in Table 3.4. For now, we are interested in just the arithmetic operators. In an algebraic expression, for example, multiplications and divisions are performed before additions and subtractions, so, as expected, multiplication and division operators have higher precedence than addition and subtraction operators. Just as in algebra, the use of parentheses can alter the precedence of operations. As a matter of style, parentheses should be used for any but the most straightforward expressions in which there is no possibility of misinterpreting the precedence rules. We will assume in this text that our definition of straightforward expressions is limited to those for which the algebraic precedence rules for addition, subtraction, multiplication, and division apply.

Table 3.3. C operators

Operator	Purpose	Example
Arithmetic Operators		
+	add (binary) or multiply by +1 (unary)	a+b, +a
-	subtract (binary) or multiply by -1 (unary)	a-b, -a
*	multiply	a*b
/	divide	a/b
%	remainder (modulus) in integer arithmetic	i%j
Assignment Operators		
=	simple assignment	x=y
<operator>=	compound assignment used with arithmetic operators	x+=y (x=x+y) x-=y (x=x-y) x*=y (x=x*y) x/=y (x=x/y) i%=j (i=i%j)
Increment/Decrement Operators [1]		
++	add one to operand	++i, i++
--	subtract one from operand	--x, x--
Relational and Logical Operators		
==	equal	a==b
!=	not equal	a!=b
<	less than	a<b
>	greater than	a>b
<=	less than or equal	a<=b
>=	greater than or equal	a>=b
!	logical NOT (unary operator)	!a
&&	logical AND	(a==b) && (c<d)
||	logical OR	(a<b) || (c>d)

[1] See the text for a discussion of the implications of applying these operators before and after the variable.

Table 3.4. Precedence of C operations

Operator(s)	Precedence
function calls	1
!, unary +, unary -, unary & [1], unary * [2]	2
type casts	3
*, /, %	4
binary +, binary -	5
<, >, <=, >=	6
==, !=	7
&&	8
||	9
=	10

[1] & is the address-of operator as used in scanf, for example.

[2] * is the dereferencing operator for pointers, a topic that will be discussed in Chapter 5.

P-3.2 demonstrates the use of some of the shorthand assignment and incrementing/decrementing operators given in Table 3.3. It is never required to use these operators, but their use is consistent with C's generally terse syntax.

P-3.2 [operator.c]

```
#include <stdio.h>
int main(void)
{
  int x,y;
  x=7; y=4;
  printf("%i %i\n",x%y,x/y);    /* (1) */
  x+=y;
  printf("%i\n",x);             /* (2) */
  x=y--;
  printf("x= %i, y= %i\n",x,y); /* (3) */
  x=--y;
  printf("x= %i, y=%i\n",x,y);  /* (4) */
  printf("%i\n",x*=y);          /* (5) */
  return 0;
}
```

Running P-3.2

```
3 1
11
x= 4, y= 3
x= 2, y= 2
4
```

From the `printf` function in the line labelled (1) in P-3.2, the modulus and division operators applied to 7 and 4 yield 3 and 1. For line (2), the result is the same as writing x=x+y, which equals 11. For the decrementing

| *prefix operator* |
| *postfix operator* |

and incrementing operators, the results depend on whether the operator appears before (***prefix operator***) or after (***postfix operator***) a variable name. For line (3), the postfix operation assigns the current value of y (4) to x and then decrements y to 3. In line (4), the prefix operation first decrements y from 3 to 2 and then assigns x this new value. The behavior of the incrementing/decrementing operators can be confusing, so they should be used with care.

The relational operators described in Table 3.3 are used to compare values and expressions. For example, the expression A < B has a value of True if A is less than B and a value of False if it's not. Such comparisons are used in the implementation of the ***IF... THEN... ELSE...*** pseudocode command: for example, "If A is less than B, then take some action...." The C implementation of this pseudocode will be discussed in Chapter 4.

Some languages support a ***logical*** or ***boolean data type*** that has True or False as its two possible values. One of these values is assigned as a result of a

| *logical data type* |
| *boolean data type* |

comparison, such as A < B, being either True or False. However, as noted in the discussion of selection structures in Chapter 4, C does not support a logical data type. Therefore, it is sometimes useful to define constants that make relational operations more clear:

```
#define TRUE 1
#define FALSE 0
```

Finally, C supports the logical operators NOT, AND, and OR. These are used to form compound relational statements,

| *truth table* |

such as, "If A equals B and C is greater than 0, then...." In view of the precedence rules, it is advisable to write such statements with parentheses even at the algorithm design stage: "If (A = B) and (C > 0), then...." This indicates that the expressions A = B and C > 0 are to be evaluated first, and the relationship between those two results will then be tested. At that point, the truth of an entire compound expression depends on ***truth tables***, as shown in Table 3.5. Again, the details of implementing relational and logical operators will be deferred to Chapter 4.

Table 3.5. Truth tables for logical expressions A and B

AND	B is True	B is False
A is True	True	False
A is False	False	False
OR	B is True	B is False
A is True	True	True
A is False	True	False

The expression (A && B) is True only if both A *and* B are True. The expression (A || B) is True if either A *or* B is True.

3.3 Type Casting

C supports the ability to convert one kind of value into another, an operation called *type casting*. When programs work with numerical data, common type casting operations include converting integer values into floating-point values before performing arithmetic operations (an *upward type cast*) and converting type double return values from math functions into type

type casting
upward type cast
downward type cast
explicit type cast
implicit type cast

float values (a *downward type cast*). Type casts can be either implicit or explicit. With an *explicit type cast*, the target data type is given in parentheses directly to the left of the value, variable, or expression that will be cast. With an *implicit type cast*, the variable on the left side of an assignment operator has a different data type than the value, variable, or expression on the right side of the assignment operator. C performs a type cast for the value, variable, or expression so it conforms to the data type of the variable on the left side of the assignment operator. This implicit type cast is performed regardless of whether it is a good idea in the context of what you are asking your program to do.

With either kind of type cast, it is possible to lose information. For example, a type float or double value, variable, or expression can be cast to an int variable, although this is usually not a good idea. For example, consider this code fragment:

```
int i;
double x=17.7;
i=x;
```

The third statement in this code assigns the type double variable x, with a value of 17.7, to the type int variable i. Because of the implicit downward type cast, the value of i is 17; this represents a loss of information, specifically the fractional part of the value 17.7.

Because of the potential for loss of information, it is important to be aware of the results of implicit (automatic) type casting, especially when multiplications and divisions are being performed. P-3.3 illustrates a typical scenario in which an upward type cast can be used to advantage.

P-3.3 [test_avg.c]

```
/* Demonstrate effect of explicit type casting. */
#include <stdio.h>

int main()
{
        int total_score,num_students;
        float average;

        printf("Enter sum of scores: ");
        scanf("%d",&total_score);
        printf("Enter number of students: ");
        scanf("%d",&num_students);

        average=total_score/num_students;
        printf("Average score (no type casting) is %.2f\n",average);

        average=(float)total_score/(float)num_students;
        printf("Average score (with type casting) is %.2f\n",average);
        return 0;
}
```

Running P-3.3

```
Enter sum of scores: 333
Enter number of students: 4
Average score (no type casting) is 83.00
Average score (with type casting) is 83.25
```

In P-3.3, the sum of several integer values is divided by the number of values to give the average as a floating-point result. There is no loss of information when integers are type cast to floating-point values. In this case, the total score has been stored as an integer, presumably because the individual scores from which the total score has been calculated are whole numbers. However, when the scores are averaged, the result will not be a whole number, in general. In the statements

```
average=total_score/num_students;
```

the result of dividing the two type int variables is the *truncated* quotient, which is not the desired result in this case; even if you want an integer result, you would probably prefer the *rounded* result from the division. That is, the division operation on two integers retains the integer quotient and throws away the remainder.

The solution in this program is to use an explicit type cast:

```
average=(float)total_score/(float)num_students;
printf("Average score (with type casting) is %.2f\n",average);
```

In this case, both the numerator and the denominator have been converted to floating-point numbers because the name of the desired data type appears in parentheses directly in front of a variable. The type cast operation has higher precedence than division, so it converts the values to the target data type before the division is performed. In this case, either

```
float(total_score)/num_students
```

or

```
total_score/(float)num_students
```

will achieve the desired result, but

```
(float)(total_score/num_students)  /* won't work */
```

won't work because the division is performed before the type cast operation.

This example should convince you that it is important to think carefully about the data type of operands, especially when division operations are being performed. In P-3.3 it would have been a better idea to declare total_score as type float or double rather than int. Then the type cast wouldn't have been necessary.

The preceding discussion should also convince you to be especially careful when you use implicit type casts. They are not usually necessary in scientific and engineering calculations, and they can sometimes produce unexpected and unwanted results. For now, you should restrict your casts to the implicit or explicit integer-to-floating-point (type float or double) casts illustrated in P-3.2 and P-3.3.

3.4 Intrinsic Functions

C supports many built-in (intrinsic) functions. Table 3.6 lists functions that enable common mathematical calculations to be performed in C. Most of the functions expect one or more type `double` arguments and return a type `double` result. Unless otherwise noted, each function requires the inclusion of the `math.h` standard header file. In your program design, you must ensure that a function is called with an appropriate argument.

Although most intrinsic math functions expect type `double` arguments, they will also accept arguments for which an upward type cast prevents loss of information. Thus the function calls `sqrt(3)` and `pow(4,3)` produce answers identical to the more proper calls `sqrt(3.)` and `pow(4.,3.)`.

Some mathematical functions can produce values that approach 0 or ±∞. For example, tan(θ) approaches +∞ as θ approaches 90°, and e^{-x} approaches 0 as x approaches +∞ or −∞. In such cases, C returns ±HUGE_VAL or 0 where HUGE_VAL is a constant defined in the `math.h` library; the actual value of HUGE_VAL varies from compiler to compiler. Note that C programs won't crash when you enter an inappropriate argument. For example, the `sqrt` function will return a value of 0 if you call it with a negative argument. This has both advantages and disadvantages. The advantage is that your program will continue to execute. The disadvantage is that your program may no longer be producing answers that make sense. Be careful!

For future reference, Table 3.7 includes some intrinsic functions for file and I/O operations. As noted, these functions require that the standard header file `stdio.h` be included in your program.

One of the functions in Table 3.7, `fflush`, hasn't been mentioned before. Its purpose is to empty (flush) an input buffer. Its typical use is to clear the keyboard buffer before more input is read: `fflush(stdin);`, where `stdin` is the name of the keyboard, the default input buffer. This is sometimes needed when a program contains multiple `scanf` statements. It is a good habit to precede a `scanf` statement with `fflush(stdin);` for any call to `scanf` after the first in a program.

The `const char *` parameter type appearing in several of the functions refers to a string constant; for example, a string containing I/O format specifiers.

Table 3.6. Standard math functions (The `math.h` standard header file is required except where noted. See P-3.4 [`math.c`].)

3.6(a) Trigonometric and hyperbolic functions

Function	Function and Parameter Type	Return Value	Example
`acos(x)`	`double`	arc cosine of x, in radians, range 0–π for $\|x\| \le 1$, otherwise 0	`acos(0.5)`
`asin(x)`	`double`	arc sine of x, in radians, range ±π/2 for $\|x\| \le 1$, otherwise 0	`asin(0.5)`
`atan(x)`	`double`	arc tangent of x, in radians, range ±π/2	`atan(0.5)`
`atan2(y,x)`	`double`	arc tangent of y/x, in radians, range π±, 0 if both x and y are 0	`atan2(-2.0,1.0)`
`cos(x)`	`double`	cosine of x radians, 0 if not successful	`cos(3.0)`
`cosh(x)`	`double`	hyperbolic cosine of x, HUGE_VAL if result is too large	`cosh(0.5)`
`sin(x)`	`double`	sine of x radians, 0 if not successful	`sin(0.5)`
`sinh(x)`	`double`	hyperbolic sine of x, ±HUGE_VAL if result is too large	`sinh(0.5)`
`tan(x)`	`double`	tangent of x radians, 0 if not successful	`tan(0.5)`
`tanh(x)`	`double`	hyperbolic tangent of x	`tanh(0.5)`

Table 3.6(b) Other math functions

Function	Function and Parameter Type	Return Value	Example
abs(x)	int	integer absolute value of x (requires stdlib.h)	abs(-7)
ceil(x)	double	smallest whole number not less than x	ceil(-3.3)
exp(x)	double	e^x, HUGE_VAL on overflow, 0 on underflow	exp(0.5)
fabs(x)	double	absolute value of x	fabs(-3.3)
floor(x)	double	largest whole number not greater than x	floor(-3.3)
fmod(x,y)	double	remainder of x/y	fmod(1.,.3)
log(x)	double	natural logarithm of x for x > 0, -HUGE_VAL if not successful	log(0.5)
log10(x)	double	base-10 logarithm of x for x > 0, -HUGE_VAL if not successful	log10(0.5)
pow(x,y)	double	x^y, 0 or ±HUGE_VAL if not successful; if x < 0, y must be a whole number	pow(2.0,3.5)
rand()	int	pseudorandom number in the range [0,RAND_MAX] where RAND_MAX is a constant defined in stdlib.h	rand()
sqrt(x)	double	square root of x for x ≥ 0, 0 if not successful	sqrt(0.5)
srand(x)	unsigned int	none—argument of 1 reinitializes random number generator, any other value sets random starting point for generating series of pseudorandom integers using rand()	srand(3)

Table 3.7. Some functions for file and I/O operations
(All functions require stdio.h standard header file.)

Name	Number and Type of Parameter(s)	Return Type	Description
fclose	1; FILE *	int	Close a file. Returns 0 if successful, EOF if not.
fflush	1; FILE *	int	Flush an input stream. Returns 0 if successful, EOF if not.
fgets	3; const char *, int, FILE *	char *	Get string input from file. Returns pointer to string if successful, NULL if not.
fopen	2; const char *, const char *	FILE *	Open a file. Returns pointer to file if successful, NULL if not.
fprintf	variable; FILE *, const char *, types matching conversion specifications	int	Write formatted output to text file. Returns number of characters printed.
fscanf	variable; FILE *, const char *, types matching conversion specifications	int	Get text file input. Returns number of values read or EOF if no values (at end of file).
printf	variable; const char *, types matching conversion specifications	int	Write formatted output to screen. Returns number of characters printed.
scanf	variable; const char *, types matching conversion specifications	int	Read formatted input from keyboard buffer. Returns number of values read.
sscanf	variable; const char *, types matching conversion specifications	int	Read formatted input from character string. Returns number of values read, EOF if at end of string.

Program P-3.4 shows how to use some of the math functions described in Table 3.6. You should run this program yourself and examine the output carefully to make sure you understand the results.

P-3.4 [math.c]

```
#include <stdio.h>
#include <math.h>
#include <stdlib.h>
void main()
{
        double pi,x,y;
        pi=atan(1.0)*4.0;
        printf("acos(0.5)   %lf\n",acos(0.5));
        printf("asin(0.5)   %lf\n",asin(0.5));
        printf("atan2(-2.0,1.0)   %lf\n",atan2(-2.0,1.0));
        printf("cos(3.0)   %lf\n",cos(3.0));
        printf("cosh(0.5)   %lf\n",cosh(0.5));
        printf("sin(0.5)   %lf\n",sin(0.5));
        printf("sinh(0.5)   %lf\n",sinh(0.5));
        printf("tan(0.5)   %lf\n",tan(0.5));
        printf("tanh(0.5)   %lf\n",tanh(0.5));
        printf("abs(-7)   %d\n",abs(-7));
        printf("ceil(-3.3)   %lf\n",ceil(-3.3));
        printf("exp(0.5)   %lf\n",exp(0.5));
        printf("fabs(-3.3)   %lf\n",fabs(-3.3));
        printf("floor(-3.3)   %lf\n",floor(-3.3));
        printf("log(0.5)   %lf\n",log(0.5));
        printf("log10(0.5)   %lf\n",log10(0.5));
        printf("pow(2.0,3.5)   %lf\n",pow(2.0,3.5));
        printf("%d   %d\n",RAND_MAX,rand());
        printf("sqrt(0.5)   %lf\n",sqrt(0.5));
        printf("%e\n",HUGE_VAL);
}
```

Running P-3.4

```
acos(0.5)   1.047198
asin(0.5)   0.523599
atan2(-2.0,1.0)   -1.107149
cos(3.0)   -0.989992
cosh(0.5)   1.127626
sin(0.5)   0.479426
sinh(0.5)   0.521095
tan(0.5)   0.546302
tanh(0.5)   0.462117
abs(-7)   7
ceil(-3.3)   -3.000000
exp(0.5)   1.648721
fabs(-3.3)   3.300000
floor(-3.3)   -4.000000
log(0.5)   -0.693147
log10(0.5)   -0.301030
pow(2.0,3.5)   11.313708
32767   41
sqrt(0.5)   0.707107
1.797693e+308
```

3.5 Simple User-Defined Functions

The C language relies heavily on program modularization, as do other high-level languages. Considering the growing importance of object-oriented languages such as C++ and Java, it is even more important to learn to think about programs as being built from pieces of code that are bound together in some kind of overall structure.

The basic subprogram structure in C is a *user-defined function*. (Indeed, as we have noted previously, even the main program in a C program is actually just a function.) Program P-3.5, which is a modification of earlier programs for calculating the area and circumference of a circle, demonstrates the use of some simple user-defined functions.

P-3.5 [circlep1.c]

```
/* Create simple functions. */
#include <stdio.h>
#define PI 3.14159265

/* function prototypes */
double area_func(double radius);
double circumference_func(double radius);

int main()
{
  double radius=3.0;
  printf("From area_func: %8.3lf\n",area_func(radius));
  printf(
  "From circumference_func: %8.3lf\n",circumference_func(radius));
  return 0;
}

double area_func(double radius)
/* PI must be available as a global constant. */
{
  return PI*radius*radius;
}

double circumference_func(double r)
/* PI must be available as a global constant. */
{
  return 2.0*PI*r;
}
```

In P-3.5, the calculations for area and circumference are performed inside the user-defined functions that follow the `main` function. A program can contain as many user-defined functions as needed. Prior

function prototype
parameter list

to the `main` function, *function prototypes* for each function are given. Each prototype consists of a single statement giving the data type of the function, the name of the function, and the *parameter list*—a list of data types with optional variable names. It is good programming style, and one we will follow in this text, to include both data types and variable names in a function prototype's parameter list, even though only data types are actually required. It is possible to write a function with no parameters—the `main` function usually doesn't have any parameters, for example. The general syntax for a function prototype is

```
data_type function_name(empty, void, or list of data types,
                with or without variable names);
```

The general syntax for implementing functions as they are used in P-3.5 is

```
data_type function_name(empty, void, or list of data types with
                variable names){

   body of function

   return return_value or expression;
}
```

The parameter list in the *function implementation* must include variable names corresponding to the names by which the

function implementation

parameters will be known locally within the function. In addition,

The parameters in a function prototype must agree in number and data type with the parameters in the function's implementation. The names do not have to be, and generally aren't, the same.

Because the parameter list of a function prototype doesn't even have to include variable names, it is clear that the list acts essentially as a placeholder for the actual values that will be used by the function.

Remember that every user-defined function must have a data type associated with it. Both functions in P-3.5 are type `double`. It is possible to give a function the `void` data type, and we will return to this possibility in Chapter 5. It is also possible as a matter of syntax to write a function without a specific data type; by default, such a function is given type `int`. It is generally considered poor programming practice to use default data types in function definitions, and we will never do it in this text.

When a function is called, the **calling arguments**, values corresponding to each item in the parameter list, are passed to the function through an **argument list**. The general syntax for calling a function is

> *calling argument*
> *argument list*

```
⟨variable_name = ⟩function_name(list of variables, constants,
                       expressions, or functions);
```

Two additional important rules about using functions are:

> The number of arguments passed to a function *must* agree with the number of parameters defined in the function prototype. The data type of the arguments passed to a function *should* agree with the number and data type of parameters defined in the function prototype. The *names* of variables in the argument list do not have to be the same, and generally are not the same, as the names in the parameter list.

> The arguments used in a call to a function can be variable names, constants, or expressions of the appropriate data type. Expressions may contain references to other functions.

Why does the rule for the data type of arguments passed to a function state only that the data type "should" agree with the function parameters? Because certain kinds of implicit or explicit type casts are allowed even though it is usually not a good idea to use them. It was noted earlier in this chapter that, for example, the statement `x=sqrt(2);` is allowed even though the argument is an integer rather than a real number. However, the statement `i=abs(-3.3);` will generate a compiler warning because the `abs` function expects type `int` arguments. If you allow the compilation to proceed in spite of the warning, the downward type cast of -3.3 to -3 will produce a result of 3 rather than 3.3. The same interpretations apply to user-defined functions. Consider this code:

```
double X(double x,int y);
int main(void) {
  printf("%lf\n",X(2,3.3));
}
double X(double x,int y) {
  return x*y;
}
```

The argument 2 passed to the x parameter is allowed and will be type cast to the real number 2.0. However, the argument 3.3 requires a downward type cast to an int value and will result in at least a warning at compile time. If the downward type cast is allowed, function X will return a value of 6, not 6.6. The general rule is:

> Implicit upward type casts that will not result in loss of accuracy are allowed as arguments, but implicit downward type casts that could result in loss of accuracy are not allowed as a matter of style even if a compiler allows such type casts.

In P-3.5, the name of the parameter in area_func is radius, but the name of the parameter in circumference_func is r. In the first case, the parameter name agrees with the name of the calling argument. In the second case, it does not. There is no justification for using different names other than to make the point of this discussion, but the disagreement is of no consequence in the program. All that matters from a syntax point of view is that the calling argument is of type double. From an algorithm design point of view, all that matters is that the calling argument contains the value of a radius, no matter what it is called. As noted in the syntax description, an argument doesn't even have to be a variable. It can also be a constant or an expression that returns a value of the appropriate data type.

Each function can return only a single value to the calling program, through a statement using the reserved word return. You shouldn't be surprised to find that

> The type of the value or expression appearing in a function's return statement should match the declared data type of the function.

Thus the values returned by the two functions in P-3.5 should be of type double. However, type casts are allowed in return statements. An upward type cast will proceed unnoticed. Some compilers will not even flag a downward type cast in this situation. In general, it is much better programming style to match the data type of a returned expression to the declared data type of the function. If you want to use a type cast, include an explicit type cast as part of the return statement.

When a function is called, its returned value is associated with the name of the function itself. Hence, function calls can be treated just like other values. In P-3.5, the values returned by the two functions are displayed directly in printf statements just by calling the functions inside a printf statement. It is also possible to assign the value returned from a function to another variable. Thus in the general syntax description, *variable_name* *should* have the same data type as the function itself, with the understanding that the kinds of implicit type casts discussed above are allowed even though they represent poor programming style. Consider this version of P-3.5's main function:

```
int main()
{
  double radius=3.0,area,circumference;
  area=area_func(radius);
  printf("From area_func: %8.3lf\n",area);
  circumference=circumference_func(radius);
  printf("From circumference_func: %8.3lf\n",circumference);
  return 0;
}
```

In this case, the values returned from the two functions are stored in the locally declared type `double` variables `area` and `circumference`. Either way of using the value returned by a function is acceptable and the choice you make depends, for example, on whether you need to do anything more with the value returned from a function than display it.

Note that in both functions in P-3.5, a comment is included to make clear the source of the value `PI`. The source of all the variables and values used in a function should always be clear, so someone looking at the source code in a function should not be required to look back at other parts of the program. In the algorithm design sense, this means that every user-defined function should have a clearly defined information interface.

In general, user-defined functions as they are used in P-3.5 are equivalent to the intrinsic math functions in the sense that they accept one or more arguments as input and provide a single output value associated with the name of the function itself. Suppose that the variables x and y are declared as type `double` in P-3.5. The statement `y=area_func(x);` is then equivalent in its syntax and use to the statement `y=sin(x);`. In the latter case, the function prototypes for math functions are included in the `math.h` header file and the implementation is provided by your C programming environment. In the former case, the prototypes and implementations are given explicitly within the source code.

It is not always necessary to use function prototypes. An alternative is to let all function implementations appear before the main program, as shown in Program P-3.6.

P-3.6 [`circlep2.c`]

```c
/* Create simple functions. */
#include <stdio.h>
#define PI 3.14159265

/* function definitions */

double area_func(double radius)
/* PI must be available as a global constant. */
{
  return PI*radius*radius;
}

double circumference_func(double radius)
/* PI must be available as a global constant. */
{
  return 2.0*PI*radius;
}

int main()
{
  double radius=3.0;
  printf("From area_func: %8.31f\n",area_func(radius));
  printf(
    "from circumference_func: %8.31f\n",circumference_func(radius));
  return 0;
}
```

The requirement for functions is that:

Either **a function prototype** *or* **the entire code for a function must appear** ***before*** **the main function.**

To put it another way, whenever a function is called ("invoked"), the compiler must know where to find it. You can think of C as using a "one pass" compiler, which means that it remembers everything it has read in a source code file—that is, it can look backward in the source code—but it can't look ahead. Thus whenever a function is called, either the function prototype or the function implementation must already have appeared in the source code file. If a function prototype appears before the `main` function, the corresponding code implementation normally appears after the `main` function. Typical C programming style is to use function prototypes, and that is the style we will usually use for programs appearing in this text.

It's important to understand the relationship between the calling arguments provided when a function is used and the function parameters that are part of the function prototype and function header statement. We have already seen that in program P-3.5 the single parameter is given a different name in each function. In P-3.6, the parameter has the name `radius` in both functions. When these functions are used in the main program, the calling argument always has the name `radius`. This is a design convenience because `radius` is a reasonable name for this quantity. To help clarify these relationships, consider the following code, which is a version of P-3.5 that works just like the original version.

```
/* Create simple functions. */
#include <stdio.h>
#define PI 3.14159265

/* function prototypes */
double area_func(double);
double circumference_func(double r);

main()
{
  double radius=3.0;
  printf("From area_func: %8.3lf\n",area_func(3.0));
  printf
    ("from circumference_func: %8.3lf\n",circumference_func(radius));
}

double area_func(double rad)
/* PI must be available as a global constant. */
{
  return(PI*rad*rad);
}

double circumference_func(double R)
/* PI must be available as a global constant. */
{
  return(2.0*PI*R);
}
```

The prototype for `area_func` has a parameter list with just a data type and no variable name. However, a variable name is required when that function is implemented. It is better style to use variable names in function prototypes, as it makes the purpose of the function clearer, assuming that meaningful names are used. In `circumference_func`, the variable name `r` in the prototype is different than the name in that function's implementation. (Remember that `r` is a different name than `R`.) When these functions are called from the `main` function, a constant argument is used in one case but a different variable name is used in the other case. Although it may be confusing from an algorithm design standpoint to use several different names for the same thing, C will not be confused.

The utility of having function parameters serve simply as placeholders for the actual values passed to the function is clear if you think about how the intrinsic math functions are used. The internal workings of intrinsic functions are hidden. You would have to see the actual source code for the intrinsic functions to know what their parameter lists look like—including the names by which their parameters are known internally to the function. However, not having this level of access doesn't prevent you from using the intrinsic functions. All you need to know to use `sin(x)`, for example, is that the single argument x must be a type `double` variable, expression, or value.

Remember that not only can argument names and parameter names be different, but the arguments don't even have to be single variable names. For the user-defined functions in programs P-3.5 and P-3.6, the following statements are all perfectly acceptable uses of `area_func` and `circumference_func`, assuming that all the variables have been appropriately declared and that x, y, r, and z have been assigned values:

```
area=area_func(r);
circumference=circumference_func(3.0);
area=area_func(x+3.*y);
circumference=circumference_func(sqrt(x*x+y*y)+log(z));
```

Here's another problem whose solution will provide more information on how to create and use simple functions.

An approximate empirical formula that relates atmospheric pressure to altitude is

$$P(h) = 1013e^{-0.12h}$$

where pressure P is in units of millibars (gm/cm²), and height h is in kilometers. The formula applies to heights less than about 80 km.

Write a program that prints a table of pressures from sea level to 80 km in 10-km steps. The values are shown in Figure 3.1.

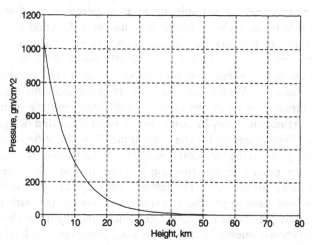

Figure 3.1. Atmospheric pressure as a function of height.

Program P-3.7 produces the required table. The code uses a simple loop structure, which we will discuss in detail in Chapter 4. For now, however, the intent should be clear even if the details are not.

P-3.7 [atm_pres.c]

```
/* Calculate table of atmospheric pressure. */
#include <stdio.h>
#include <math.h>
double Pressure(double h);

int main()
{
    int height;

    printf("height    pressure\n");
    printf("  km      gm/cm^2\n");
    printf("----------------\n");
    for (height=0; height<=80; height+=10)
        printf("%6i %10.3f\n",height,Pressure((double)height));
    return 0;
}
double Pressure(double height)
{
    return 1035.0*exp(-0.12*height);
}
```

Running P-3.7

Problem Discussion

Program P-3.7 contains several features of interest. Recall that in programs P-3.5 and P-3.6, the parameters in the function prototypes, the actual function headers, and the arguments used when the functions were called from the main program all had the same data types, even if their names were different. In P-3.7 this is no longer true. The function prototype uses a double parameter named h. It would actually be better programming style to give this "placeholder" parameter a more meaningful name, but this choice has been made to emphasize the fact that parameter names in a function prototype need not be the same as the parameter names in the actual function header or the argument names used when the function is invoked in the program. Remember that it is not the names of the parameters in a function prototype that are important, only their data types.

In the function header for Pressure in P-3.7, the parameter has, as it must, the same data type (double) as in the function prototype, but a different name (height) that will be used locally. The variable name height is also used in the main program, but there it is type int, which (as will be discussed in Chapter 4) is appropriate for its use as the loop control variable for generating the table. In the call to function Pressure, height is explicitly cast to double so it will agree with the data type in Pressure's parameter list.

The explicit type cast (double)height in the parameter list of Pressure is good programming style but not actually required. That is, an implicit cast from int to double is allowed.

P-3.7 also shows how variable definitions are localized within functions. The type double variable height in the parameter list and the implementation of function Pressure is local to—that is, known to—only that function, which does not know or care about the definition of height as an integer in the main function.

3.6 Applications

3.6.1 Refraction of Light

1 Define the problem.

Snell's Law describes the refraction (bending) of light as it passes from one medium to another. If the refractive index of the incident medium is n_i and that of the refracting medium is n_r, the angle of incidence i and angle of refraction r of a ray of light, measured from the perpendicular to the boundary between the two mediums, are related by

$$n_i \sin i = n_r \sin r$$

Figure 3.2 illustrates the geometry and Figure 3.3 gives some typical data.

Write a program that asks the user to provide two refractive indices and the angle of an incident ray and then calculates the angle of a refracted ray.

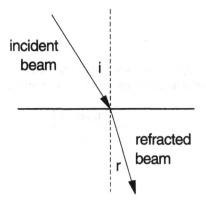

Figure 3.2. Geometry for Snell's Law of refraction.

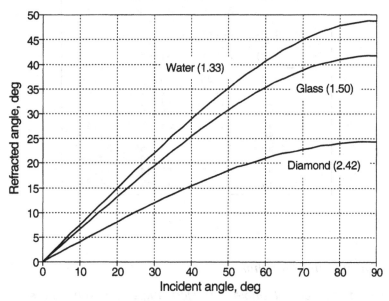

Figure 3.3. Angle of refraction as a function of angle of incidence.

2 Outline a solution.

1. Prompt the user to supply two indices and an incident angle.
2. Apply Snell's Law to determine the angle of the refracted ray:

$$r = \sin^{-1}\left(\frac{n_i \sin(i)}{n_r}\right)$$

3. Display the output.

Table 3.8 gives the angles of refraction for some common materials when a light ray is directed from air, which has a refractive index equal to 1, into the material. These data are shown in Figure 3.3.

Table 3.8. Calculations for Snell's Law

Angle of incidence (from air)	Angle of refraction for: Refractive index:		
	1.33 Water	1.50 Glass	2.42 Diamond
0	0.00	0.00	0.00
10	7.50	6.65	4.11
20	14.90	13.18	8.12
30	22.08	19.47	11.92
40	28.90	25.37	15.40
50	35.17	30.71	18.45
60	40.63	35.26	20.97
70	44.95	38.79	22.85
80	47.77	41.04	24.01
90	48.75	41.81	24.41

3 Design an algorithm.

DEFINE (n_i, n_r, incident_angle, refracted_angle as real numbers,
π and DegToRad (conversion from angles to radians) as real)
ASSIGN DegToRad = $\pi/180$
WRITE ("Give index of refraction for incident and refracting medium:")
READ (n_i, n_r)
WRITE ("Give incident angle, in degrees:")

READ *(incident_angle)*
(Convert to radians before doing trig calculations.)
ASSIGN *refracted_angle = sin⁻¹(nᵢ /nᵣ•sin(incident_angle•DegToRad))*
(Display output in degrees.)
WRITE *("Refracted angle is", refracted_angle/DegToRad)*

This algorithm specifically includes the conversions between degrees and radians. This is optional for the algorithm design but essential for a C program.

4 Convert the algorithm into a program.

P-3.8 [refract.c]

```
/* REFRACT.C */
/* Do refraction calculations using Snell's Law */

#include <stdio.h>
#include <math.h>

int main(void)
{
    double ni,nr; /* indices of refraction (dimensionless) */
    double incident,refracted; /* angles from perpendicular (deg) */
    double pi,deg_to_rad;

    pi=4.0*atan(1.0);
    deg_to_rad=pi/180.0;
    printf("Give indices of refraction for incident and refracting
        medium,\n");
    printf("separated by one or more spaces: ");
    scanf("%lf %lf",&ni,&nr);
    printf("What is the angle of incidence? ");
    fflush(stdin);
    scanf("%lf",&incident);
    refracted=asin(ni/nr*sin(incident*deg_to_rad));
    printf("refracted angle = %.2lf degrees",refracted/deg_to_rad);

    return 0;
}
```

Running P-3.8

```
Give indices of refraction for incident and refracting medium,
separated by one or more spaces: 1 1.5
What is the angle of incidence? 20
refracted angle = 13.18 degrees
```

5

Verify the operation of the program.

Check your results with a hand calculator. Compare your values with those in Table 3.8.

3.6.2 Inverse Hyperbolic Functions

1

Define the problem.

Although C includes the hyperbolic functions among its intrinsic functions, it doesn't include the inverse hyperbolic functions

$$\sinh^{-1}(x) = \ln[x + (x^2 + 1)^{1/2}]$$
$$\cosh^{-1}(x) = \ln[x + (x^2 - 1)^{1/2}]$$
$$\tanh^{-1}(x) = \ln[(1 + x)/(1 - x)]/2$$

Write a program that displays the hyperbolic functions and their inverses, using user-defined functions for the inverse functions. Based on results from your program, make a table for the inverse hyperbolic functions which shows the theoretical range for arguments and the range of values returned for each function. These three functions are plotted in Figure 3.4.

2

Outline a solution.

1. Ask the user to provide a real number.
2. Display the intrinsic hyperbolic functions.
3. Use each of the results as the argument in the corresponding inverse hyperbolic function and display the results.

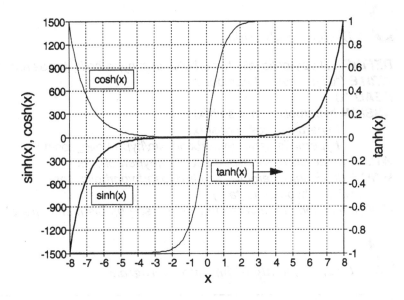

Figure 3.4(a). Hyperbolic functions.

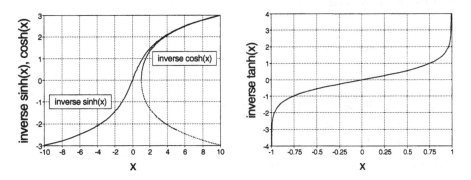

Figure 3.4(b). Inverse hyperbolic sine and cosine.

Figure 3.4(c). Inverse hyperbolic tangent.

3 Design an algorithm.

DEFINE *(x, hyperbolic_sin, hyperbolic_cos, hyperbolic_tan as real numbers)*
WRITE *("Give any real number.")*
READ *(x)*
ASSIGN *hyperbolic_sin = sinh(x)*
        hyperbolic_cos = cosh(x)
        hyperbolic_tan = hyperbolic_sin/hyperbolic_cosine
WRITE *(hyperbolic_sin,hyperbolic_cos,hyperbolic_tan)*
WRITE *(InvSinh(hyperbolic_sin),InvCosh(hyperbolic_cos),*
     InvTanh(hyperbolic_tan))
(Define functions for inverse functions—see problem statement.)

4 Convert the algorithm into a program.

P-3.9 [hyperbol.c]

```c
#include <stdio.h>
#include <math.h>

double inv_sinh(double z)
{
  return log(z+sqrt(z*z+1.0));
}
double inv_cosh(double z)
{
  double sign=1.0;

  if (z < 0.0) sign=-1.0;
  return sign*log(z+sqrt(z*z-1.0));
}

double inv_tanh(double z)
{
  return log((1.0+z)/(1.0-z))/2.0;
}

int main(void)
{
  double x,hyperbolic_sin,hyperbolic_cos,hyperbolic_tan;

  printf("Give a real number: ");
  scanf("%lf",&x);
  hyperbolic_sin=sinh(x);
  hyperbolic_cos=cosh(x);
  hyperbolic_tan=hyperbolic_sin/hyperbolic_cos;
  printf("        Hyperbolic sin,cos,tan: %10.5lf %10.5lf %10.5lf\n",
hyperbolic_sin,hyperbolic_cos,hyperbolic_tan);
  printf("Inverse hyperbolic sin,cos,tan: %10.5lf %10.5lf %10.5lf\n",
```

```
inv_sinh(hyperbolic_sin),inv_cosh(hyperbolic_cos),
        inv_tanh(hyperbolic_tan));
  return 0;
}
```

Running P-3.9

```
Give a real number: .5
        Hyperbolic sin,cos,tan:   0.52110   1.12763   0.46212
Inverse hyperbolic sin,cos,tan:   0.50000   0.50000   0.50000
```

5 Verify the operation of the program.

You can assume that the hyperbolic functions work correctly. Therefore, your program should return the original input if the inverse hyperbolic calculations are done correctly and the functions are used appropriately.

In response to the second part of the problem, Table 3.9 presents argument and function ranges for the inverse hyperbolic functions. Make sure the results from your program are consistent with these tabulated values.

Table 3.9. Argument and value ranges for inverse hyperbolic functions

Function	Argument Range	Function Range
$\sinh(x)$	$(-\infty,\infty)$	$(-\infty,\infty)$
$\cosh(x)$	$(-\infty,\infty)$	$[1,\infty)$
$\tanh(x)$	$(-\infty,\infty)$	$(-1,1)$
$\sinh^{-1}(x)$	$(-\infty,\infty)$	$(-\infty,\infty)$
$\cosh^{-1}(x)$	$[\pm1,\pm\infty)$	$[0,\infty)$
$\tanh^{-1}(x)$	$[-1,1]$	$(-\infty,\infty)$

Problem Discussion

Function `inv_cosh` in P-3.9 is notable because it is the first function we have written that contains a local variable, `sign`. Any function can contain one or more locally declared variables. A quantity that is needed for a function to do its job but that isn't part of the input required for the function should be defined locally. In this case, variable `sign` is part of the implementation, but it is of no interest to the user of the function. Thus this variable does *not* belong in the function's parameter list. A common mistake by beginning programmers is to put local variables in a function's parameter list.

Variables declared locally within a function exist only within that function. Thus, the variable name sign is unknown to other parts of P-3.9. This means that local variable names can be reused for other purposes in several parts of a program without causing problems. Whether this is a good idea depends on whether it is apt to be confusing.

P-3.9 is an excellent example of a program that appears very simple in its implementation but that actually contains several potential programming problems. First of all, cosh⁻¹(x) requires that its argument be greater than or equal to 1, and it always returns a non-negative value. Because cosh(x) is always greater than or equal to 0, regardless of the sign of x, cosh⁻¹(cosh(x)) will return a positive result even if x is negative. This means that the inverse function won't give back the original value of x unless the original sign of x is retained and used as part of the inverse calculation. The function makes use of C's implementation of the *IF...THEN* command even though we haven't discussed this yet.

A more serious problem concerns the accuracy of the underlying computations for numbers of type double. An obvious trouble spot is the calculation for the inverse hyperbolic tangent, which contains $1 - z$, where $z = \tanh(x)$ when the function is calculated in the program. How big, in absolute magnitude, does x have to be before tanh(x) is so close to 1 that the $1 - z$ in the denominator results in an apparent division by zero, or before it's so close to 1 that the calculation is no longer sufficiently accurate? The answer is, "Not very big!" Why? Because tanh(x) is very close to 1 for any value larger than about 3. Table 3.10 gives some representative values for the hyperbolic functions. With the compiler used for the programs in this text, setting x to 20 causes the program to crash with a divide-by-0 error.

Table 3.10. Values for hyperbolic functions

x	sinh(x)	cosh(x)	tanh(x)
0	0.00000	1.00100	0.00000
1	1.17520	1.54308	0.76159
2	3.62686	3.76220	0.96403
3	10.01787	10.06766	0.99505
4	27.28992	27.30823	0.99933
5	74.20321	74.20995	0.99991
6	201.71316	201.71564	0.99999
7	548.31612	548.31704	1.00000

Similar computational problems arise in the sinh and cosh calculations because the exponential function e^x causes an ***arithmetic overflow*** error for large values of x.

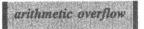

These kinds of computational problems occur because the accuracy of arithmetic calculations is limited by the accuracy with which real numbers are represented in C.[1] Their impact can be minimized by using C data type declarations that allow more accurate calculations, but they can't really be solved in C or in any other procedural language, for that matter. As is so often the case, *you* are responsible for appropriate use of a programming language. In many situations, a loss of accuracy in calculations means that you should reformulate your problem and its solution, rather than worrying about the limitations imposed by the programming language. This topic is covered in courses on numerical analysis, but is beyond the scope of this text.

3.7 Debugging Your Programs

3.7.1 Problems With Data Types and Casting

As has been stressed throughout this chapter, it is essential to choose appropriate data types for representing data. Avoid using integer data types to represent physical quantities, even when the values of those quantities are expressed as whole numbers. Ignoring this rule can lead to programming errors that are difficult to find because they don't produce error messages. Consider this problem:

Convert a time expressed in hours, minutes, and seconds, in the format hh:mm:ss, to decimal hours.

The required calculation is

$$hours = hh + mm/60 + ss/3600$$

However, if this formula is translated verbatim into C as

```
int hh,mm,ss;
double hours;
...
hours=hh+mm/60+ss/3600;
```

---

[1]This problem is not restricted to C.

the result is wrong because of the integer divisions mm/60 and ss/3600. This can be fixed by rewriting the assignment statement as

```
hours=hh+mm/60.0+ss/3600.0;
```

to force the division to produce a floating-point result. It would also be a much better idea as a matter of style to declare hh, mm, and ss as double rather than int.

3.7.2 Problems With Intrinsic Functions

For intrinsic functions, some common errors include:

1. Misspelling a function name or using uppercase letters in the name of the function
    For example, C doesn't recognize sine(x) or Sin(x) as equivalent to sin(x).

2. Forgetting to include the math.h header file
    If you are using the cc compiler, remember that, in addition to including the header file in your source code, you must also link the math library by using the -lm option in the compile command: cc test.c -otest.exe -lm. (The "l" is a lowercase L and not the number 1.)

Some more subtle errors include:

1. Supplying arguments of the wrong data type
    Most math functions expect type double arguments. When in doubt, use an explicit type cast: y=sin((double)x);, for example.

2. Using degrees as input to trigonometric functions and interpreting output from the inverse functions as degrees
    The trigonometric functions expect input in radians and the inverse functions produce output in radians. When a program does a lot of internal processing of trigonometric functions, the errors resulting from using degrees rather than radians are often virtually undetectable. C is perfectly willing to calculate sin(30.0), but it interprets the argument as 30 radians, not 30 degrees.

3. Supplying arguments with inappropriate values

Rather than causing a program crash, C functions typically return a value even when the input argument is inappropriate. For example, the sqrt function will return a value (0) even when its argument is negative. This may be good or bad, depending on your expectations for a program, but it is the responsibility of the programmer to provide adequate and appropriate protection against calling math functions with inappropriate arguments, or at least to provide safeguards against misusing what are essentially error-message returns from functions as valid values.

3.7.3 Problems With User-Defined Functions

The same potential exists for problems with user-defined functions as with intrinsic functions. However, we will be less diligent than the authors of C's intrinsic functions about writing "bulletproof" functions that return a value under all conditions of use or misuse. Instead, we will generally assume that the programmer and the program user will take joint responsibility for meeting the input expectations of a function.

It is important, of course, to be careful to provide arguments of the required data type. Additionally, it is important to use meaningful names in argument and parameter lists so that you will be less likely to use the wrong variables when you are writing code. If a program calls a function with arguments that have the correct data type but not the intended values, there is no way for the C environment to detect this as an error.

3.8 Exercises

In each of these exercises, you should perform the required calculations inside an appropriate function even if the problem statement doesn't specifically mention such a function. In fact, in all your future programs, it is *assumed* that you will use functions to modularize calculations without being asked specifically to do so. Typically, the main function will prompt the user for input values and display the output from the function. That is, the function that does the calculations will not include input or output statements. The main function can also get input values from an external data file and write output to a separate file if so specified by your instructor.

For additional practice, the exercises in Chapter 2 can be rewritten so that calculations are done in one or more functions of the kind discussed in this chapter.

1. A simple pendulum consisting of a mass swinging at the end of a massless string undergoes simple harmonic motion as long as the displacement of the mass from the vertical is very small compared to the length of the string. The period T of a simple pendulum is independent of its mass and is given by $T = 2\pi\sqrt{L/g}$, where the length L is given in meters and $g = 9.807$ m/s². (See Figure 3.5.) Write a program that will determine (a) the period of a pendulum with a specified length, and (b) the pendulum length required to produce a period of 1 second. [pendulum.c]

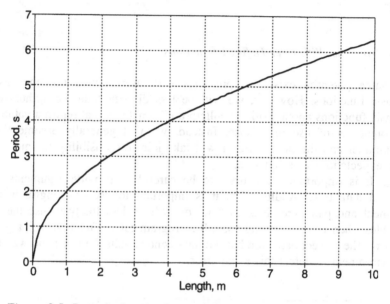

Figure 3.5. Period of a simple pendulum as a function of length.

2. Write a program that asks the user to enter a currency amount and then calculates how many dollar bills, quarters, dimes, nickels, and pennies are required to return this amount in change. Assume that the minimum total number of coins should be returned. This means that your program should return first the maximum number of one-dollar bills, then the maximum number of quarters, then dimes, and so forth. That is, even though you obviously could return $0.66 in change as, for example, six dimes and six pennies, the program should tell you to return this change as two quarters, one dime, one nickel, and one penny. This restriction actually makes the problem easier to solve. [change.c]

3. The terminal velocity v_f of a single-stage rocket intended to launch a payload into earth orbit is

$$v_f = v_{exhaust}\ell n(m_i/m_f)$$

where $v_{exhaust}$ is the speed of the gas exhaust from the rocket nozzle, m_i is the original weight of the rocket including its fuel, and m_f is the final weight of the rocket when all its fuel is gone. Write a program that gives the terminal velocity of a single-stage rocket when its initial mass, final mass, and gas exhaust speed are given. As an example, suppose a rocket engine produces an exhaust speed of 3000 m/s and the fuel in such a rocket is 75 percent of the total launch weight.

Extra Credit:
Higher terminal velocities, such as are required for lunar and interplanetary missions, can be obtained by using multiple rocket stages. The Saturn V, used for the Apollo missions to the moon, was a three-stage rocket. The first stage of a three-stage launch system consists of the rocket engine, its fuel and tanks, plus a payload consisting of two more complete rocket stages. When the fuel from the first stage is gone, the engine and its empty tanks are jettisoned. Then the second-stage rocket ignites. This process is repeated for the third stage. When the third-stage engine and tanks are jettisoned, all that is left is the mission payload. Write a program that calculates the terminal velocity of the payload of a three-stage rocket, given some appropriate assumptions about the three stages.

4. Paleontologists have discovered several sets of dinosaur footprints—preserved in ancient river beds, for example. Is it possible to deduce from these footprints the speed at which dinosaurs walked or ran? The two pieces of information that can be determined directly from the footprints are the length of the dinosaur's foot and the length of its stride, which is defined as the distance between the beginning of a footprint made by one foot and the beginning of the next footprint made by that same foot.
One way to approach this problem is to examine the relationship between size, stride, and speed in modern animals. Because of the dynamic similarities in animal motion, an approximate linear relationship between relative stride and dimensionless speed applies to modern bipedal and quadrupedal animals as diverse and differently shaped as humans, ostriches, camels, and dogs:[2]

$$s = 0.8 + 1.33v$$

Relative stride s is defined as the ratio of stride length to leg length, s=S/L. Dimensionless speed v is defined as the speed divided by the square root of leg length times the gravitational acceleration g: $V/\sqrt{Lg}$. Although it might seem at first analysis that gravitational acceleration shouldn't influence an animal's speed

---

[2]The quantitative relationship between relative stride length and dimensionless speed can be obtained from data given in R. McNeill Alexander, *Dynamics of Dinosaurs & Other Extinct Giants*, Columbia University Press, New York, 1989.

on level ground, this isn't true, as gravity influences the up and down motions of the body required even for walking.

Leg length from ground to hip joint for dinosaurs of a known species can be determined from fossils. However, even when the dinosaur species responsible for a particular set of tracks is unknown, its leg length can be inferred by multiplying the footprint length by four. This is another relationship that is approximately true for a wide range of modern animals. (You should try it for humans.)

As an aside, note that the use of dimensionless ratios is common in engineering as a way to scale phenomena from one size to another. These ratios are required in aeronautical engineering, for example, in which it is necessary to perform wind tunnel testing on models of real aircraft that are much smaller than the real thing.

Write a program that uses the equation described here to calculate the speed of a dinosaur based on measurements of its footprint and stride length. Use metric units. Test your program with a large footprint 0.64 m long and a stride length of 3.3 m. [dinosaur.c]

Extra Credit:

Based on similar calculations for humans, which you can easily do for your own stride, can you speculate whether the dinosaur in the example was running or walking? Try to justify your answer.

5. Write a program that asks the user to supply the mass and velocity of an object and then calculates and prints the kinetic energy and linear momentum of that object. The kinetic energy is $mv^2/2$, and the momentum is mv. Use metric units (mass in kilograms, velocity in meters per second, energy in joules). Use a function for each calculation. [kinetic2.c]

Extra Credit:

Include code for functions that will convert the kinetic energy and momentum into their British system equivalents. The British unit of energy is ft-lb, and the unit of momentum is slug-ft/s. 1 ft-lb = 1.356 joule; 1 slug = 14.59 kg; 1 ft/s = 0.3048 m/s.

6. It is well known that cold weather feels even colder when the wind is blowing. This effect gives rise to what is commonly described as the windchill temperature—the temperature of still air that produces the same feeling of coldness as a person experiences when exposed to a combination of temperature and wind. A formula commonly used to compute the windchill temperature T_{wc} in °F, for ambient temperature T in °F and wind speed V in miles per hour, is

$$T_{wc} = (0.279\sqrt{V} + 0.550 - 0.0203\,V)(T - 91.4) + 91.4$$

where T < 91.4° F and V ≥ 4 mph.[3] Write a program that accepts as input the temperature and wind speed and then calculates and displays the windchill temperature. [windchil.c]

7. Radioactive elements decay at a rate characterized by their half life, defined as the time required for the original quantity of radioactive material to decrease by half. (The decayed material doesn't disappear, of course. The process produces decay products that may themselves be stable or unstable.) For example, radon has a half life of 3.8 days. If there are originally 100 mg of radon gas in an enclosed container, there will be 50 mg after 3.8 days, 25 mg after 7.6 days, etc. The process of radioactive decay can be described by the formula

$$A(t) = A_o e^{-t/t_o}$$

where A_o is the initial amount, $A(t)$ is the amount after time t, and t_o is proportional to the half life t_{half}. To relate t_o to t_{half}, set $A(t) = A_o/2$ and take the logarithm of both sides:

$$A/2 = A_o e^{-t_{half}/t_o}$$
$$t_o = -t_{half}/\ell n(1/2)$$

For radon, t_o is about 5.48 days. Figure 3.6 shows the radioactive decay curve for radon.

Write a program that calculates and prints the amount of radon remaining from a given original sample mass after a specified number of days. Include the calculation for t_o in the program rather than doing it by hand ahead of time. [halflife.c]

Extra Credit:
(a) Half lives vary over a wide range, from small fractions of a second to thousands of years. Modify your program so it will let the user provide both the half life, in appropriate time units, and the elapsed time in the same units, so the program will work for elements other than radon. (This would be a better way to write the original program too, because it represents a more general approach to the problem.)

(b) You may prefer to write $A = A_o(1/2)^{t/t_{half}}$ to calculate radioactive decay. Modify your program accordingly.

---

[3] Author's note: I found this formula on the Web in about five minutes by searching for "windchill" at www.yahoo.com.

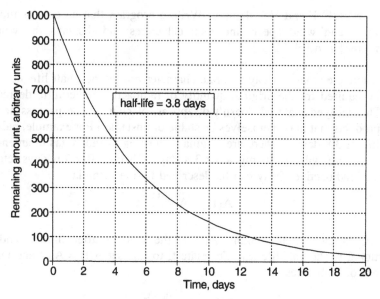

Figure 3.6. Radioactive decay of radon.

8. Under natural conditions of ample food supplies, adequate living space, and a stable environment, animal populations grow exponentially, as illustrated for the global human population in Figure 3.7. That is, the projected population at some future time will be proportional to the current population.where y_0 and y are initial and final years, and g is the net annual growth rate as determined by the difference between births and deaths.

A simple model for extrapolating an initial population P_0 into the future is:

$$P_y = P_0(1 + g)^{y-y_0}$$

Write a program that uses this formula in a function to calculate the growth rate needed to achieve a specified population at some time in the future. In 1992, the global human population was about 5.4×10^9 people. Some estimates predict that global population will be about 8.5×10^9 in the year 2025. It is not at all clear that the natural conditions required to support exponential growth will continue to exist for the human population. Food shortages, overcrowding, poor economic conditions, war, and environmental degradation can significantly affect both birth and death rates. [`populatn.c`]

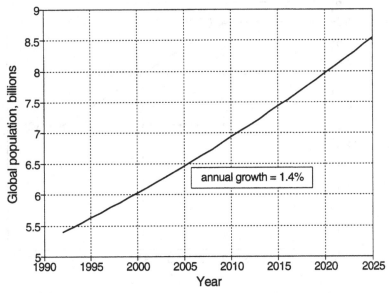

Figure 3.7. Exponential growth of global human population.

9. The loudness of a sound is measured in decibels (dB) on an arbitrary scale that relates perceived loudness to the ratio of the intensity of a sound to the intensity of the weakest audible sound I_o, which is about 10^{-12} W/m^2:

$$\text{Loudness} = 10\log_{10}(I/I_o)$$

Intensity is a physically measurable quantity, but loudness is a subjective human perception. The perception of loudness has approximately the logarithmic relationship indicated by the equation, but it varies among individuals. Write a program that uses a function to calculate the intensity of sounds 10, 100, and 1000 times more intense than the weakest audible sound. [noise.c]

Extra Credit:
    Modify your program to calculate and display the intensity of a sound with a specified dB value. What is the intensity of a sound of 100 dB, which is loud enough to cause permanent hearing damage?

10. Given the (x,y) coordinates of two points in a plane, write a program that calculates (a) the shortest distance between the two points, and (b) the (x,y) coordinates of a point halfway between the two points lying on a straight line joining the points. (See Figure 3.8.) [points.c]

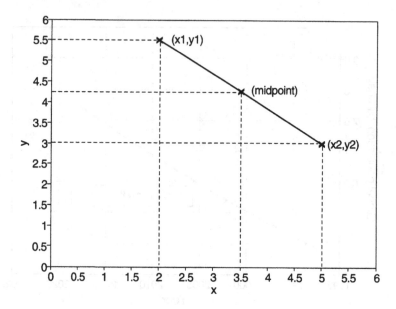

Figure 3.8. Distance between two points in a plane.

Extra Credit:

Modify your program so it also calculates the slope of the line joining two points in a plane. What restriction will this calculation impose on the location of the two points?

11. The efficiency of solar energy systems depends critically on the ability to track the sun's position. One required value is the solar elevation angle ε—the angle to the sun measured upward from the local horizontal. This angle depends on the latitude of the subsolar point (solar declination) δ, the observer's latitude λ, and the hour angle β, where hour angle is the angle from the observer's meridian to the subsolar meridian. (β = 0° occurs at local high noon, which generally differs from clock noon by a few minutes. One hour of clock time corresponds to approximately 15° of hour angle. A meridian is a line of constant longitude running from the north pole to the south pole.) The latitude of the subsolar point is seasonally dependent, with a range of ±23.4°. The largest positive value occurs at northern hemisphere midsummer, and the largest negative value occurs at southern hemisphere midwinter. The solar elevation angle for any solar declination, latitude, and hour angle is given by:

$$\varepsilon = 90° - \cos^{-1}(\cos\delta\cos\lambda\cos\beta + \sin\delta\sin\lambda)$$

Write a program that asks the user to supply an observer's latitude and the solar declination and then calls a function to calculate the solar elevation angle. Do this for hour angles of 60°, 30°, and 0° (corresponding approximately to 8 am, 10 am, and noon in clock time). Use your program to determine the range of high noon (maximum) elevation angles as a function of season at a specified latitude. What happens in the polar regions, where the sun may not shine at all during part of the year? Figure 3.9 shows the elevation angle for 40°N latitude in the summer and winter. [elevatin.c]

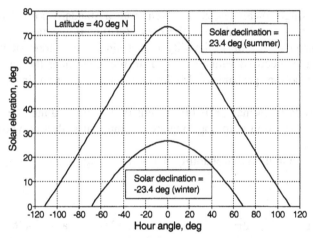

Figure 3.9. Solar elevation angle in winter and summer at 40°N latitude.

12. The well-known factorial function n! is defined as

$$n! = n \cdot (n - 1) \cdot (n - 2) \cdot \ldots \cdot 2 \cdot 1$$

For example, $5! = 5 \cdot 4 \cdot 3 \cdot 2 \cdot 1 = 120$. For large values of n, this is a very impractical calculation. However, n! can be approximated for large values of n with Stirling's formula:

$$n! \approx (n/e)^n (2n\pi)^{1/2}$$

Write a program that requests a value of n and calculates n! using Stirling's approximation. How close is Stirling's approximation for values of n! you can calculate yourself by hand? This approximation is especially useful when calculating the ratio of two large factorials, as required for certain problems in probability theory.

Hint: Declare n as a real number, not an integer. [`stirling.c`]

Extra Credit:
What is the largest value of n for which n! can be calculated from its definition—that is, not from Stirling's approximation—when n is declared as the default `int` data type? How about the `long` integer type? Can you establish the maximum value of n for which you can use Stirling's approximation? The answers to these questions are system-dependent.

13. Suppose a single measurement is taken from a standard normal (Gaussian) distribution. For such a distribution, the mean (arithmetic average) is 0 and the standard deviation is 1. The probability that a single measurement will be no greater than some specified value z is equal to the area under the curve defined by the standard normal probability density distribution function, integrated from $-\infty$ to z.

The standard normal probability density function cannot be integrated analytically. One solution is to approximate the integral with a polynomial:

$$\text{cumulative probability} \approx 1 - r(a_1 t + a_2 t^2 + a_3 t^3)$$

where

$$r = e^{-z^2/2}/\sqrt{2\pi} \qquad t = (1 + 0.3326z)^{-1} \qquad a_1 = 0.4361836$$
$$a_2 = -0.1201676 \qquad a_3 = 0.9372980$$

The error resulting from using this approximation for appropriate values of z is no more than about 10^{-4}.

Write a program that includes a function to calculate cumulative probability for a specified value of z using this approximation. What restrictions, if any, should you place on the allowed values of z? [`normal2.c`]

Extra Credit:
The standard normal variable z is related to measurements of normally distributed quantities taken from populations whose sample mean m and standard deviation s have values other than 0 and 1 by

$$z = \frac{x - m}{s}$$

Modify your program so that it will calculate the probability that a single measurement from a normally distributed population with sample mean m and standard deviation s will not exceed the mean by more than some specified amount.

14. (a) A production machine in use for several years is known to have produced thousands of ball bearings with a mean diameter μ of 0.5 cm and a standard deviation σ of 0.01 cm. A recent sample of 50 ball bearings had a mean diameter m of 0.495 cm and a standard deviation s of 0.012 cm. Is it possible to conclude on the basis of this single sample that the performance of the machine has changed?

This is a common problem in statistics involving formulating a null hypothesis, which in this case is that the random sample has been drawn from a population whose mean is 0.500 cm. Then the data are examined and the hypothesis is either accepted or rejected. The calculation is based on the z score:

$$z = \frac{m - \mu}{\sigma/\sqrt{N}}$$

where N is the sample size. In general, statistical calculations distinguish between the population statistics, μ and σ, and the sample statistics, m and s. As implied by their names, sample statistics are based on a single random sample and population statistics are based on an entire population. The latter value is usually not available in practice, and perhaps not even in principle, but statistics based on a very large sample, as in this problem, are typically assumed to be equal to the population statistics. The hypothesis about a sample that is small compared to the total population is accepted or rejected at a certain confidence level based, in this case, on values of z for a two-tailed significance test, as given in Table 3.11 for commonly used significance levels.

Table 3.11. Calculations for two-tailed tests of significance

Level of Significance	0.10	0.05	0.01	0.005	0.002
Critical z Values	±1.645	±1.96	±2.58	±2.81	±3.08

The levels of significance represent the probability of being wrong in rejecting the hypothesis, or making what is referred to as a Type I error. The smaller the level of significance, the less likely that a Type I error will be made. For this problem,

$$z = (m - \mu)/(\sigma N^{1/2}) = (0.495 - 0.500)/(0.01/7.071) = -3.54$$

Thus the hypothesis can be rejected with a very low probability of making a Type I error. That is, it is very unlikely that the performance of the machine in question has *not* changed. Note that the sample standard deviation is not used in this problem.

(b) A manufacturer purchases a ball bearing machine that is *claimed* to produce ball bearings with a mean diameter of 0.5 cm and a standard deviation of 0.01 cm. A sample of 50 ball bearings from the machine has a mean m of 0.495 cm and a standard deviation s of 0.012 cm.

    This problem is similar to that in (a). The difference is that the population statistics, based on a very large sample, have not been determined. The hypothesis is still that the sample is taken from a population whose mean μ is 0.500 cm. However, to calculate the z score, use the sample standard deviation as an *estimate* of the population standard deviation:

$$z = \frac{m - \mu}{s/\sqrt{N}}$$

For this problem,

$$z = (m - \mu)/(sN^{1/2}) = (0.495 - 0.500)/(0.012/7.071) = -2.95$$

Thus it is highly unlikely that the machine is performing according to its stated specifications. Note that in this version of the problem, the claimed population standard deviation is not used.

    For parts (a) and (b) of this problem, write and test a function that calculates the z score when the sample mean, population mean, population or sample standard deviation, sample size, and critical z value are specified. Note that the function does not "care" whether the standard deviation passed as input is the population or sample standard deviation.

15. The day of the year n in the range 1–366 for a specified month m (1–12), day d (1–31), and four-digit year y[4] is given by

$$n = \langle 275m/9 \rangle - \langle (m + 9)/12 \rangle (1 + \langle (mod(y,4) + 2)/3 \rangle) + d - 30$$

where $\langle ... \rangle$ means that a division is to be truncated to a whole number (for example, $\langle 11/3 \rangle = 3$), and mod is the remainder from integer division (for

---

[4] At the time this manuscript was being written, the Y2K problem (the inability of older computer software to process years later than 1999) was receiving lots of attention in the press. Hence it seemed like a good idea to insist on four-digit years.

example, mod(11/3) = 2). As written, the formula is valid for any year, including leap years, except for those centurial years that are not evenly divisible by 400. Thus the formula applies to the year 2000, which is a leap year, but not to 1900 or 2100, which are not leap years even though they are evenly divisible by 4.

Write a program with a function that calculates and returns the day of the year for a specified month, day, and year.

Extra Credit:

Modify your function so that it returns the correct value for centurial years not evenly divisible by 400. For example, your function should take into account the fact that 2100 is not a leap year. You can look ahead to Chapter 4 to see how to implement an *IF... THEN... ELSE...* statement that will allow your code to respond appropriately in centurial years that are not leap years.

16. A cylindrical liquid storage tank of radius R and length L is buried underground on its side; that is, with its straight sides parallel to the ground. In order to determine how much liquid remains in the tank, a dip stick over the centerline of the tank is used to measure the height of the liquid in the tank. The formula for the area A of a circle of radius R with a cap cut off horizontally at height D from the bottom of the circle is

$$A = R^2 \cos^{-1}\left(\frac{R - D}{R}\right) - (R - D)\sqrt{2RD - D^2}$$

Write a program that reads several values of R, L, and D from a file and calculates the volume in the tank for each set of values.

Selection and Repetition Constructs

4.1 Relational and Logical Operators

Like other high-level programming languages, C has the ability to make decisions by comparing values. Two values can be tested for equality, for example, and one block of statements can be executed if the values are equal. Another block of statements, or no statements at all, can be executed if the values aren't equal. The purpose of such decision-making statements should already be clear from the discussion of pseudocode commands in Chapter 1. Also, we have already used some implementations of the pseudocode *IF...THEN...ELSE* statement in Chapters 2 and 3 in code for reading files. For instance, in the statements

```
status=fscanf(infile,...);
if (status == EOF) break;
```

and

```
infile=fopen(name,"r");
if (infile == NULL)
  printf("Can't find file.");
else
  ...
```

`if...` statements are used to respond appropriately when the end-of-file mark is found or when the program can't find a requested file.

Table 4.1 summarizes the operators required to implement decision-making statements. It contains the same operators given previously in Table 1.3, with the addition of the C symbols for those operators. Expressions having more than one relational operator are evaluated according to certain precedence rules in the same sense that multiplication and division operations are performed before addition and subtraction. The relational and logical operators have been given in Table 4.1 in order of descending precedence, with level 1 having the highest precedence. Relational and logical operators also have precedence relative to other kinds of operations, as previously shown in Table 3.4 in Chapter 3.

Precedence rules for relational and logical operators can be difficult to remember. Consequently, as a matter of style, we will be consistent about using parentheses to make clear the order in which operations should be performed. Even when parentheses aren't required, they can often help clarify a statement's intent, and they can also be used to override the natural precedence whenever that is desired.

Table 4.1. Relational and logical operators

Math Symbol	Meaning	C Symbol(s)	Precedence
not	logical "not"	!	1
≤	less than or equal to	<=	2
≥	greater than or equal to	>=	2
<	less than	<	2
>	greater than	>	2
=	equal to	==	3
≠	not equal to	!=	3
and	logical "and"	&&	4
or	logical "or"	||	5

As noted in Chapter 3, C does not support a separate data type for manipulating logical expressions. Instead, C evaluates a relational statement and assigns a value of 1 if it is True and a value of 0 if it is False. Consider the code fragment

```
a=3;
b=4;
c=5;
printf("%i\n",(a<=3)+(a<b)+(a==c));
```

What value is displayed by the printf statement? With the assignment statements shown, a is less than or equal to 3, a is less than b, and a is not equal to c. Thus the three relational expressions have values of 1, 1, and 0, and a 2 will be displayed. We will generally restrict our use of relational expressions to writing selection constructs, and we will not use the values associated with logical expressions in this way.

The interpretation of relational and logical operations is straightforward, but there are two common pitfalls in tests for equality. First, it is easy to forget that the = sign by itself is *not* the relational operator for equality. The expression a=b won't produce a syntax error when it is used in an if... statement, but it is *not* the same expression as a==b. This is because, in C, assignment statements themselves have values, even though we don't usually think of them in that way.

Thus an assignment statement a=b has a value that depends on the value of b. Consider this code fragment:

```
int a=3,b=-4;
printf("%i\n",a=b);
```

This code prints a value of –4 because the expression a=b has a value of –4. In the relational sense, the assignment a=b as it appears in this code fragment will be interpreted as True because C interprets *any* nonzero value (even a negative value) as True.

The second pitfall involves testing real numbers for equality. If A and B are type float or double, it is generally poor programming practice to test them for equality. This is because C and other languages represent real numbers only approximately and, hence, arithmetic with real numbers is inexact. The algebraic expression (10/3)(3) is obviously equal to 10 in the algebraic sense. However, when C evaluates this expression, it first performs the division: 10/3=3.333333.... Multiplying this result by 3 yields 9.999999..., which is not exactly equal to 10. Some compilers and some languages may be better than others about interpreting this source code representation of an algebraic expression, but the *potential* for problems can never be eliminated entirely.

If you wish to test real numbers for equality, especially when those numbers are obtained as the result of arithmetic operations, it is much better programming practice to test the absolute value of their difference against some suitably small value, as with the statement fabs(A-B) < small_value. An appropriately small value would be 10^{-6} or 10^{-7}, but 10^{-20} would be inappropriate because real arithmetic is not done at this level of precision with float or double variables, and also because such calculations are probably meaningless in the physical or mathematical sense.

4.2 Selection (*IF...THEN...ELSE...*) Constructs

The relational operations described in the previous section are used with the *IF...THEN...ELSE...* pseudocode command discussed in Chapter 1. This pseudocode has a straightforward implementation in C. Its general syntax is

```
if (condition_1)
    {
        statements
    }
else if (condition_2)
    {
        statements
    }
else if (condition_3)
    {
        statements
    }
...
else
    {
        statements
    }
```

where each *condition* represents a relational expression. Note that the **THEN** part of the **IF...THEN...** pseudocode command is implied in C; there is no "then" word in the C language. Each branch of the if... statement can be associated with a block of statements set off with curly braces, {...}, but a single statement doesn't have to be enclosed in braces.

Program P-4.1 illustrates several typical statements using logical and relational operators. It includes several features of interest. Because C doesn't have a separate logical (boolean) data type, the values TRUE and FALSE have been assigned values 1 and 0 in define statements. This makes True and False assignments easier to write and understand. Also, the if... statements involving character responses test for both lowercase and uppercase responses. This is optional, but it helps to make the program a little more "idiot proof." Finally, note the fflush(stdin); statements appearing before each scanf statement that looks for a character typed at the keyboard. This is necessary to ensure that the keyboard buffer is empty so that the character a user types will be the first character in the buffer. Otherwise, a blank space or end-of-line character from any previous scanf statement will remain in the buffer, and any new character the user types will not be detected; this is a subtle point that is easy to forget, and it can lead to programs that appear to be written properly, but which won't work as expected. It is unnecessary to flush the keyboard buffer if a scanf statement is expecting only numerical values, because blanks are ignored (or skipped over, more precisely) when scanf searches for a numerical value.

P-4.1 [selectin.c]

```c
/* Demonstrate various selection structures */

# include <stdio.h>
# define TRUE 1
# define FALSE 0

main()
{
  int resting_heart_rate,temperature,raining;
  char plane_type,rain;

  printf("What is your resting heart rate? ");
  scanf("%d",&resting_heart_rate);
  if (resting_heart_rate > 56 )
      printf("You need more exercise.\n");
  else
      printf("You are in good shape.\n");

  printf("What is the aircraft type, [b]omber or [c]argo? ");
  fflush(stdin);
  scanf("%c",&plane_type);
  if ( (plane_type == 'b') || (plane_type == 'B') )
      printf("The aircraft is a bomber.\n");
  else if ( (plane_type == 'c') || (plane_type == 'C') )
      printf("The aircraft is a cargo plane.\n");
  else
      printf("I don't know what this aircraft is.\n");
  printf("How hot is it (deg F)? ");
  scanf("%i",&temperature);
  printf("Is it raining (y or n)? ");
  fflush(stdin);
  scanf("%c",&rain);
  if ( (rain == 'y') || (rain == 'Y') )
    raining=TRUE;
  else raining=FALSE;
  if ( (temperature > 85) && !raining )
    printf("Let's go swimming!\n");
  else
    printf("We'll stay inside.\n");
  return(0);
}
```

Running P-4.1

```
What is your resting heart rate? 70
You need more exercise.
What is the ship type, [c]ruiser or [f]rigate? f
The ship is a frigate.
How hot is it (deg F)? 93
Is it raining (y or n)? n
Let's go swimming!
```

Here is a typical programming problem that requires a simple decision structure.

Income taxes are assessed according to the following formula:

For incomes ≤ \$50,000, the rate is 7%
For incomes > \$50,000, the rate is 7% on the first \$50,000 and 10% on the
    amount greater than \$50,000.

The pseudocode for the critical part of the code is:

IF *(income ≤ \$50,000)* **THEN**
        tax = \$50,000•0.07
ELSE
        tax = \$50,000•0.07+(income - \$50,000)•0.10

A common mistake is to write this pseudocode instead:

IF *(income ≤ \$50,000)* **THEN**
        tax = income•0.07
ELSE
        tax = income•0.10

Make sure you understand why the second algorithm is wrong! Program P-4.2 gives a program to solve this problem.

P-4.2 [`taxes.c`]

```
/* Simple decision structure.   TAXES.C */
#include <stdio.h>
#define LOW_RATE 0.07
#define HIGH_RATE 0.10
#define CUTOFF_INCOME 50000.0

int main()
{
  double income, tax;

  printf("Give income: $");
  scanf("%lf",&income);
  if (income <= CUTOFF_INCOME)
    tax=income*LOW_RATE;
  else
    tax=CUTOFF_INCOME*LOW_RATE+(income-CUTOFF_INCOME)*HIGH_RATE;
  printf("On an income of $%.2lf, the tax is $%.2lf\n",income,tax);
  return 0;
}
```

Running P-4.2

```
Give income: $73000
On an income of $73000.00, the tax is $5800.00
```

The interpretation of multiple-alternative if... statements can be confusing. Consider the following table that relates loudness in decibels to human perception:

Loudness (dB)	*Perception*
≤50	quiet
51-70	intrusive
71-90	annoying
91-110	very annoying
>110	uncomfortable

Suppose the goal of a program is to ask the user to provide a decibel level and then to respond with an appropriate message. If the tests are arranged in the order shown, the pseudocode could be written like this:

IF *(dB ≤ 50)* **THEN WRITE** *(quiet)*
ELSE IF *(dB > 50 and dB ≤ 70)* **THEN WRITE** *(intrusive)*
ELSE IF *(dB > 70 and dB ≤ 90)* **THEN WRITE** *(annoying)*
and so forth...

For a value of 88 dB, for example, it is not true that the value is less than or equal to 50 or is in the range 51-70. The second **ELSE IF...** branch is the only one that returns a True result, and this will be the only branch executed. However, the desired result can be achieved more simply like this:

IF *(dB ≤ 50)* **THEN WRITE** *(quiet)*
ELSE IF *(dB ≤ 70)* **THEN WRITE** *(intrusive)*
ELSE IF *(dB ≤ 90)* **THEN WRITE** *(annoying)*
ELSE IF *(dB ≤ 110)* **THEN WRITE** *(very annoying)*
ELSE WRITE *(uncomfortable)*

Suppose the noise level is 75 dB. This is greater than 50 but less than 70, so the second branch will be executed. However, 75 is also less than the values in the statements in the third and fourth branches. Does this mean that each of the other branches will also be executed? No, because

Only *one* branch from a compound *IF...* statement—the first one for which the controlling expression is true—will be executed.

The second pseudocode algorithm doesn't require that both the upper and lower limits on the range be specified, and therefore it's shorter and less cluttered than the first alternative. This behavior, as described in pseudocode, also applies to the programming language implementation of *IF...* statements. Programs that implement the first kind of pseudocode will certainly work, but this kind of code usually means that a programmer doesn't understand how *IF...* statements work. Program P-4.3 gives C code for the noise level problem.

P-4.3 [decibels.c]

```c
/* Illustrate multiple-alternative decisions. */

#include <stdio.h>

main()
{
  int noise_db;

  printf("Enter the noise level as integer decibels: ");
  scanf("%i",&noise_db);

  if ( noise_db <= 50)
      printf("%i dB is quiet.",noise_db);
  else if (noise_db <= 70)
      printf("%i dB is intrusive.",noise_db);
  else if (noise_db <= 90)
      printf("%i dB is annoying.",noise_db);
  else if (noise_db <= 110)
      printf("%i dB is very annoying.",noise_db);
  else
      printf("%i dB is uncomfortable.",noise_db);
  return(0);
}
```

Running P-4.3

```
Enter the noise level as integer decibels: 105
105 dB is very annoying.
```

4.3 Choosing Alternatives From a List of Possibilities

When there are many possible program branches to be considered, it is often easier to construct what amounts to a table of choices, using an implementation of the **CHOOSE** pseudocode command discussed in Chapter 1. Consider the statement in P-4.1, which was implemented as a three-branch if... statement to select an aircraft type. There were only three possibilities: bomber, cargo, and unknown. Such a list of choices is cumbersome to expand. Program P-4.4 illustrates an alternative, with a new choice added.

P-4.4 [planes.c]

```
# include <stdio.h>
int main()
{
  char plane_type;
  printf(
    "What is the aircraft type, [b]omber, [c]argo, or [f]ighter? ");
  scanf("%s",&plane_type);
  switch(plane_type) {
      case 'b':
      case 'B':
              printf("bomber\n");
              break;
      case 'c':
      case 'C':
              printf("cargo\n");
              break;
      case 'f':
      case 'F':
              printf("fighter\n");
              break;
      default:
              printf("unknown\n");
      }
  return 0;
}
```

P-4.4 uses the switch keyword to create another kind of selection construct. Its general syntax is

```
switch(controlling expression)
{
    case value:
    ⟨case value:⟩
            statements
            ⟨break; or return;⟩
    ⟨more case values and statements⟩
    default:
            statements
}
```

where each value is an ordinal constant. The default: branch is optional.

The switch construct differs significantly from C's if... construct. Recall that in a multibranched if... statement, only the *first* True branch is executed. However,

> In a switch statement, *every* statement following a case label equal to the
> controlling expression is executed until a break or return is encountered.

This rule explains why multiple statements following one or more case labels
aren't grouped in a statement block with braces, {...}, as they are for an
if... statement.

If you think of each case label (or group of case labels) as representing
the start of a branch to be taken, as is certainly reasonable from an algorithm
design viewpoint, the break; statement is required to ensure that only one
branch—that is, only one set of statements—within the structure is executed. This
is different from an if... construct, in which no break statement is required
to ensure that only one branch is taken. In terms of syntax, the break; or
return; statement associated with each case value is optional, but it is almost
always required as a matter of algorithm design.

The data type of the controlling expression in the switch statement must
be ordinal (countable), which means that it may have an int or char type, but
not a floating point data type such as float or double. Also, the controlling
expression may not be a *string* of characters.[1] This also means that the values
appearing in the case labels must have appropriate data types. This restriction
precludes the use of a switch structure when decisions must be based on
floating-point values or on ranges of values (rather than individual values).
However, this construct is a good choice whenever decisions can be based on
single ordinal values.

Although it is perhaps not obvious and may not be a good idea as a matter
of style, C allows case labels associated with a switch statement to contain a
mixture of integer and character values regardless of whether the controlling
expression is of type int or char. This is possible because of C's willingness
to perform implicit type casting whenever required. Thus, this code fragment
causes no compilation problems even though the case labels mix data types in
what appear to be potentially inappropriate ways:

```
char ch;
int i;
switch (ch) {
  case 1:;
  case 'a':;
  break;
}
switch (i) {
  case 1:;
  case 'a':;
}
```

---

[1] The reason is that character strings, as opposed to single characters, are not ordinal. For example,
the next character after k is l, but there is no way to tell what comes after the word kitten.

4.4 Repetition (*LOOP...*) Constructs

In Chapter 1, the pseudocode concept of a loop structure was described. Loop structures are required to implement the third of the three program control structures—sequence, selection, and repetition. This concept is so pervasive in programming that we used some loop constructs as early as Chapter 2 in code to read external data files. The **LOOP** *(conditions)...***END LOOP** pseudocode command includes a "plain English" description of the conditions that define when (or if) the statements inside the loop are executed. In the C implementation, this description can be implemented in two basic ways.

4.4.1 Count-Controlled Loops

The simplest loop, in concept, is the ***count-controlled loop***. This is appropriate when the program knows ahead of time or can determine how many times the statements inside the loop should be executed. Consider this problem:

> Write a program that prints a table of angles and their sine, cosine, and tangent over the range [0°, 180°] in increments of 5°.

It is easy to determine that this table will contain 37 rows. You can perform the calculation by hand or let your program do it: 180/5 + 1. Because the limits on the loop are known ahead of time, a count-controlled loop is appropriate. The pseudocode might look like this:

LOOP *(for i = 0 to 36)*
    ASSIGN *angle = 5•i*
    WRITE *(angle, sin(angle), cos(angle), tan(angle))*
END LOOP

When you implement this algorithm in C, remember to convert angles to radians (because that's what the trigonometric functions expect as input), and you should also take into account the fact that the tangent of $\pi/2$ radians is undefined. The general syntax for a count-controlled loop in C is

```
for (initialization expression; repetition control condition;
        update expression)
{
   statements
}
```

The loop starts with the reserved word `for`. Execution of the loop is controlled by the value of an integer *loop counter*. Inside the parentheses following the `for`, the initial
value of the counter is given first. Then a relational expression is given. As long as this expression is true, the loop counter will be updated according to the update expression and the statements inside the loop will be executed. If there is only one statement, the braces aren't needed. If the loop repetition expression is false the first time it is evaluated, the loop will terminate without executing the statements inside the loop. When the loop terminates, program control is transferred to the statement that immediately follows the loop.

The update expression defines how the loop variable will be changed at the end of each trip through the loop. A common update expression, although by no means the only legitimate one, increments the loop counter by one for each trip through the loop.

A typical use of loops is to generate a table of values. Program P-4.5 shows one way to implement a loop that generates and displays a table of trigonometric values.

P-4.5 [`trigtabl.c`]

```
/* Generate a table of trig values.   Demonstrates count-controlled
loops. */
#include <stdio.h>
#include <math.h>

int main()
{
  double angle,deg_to_rad;
  int i;

  deg_to_rad=4.0*atan(1.0)/180.0;
  printf("  i    x    sin(x)   cos(x)   tan(x)\n");
  printf("----------------------------\n");
  for (i = 0; i <= 36; i++) {
    angle=i*5.0;
    printf("%3i %4.0lf",i,angle);
    angle=angle*deg_to_rad;
    if (i*5 != 90) {
      printf(
          "%9.4lf%9.4lf%9.4lf\n",sin(angle),cos(angle),tan(angle));
    }

    else {
      printf("%9.4lf%9.4lf\n",sin(angle),cos(angle));
    } /* end if... */
  }  /* end for... */
  return 0;
}
```

Running P-4.5

```
  i     x   sin(x)   cos(x)   tan(x)
  ---------------------------------------
  0     0   0.0000   1.0000   0.0000
  1     5   0.0872   0.9962   0.0875
  2    10   0.1736   0.9848   0.1763
  3    15   0.2588   0.9659   0.2679
  4    20   0.3420   0.9397   0.3640
  5    25   0.4226   0.9063   0.4663
  6    30   0.5000   0.8660   0.5774
  7    35   0.5736   0.8192   0.7002
  8    40   0.6428   0.7660   0.8391
  9    45   0.7071   0.7071   1.0000
 10    50   0.7660   0.6428   1.1918
 11    55   0.8192   0.5736   1.4281
 12    60   0.8660   0.5000   1.7321
 13    65   0.9063   0.4226   2.1445
 14    70   0.9397   0.3420   2.7475
 15    75   0.9659   0.2588   3.7321
 16    80   0.9848   0.1736   5.6713
 17    85   0.9962   0.0872  11.4301
 18    90   1.0000   0.0000
 19    95   0.9962  -0.0872 -11.4301
 20   100   0.9848  -0.1736  -5.6713
 ...
```

In P-4.5, the loop counter i is given an initial value of 0, the repetition condition is given as i <= 36, and i is incremented by 1 after each trip through the loop. Thus, the statements inside the loop will be executed for values of i between 0 and 36, inclusive. This interpretation of the loop termination condition makes clear that the loop counter update expression is executed at the *end* of the loop rather than at the beginning. If the counter is incremented at the beginning of the loop, the first value in the statement angle=i*5.0 will be 1 rather than 0. The last time the statements inside the loop are executed, i will have a value of 36. At the end of the calculations, the incremented value will be 37. When the loop repetition expression is evaluated, it will now be False and the loop will terminate.

An alternative repetition condition could be i != 37, although this choice is less clear than the one used. Also, the update expression could be i=i+1, i+=1 or ++i rather than i++.

Why does the loop counter use an integer in the range [0, 36] rather than the angle values themselves? As a matter of syntax, C allows the use of real numbers as loop control variables, so the loop could in principle be written like this:

```
for (angle = 0.0; angle <= 180.0; angle += 5.0) {/* poor style! */
    printf("%4.0lf",angle);
    ...
```

However, the practice of using noninteger loop control variables is strongly discouraged because the approximations inherent to real number arithmetic mean that the calculated values of real loop counters can sometimes lead to unexpected results. The loop controls on angle *seem* reasonable, but it is *possible* that the "final" incrementing operation could give a result of 179.99999, for example, rather than exactly 180. In that case, the statements inside the loop would be executed one more time than expected.

As a matter of good programming style, you should always use integer loop control variables.

Even in view of this style rule, there is at least one more reasonable alternative for constructing the loop in P-4.5:

```
for (i = 0; i <=180; i+=5) {
  printf("%4i",i);
  angle=(double)i*deg_to_rad;
  if (i != 90) {
    printf(
        "%9.4lf%9.4lf%9.4lf\n",sin(angle),cos(angle),tan(angle));
  }
  else {
    printf("%9.4lf%9.4lf\n",sin(angle),cos(angle));
  } /* end if... */
}   /* end for... */
```

In this implementation, the loop counter takes on the integer values 5, 10, 15, and so on. The assignment statement

```
angle=(double)i*deg_to_rad;
```

converts the angle to radians. The (double) makes clear the type cast that is performed, but it's not required because deg_to_rad is already a real value.

Here's another question about loop controls. Is it allowed to reassign the value of the loop counter variable *inside* the loop? For example, is it possible to write

```
for (i = 0; i != 37; i++) {
  ...
  i+=3;
}   /* end for... */
```

The answer in C is, "Yes, you can do that." However, this is generally considered to be very poor programming style because altering the loop counter variable inside the loop overrides the conditions established for loop termination as part of the for... statement.

> As a matter of good programming style, the value of a loop counter variable should never appear on the left side of an assignment operator inside the loop.

This style rule applies as well to implied assignment statements such as i++.

What is the value of the loop counter variable *after* the loop is terminated? In P-4.5, i has a value of 37 because that is the value required to terminate the loop. However,

> It is poor programming style to use the value of a loop counter variable after a loop is terminated. As a matter of good programming style, you should always consider a loop counter variable to be undefined after the loop it controls is terminated.

It is, however, OK to reuse the loop counter variable itself in another loop or even for some other purpose, by reassigning its value. Thus the code fragment

```
for (i=1; i<=10; i++)
  printf("%i\n",i);
j=i+5;
```

is allowed as a matter of syntax, but is considered poor programming style because the value of i is used after the loop is terminated. As a result of this code, j will have a value of 16 rather than 15 because i has a value of 11 when the loop terminates; this may or may not be what you intended. This code fragment is much better:

```
end_value=10;
for (i=1; i<=end_value; i++)
  printf("%i\n",i);
j=end_value+6;
```

assuming that, in fact, you wish j to have a value of 16 rather than 15.

It is possible to nest loops one inside the other. Consider this code:

```
for (row=1; row<=4; row++) {
  printf("row # %2i,",row);
  for (col=1; col<=5; col++) {
    printf("%2i",col); }
  printf("\n");
}
```

The output of this typical approach to producing a two-dimensional table of values looks like this:

```
1  1  2  3  4  5
2  1  2  3  4  5
3  1  2  3  4  5
4  1  2  3  4  5
```

The inner loop is executed completely four times, once for each trip through the outer loop. The variable `row` is used to number each row in the table, and `col` is used to number columns. Each time the inner loop is executed, its counter variable `col` is automatically reset to 1. The curly braces are not necessary for the inner loop, which contains only one statement, but they serve as a reminder that you can include as many statements as you need to take the required action inside the inner loop. Note that the line-feed character `\n` is printed after the end of the inner loop, but still inside the outer loop.

You can have as many levels of nested loops as your program needs. You should not be surprised to learn that

> **Each counter variable in two or more nested loops must have a different name.**

In order to minimize logical errors in your code, it is important to assign meaningful names to counter variables in nested loops. That is why the counter variables in the above example are called `row` and `col` rather than something less descriptive such as `i` and `j`.

Finally, it is possible to construct loops that count down rather than up. This requires only that the terminating expression and the update expression be consistent. For the code

```
for (i=10; i>=0; i--)
   {...}
```

`i` takes on values 10, 9, ..., 1, 0.

4.4.2 Conditional Loops

It is often the case that the number of times the statements inside a loop must be executed cannot be determined ahead of time. In that case, a *conditional loop* must be used. There are two possibilities. In a *post-test loop*, statements inside the loop are always executed at least

> conditional loop
> post-test loop
> pre-test loop

once. At the bottom of the loop, a decision is made whether to continue. In a *pre-test loop*, a decision whether to execute statements inside the loop is made at the top of the loop. This means that statements inside a pre-test loop might never be executed.

Pre-Test Loops

The general syntax for pre-test loops is

```
while (loop repetition condition)
{
  statements
}
```

The braces are required only for multiple statements.
As an example, consider this problem:

Write a program that calculates the period of an earth-orbiting satellite in a circular orbit with a user-specified altitude and displays the starting time for each orbit during one day. Assume that the first orbit starts at a time of 0. The equation for the period T is

$$T = 2\pi a \sqrt{a/G}$$

where a is the radius of the orbit in km and G is the earth's gravitational constant, 398601.2 km^3/sec^2. The (equatorial) radius of the earth is 6378 km. There are 86,400 seconds in one day. Don't forget that the value of a in the formula is the earth's radius plus the user-specified altitude.

This problem can be formulated in terms of a pre-test loop, which should keep executing as long as the elapsed time is less than one day:

LOOP *(as long as the total time is less than one day)*

...

END LOOP

Program P-4.6(a) shows how to implement this algorithm as a pre-test loop.

P-4.6(a) [orbits1.c]

```
/* Print information about earth orbits. */
/* Use a pre-test loop. */

#include <stdio.h>
#include <math.h>

#define PI 3.1415927
#define G 398601.2            /* km^3/s^2 */
#define EARTH_RADIUS 6378.0 /* km */
```

```
#define DAY 86400.0              /* seconds */

int main()
{
        double period,altitude,total_time=0.0;
        int orbit_number=0;

        printf("What is the altitude (km)? ");
        scanf("%lf",&altitude);
        period=2.0*PI*(EARTH_RADIUS+altitude)*
                sqrt((EARTH_RADIUS+altitude)/G);
        printf("The orbital period is %.1lf seconds.\n",period);
        while (total_time < DAY) {
          orbit_number++;
          printf("Orbit #%2i starts at time %7.1lf seconds.\n",
                  orbit_number,total_time);
          total_time+=period;
        }
  return 0;
}
```

Running P-4.6(a)

```
What is the altitude (km)? 1000
The orbital period is 6306.9 seconds.
Orbit # 1 starts at time      0.0 seconds.
Orbit # 2 starts at time   6306.9 seconds.
Orbit # 3 starts at time  12613.9 seconds.
Orbit # 4 starts at time  18920.8 seconds.
Orbit # 5 starts at time  25227.8 seconds.
Orbit # 6 starts at time  31534.7 seconds.
Orbit # 7 starts at time  37841.6 seconds.
Orbit # 8 starts at time  44148.6 seconds.
Orbit # 9 starts at time  50455.5 seconds.
Orbit #10 starts at time  56762.4 seconds.
Orbit #11 starts at time  63069.4 seconds.
Orbit #12 starts at time  69376.3 seconds.
Orbit #13 starts at time  75683.3 seconds.
Orbit #14 starts at time  81990.2 seconds.
```

Note that this particular pre-test loop will always execute at least once because total_time is initialized to 0.

Post-Test Loops

The general syntax for post-test loops is

```
do
{
   statements
}
while (loop repetition condition)
```

As before, braces are required only for multiple statements. The statement(s) in this loop are always executed at least once because the repetition condition isn't tested until the end of the loop.

The problem from the previous subsection can easily be formulated as a post-test loop, as shown in P-4.6(b).

P-4.6(b) [orbits2.c]

```
/* Print information about earth orbits. */
/* Use a post-test loop. */

#include <stdio.h>
#include <math.h>

#define PI 3.1415927
#define G 398601.2            /* km^3/s^2 */
#define EARTH_RADIUS 6378.0 /* km */
#define DAY 86400.0           /* seconds */

int main()
{
      double period,altitude,total_time=0.0;
      int orbit_number=0;

      printf("What is the altitude (km)? ");
      scanf("%lf",&altitude);
      period=2.0*PI*(EARTH_RADIUS+altitude)
            *sqrt((EARTH_RADIUS+altitude)/G);
      printf("The orbital period is %.1lf seconds.\n",period);
      do {
            orbit_number++;
            printf("Orbit #%2i starts at time %7.1lf seconds.\n",
                orbit_number,total_time);
            total_time+=period;
      }
      while (total_time < DAY);
   return 0;
}
```

The output from P-4.6(b) is identical to that for P-4.6(a).

Sometimes you must think carefully about how to design a loop and its terminating conditions properly. Consider this problem, to which we will apply the entire five-step problem-solving process.

1 Define the problem.

A small elevator can safely carry a load of no more than 500 pounds. If this load limit is exceeded, the elevator cable will snap and all the occupants will be killed. Initially the elevator is empty and several people are waiting in line. There is a scale outside the elevator door so that each person can be weighed to determine whether he or she will be allowed on the elevator. To make the problem easier, assume that if the next person in line will cause the load limit to be exceeded, the elevator doors will close. That is, no attempt is made to search farther back in the line for a lighter person who will not cause the load limit to be exceeded. Write a program to simulate this situation.

2 Outline a solution.

The load initially is 0. Then, inside a loop, the program accepts proposed weights typed at the keyboard. For each new value, the algorithm must calculate a proposed new total load. If this proposed total does not exceed the maximum, then the actual total load becomes the proposed total load. The loop should continue as long as the proposed new load does not equal or exceed the load limit.

3 Design an algorithm.

Here is an algorithm for the critical loop structure. It involves proposing a new load based on the next weight and then responding appropriately.

LOOP *(as long as actual new load or unacceptable proposed new*
load does not equal or exceed the load limit)
    READ *(new_weight)*
    ASSIGN *proposed_load = current_load + new_weight*
    IF *(proposed_load ≤ limit)* **THEN**
        ASSIGN *current_load = proposed_load*
    ELSE *(print message indicating that new_weight is not allowed)*
END LOOP

It should also be possible to implement this loop as a pre-test loop. It will still be necessary to think carefully about how to terminate the loop.

4 *Convert the algorithm into a program.*

P-4.7 [elevator.c]

```c
/* Purpose: To allow individuals to enter an elevator one by one
   as long as the total weight doesn't exceed a specified maximum.
*/
#include <stdio.h>
#define MAX 500

int main(void)
{
  int total_load=0,wt,proposed_load;

  do {
    printf("Give new proposed weight: ");
    scanf("%i",&wt);
    proposed_load=total_load+wt;
    if (proposed_load <= MAX) {
      total_load=proposed_load;
      printf("new = %4i total = %4i\n",wt,total_load);
    }
    else
      printf("NOT ALLOWED. This will give a total load of %i.\n",
             total_load+wt);
  } while (proposed_load < MAX);

  return 0;
}
```

Running P-4.7

```
Give new proposed weight: 100
new =  100 total =  100
Give new proposed weight: 200
new =  200 total =  300
Give new proposed weight: 175
new =  175 total =  475
Give new proposed weight: 99
NOT ALLOWED. This will give a total load of 574.
```

5 *Verify the operation of the program.*

The single sample output shown here is insufficient to test the program thoroughly. You should also test a case for which the first proposed weight exceeds 500 pounds and one for which the weights add up to exactly 500 pounds.

Loops for Input Validation

In interactive programs that require user input, it is often important to perform some validation tests on keyboard input before using it. Consider the beginning of a typical problem statement:

Write a program that asks a user to enter a dollar amount and then...

For this discussion, we don't care what will be done with the dollar amount. However, we are concerned that a user may enter a dollar amount as $10,000 or 10,000 rather than 10000, even if the input prompt is specific about the program's expectations. We know that C won't accept the first two examples as valid numbers. Our goal is to scan the input before trying to interpret it as a number. If the input is inappropriate, the program should give the user another chance. Program P-4.8 presents one solution to this problem.

P-4.8 [dollars.c]

```c
/* Perform input validation on numerical data. */
#include <stdio.h>
#include <string.h>
#define TRUE 1
#define FALSE 0

int main()
{
        double dollars;
        char test_string[80],final_string[80];
        int i,good_data;

        do
        {
          printf("Give a dollar amount with no commas: $");
          scanf("%s",&test_string);
          good_data=TRUE;
          i=-1;
          while ( (i <= strlen(test_string)-1) && (good_data) )
          {
            i++;
            if ( (test_string[i] == ',') || (test_string[i] == '$') )
              good_data=FALSE;
          }
          if (! good_data)
            printf("Your input of %s is unacceptable.  Try again.\n",
                   test_string);
          else
            printf("Your input of %s is acceptable.\n",test_string);
        }
        while (! good_data);
        return 0;
}
```

The code in P-4.8 involves some new syntax that we won't discuss in detail until Chapter 6. Basically, each character in a string of characters can be accessed individually (starting with the first character, which C addresses as character 0) and tested to see whether it is a comma or a dollar sign. The `for`... loop is controlled by the standard C function `strlen`, which needs access to the `string.h` header file and which counts the number of characters in the user's input, excluding the terminating character.

4.5 Applications

4.5.1 Solving the Quadratic Equation

1 *Define the problem.*

Write a program that solves the quadratic equation $a^2x + bx + c = 0$ for its real roots, using user-specified values for a, b, and c.

2 *Outline a solution.*

The well-known solution to the quadratic equation is

$$\frac{-b \pm \sqrt{b^2 - 4ac}}{2a}$$

When you apply this solution to finding real roots, there are three possibilities:

1. If the discriminant is positive, there are two real roots.
2. If the discriminant is zero, there is one real root.
3. If the discriminant is less than zero, there are no real roots.

3 *Design an algorithm.*

The critical part of the algorithm is the test applied to the discriminant:

IF (discriminant > 0) **THEN**
    ASSIGN two real roots according to the formula
ELSE IF (discriminant = 0) **THEN**
    ASSIGN one real root equal to -b/2a
ELSE
    there aren't any real roots

 Convert the algorithm into a program.

P-4.9 [quadratc.c]

```c
/* Quadratic equation with test for discriminant. */

#include <stdio.h>
#include <math.h>

int main(void)
{
  double a,b,c,discriminant,root1,root2,LIMIT=1e-6;

  printf("Enter coefficients for ax^2+bx+c: ");
  scanf("%lf %lf %lf",&a,&b,&c);
  discriminant=b*b-4.0*a*c;
  printf("discriminant = %lf\n",discriminant);
  if (discriminant > LIMIT ) {
    root1=(-b+sqrt(discriminant))/2.0/a;
    root2=(-b-sqrt(discriminant))/2.0/a;
    printf("root1 = %lf, root2 = %lf\n",root1,root2);
  }
  else if (fabs(discriminant) <= LIMIT) {
    root1=-b/2.0/a;
    root2=0.0;
    printf("The single real root = %lf\n",root1);
  }
  else
    printf("There are no real roots.\n");
    root1=0.0;
    root2=0.0;

  return 0;
}
```

Running P-4.9

```
Enter coefficients for ax^2+bx+c: 1 2 3
discriminant = -8.000000
0
There are no real roots.
```

There are no real roots for the quadratic equation $x^2 + 2x + 3 = 0$.

In the implementation of the algorithm, it is necessary to think carefully about the implications of concluding that the discriminant is 0. Suppose that the discriminant $b^2 - 4ac$ is *algebraically* equal to 0. It is not a good idea to assume that this value will always be *numerically* equal to 0 because of the limitations on the precision of real arithmetic. This problem is not so bad if the discriminant is a very small *positive* number rather than 0; then your program will report that there are two nearly identical real roots. However, this could be a serious problem if the discriminant is a very small *negative* number. Then your program will report that there are no real roots when, in fact, there is one real root. Program P-4.9 protects against this potential problem by testing the absolute value of the discriminant against the hard-coded small value LIMIT. In this implementation, a discriminant that is less than or equal to 10^{-6} is considered to be 0.

5 *Verify the operation of the program.*

The obvious verification steps require supplying sets of coefficients that test all three branches in the if... statement. It would be interesting to find a case where the discriminant is algebraically equal to 0 but is represented numerically as a very small negative number.

4.5.2 *Maximum Deflection of a Beam With Various Support/Loading Systems*

1 *Define the problem.*

The problem of calculating the maximum deflection of a beam supported at both ends and subject to a load concentrated at the center of the beam has already been treated as an application in Section 2.5.1. In this application, the calculations will be extended to cover several support/loading configurations.

2 *Outline a solution.*

Table 4.2 gives formulas for four support/loading options, including the one discussed previously in Section 2.5.1.

Table 4.2. Maximum deflection of a beam subject to
various support and loading conditions

Loading and Support [1]	Schematic	Maximum Deflection
Supported at each end, concentrated force F	F ↓ /\ /\ <------- L ------->	$-FL^3/(48EI)$ at L/2
Supported at each end, distributed weight W	W ↓↓↓↓↓↓↓↓↓↓ /\ /\	$-5WL^3/(384EI)$ at L/2
Supported at one end, concentrated force F at free end	F ↓	$-FL^3/(3EI)$ at free end
Supported at one end, distributed weight W	W ↓↓↓↓↓↓↓↓↓↓	$-WL^3/(8EI)$ at free end

[1] For this table, force F and weight W have units of lb; length L, in; elasticity E, lb/in^2; and moment of inertia, in^4.

3   Design an algorithm.

Here is one way the support/loading options might be incorporated into an algorithm, assuming that values for F (or W), L, E, and I are already available.

WRITE *(menu describing four possible support systems, with input prompt)*
READ *(choice of support system 1-4)*
CHOOSE *(based on support/load ID)*
     1: **ASSIGN** *deflection = $-FL^3/(48EI)$*
     2: **ASSIGN** *deflection = $-5WL^3/(384EI)$*
     3: **ASSIGN** *deflection = $-FL^3/(3EI)$*
     4: **ASSIGN** *deflection = $-WL^3/(8EI)$*
     anything else: **WRITE** *("Input error.")*
(end CHOOSE)
WRITE *(deflection)*

Convert the algorithm into a program.

P-4.10 [beam2.c]

```c
#include <stdio.h>

char MakeChoice(void);
double CalculateDeflection(char ch,double L,double F,
                           double E,double I);
int main(void)
{
  double length,force,elasticity,mom_of_inertia,deflection;
  char choice,more='y';
  do {
    printf("Give length (ft), force (lb),\n");
    printf("elasticity (lb/in^2), moment of inertia (in^4): ");
    scanf("%lf %lf %lf %lf",
          &length,&force,&elasticity,&mom_of_inertia);
    choice=MakeChoice();
    deflection=CalculateDeflection(choice,length*12.,force,
                                   elasticity,mom_of_inertia);
    printf("\nThe deflection is %.3lf inches\n",deflection);
    printf("\nMore (y/n)? ");
    fflush(stdin);
    scanf("%c",&more);
  } while (more == 'y');
  return 0;
}

char MakeChoice(void)
{
  char ch;
  printf("\n");
  printf("1 - supported at both ends, central load\n");
  printf("2 - supported at both ends, distributed load\n");
  printf("3 - supported at one end, loaded at free end\n");
  printf("4 - supported at one end, distributed load\n");
  printf("\n");
  printf("Choose one... ");
  fflush(stdin);
  scanf("%c",&ch);
  return ch;
}

double CalculateDeflection(char ch,double L,double F,
                           double E,double I)
{
  printf("Choice: %c %lf %lf %lf %lf\n",ch,L,F,E,I);
  switch(ch) {
    case '1':
      return -F*L*L*L/48./E/I;
    case '2':
      return -5.*F*L*L*L/384./E/I;
    case '3':
      return -F*L*L*L/3./E/I;
```

```
case '4':
  return -F*L*L*L/8./E/I;
default:
  printf("Inappropriate support/loading option.\n");
  return 0;
  }
}
```

5 *Verify the operation of the program.*

Representative values for the elasticity E and moment of inertia I are 3×10^7 lb/in^2 and 800 in^4, for which the deflection of a beam supported at each end and subjected to a central load of 50,000 lb is about 0.6 in. You should check calculations by hand for each of the four support/loading options.

Problem Discussion

P-4.10 is an excellent example of a program that can benefit from modularization. The main function guides selection of one or more support/loading options and a separate function performs the actual deflection calculations. Separation of the code in this way is much better programming style than putting all the code required to support the menu options and deflection calculations inside the main function. The function to calculate the deflection includes a switch construct to perform the appropriate calculation, as well as a provision for responding to inappropriate input.

The main program contains a conditional loop. It is optional in this program, but its purpose is to give the user a chance to perform more than one calculation without having to reexecute the program. This is a typical structure for menu-driven programs.

4.5.3 Refraction of Light

1 *Define the problem.*

Refer to the application in Section 3.6.1 for a discussion of Snell's Law, which gives the angle of a refracted ray of light as a function of the angle of the incident ray at the interface between two materials with different refractive indices:

$$n_i\sin(i) = n_r\sin(r)$$

Table 3.8 in Section 3.6.1 gives angles of refraction for a ray of light passing from air into three different materials over a range of incident angles from 0° to 90°. Write a program that will produce the results given in that table.

2 *Outline a solution.*

1. Specify the refractive index for each of the three materials in Table 3.8. They can be hard-coded within the program or read from a data file.
2. Use a count-controlled loop to generate the incident angles. Within the loop, calculate refracted angles for an air-material interface with each of the three materials.

3 *Design an algorithm.*

DEFINE *(incident_angle, water_angle, glass_angle, diamond_angle as real numbers; π and DegToRad (conversion from angles to radians) as real numbers; water_index, glass_index, diamond_index, air_index as real numbers)*

ASSIGN *DegToRad = π/180*
      water_index = 1.33
      glass_index = 1.50
      diamond_index = 2.42
      air_index = 1.00
WRITE *(headings)*
LOOP *(incident_angle = 0 to 90, steps of 5)*
    ASSIGN *incident_angle = incident_angle • DegToRad*
      water_angle =
        sin⁻¹[(air_index/water_index)*sin(incident_angle)]
      glass_angle =
        sin⁻¹[(air_index/glass_index)*sin(incident_angle)]
      diamond_angle =
        sin⁻¹[(air_index/diamond_index)*sin(incident_angle)]
  (Display angles in degrees)
    WRITE *(incident_angle,water_index/DegToRad,*
        glass_index/DegToRad, diamond_index/DegToRad)
END LOOP

Convert the algorithm into a program.

P-4.11 [snell.c]

```c
/* Snell's Law */

#include <stdio.h>
#include <math.h>
#define PI 3.14159
#define FILENAME "snell.dat"

int main(void)
{
  double n_inc=1.0,a_inc,ref_1,ref_2,ref_3;
  double n_1,n_2,n_3;
  double deg_to_rad;
  int i;
  char name_1[10],name_2[10],name_3[10];
  FILE *snell_in;

  snell_in=fopen(FILENAME,"r");
  fscanf(snell_in,"%s %lf %s %lf %s %lf",name_1,&n_1,name_2,&n_2,
         name_3,&n_3);
  fclose(snell_in);
  printf("Indices of refraction for: \n");
  printf("%10s %.2lf\n%10s %.2lf\n%10s %.2lf\n",name_1,n_1,
         name_2,n_2,name_3,n_3);
  deg_to_rad=PI/180.0;
  printf("\n Incident Refracted angle (deg)\n");
  printf("   (air)    %9s %9s %9s\n",name_1,name_2,name_3);
  printf("-----------------------------------------\n");
  for (i=0; i <= 90; i+=10) {
    a_inc=(double)i*deg_to_rad;
    ref_1=asin(n_inc*sin(a_inc)/n_1)/deg_to_rad;
    ref_2=asin(n_inc*sin(a_inc)/n_2)/deg_to_rad;
    ref_3=asin(n_inc*sin(a_inc)/n_3)/deg_to_rad;
    printf("%8.2lf   %9.2lf %9.2lf %9.2lf\n",
           a_inc/deg_to_rad,ref_1,ref_2,ref_3);
  }

  return 0;
}
```

Running P-4.11

```
Indices of refraction for:
    water 1.33
    glass 1.50
  diamond 2.42

Incident Refracted angle (deg)
  (air)       water     glass    diamond
------------------------------------------
   0.00        0.00      0.00      0.00
  10.00        7.50      6.65      4.11
  20.00       14.90     13.18      8.12
  30.00       22.08     19.47     11.92
  40.00       28.90     25.37     15.40
  50.00       35.17     30.71     18.45
  60.00       40.63     35.26     20.97
  70.00       44.95     38.79     22.85
  80.00       47.77     41.04     24.01
  90.00       48.75     41.81     24.41
```

5 *Verify the operation of the program.*

Verify the tabulated values with a hand calculator in addition to comparing your results with the values in Table 3.8.

Problem Discussion

In P-4.11, the names of the three materials and their refractive indices have been stored in an external text file. This arrangement makes it easy to change the materials, but not the total number of materials. The input values are echoed in the program's output. Note how the values for the angles are generated from the integer loop counter.

4.5.4 Oscillating Frequency of an LC Circuit

1 *Define the problem.*

An electrical circuit that contains an inductance L (henrys, H) and a capacitance C (farads, F) in series oscillates at a characteristic frequency

$$f = \frac{1}{2\pi\sqrt{LC}}$$

Write a program that generates a table of oscillating frequencies for a two-dimensional table of L and C values. Let the L values form the rows of the table and the C values form the columns. Such a circuit can be used to tune radios or TVs. The table for this problem should include values for a circuit to be used in a radio that receives AM-band radio stations—frequencies on the order of 1000 kHz.

2 *Outline a solution.*

A circuit containing an inductance of 2.5 mH and a capacitance of 10 pF oscillates at about 1000 kHz. Therefore the range of C values should be 2 to 20 pF in steps of 2 pF, and the range of inductance should be 1 to 4 mH in steps of 0.5 mH.

1. Generate appropriate column headings for the table.
2. Create a nested loop. The outer loop will step through the inductance values and the inner loop will step through the capacitance values.
3. Just inside the outer loop, but outside the inner loop, display the inductance value generated by the outer loop. Do not print a new-line character.
4. The calculation for the frequency at a particular set of inductance-capacitance values goes inside the inner loop. Display the result.
5. Just after termination of the inner loop, print a new-line character.

3 *Design an algorithm.*

The critical part of the algorithm is the nested loop to generate the table:

LOOP *(for C = 2 to 20 pF, in steps of 2 pF)*
    WRITE *(C, no carriage return)*
END LOOP
WRITE *(carriage return)*
LOOP *(for L = 1.0 to 4.0 mH, in steps of 0.5 mH)*
    WRITE *(L, no carriage return)*
    LOOP *(for C = 2 to 20 pF, in steps of 2 pF)*
        Calculate and display oscillating frequency, no carriage return
    END (inner) LOOP
    WRITE *(carriage return)*
END (outer) LOOP

Convert the algorithm into a program.

P-4.12 [lc.c]

```
/* LC.C  Oscillating frequency of an LC circuit. */
#include <stdio.h>
#include <math.h>
#define C0 0.0
#define nC 10
#define dC 2.0
#define L0 0.0005
#define nL 6
#define dL 0.0005
#define PI 3.141596
int main(void)
{
  int row,col;
  double L, C, f;
  printf("OSCILLATING FREQUENCY (kHz) OF AN LC CIRCUIT\n");
  printf("           C(pF)=\n");
  printf("L(H)= ");
  for (col=1; col<=nC; col++) {
    C=C0+dC*col;
    printf("%5.0lf",C);
  }
  printf("\n");
  for (row=1; row<=nL; row++) {
    L=L0+dL*row;
    printf("%6.4lf",L);
    for (col=1; col<=nC; col++) {
      C=C0+dC*col;
      f=0.5/PI/sqrt(L*C*1e-12);
      printf(" %4.0lf",f/1000.0);
    }
    printf("\n");
  }
  return 0;
}
```

Running P-4.12

| OSCILLATING FREQUENCY (kHz) OF AN LC CIRCUIT | | | | | | | | | |
| C(pF)= | | | | | | | | | |
L(H)= 2	4	6	8	10	12	14	16	18	20
0.0010 3559	2516	2055	1779	1592	1453	1345	1258	1186	1125
0.0015 2906	2055	1678	1453	1299	1186	1098	1027	969	919
0.0020 2516	1779	1453	1258	1125	1027	951	890	839	796
0.0025 2251	1592	1299	1125	1007	919	851	796	750	712
0.0030 2055	1453	1186	1027	919	839	777	726	685	650
0.0035 1902	1345	1098	951	851	777	719	673	634	602

5 Verify the operation of the program.

A crucial check is to make sure that a circuit with L = 2.5 mH and C = 10 pF oscillates at about 1000 kHz. It is easy to get the wrong answers for this problem if you are not careful about converting quantities into the appropriate units; for example, picofarads to farads in the case of capacitance. If one set of values produces the correct answer, you can be reasonably confident that the other results are also correct.

Problem Discussion

P-4.12 is a typical use of nested loops to generate tabulated values. Note how a single loop is used before the nested loop to generate the capacitance values across the columns of the table. Make sure you understand how the \n character is used to control the location of line feeds at the end of lines within the table. The program uses several #define directives for constant values that are used to control the operation of the nested loops. It is better programming style to define these values in this way than to hard-code the needed values in the loops themselves.

4.5.5 Calculating Radiation Exposures for a Materials Testing Experiment

1 Define the problem.

In a test of the effects of radiation on materials, an experiment protocol requires that:

(1) a sample be subjected to several bursts of radiation of random intensity, each of which must not exceed some specified maximum value; and
(2) the sum of all radiation delivered to the sample must not exceed a specified limit for total exposure.

Write a program to simulate this experiment by generating a sequence of random exposure levels that satisfy this protocol.

2 Outline a solution.

1. Supply the maximum intensity for a single exposure and the limit on total cumulative exposure; the former must be less than the latter. These values may be hard coded.
2. Initialize the cumulative exposure to 0 and select a random exposure value—call this value the current value.
3. Construct a loop that allows the execution of statements inside the loop only if the cumulative exposure plus the current value doesn't exceed the allowed total cumulative exposure.
4. Inside the loop, add the current value to the cumulative exposure. Print the current and cumulative exposures. Select a new current exposure value.
5. Outside the loop, after it terminates, print the current exposure value along with a message indicating that this exposure would have exceeded the allowed maximum.

3 Design an algorithm.

Here is a design for the critical loop structure.

LOOP *(as long as proposed_exposure is less than max_total)*
    ASSIGN *current_exposure = random value, ≤ max_single*
    ASSIGN *proposed_exposure = cum_exposure + current_exposure*
    IF *(proposed_exposure ≤ max_total* **THEN**
        ASSIGN *cum_exposure = proposed_exposure*
    ELSE
        display appropriate message
END LOOP
WRITE *(current exposure, "is too big")*

4 Convert the algorithm into a program.

P-4.13 [dose.c]

```
#include <stdio.h>
#include <stdlib.h>
#include <time.h>
#define MAX_TOTAL 1000.0
#define MAX_DOSE 200.0
```

```
int main(void)
{
  int i;
  double total_dose=0.0, proposed_total, dose;

  srand((unsigned)time(NULL)); /* initialize random # generator */
  printf("R A D I A T I O N    S I M U L A T I O N    T E S T\n");
  printf("     The maximum total dose for this test is %5.01f.\n",
    MAX_TOTAL);
  printf("The maximum individual dose for this test is %5.01f.\n\n",
    MAX_DOSE);
  printf("    dose   total\n");
  printf("---------------\n");
  do {
    dose=MAX_DOSE*rand()/RAND_MAX;
    proposed_total=total_dose+dose;
    if (proposed_total <= MAX_TOTAL) {
      total_dose+=dose;
      printf("%8.01f%8.01f\n",dose,total_dose);
    }
    else
      printf(
      "The proposed dose of %.01f will exceed the max.  End test.\n",
      dose);
  } while ( proposed_total < MAX_TOTAL);
  return 0;
}
```

Running P-4.13

```
R A D I A T I O N    S I M U L A T I O N    T E S T
     The maximum total dose for this test is  1000.
The maximum individual dose for this test is   200.

   dose   total
---------------
     45      45
     66     111
     62     173
     14     186
     80     266
      1     267
    126     392
     57     449
    137     586
    197     783
     54     838
     62     899
The proposed dose of 122 will exceed the max.  End test.
```

5 *Verify the operation of the program.*

This problem is similar to the "elevator" problem described in Section 4.4. The goal of your program testing must be to ensure that the specified maximum limit is never exceeded. The only straightforward way to do this is to observe the operation of P-4.13 many times. However, it is also worth temporarily replacing the random levels generated in the program with user-supplied levels. That way you can test specific combinations of levels. What happens if the first proposed intensity is greater than the maximum allowed intensity? What happens if the cumulative exposure is exactly equal to the total allowed exposure? These are questions that are difficult to answer when each exposure is chosen randomly, but you can test the program's response if you can select the exposures yourself.

Problem Discussion

There are several features of P-4.13 that are worth studying. First, note that no physical units have been specified in the problem statement or program. In this simulation, the units don't matter as long as the user-supplied values are given in consistent units.

Second, this program requires a sequence of random numbers. Programming languages don't have access to truly random numbers, but C and other high-level languages

random number generator
pseudorandom number

include a software-based ***random number generator*** that can be used to produce sequences of ***pseudorandom numbers*** that *appear* to be random.

In P-4.13, the statement

```
dose=MAX_DOSE*rand()/RAND_MAX;
```

inside the loop generates the random values using the C function `rand`. This function generates a random integer uniformly distributed between 0 and the largest possible integer for the C implementation being used. This maximum value is stored in the predefined value RAND_MAX. The calculation in this statement requires access to the `stdlib.h` header file. Note that the calculation `rand()/RAND_MAX` by itself will return a value of 0 because both the numerator and denominator are integers! However, because MAX_DOSE has been defined as a real number, dose will be assigned a value between 0 and MAX_DOSE.

The purpose of the statement

```
srand((unsigned)time(NULL));
```

before the loop is to reinitialize ("seed") the random number generator each time the program is run. To do this, the intrinsic function `srand` accesses a value in your computer's system clock, which essentially starts the sequence of random numbers from a random position every time the program is executed. Access to the system clock requires inclusion of the `time.h` header file.

4.6 Debugging Your Programs

Students often have trouble with selection and repetition statements. It is important to separate algorithm design problems from implementation problems. Here are some questions you should ask yourself when your code doesn't work.

1. Do I understand what a selection construct is supposed to accomplish in the context of a particular problem? When I choose paths covering a range of values, have I designed the algorithm so that all possible values are included, without any overlap? Have I chosen appropriately beween "or" and "and" in designing relational tests? Have I organized responses to a variety of conditions in a logical way to minimize unnecessarily long and convoluted selection constructs? Have I made a conscious choice between **IF**... and **CHOOSE**... algorithms and used the latter whenever possible, to produce more readable code?

2. When I implement an **IF**... algorithm, have I been careful to group statements within curly braces for each branch of the selection construct? Once the code is working, have I tested each branch of the construct?

3. When I implement a **CHOOSE**... algorithm with a `switch` construct, have I provided code for all possible values of the ordinal case expression, including a `default` path for out of range responses? Have I included `break` statements at the end of the code for each path?

4. Do I understand what a repetition construct is supposed to accomplish in the context of a particular problem? Have I chosen appropriately among count-controlled, pre-test, and post-test loops? For count-controlled loops, have I made appropriate use of *integer* loop variables?

5. When I implement a count-controlled loop, have I made sure that the initial value of the loop counter, the repetition condition, and the update expression are internally consistent? Have I avoided changing the value of the loop counter inside its loop or using a loop counter outside its loop? Have I reused loop counter names in order to avoid needless proliferation of variable names?

6. When I implement a conditional loop, have I chosen appropriately between while... (pre-test) and do... while (post-test) syntax? When a counter must be updated inside the loop, have I done this at an appropriate place relative to the code that uses the counter? (This can be a problem in loops that read and process data from files.) Am I sure that the terminating condition is appropriate and will *always* be satisfied? Inappropriate terminating conditions can result in *infinite loops* that will continue to execute forever, or at least until you interrupt your program with some system-dependent series of commands.

4.7 Exercises

1. Electric utility rates in the Philadelphia area are among the highest in the country. Monthly charges for residential customers who use electric resistance heating or an electric heat pump are calculated as follows:

Service Charge:	$5.08
Energy Charge:	
Winter:	$0.1345/kWh for first 600 kWh
	$0.0679/kWh for additional kWh
Summer:	$0.1345/kWh for first 500 kWh
	$0.1530/kWh for additional kWh

The service charge appears on each month's bill. The energy charge changes from summer to winter; the summer rate structure applies from June through September and the winter rate structure applies during all other months.

Write a program that asks the user to specify the month, expressed as an integer between 1 and 12, and the number of kWh (kilowatt hours) used during that month and then calls a function to calculate the monthly bill.

Use a `switch` construct to choose between summer and winter rate structures and an `if...` statement to perform the required calculation based on monthly usage. For this program, even though it's not a good idea in general, you may assume that the month passed to the function is never outside the range 1 to 12; this means that you can specify `case` values of 6, 7, 8, and 9 for the summer months and use the `default:` case to process the winter months. [peco.c]

2. A tray is formed from a sheet of metal by cutting equal squares from each corner and bending the sides up. Given the length and width of the original sheet, what size square corner cut gives a tray with maximum volume? Write a program that will provide an approximate answer to this question by starting with a user-specified size for the sheet

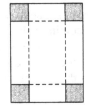

and calculating the volumes based on a series of cut sizes in 0.1-inch increments. Ignore the fact that bending the sheet will result in a small loss in the height of the sides. [tray_vol.c]

Extra Credit:
If you have had an introductory course in differential calculus, you should be able to determine the exact answer to this problem. Compare it to the result from your program.

> An understanding of elementary calculus is required.

3. (a) The population of a certain animal is 1,000,000 at the beginning of the year. During each year, 6% of the animals alive at the beginning of the year die. The number of animals born during the year that survive to the end of the year is equal to 1% of the population at the beginning of the year. Write a program that prints out the births, deaths, and total population at the end of each year and stops when the population falls to 10% or less of the original population.
Hint: Populations can have only integer values.

(b) Assuming the death rate stays the same as in part (a), what is the birth rate required for the population to double in 20 years? Starting with the original population of 1,000,000, print the births, deaths, and total population at the end of each year for 20 years, using the newly calculated birth rate. The population after 20 years will be twice the original population when $2 = (1 + r)^{20}$, where r is the overall population growth rate; that is, the birth rate minus the death rate.

You may include both parts of the problem in a single program. [populatn.c]

4. The average temperature of the earth/atmosphere system as viewed from space depends on the solar constant S_o, which is about 1368 W/m^2, and the earth's albedo (reflectivity). Assuming the earth acts like a blackbody (a perfect radiator), the temperature is related to the solar constant by

$$S_o(1 - \alpha)/4 = \sigma T^4$$

where σ is the Stefan-Boltzmann constant, 5.67×10^{-8} W/(m$^2 \cdot$K^4), and α is the earth's albedo, about 0.30. (Albedo is a dimensionless measure of the fraction of incoming solar energy reflected by the earth/atmosphere system.)

Write a program that calculates the temperature as a function of changes in the solar constant over the range ±10%. Note that the temperature of the earth/atmosphere system as viewed from space is *not* the same as the average surface temperature of the earth, which is about 15°C, because of the well-known greenhouse effect of the earth's atmosphere. [earthatm.c]

5. The wavelengths of the Balmer series of lines in the hydrogen spectrum are given by

$$\lambda = \frac{3646\,n^2}{n^2-4}$$

where n is an integer having values greater than 2. Write a program that generates the first 10 wavelengths in the Balmer series. [balmer.c]

6. The resistivity ρ of tungsten wire is roughly 100×10^{-6} ohm-cm at the operating temperature of a lightbulb filament. Suppose a lightbulb consumes 100 W of power on a 110-volt circuit. The power can be expressed in terms of the voltage V and resistance R of the filament as

$$\text{Power} = V^2/R = V^2/(\rho L/A)$$

where L is the length of the filament in cm and A is the cross-sectional area in cm^2.

Write a program that generates a table of *reasonable* lengths and diameters that will give the required resistance. It is up to you to decide what "reasonable" means. [tungsten.c]

7. Write a program that calculates and displays the square root, cube root, fourth root, and fifth root of the integers 2 through 20. Your table should look something like this:

```
n 2       3       4       5
2 1.4142 1.2599 1.1892 1.1487
3 1.7321 1.4422 1.3161 1.2457
...
20 4.4721 2,7144 2.1147 1.8206
```

Be sure to use appropriate format specifiers so the decimal points in the table line up. [rootable.c]

8. The series

$$\sum_{n=0}^{\infty} \frac{z^n}{n!} = \frac{1}{0!} + \frac{z}{1!} + \frac{z^2}{2!} + \frac{z^3}{3!} + \cdots$$

converges for any value of z. That is, an individual term $z^n/n!$ approaches 0 and the sum of all the terms approaches a definite value as n approaches infinity. Write a function, and a program to test it, that accepts as input a value of z and returns as output an estimate of the value of the series for that value of z. Use a conditional loop that terminates when the absolute value of an individual term is smaller than some hardcoded small value. Note that you can compute individual terms in the series without actually calculating n! explicitly. The nth term is just the $(n-1)^{th}$ term times z/n.

Your results can easily be checked once you recognize what this series represents; you will find it in any tabulation of series expansions for common mathematical functions. [series.c]

9. An external text file contains real numbers:

```
7.7
6.6
4.9
5.9
8.1
```
(and so forth)

Write a program that reads this file and calculates the average m and standard deviation s for all the values in the file, using the formulas

$$m = \sum_{i=1}^{n} x_i \qquad s = \sqrt{\frac{\sum_{i=1}^{n} x_i^2 - \left(\sum_{i=1}^{n} x_i\right)^2 / n}{n-1}}$$

10. One of the concerns in connection with global warming is that the average sea level may rise. Suppose you are a civil engineer who has been asked to estimate the potential loss of land along a coastline. Write a program that relates a sea level rise of R cm to loss of land, in units of km^2/km and acres/mi, along a coastline with a specified range of grades. A grade of 0.1%-10% with respect to the sea, in increments of 0.1%, is reasonable.

If the coastline makes an angle θ with the sea, the distance lost from the original coastline, measured along the sloping ground, is $R/\sin(\theta)$. The grade is defined as $100 \cdot \tan(\theta)$ percent. Suppose the sea level rises 10 cm (about 4 in). A 1° slope (about 1.75% grade) means that the coastline will recede about 5.7 m, with a loss of about 0.0057 km^2 per km of coastline, or about 2.3 acres per mile of coastline. (There are 1609.3 m/mile and 640 acres/mile^2.) [sea_levl.c]

11. Simulation studies in science, mathematics, and engineering often require random numbers from a so-called normal distribution. Such numbers have a mean of 0 and a standard deviation of 1. (The standard deviation is a measure of the spread of values in a distribution.) C's random number generator produces uniformly distributed integers that are easily convertible to uniformly distributed real numbers in the range [0,1), rather than normally distributed numbers. (Recall the application in Section 4.5.5.)

Fortunately, there is a simple way to generate a pair of normally distributed numbers x_1 and x_2 from a pair of uniformly distributed numbers u_1 and u_2 in the range (0,1]:

$$x_1 = \sqrt{-2\ell n(u_1)}\cos(2\pi u_2)$$
$$x_2 = \sqrt{-2\ell n(u_1)}\sin(2\pi u_2)$$

Write a program that uses this formula to generate a sample of 200 normally distributed numbers. You can check the numbers to see if they actually appear to be normally distributed by calculating their mean and standard deviation, using the equations given in Exercise 9.

Accumulate the sums of x and x^2 inside the loop and use the sums to calculate the mean and standard deviation when the loop is complete. The mean and standard deviation (or the average of the means and standard deviations from several sets of numbers) will be close to 0 and 1, but they won't be exactly 0 and 1. There are quantitative statistical tests for a normal distribution, but they are beyond the scope of this problem.

Hint: Remember that this algorithm generates random numbers in pairs, so a `for...` loop from 1 to 100 generates 200 random numbers, not 100.

The formulas for generating normally distributed numbers require uniform numbers in the range (0,1], rather than [0,1], because ln(0) is undefined. In the implementation, the upper limit of the range is of no concern. However, it's possible that a value of exactly 0 might be generated. Therefore, your program should protect itself against this possibility, no matter how unlikely, by testing u_1 and replacing it with a very small number if its generated value is exactly 0. [random.c]

12. One way to estimate the square root of a number n is to use Newton's algorithm. For this algorithm, the value of the initial guess is relatively unimportant; guess = n/2 is a reasonable choice. Then calculate a new estimate by calculating a new guess:

$$guess = (guess + n/guess)/2$$

Continue to make new estimates until the absolute value of the difference between guess^2 and n differs from the original number by less than some specified small amount. Write and test a function that implements this algorithm. [newton.c]

13. The Internal Revenue Service acknowledges that the value of equipment used in manufacturing and other businesses declines as that equipment ages. Therefore, businesses can gain a tax advantage by depreciating the value of new equipment over an assumed useful lifetime of n years. At the end of n years, the equipment may have either no value or some small salvage value. Depreciation can be computed three ways:

1. *Straight-line depreciation.* The value of an asset minus its salvage value depreciates by the same amount each year over its useful life of n years.
2. *Double-declining depreciation.* Each year, the original value of an asset minus previously declared depreciation (its book value) is diminished by 2/n.
3. *Sum-of-digits depreciation.* Add the integers from 1 through n. The depreciation on the original value of an asset minus its salvage value allowed in year i is (n - i) + 1 divided by the sum of the digits.

Write a program that calculates the depreciation available for years 1 through n. Assume that the salvage value is some small percentage (perhaps a value in the range 5 to 10 percent) of the original value. Table 4.3 gives some sample output for an asset originally valued at $1000 with a lifetime of 7 years and an assumed salvage value of $100.

Table 4.3. Sample depreciation table

```
        Original value     $1000
        Salvage value      $ 100
        Lifetime               7 years
```

Year	Straight line	Asset value	Double declining	Asset value	Sum of digits	Asset value
1	128.57	871.43	285.71	714.29	225.00	775.00
2	128.57	742.86	204.08	510.20	192.86	582.14
3	128.57	614.29	145.77	364.43	160.71	421.43
4	128.57	485.71	104.12	260.31	128.57	292.86
5	128.57	357.14	74.37	185.93	96.43	196.43
6	128.57	228.57	53.12	132.81	64.29	132.14
7	128.57	100.00	37.95	94.86	32.14	100.00

Note that the yearly depreciation for the double-declining method doesn't depend at all on the salvage value. This means that not all the depreciation can actually be taken in the seventh year if the asset really has a salvage value of $100. [deprecia.c]

Extra Credit:

Businesses often like to maximize depreciation when equipment is new in order to produce the greatest immediate tax advantage. Which method should they choose? If businesses can change the method by which they calculate depreciation at any time during the life of an asset, when (if ever) should they change methods? (The answer to this question depends on the salvage value of the asset.)

14. Consider the following piecewise-continuous function, which is shown in Figure 4.1:

$$f(x) = \begin{array}{l} x, \ 0 \le x \le 30 \\ 30 + (x - 30)^2/100, \ 30 < x \le 80 \\ 55 + (x - 80)/2, \ x > 80 \end{array}$$

Write a program that calculates values of this function for values of x in the range 0 to 100 in steps of 5 units. [piecewse.c]

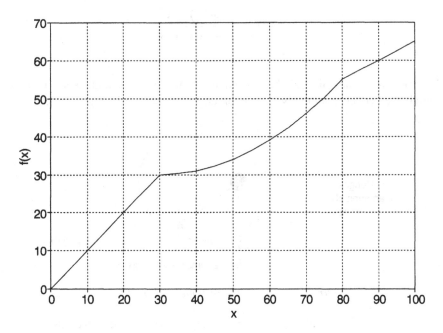

Figure 4.1. Graph of a piecewise-continuous function.

15. In orbital mechanics, the angular position of an orbiting object as a function of time must be calculated. For a circular orbit, the calculation is simple because the position is directly proportional to time. For noncircular orbits, the calculation is more complicated.

First, some definitions. The time required for an orbiting object to complete one revolution is called its period. The mean anomaly is the angular position an object would have if it were in a circular orbit with the same period. Mean anomaly is directly proportional to time.

The eccentric anomaly E_c is related to the mean anomaly M through a transcendental equation:

$$M = E_c - e \cdot \sin(E_c)$$

where both angular quantities must be expressed in radians rather than degrees and the eccentricity e is a measure of the shape of the orbit. The range of e is 0 to 1, with circular orbits having an eccentricity of 0.

The true anomaly θ is related to the eccentric anomaly through the equation

$$\cos(\theta) = \frac{\cos(E_c) - e}{1 - e\cos(E_c)}$$

Therefore, true anomaly can be related to mean anomaly, and hence to time, through the eccentric anomaly. The geometry is illustrated in Figure 4.2.

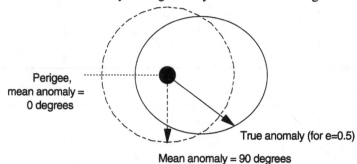

Figure 4.2. Geometry of noncircular orbits.

The equation involving M (Kepler's equation) can't be solved directly for eccentric anomaly, but it can be solved iteratively:

1. As a first guess, assume $E_c = M$.
2. Inside a loop, save the current value of E_c: $E_{old} = E_c$.
3. Recalculate E_c: $E_c = M + e \cdot \sin(E_c)$.

4. Repeat steps 2 and 3 until the absolute magnitude of E_c minus E_{old} is less than some specified small value (10^{-5} or 10^{-6} are reasonable choices).

Write a program that uses this algorithm to calculate true anomaly as a function of mean anomaly for values of mean anomaly in the range $0°-360°$ degrees, in increments of $5°$, for these values of eccentricity: 0.1, 0.25, 0.50, 0.75, and 0.90.

Hints:

1. All angular calculations must be done in radians. If you wish to display results in degrees, convert angles to degrees within output statements.

2. It is possible for arithmetic errors to occur when the mean anomaly is $180°$ because the argument of the arccosine function must never exceed 1. As the eccentric anomaly approaches $180°$, the calculation for $\cos(\theta)$ might produce a value slightly greater than 1. Account for this possibility by testing the value of $\cos(\theta)$ before you take its arccosine. Also, the arccosine function doesn't produce values in the range 0 to 2π ($0°$ to $360°$). You can use the values of mean anomaly to make sure your program produces answers in the appropriate range; whenever the mean anomaly is greater than $180°$, the true anomaly must also be greater than $180°$. [kepler2.c]

16. A satellite flying over a cloudless desert carries an instrument that measures the longwave radiance reflected in the direction of the instrument from a particular spot on the desert's surface. The instrument records the radiance L as a function of zenith angle θ relative to the spot on the surface. An empirical model is used to interpret the measured radiance as a function of zenith angle and the radiance L_o that would be measured from a satellite passing directly over the site:

$$L = L_o \sec(\theta)^x, \quad \theta \leq 60°$$
$$L = L_o \sec(\theta)^x - a[\sec(\theta) - \sec(60°)], \quad \theta > 60°$$

where x and a are empirically determined constants. The secant of the zenith angle is proportional to the amount of atmosphere between the satellite and the ground (the atmospheric path length). The model reflects the fact that the radiance observed by a satellite is limb darkened because the satellite must look through more atmosphere as the zenith angle increases. At large zenith angles, an additional term is required to account for the rapidly decreasing transparency of the atmosphere to longwave radiation.

Table 4.4 gives empirical model parameters for three desert surfaces derived from measurements taken in January. This is winter in the northern hemisphere, which explains why the value of L_o is higher for Australian deserts than it is for the two northern hemisphere deserts. Because the satellite measures longwave radiance, a larger radiance means that the surface is warmer. Figure 4.3 shows predicted radiances for these surfaces.

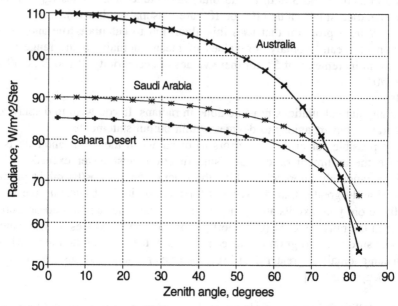

Figure 4.3. Predicted longwave radiances for three desert sites.

Table 4.4. Model parameters for longwave radiance from deserts

Desert Location	Overhead Radiance, W/m²/ster	x	a
Australia	110	-0.2116	3.184
Sahara	85	-0.0998	1.854
Saudi Arabia	90	-0.0974	1.241

Write a program that will calculate predicted values of radiance as a function of satellite zenith angle for the three sets of model parameters given in Table 4.4. What happens as the zenith angle approaches 90°? What can you conclude about the validity of the model as the satellite approaches the horizon? What might you conclude about the fact that, as the zenith angle increases, the differences in radiances observed from different surfaces tend to decrease? [limbdark.c]

17. A rectangular container with specified length, width (as viewed from the side), and depth contains a liquid (molten metal, for example). The container is rotated

about an axis parallel to the depth dimension at a constant angular rate, and the contents of the container spill into a mold. Write a program that will calculate the total volume of liquid poured into the mold as a function of container angle. Also, calculate an approximation to the "instantaneous" rate at which liquid pours from the container as a function of container angle and rotation rate.

Hints: Rotate the container in equal angular increments and calculate the resulting volume that has been emptied from the container. Subtract from this the volume at the previous angular value and divide by the angle increment. If the angle changes at a constant rate with respect to time, this calculation gives an approximation of the changing volume rate with respect to time.

Divide the calculations into two parts. First calculate angles from the time the container starts to rotate to the time the liquid level reaches the bottom corner of the container. Then calculate angles between this point and 90°, at which time the container is empty. The angle at which this transition occurs is given by

$$\tan(\theta) = \text{height/width}$$

[pouring.c]

Extra Credit:

1. Suppose you need to pour liquid at a constant rate. Modify your program to calculate how the angle must change with respect to some arbitrary time unit. One way to visualize this problem discretely rather than continuously is to imagine that the molten metal is used to fill 100 identical molds; that is, each mold uses 1% of the liquid. How much should the angle increase to fill each mold? Clearly, the change in angle required to fill each mold is *not* constant.

2. Suppose the container is cylindrical rather than rectangular. The equations for emptying the first half of the container are easy because the volume at any angle is simply half a

A good understanding of integral calculus is required.

cylinder whose height is measured at the point where the liquid intersects the side. However, after the liquid reaches the bottom corner of the container, the shape becomes a conic section, the volume of which is harder to calculate.

18. A simple model of population growth assumes that a new population p' is linearly related to the current population p; that is, p' = rp. Such a population will increase or decrease monotonically, depending on the value of r. Biologists have long recognized that populations are usually bounded in some way. For example, as populations grow, limited food resources may constrain further growth. Conversely, once populations shrink, those same food resources may be able to support a population that can start to grow again.

Here is a simple equation that models this bounded behavior:

$$p' = rp(1 - p)$$

where, for simplicity, the population has a value in the range [0,1]. Clearly, this model has the desired properties of bounding p'. As p grows, 1-p shrinks, and vice versa. Suppose r = 2. Here are the first few values from iterating this equation with an initial value of p = 0.2:

cycle	p	p'
1	0.20	0.32000
2	.32	.43520
3	.4352	.49160
4	.4916	.49986
5	.49986	.50000

One remarkable property of this function is that for r = 2, the population stabilizes at a value of 0.5 for *any* value of initial population p in the range (0,1) (that is, for any value between, but not including, 0 and 1).

For many years, however, some interesting properties of this disarmingly simple equation went unnoticed. Suppose p = 3.2. Iterate on the equation, starting with p = 0.9 (an arbitrary choice):

cycle	p	p'
1	0.90000	0.28800
2	.28800	.65618
3	.65618	.72195
4	.72195	.64237
...		
37	.79946	.51305
38	.51305	.79945
39	.79945	.51305
40	.51305	.79945

Now the population no longer stabilizes at a single value. Instead, it cycles back and forth between two values. Figure 4.4 shows the first 20 population values.

For r = 3.5, the population cycles among four different values. For a slightly higher value, it cycles among eight values. For r just in excess of 3.57, the population oscillates randomly. As r continues to increase, other cycles emerge, only to disappear into randomness as r continues to increase. What is the upper limit on r in order for the population to remain bounded; that is, to oscillate between fixed limits? What is the maximum value of r for which the population is *stable* rather than *bounded*?

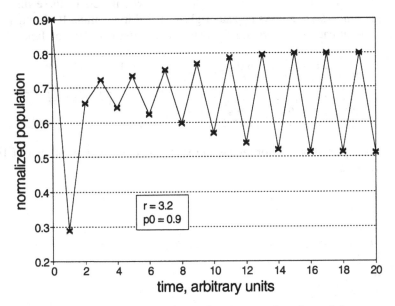

Figure 4.4. Normalized population as a function of time.

The discovery that an apparently simple dynamical system can produce this odd kind of random behavior gave birth to what is now known as chaos theory. This theory has found applications in many fields of science and has had a profound effect on science during the second half of the twentieth century.

Fortunately, it is easy to investigate the behavior of this remarkable population equation. Write a program that requests values for r and p, where the value of p must be between 0 and 1. Calculate future populations in a count-controlled loop. The lower limit on r is 0, but what is the upper limit? Can you find the smallest value of r for which the population (a) no longer converges on a single value; (b) oscillates between two or more values; (c) is still bounded but appears to be random? [popchaos.c]

19. A heat wave occurs whenever the high temperature is at least 90°F for at least three consecutive days. Using the file weather.dat, print the date and high temperature for any day on which the high temperature was at least 90°F. If that day was part of a heat wave, print an appropriate message after the high temperature for the third day, which is the first day on which the heat wave can be recognized. The message should include the number of days in the current heat wave, starting with day 3. Keep track of the total number of days with highs of at least 90°F and display this value when you have processed all the days.

In the file `weather.dat`, the data are given in sets of three lines. The daily high temperature always appears right-justified in columns 10 through 12 of the first line in each set. Here are the data for the first two days of June 1997.

```
06/01/97   79   3:16p   62   6:56a   97 1895   44 1984   78   58
           29.92r 29.90f 29.83f 29.88s
          100   63   0.00   0.00 14.09 16.95 g 33 oz   80   5:34a   8:24p
06/02/97   63   1:01a   57   8:00p   98 1925   46 1907   78   58
           29.89r 29.95r 29.96s ------
          100   92   0.63   0.63 14.72 17.07 g 33 oz 100   5:33a   8:24p
```

Here is some partial output for temperatures recorded during the summer of 1997. [heatwave.c]

```
06/21/97 94
06/22/97 93
06/24/97 91
06/25/97 96
06/26/97 93 OFFICIAL HEAT WAVE, day 3
06/28/97 90
07/03/97 92
07/04/97 91
07/09/97 93
07/13/97 94
07/14/97 94
07/15/97 98 OFFICIAL HEAT WAVE, day 3
07/16/97 96 OFFICIAL HEAT WAVE, day 4
07/17/97 97 OFFICIAL HEAT WAVE, day 5
07/18/97 97 OFFICIAL HEAT WAVE, day 6
07/27/97 94
07/28/97 91
```

20. The student body of a university is 60 percent women. Within this student body, 25 percent of the women and 15 percent of the men are majoring in some branch of engineering. If a student chosen at random is majoring in engineering, what is the probability that the student is a woman?

Write a program to solve this problem by simulating a specified large number of trials, where a trial is defined as selecting a student, randomly assigning gender with the specified probability, and determining whether the student is majoring in engineering, with a probability based on gender. Keep count of the number of simulated male and female students who are studying engineering. The probability that a student majoring in engineering is a woman is the ratio of the number of women majoring in engineering to the total number of students majoring in engineering. If you have had a probability and statistics course, you should be able to compare the results of this simulation to the theoretical probability. [students.c]

21. Assume that a simple two-chromosome model of gender determination holds for humans—XX = female, XY = male—and that the probability of inheriting a Y chromosome from a male parent is 50 percent.

(a) Write a program that you can use to fill in Table 4.5, giving child gender distributions for four-child families.[2]

(b) Suppose that the probability of inheriting an X chromosome from a male parent is only 40 percent? How will this affect the values in Table 4.5? What is the population distribution of males and females after 10 generations? After 100 generations? Write a program that will help you answer these questions.

Table 4.5. Expected child gender distributions for four-child families

Number of Boys	Number of Girls	Percent Occurrence
4	0	
3	1	
2	2	
1	3	
0	4	

Note: See the discussion of simulations in Exercise 20. [chromo.c]

---

[2]This is a standard problem from probability and statistics.

22. A factory assembly line consists of four machines producing the same product. Production statistics for the machines are given in Table 4.6.

Table 4.6. Statistics for production machinery

Machine	Percent of Total Production	Percent Defective Output From This Machine
A	10	0.1
B	20	0.05
C	30	0.5
D	40	0.2

What is the probability that a product chosen randomly from the total assembly line production will be defective? If a randomly chosen product from the assembly line is found to be defective, what is the probability that the item was produced by machine A? By B? By C? By D?

Write a program to solve this problem by simulating the selection of a large number of products, assigning each product to a machine, and determining if it is defective.

Hint: See the discussion of simulations in Exercise 20. [factory.c]

23. A factory manufactures N widgets per year. The storage cost of raw materials for widgets is D dollars per widget per year. The cost to order raw materials for widgets is O dollars regardless of the amount of raw material ordered.

(a) Write a program that will determine:

(1) how many units of raw material U the factory should order at one time in order to minimize the total yearly cost to maintain an inventory of raw materials for making widgets;
(2) the minimum total yearly inventory cost.

Assume that the total yearly inventory cost to store raw material for widgets is given by

$$C = D \ (U/2) + O \ (N/U)$$

where U/2—half the size of each order—is the average number of raw material units stored during the year.[3] Use N = 10,000 widgets per year, D = $1000 per raw material unit per year, and O = $100 per order as a test case.

This optimization problem can easily be solved with calculus: Set the derivative of C equal to 0 and solve for U. However, it is also easily solved simply by trying all

> An understanding of elementary calculus is required.

values of U from 1 to 10,000 and saving the value of U that gives the minimum total cost. If you have had a course in differential calculus, you should check your program's numerical solution against the analytical solution.

(b) The numerical solution has the advantage that it is easy to modify. Add code to your program that will determine how many units of raw material to order at one time when the order cost is O plus a term that depends on the number of units ordered. Use an additional order charge of $0.50 per unit as a test case. [eoq.c]

24. There is not much justification for writing code to do single-variable optimizations, as in Exercise 23, other than as a programming exercise. However, with more variables, the calculus required to find the analytic optimum solution even for an unconstrained problem becomes more unwieldy. When the variables are constrained, then different approaches are required. One typical multivariable problem from economics is maximizing total profit on sales of more than one item as a function of the cost to advertise each item, when the total advertising budget is constrained not to exceed a specified amount. Suppose a retailer wishes to maximize total profit on the sales of two items, A and B. Economic research has shown that the profit for two products A and B, as a function of advertising expenditures x for product A and y for product B, can be expressed as

$$P_A = -a_A x^2 + b_A x + c_A$$
$$P_B = -a_B y^2 + b_B y + c_B$$

A reasonable initial assumption is that profit is directly proportional to the amount of money spent on advertising. However, these equations reflect the fact that at some point, additional advertising is counterproductive and can even result in losses rather than profits.

Write a program that will determine the optimum amount of money to spend for advertising products A and B such that the total profit, $P_A + P_B$, is maximized. Your output should include at least this test case:

---

[3]This is a standard economic order quantity model from economics.

$$a_A = 2 \qquad a_B = 0.5$$
$$b_A = 40 \qquad b_B = 60$$
$$c_A = 2000 \qquad c_B = 3000$$
$$x + y \leq 25$$

Can you increase profits for this case by increasing the total amount spent on advertising? Use your program to determine the total advertising budget that will produce the maximum total profits for these two profit models. (You can do this simply by trying different values in place of 25. Your program doesn't have to find this optimum value on its own.)

Hints: Assume the advertising expense variables x and y are integers, with units (thousands or millions of dollars?) such that the value of these variables will not exceed the range of data type int. Use nested loops to try all appropriate combinations of x and y. [prof_max.c]

More About Modular Programming

5.1 Defining Information Interfaces in C

User-defined functions, as an implementation of the *CALL* and *SUBPROGRAM* pseudocode statements, were first introduced in Chapter 3. In that discussion, functions, including C's intrinsic functions, had a simple information interface. The input consisted of one or more values, and the output consisted of a single value associated with the name of the function through the use of a `return` statement. Thus, assuming that a, b, and c are declared and given appropriate values, these kinds of statements are possible:

```
y=user_function(a,b,c);
```

and

```
printf("%lf\n",user_function(a,b,c));
```

With this function interface, information flows into the function from the argument list specified when the function is called, along a "one-way street" through the parameter list. The result generated by the function is associated with the name of the function, which can be used in an assignment statement or by itself.

In general, subprogram implementations need to be more flexible than this. Consider a programming problem in which a large computational task will be divided into several smaller tasks under the control of a main program. Each small task is associated with a subprogram. Some of the subprograms may be called by the main program and some may be called by other subprograms. Each subprogram may require multiple inputs to do its job and may return multiple outputs. Such a model is illustrated in Figure 5.1.

In this program, the controlling program (the `main` function in a C implementation) calls subprograms 1, 3, 4, and 5 directly. Subprogram 1 calls subprogram 2. Subprogram 5 is called by subprogram 4 as well as by the controlling program.

Input to and output from these subprograms are indicated by the arrows in Figure 5.1. We already know that we can provide multiple inputs to C functions, but we would like not to be restricted to a single output. In the algorithm design sense, the In arrow should provide a symbolic path for whatever information a subprogram needs to do its job and the Out arrow should provide a path for all the results of calculations done within that subprogram.

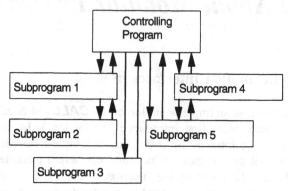

Figure 5.1. Function interface model.

Before we explore a more general information interface model for C functions, we should consider once again the simple function model of Chapter 3. An important consequence of passing information along a "one-way street" through a parameter list is that, although the values of parameters can be changed inside a function, the values of the arguments corresponding to those parameters will *not* be affected by any local changes. Consider this proposed change to the function area_func, which first appeared in program P-3.5:

```
double area_func(double radius)
/* PI must be available as a global constant. */
{
   radius=0.0;
   return PI*radius*radius;
}
```

The value returned by the function is 0 because the *local* value of radius has been changed to 0, for no reason other than to make a point. However, the value of the argument corresponding to radius in the calling function will remain unchanged. (You should verify this by making the indicated change to P-3.5 and displaying the value of radius in the main function after the call to area_func.)

The function interface model described here is called *pass-by-value*. C protects the original values of the arguments   **pass-by-value** by making a *copy* of those values rather than using the original values themselves. The process is illustrated schematically in Figure 5.2. Note that it is only *copies* of the arguments a, b, and c which are passed to the

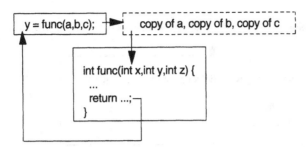

Figure 5.2. Pass-by-value function interface model.

parameter list. Remember that the names in the argument and parameter list and parameter lists are independent of each other. In Figure 5.2, the parameter names x, y, and z are (but don't have to be) different from the argument names a, b, and c.

A consequence of the fact that values of arguments associated with items in a parameter list cannot be changed by a call to a function is that functions cannot return "output" values, in the algorithm design sense, through the parameter list. Consider again the simple problem solved in programs P-3.5 and P-3.6: given a radius, calculate the area and circumference of a circle. Those programs defined two functions, each of which returned one quantity. Is it possible to overcome the single-output restriction on functions and combine both these calculations in a single function? Yes, and Figure 5.3 presents a model for implementing multiple return values in C.

In this case, the function contains four parameters. The first two are passed by value, with copies of arguments a and b being passed to the parameters x and y. The second two arguments are the *addresses* of the variables c and d; hence the use of the & operator. The corresponding parameters r_ptr and s_ptr are *pointers* to the locations of values of type int. Note that the data type of func_by_ref is void. This is because the function does not contain a return statement. Instead, calculated values are returned indirectly through the parameter list. How is this possible if the values of arguments are passed to the parameter list along a "one-way street?" The answer lies in the use of pointers in the parameter list.

When func_by_ref is called, the third and fourth arguments are addresses rather than values. Within function circle_stuff, the appearance of the ***indirection operator*** * with the names r_ptr and s_ptr in the parameter list indicates that these names are not meant to be given values directly, as variables. It is not the values of these pointers which will be changed inside the function, but *the contents of the memory locations to which the pointers point.*

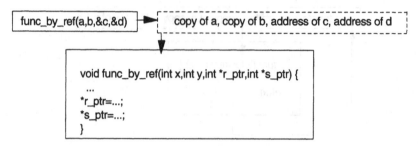

Figure 5.3. Pass-by-reference function interface model.

Hence, the quantities on the left side of the two assignment statements in `func_by_ref`,

```
*r_ptr=...;
*s_ptr=...;
```

are references to the memory locations that will hold the results of the calculations on the right side of the assignment operation. Based on the syntax of the parameter list in `func_by_ref`, assignment statements such as `r_ptr=...;` make no sense and will generate a syntax error; such a statement would be an attempt to change not a value, but a memory address. Also, because `func_by_ref` does not include a `return` statement, it makes no sense for this function to appear on the right side of an assignment statement.

Through the use of pointers to change the contents of memory locations, C has overcome the limitations of the pass-by-value subprogram model. The **pass-by-reference** ability to operate on a memory location passed as a parameter is called *pass-by-reference*. (This is why the function in Figure 5.3 is called `func_by_ref`.) With pass-by-value and pass-by-reference models, parameters can be described as "input" or "output" with a specific meaning as defined by the language syntax: quantities passed by value (which may be expressions or values as well as variables) are always input, whereas variables passed by reference are output in the sense that changes to their values inside a subprogram are passed back to the calling subprogram.

You can conclude that C only *simulates* pass-by-reference because the address of a variable must be passed as an argument, rather than just the variable name, and because the indirection operator must be used when assigning values by changing the contents of memory locations.[1] However, from the algorithm design point of view, the availability of pointers and the indirection operator at least allows C programmers to design algorithms in which parameters have either an "input" or "output" attribute.

To see how pass-by-reference works in practice, we will now return to the task of combining the calculations of the area and circumference of a circle into a single function, as shown in P-5.1.

P-5.1 [circlep3.c]

```
#include <stdio.h>
#define PI 3.14159265
void circle_stuff(double radius, double *a_ptr, double *c_ptr);
int main(void)
{
    double radius=3.0;
    double area, circumference;

    circle_stuff(radius, &area, &circumference);
    printf("%8.3f %8.3f\n",area, circumference);
    return 0;
}
void circle_stuff(double radius, double *a_ptr, double *c_ptr)
{
    *a_ptr=PI*radius*radius;
    *c_ptr=2.0*PI*radius;
}
```

In P-5.1, the function circle_stuff has been given the data type void. As indicated in the discussion of Figure 5.3, the void declaration means that this function will not return a value in the sense that there is no return statement in the function. Instead, we will use pointers as an alternate way of accessing values in memory, following the model shown in Figure 5.3. The goal of function circle_stuff is to calculate the area and circumference and then to pass these values back to the calling function. However, in P-5.1, the *values* of area and circumference do not appear in the argument list when function circle_stuff is called; instead, through the use of the & (address of) operator, the addresses of the *memory locations* used by area and circumference are passed in the argument list. In function circle_stuff's parameter list, the memory locations specified in the calling argument list are associated with pointers, using the notation double *a_ptr, double c_ptr.

Within function circle_stuff, the appearance of the indirection operator * with the names a_ptr and c_ptr in the parameter list indicates that these names are not meant to be given values directly, as variables. It is not the

---

[1]Some languages, such as Pascal and C++, offer a more transparent implementation of pass-by-reference.

values of these pointers which will be changed inside the function, but *the contents of the memory locations to which the pointers point.* Hence, the quantities on the left side of the two assignment statements in circle_stuff,

```
*a_ptr=PI*radius*radius;
*c_ptr=2.0*PI*radius;
```

are references to the memory locations that will hold the results of the calculations on the right side of the assignment operation. In P-5.1, these locations correspond to the addresses of a_ptr and c_ptr. Because these pointers are associated with the addresses of area and circumference, the values of these variables have been changed, even though this change never involved the variable names area and circumference (or their local names in a function) appearing on the left side of an assignment statement.

The concept of assigning values indirectly through pointers can be difficult to understand, and it may help to look at an example unrelated to how pointers are used in P-5.1. Consider program P-5.2:

P-5.2 [ptr_demo.c]

```
#include <stdio.h>
int main(void) {
    int i=2,j=3,*i_ptr,*j_ptr;

    i_ptr=&i;
    j_ptr=&j;
    printf("%i %i %i %i %i %i\n",i,j,*i_ptr,*j_ptr,
            *i_ptr+*j_ptr,(*i_ptr)*(*j_ptr));
    return 0;
}
```

In P-5.2, the data declaration statement includes two pointers associated with values of type int—*i_ptr and *j_ptr. When pointers are declared, they are said to be bound to their

dereferencing
dereferencing operator

declared data type. In the two assignment statements following the declaration statement, i_ptr and j_ptr are assigned values equal to the addresses of i and j. As demonstrated by the printf statement, it is possible to access the values associated with i and j either directly, in the usual way, or indirectly by *dereferencing* the pointer to the memory location in which i or j is stored, using the *dereferencing operator* (*). It is also possible to perform arithmetic operations using these memory locations, such as *i_ptr+*j_ptr and (*i_ptr)*(*j_ptr). In the second of these statements, the parentheses are optional and are used just to make clear the multiple uses of the * character; the fact that C correctly interprets such a statement without extra parentheses implies that the dereferencing operation has precedence over the multiplication operator (recall Table 3.4 in Chapter 3, which gave the precedence rules for C operators) and that C can appropriately interpret the asterisks used in this context.

It is easy to confuse the multiple uses of the asterisk symbol. Depending on context, it can be interpreted as the multiplication operator (a*b), an operator that creates a pointer bound to a specified data type (int *a;), or (as in this case), an indirection operator that accesses the contents of a memory location to which a pointer points (*a=3.0;).

In a program such as P-5.2, there is no reason to do arithmetic using pointers other than as a demonstration of what it means to access memory locations indirectly in this way. However, this approach *is* required in function circle_stuff in P-5.1 in order to provide a means of returning multiple results to a calling function.

In P-5.1, the names of pointer parameters are given the suffix _ptr. This can be helpful for understanding the code, but it is certainly not necessary. There is nothing wrong with this function implementation, in which the pointers have physically meaningful names:

```
void circle_stuff(double r, double *area, double *circumference);
{
   *area=PI*r*r;
   *circumference=2.0*PI*r;
}
```

Removing the _ptr suffix doesn't alter the fact that it is still necessary to use the indirection operator to assign values; the name of the parameter has nothing to do with the syntax of its use.

It may help to consider C's simulation of pass by reference on two different levels. At one level you can be aware of how C uses pointers to change memory locations indirectly. As an implementation aid, you can use _ptr suffixes on appropriate parameters and you will be aware that when you use the indirection operator you are accessing the memory locations to which the pointers point. At another level you can think of the * symbol appearing in the parameter list to define a pointer, and within the function when assignments are made through indirection, as a purely notational device for distinguishing between input to and output from the function. C doesn't actually make the distinction between input and output as a part of its syntax, but it can be useful to think in these terms when you implement algorithm designs.

It is critical to understand how P-5.1 works because it provides a window onto C's extensive use of pointers and illustrates an essential piece of the information flow model for C programs. In C, a programmer can, and sometimes must, write code that uses pointers to make changes directly in memory locations. This model, which bypasses the layer of insulation that a variable name provides between a program and user-accessible computer memory locations, is in some ways simpler and in other ways conceptually more difficult and dangerous. As a minimum, it imposes an extra burden on the programmer, for it is relatively easy in C to crash some computer operating systems by using pointers to manipulate the contents of memory. The same kind of damage is more difficult to inflict with languages such as Pascal that are more restrictive about how they let programmers use pointers.

5.2 Menu-Driven Programs

A typical modular program structure is one in which the main program requests user input to choose one of several tasks for the program to perform. Using an `if...` or `switch` construct, as discussed in Chapter 4, program control is transferred to one of several subprograms. Once the overall layout of the program is established, the subprograms can be written separately, one at a time. By using pass-by-values and pass-by-reference function interface models, as described in Section 5.1, C gives programmers a great deal of flexibility to design modular programs.

Here is a problem that lends itself to a menu-driven approach.

Newton's Law of Cooling describes the change in temperature as a function of time of a body that is warmer than the ambient temperature. Not surprisingly, the temperature decay is exponential, with the temperature approaching the ambient temperature T_a in the limit as t approaches infinity:

$$T(t) = T_a + (T_0 - T_a)e^{-kt}$$

Write a program that offers a user two choices:

(1) Given values of T_0, T_a, and k, calculate the temperature at a specified time.

(2) Given three temperatures observed at three distinct times, calculate T_0, T_a, and k.

The first of these calculations is trivial—it involves simple substitution into the formula—but the second is much harder. In order to obtain a solution for the second calculation, assume that the time intervals between temperature measurements are equal; that is, that $t_3 - t_2 = t_2 - t_1 = t_1 - t_0 = \Delta t$. This means that k will be in units of $1/\Delta t$ rather than per second, for example. The solutions are tedious to work out by hand, but they are easy to obtain with symbolic algebra software such as Maple V®. Here are the results from a Maple V® session.

```
> T:=t->Ta+(T0-Ta)*exp(-k*t);

                    T := t -> Ta + (T0 - Ta) exp(- k t)

> solve({T(1)=T1,T(2)=T2},{Ta,k});

                                                        2
                   - T2 + T1            T0 T2 - T1
        {k = - ln(---------),   Ta = ---------------}
                   T0 - T1            T0 - 2 T1 + T2

> solve({subs(T0=T1,T(1)=T2),subs(T0=T1,T(2)=T3)},{Ta,k});

                                2
                   T1 T3 - T2            - T3 + T2
        {Ta = ---------------,   k = - ln(---------)}
                T1 - 2 T2 + T3            - T2 + T1

> solve(T(1)=T1,T0);

            Ta - exp(- k) Ta - T1
        - ----------------------
                 exp(- k)
```

First solve for T_a and k using the first temperature, T_1, in place of T_0, T_2 in place of T_1, and T_3 in place of T_2:

$$k = -\ell n\left(\frac{T_2 - T_3}{T_1 - T_2}\right)$$

$$T_a = \frac{T_1 T_3 - T_2^2}{T_1 - 2T_2 + T_3}$$

Finally, solve for T_0 using T_1. This solution can also be used to find the temperature at any time previous to t_1, with time t measured in units of Δt. To put it another way, the initial temperature can be measured at any desired time (in units of Δt) along the exponential temperature decay curve:

$$T_0 = (T_1 - T_a)/e^{-kt} + T_a$$

Program P-5.3 implements this solution.

P-5.3 [cooling.c]

```c
#include <stdio.h>
#include <math.h>

/* function prototypes */
void get_k(double T1, double T2, double T3,
           double *k, double *T_ambient, double *T0);
double get_t(double T0, double T_ambient, double k, double t);

int main()
{
  char flag,again;
  double T0,T_ambient,T1,T2,t1,t2,T3,t3,k,t;

  do {
    again='n';
    printf("[k]: Solve for k, initial T, and ambient T,\n");
    printf("     given T at three equally spaced times.\n");
    printf("[t]: Solve for T at specified time, given intial T,
ambient T, and k.\n");
    fflush(stdin);
    scanf("%c",&flag);
    switch (flag) {
      case 't':
      case 'T':
      printf("Give initial T, ambient T, k, and time: ");
      fflush(stdin);
      scanf("%lf %lf %lf %lf",&T0,&T_ambient,&k,&t);
      printf("T = %lf\n",get_t(T0,T_ambient,k,t));
      break;
      case 'k':
      case 'K':
      printf("Give T1, T2, T3: ");
      fflush(stdin);
      scanf("%lf %lf %lf",&T1,&T2,&T3);
      get_k(T1,T2,T3,&k,&T_ambient,&T0);
      printf(
          "k = %lf, T_ambient =  %lf, To = %lf\n",k,T_ambient,T0);
      break;
      default:
      printf("INPUT ERROR.  Try again...\n");
    }
    printf("Do again (y or n)?\n");
    fflush(stdin);
    scanf("%c",&again);
  } while (again == 'y');
  return 0;
}

double get_t(double T0, double T_ambient, double k, double t)
{
  return(T_ambient+(T0-T_ambient)*exp(-k*t));
}
```

```
void get_k(double T1, double T2, double T3, double *k, double *Ta,
double *T0)
{
  *k = -log((T2-T3)/(T1-T2));
  *Ta = (T3*T1-T2*T2)/(T1+T3-2.0*T2);
  *T0 = (T1+exp(-*k)**Ta-*Ta)/exp(-*k);
}
```

Running P-5.3

```
[k]: Solve for k, initial T, and ambient T,
     given T at three equally spaced times.
[t]: Solve for T at specified time, given intial T, ambient T,
and k.
t
Give initial T, ambient T, k, and time: 500 30 .5 1
T = 315.069410
Do again (y or n)?
y
[k]: Solve for k, initial T, and ambient T,
     given T at three equally spaced times.
[t]: Solve for T at specified time, given intial T, ambient T,
and k.
t
Give initial T, ambient T, k, and time: 500 30 .5 2
T = 202.903337
Do again (y or n)?
y
[k]: Solve for k, initial T, and ambient T,
     given T at three equally spaced times.
[t]: Solve for T at specified time, given intial T, ambient T,
and k.
t
Give initial T, ambient T, k, and time: 500 30 .5 3
T = 134.871175
Do again (y or n)?
y
[k]: Solve for k, initial T, and ambient T,
     given T at three equally spaced times.
[t]: Solve for T at specified time, given intial T, ambient T,
and k.
k
Give T1, T2, T3: 315.06 202.90 134.87
k = 0.499978, T_ambient = 29.996198, To = 499.976443
Do again (y or n)?
n
```

The main program in P-5.3 presents a menu of choices and asks the user to select one option. Then a `switch` construct is used to obtain the required user input and access a function that performs the required calculations. The `default` case handles inappropriate user input. The subprograms in P-5.3 include a function (`get_t`) that returns a single value and a type `void` function `get_k` that returns output by modifying the contents of several locations to which pointers point.

The output displayed for P-5.3 is intended to check the operation of the program. The user chooses the t option three times and selects an initial temperature of 500, an ambient temperature of 30, a time constant of 0.5, and times of 1, 2, and 3. The temperature units are arbitrary, but the ambient temperature corresponds to a warm room if the temperature units are degrees centigrade. The time units are also arbitrary, and could represent anything from seconds to days. The program calculates the temperatures at each of those three times. Then, the user chooses the k option and specifies the three temperatures previously found. If the program is working properly, it should return the same initial temperature, ambient temperature, and time constant as the user originally specified. This is, in fact, what happens.

5.3 More About Function Interfaces

As discussed in Section 5.1 and illustrated by functions `circle_stuff` from P-5.1 and `get_k` from P-5.3, the argument/parameter list interface in C functions is complicated by the fact that C allows, and sometimes requires, direct access to memory locations through pointers. Suppose a function, `function_A`, is called from a main program, and the input argument(s) to that function will be variables local to the main program. That is the model we have used up to the present. Now, however, suppose `function_A` is called from some other function, `function_B`. In that case, the arguments appearing in calls to a function could be a combination of variables local to `function_B` and input parameters appearing in `function_B`'s parameter list. In the latter case, the parameters are passed through as arguments in a call to `function_A`. A third possibility is that one or more arguments in the call to `function_A` also appear as output parameters in `function_B`'s parameter list.

Program P-5.4 illustrates the third possibility. It is yet another version of a program that calculates the area and circumference of a circle. In previous versions, the radius was determined outside function `circle_stuff` (in the main program) and passed as input to this function. In this case, however, the request for the user to provide a radius appears within `circle_stuff`, and the value is passed back to the main program (as output) in addition to being used to calculate the area and circumference.

P-5.4 [`circl_p2.c`]

```
#include <stdio.h>
#define PI 3.14159265

/* function prototypes */
void circle_stuff(double *radius,
                  double *area, double *circumference);
```

```
int main(void)
{
  double radius, area, circumference;

  circle_stuff(&radius, &area, &circumference);
  printf( "%8.3lf %8.3lf %8.3lf\n",radius,area,circumference);
  return(0);
}
void circle_stuff(double *radius_ptr,
                  double *area_ptr, double *circumference_ptr)
{
  printf("Give radius: ");
  scanf("%lf",radius_ptr);
  *area_ptr=PI*(*radius_ptr)*(*radius_ptr);
  *circumference_ptr=2.0*PI*(*radius_ptr);
}
```

In P-5.4, all three parameters in `circle_stuff` have been given names consistent with their status as pointers. This certainly isn't necessary, as noted in the discussion of P-5.1, but it will be helpful for this discussion. The critical line of code in this function is the call to `scanf` in `circle_stuff`, which is printed in bold italics. Previously, whenever we have used `scanf` in a program, we have used the address-of operator to store output values from `scanf` in the memory locations associated with particular local variable names. In this case, the formal parameter `radius_ptr` in `circle_stuff` *already* contains the address of a memory location—it is a pointer and not a "value." Because `scanf` stores its output values in one or more memory locations specified by the programmer, the appropriate calling argument is `radius_ptr` rather than `&radius_ptr`.

What about the calculations for area and circumference done in `circle_stuff` in the two lines following the call to `scanf`? These calculations need to access not the value of `radius_ptr` itself—it contains the address of a memory location—but the value in the location to which `radius_ptr` points. This value is obtained by using the indirection operator `*`. Note that, again, the asterisk symbol has two different meanings in the assignment statements. Used as a unary operator, it is the indirection operator that obtains a value from a location referenced by a pointer. Used as a binary operator, it is the multiplication operator. Recall that the parentheses in, for example, `*(*radius_ptr)` help to clarify this distinction, but they aren't actually required because the interpretation of the asterisk will be clear to a C compiler in context.

Where do the calculations for area and circumference go? Not into local variables, but into the memory locations pointed to by `area_ptr` and `circumference_ptr`, as accessed through the indirection operator.

At the risk of belaboring the points raised by P-5.4, consider the modification to `circle_stuff` shown in P-5.5.

P-5.5 [`circl_p3.c`] (partial)

```
void circle_stuff(double *radius_ptr,
                double *area_ptr, double *circumference_ptr)
{
  double r;

  printf("Give radius: ");
  scanf("%lf",&r);
  *area_ptr=PI*r*r;
  *circumference_ptr=2.0*PI*r;
  *radius_ptr=r;
}
```

In P-5.5, the local variable r is used for the radius, hence the use of &r in the scanf function. However, in order to pass this value back to the calling program, the last statement in the function uses the indirection operator to store the value of r in the location to which radius_ptr points. There is no good reason to define a local variable to use in this way—there's nothing terribly wrong with the code, either, and it's a little easier to read—but the code in P-5.5 may help to clarify the difference between variable names that refer to values and names that refer directly to memory locations; that is, the difference between variables and pointers.

5.4 Recursive Functions

There are several functions in science and engineering mathematics that are most easily defined recursively. A simple example is the factorial function n!, which is defined for non-negative integer values of n as

$$0! = 1! = 1 \qquad n! = n \bullet (n - 1)!, \ n > 1$$

The definition of n! in terms of n and $(n - 1)!$ isn't as circular as it seems because of the specific definitions for 0! and 1!. (The first of these, $0! = 1$, is just a mathematically convenient definition.) Thus, if 4! is defined in terms of 4 and 3!, 3! can be calculated in terms of 2!, and 2! in terms of 1!, the value of which is known. Thus any value of n! can be bootstrapped from previous values.

This definition of the factorial function can be implemented in C, as it can in many other languages, as a **recursive algorithm**, that is, in terms of an algorithm that calls itself. It is sometimes difficult to follow the detailed behavior of recursive algorithms, so it is usually better simply to try to write the algorithm in the most natural possible way and trust the programming environment to handle the details. Recursive algorithms are usually very short. Program P-5.6

| recursive algorithm |

demonstrates how easily the recursive definition of the factorial function can be translated into C.

P-5.6 [`factoral.c`]

```
#include <stdio.h>

long factorial(int n);

int main(void)
{
   int n;

   printf("Give an integer: ");
   scanf("%i",&n);
   printf("%ld\n",factorial(n));
   return 0;
}

long factorial(int n)
/* Assumes n is always >= 0. */
{
   if (n <=1 )
      return (long)1;
   else
      return (long)n*factorial(n-1);
}
```

Function `factorial` in P-5.6 follows a typical pattern for recursive algorithms. It has code that generates a recursive call to the function and a terminating condition that allows a specific calculation to be completed. In general, all recursive algorithms must have at least one terminating condition and at least one recursive call that is executed whenever the terminating condition isn't satisfied. In this case, the recursive call is simply the recursive definition translated into C syntax. The code in P-5.6 assumes that `factorial` will never be called with a negative argument. If it is, however, the function will still return a value of 1.

The value of n! grows rapidly with n, and the declaration of the `factorial` function as `long` allows much larger values of n to be specified than would be the case with an `int` data type. (The limitations on size are implementation-dependent.)

It is perhaps not obvious that the syntax in P-5.6 should work. Indeed, the programming environment provides a great deal of behind-the-scenes help to support recursion. Each call to `factorial` generates activity that keeps track of the local values of input parameters, among other things. It is C's ability to keep track of these local values on its own that makes recursive functions look so simple.

In the first call to `factorial`, from P-5.6's `main` function, the local value of n is whatever the user specifies through the `scanf` statement. The multiplication `(long)n*factorial(n-1)` is delayed by the recursive call, for which the argument is `n-1`. As a result, the new local value of n will be the current value of n − 1. The calculation in the `return` statement will continue to be deferred by the recursive calls until, eventually, the local value of n will be 1, and the `return 1;` statement will be executed. Next, C will perform all the deferred calculations that have been created by the recursive calls before control is returned to the calling program. The value of 2! will be calculated as 2•1, 3! as 3•2, 4! as 4•6, and so forth.

Recursive algorithms aren't restricted to a single recursive call within a function. Consider the well-known Fibonacci series: 1 1 2 3 5 8 13 21..., which can be defined recursively as

$$f_1 = f_2 = 1$$
$$f_n = f_{n-1} + f_{n-2}$$

This definition is straightforward to implement as a recursive function, as shown in P-5.7.

P-5.7 [`fibonaci.c`]

```
#include <stdio.h>

int fibonacci(int n);

int main(void)
{
  int n;

  printf("Which term? ");
  scanf("%i",&n);
  printf("%i\n",fibonacci(n));
  return 0;
}

int fibonacci(int n)
{
  if (n <= 2) return 1;
  else return fibonacci(n-1)+fibonacci(n-2);
}
```

Recursive algorithms are often inefficient in their use of computer resources. In the case of the factorial function, it is so easy to calculate n! iteratively, with a loop, that writing recursive code doesn't make much sense. A function to generate Fibonacci numbers is only a little harder to write iteratively. In fact, any problem that can be solved recursively can also be solved iteratively. However, there are some kinds of problems for which a recursive algorithm is *much* simpler to write than an iterative algorithm. In those cases, it is very helpful to be able to use recursive algorithms to write programs that are as simple as possible at the source code level. For the kinds of problems addressed in this text, inefficient use of computing resources is usually not a significant factor in how a computer program performs. An interesting example of the power of recursive algorithms will be presented as an application later in this chapter.

5.5 Using Prewritten Code Modules

One of the major advantages of writing modularized programs is that you can reuse code previously written to perform specific tasks. Obviously, this avoids "reinventing the wheel" for many kinds of programming tasks. For languages widely used in scientific and engineering programming, such as C and Fortran, there are many commercial libraries of subprograms for solving common and perhaps difficult programming problems. However, you can and should create your own libraries of reusable code based on your own needs. Special care is required when you write code for libraries. It is, of course, essential to make sure that the code works properly under specified conditions. In addition, you should design and document function interfaces so they are as easy as possible to incorporate into programs.

To demonstrate how to create reusable code, we will consider a simple example from the previous section in this chapter—calculating the nth term in the Fibonacci series. We will modify P-5.7 so that the function to calculate a specified term in the Fibonacci series is not included explicitly in the program. That is, we would like to assume that this code has already been written and can simply be used in any program that needs a Fibonacci number.

The simplest modification we can make to P-5.7 is to create a source code file containing the function `fibonacci` and simply `#include` it in the source code file containing the main function. This approach is used in P-5.8(a). The code for function `fibonacci`, stored in file `fib_func.c`, is given in P-5.8(b).

P-5.8(a) [`fibonac3.c`]

```
#include <stdio.h>
#include "fib_func.c"

int main(void)
{
  int n;

  printf("Which term? ");
  scanf("%i",&n);
  printf("%i\n",fibonacci(n));
  return 0;
}
```

P-5.8(b) [fib_func.c]

```
/* Fibonacci function source code. */
int fibonacci(int n)
{
  if (n <= 2) return(1);
  else return(fibonacci(n-1)+fibonacci(n-2));
}
```

Remember that the angle brackets < ... > in #include directives tell your program to look for standard header files in a directory specified by the programming environment. You don't have to know or specify the name of this directory. However, when you #include files of your own, such as fib_func.c, you must specify both the directory and the file name—a complete path through directories and subdirectories in MS-DOS or UNIX terminology, or folder specification in Windows or Macintosh terminology.

When you #include a source code file, that file is literally copied into the specified location at compile time. In the case of P-5.8(a), the file given in P-5.8(b) is copied into P-5.8(a) right before the main function. Thus, at compile time, P-5.8(a) is completely equivalent to P-5.7.

The second method of incorporating prewritten code takes advantage of the fact that C source code can be compiled, assuming it is free of syntax errors, even if the code doesn't contain a main function. This means that entire files of functions can be compiled into *object code* and then linked to another program that contains a main function.

In this case, we will compile the function shown in P-5.8(b). On a UNIX system using the cc compiler, type

```
cc fib_func.c -c
```

The -c option produces an object file called fib_func.o, but it prevents the compiler from trying to generate an executable binary file; this isn't possible because fib_func.c doesn't contain a main function.

Program P-5.9(a) shows how to use the object file fib_func.o.

P-5.9(a) [fib_main.c]

```
#include <stdio.h>
extern int fibonacci(int n);

int main(void)
{
  int n;
```

```
    printf("Which term? ");
    scanf("%i",&n);
    printf("%i\n",fibonacci(n));
    return 0;
}
```

The main function in P-5.9(a) contains a reference to function fibonacci, but the source code for this function does not appear anywhere in this code, either explicitly or implicitly through an #include directive. However, the function prototype for fibonacci includes the extern reserved word, which tells the program that the function will be found externally, in a precompiled file that will be linked with this code after it is compiled.

By default, functions appearing in a function prototype but not found in the source code file are assumed to be external. Thus, the extern word appearing in the function prototype for fibonacci clarifies the status of this function, but the word isn't actually required.

In this case, we will assume that the external function P-5.9(a) is looking for is fib_func.o, the compiled fib_func.c file. (On MS-DOS systems, .OBJ is the default file name extension for object files.) To create the executable file fib_main.exe on UNIX systems using the cc compiler, type

```
cc fib_main.c fib_func.o -ofib_main.exe
```

The specific steps required to link a file containing a main function with other precompiled files vary from environment to environment. For this simple example, a single command suffices. For large and complex programs, the C programming environment typically includes some kind of "make" facility that can be used to direct the linking of several files to create an executable program; consult the documentation for your system.

Especially for large programs, it is common practice to create a separate header file that gives the function prototypes for all required user-defined functions, just as header files are included for standard library functions. To do this for P-5.9(a), create a text file called fib_func.h, containing the single line:

```
extern int fibonacci(int n);
```

Then modify the source code file to look like this:

P-5.9(b) [fib_main.c (modified)]

```
#include <stdio.h>
#include "fib_func.h"
int main(void)
...
```

The modification in P-5.9(b) now contains a reference to a header file, fib_func.h, that works just like standard library header files. The only difference is that you must give an explicit directory (path) reference for the file, with its path and name in quotation marks, because a header file you create yourself is probably not in the same directory as the standard header files.

What is the point of creating separate header files? For this simple program, there isn't any reason to create a separate header file for a single function reference. However, suppose you have created a large code library that contains many different functions. You wish to distribute the library without distributing the source code. By distributing the object code for the library along with a header file, you can document the use of functions in the library, through comments and function prototypes in the header file, without revealing the contents of the source code.

5.6 Using Functions as Arguments and Parameters

Suppose the purpose of a user-defined function is simply to evaluate a mathematical function and display the result. This is straightforward for intrinsic functions. For example, P-5.10(a) prints values of sin(x) for angles at a specified increment between specified lower and upper limits, where conversion includes the conversion of angles from degrees to radians.

P-5.10(a) [func_ar1.c]

```
#include <stdio.h>
#include <math.h>
#define PI 3.14159

void print_f(int lower,int upper,int step,double conversion);

int main(void)
{
   print_f(0,10,1,5.*PI/180.);
   return 0;
}

void print_f(int lower,int upper,int step,double conversion) {
   int i;
   double x;

   for(i=lower; i<=upper; i+=step) {
     x=i*conversion;
     printf("%2i %5.2lf %10.3lf\n",i,x,sin(x));
   }
}
```

If you wish to perform the same task for a user-defined function, the obvious way to do it is to define the function and call it, as in P-5.10(b).

P-5.10(b) [`func_ar2.c`]

```
#include <stdio.h>
#include <math.h>
void print_f(int lower,int upper,int di,double conversion);
double f_of_x(double x);

int main(void)
{
  print_f(0,10,1,.5);
  return 0;
}

double f_of_x(double x) {
  return sqrt(x);
}

void print_f(int lower,int upper,int di,double conversion) {
  int i;
  double x;

  for(i=lower; i<=upper; i+=di) {
    x=i*conversion;
    printf("%2i %5.2lf %10.3lf\n",i,x,f_of_x(x));
  }
}
```

A potential problem is that if you wish to change the name of the function to be evaluated and displayed, you have to recode `print_f`. This may not seem like a significant problem for programs you write yourself. However, suppose function `print_f` is replaced by a function that performs some more significant and complicated calculation that you wish to distribute to other programmers. Now those programmers must know the details of that code and they must create a function such as `f_of_x` whose name agrees with your code.

Although this still may seem like a minor problem, it can be avoided altogether by including in the parameter list the name of the function being evaluated. This is possible in C because the name of a function is actually a pointer to the code for that function. Program P-5.10(c) modifies P-5.10(b) to include in `print_f`'s parameter list the name of the function to be evaluated and displayed. The function `f` can be either an intrinsic or a user-defined function. The only restriction on `f` is that, according to the parameter list, it must be called with a single type `double` argument and must return a type `double` result.

P-5.10(c) [func_ar3.c]

```
#include <stdio.h>
#include <math.h>

void print_f(int lower,int upper,int di,double conversion,
             double (*f)(double x));
double f_of_x(double x);

int main(void)
{
  print_f(0,10,1,.5,f_of_x);
  return 0;
}

double f_of_x(double x) {
  return sqrt(x);
}

void print_f(int lower,int upper,int di,double conversion,
             double (*f)(double x)) {
  int i;
  double x;

  for(i=lower; i<=upper; i+=di) {
    x=i*conversion;
    printf("%2i %5.2lf %10.3lf\n",i,x,f(x));
  }
}
```

In the function reference double (*f)(double x), the parentheses around *f are required in order for C to interpret the asterisk properly. The dummy parameter list provides information about arguments to be supplied to the function.

Although the differences among the various versions of P-5.10 may seem to be minor matters of programming style, they are actually extremely important. In P-5.10(c), print_f now works with *any* appropriate function and is therefore completely portable to other programs without modification. Portability is essential in large-scale programming projects and should be maximized whenever possible. In P-5.9(b), the function to be evaluated inside print_f is given an alias name by which it will be known locally inside print_f. Thus the users of print_f don't have to have access to the code *inside* printf_f. They need be told only that a proper call to print_f includes the address of a function that requires a single type double argument and returns a single type double result. This requirement is obvious from an examination of print_f's prototype.

It is worth noting that although print_f's parameter list calls for a type double function with a single input argument, a function in a parameter list can, in general, return any desired data type and can have any required number of input arguments. Again, this information is conveyed by the function prototype.

An important application of passing pointers to functions to other functions is to perform numerical integration on mathematical functions that lack an analytical integral. In order to increase the portability of such code, the numerical integration function should be written so that the programmer can simply pass to the integration function the name of the mathematical function whose integral is sought. An example of this technique using Trapezoidal Rule integration will be given in Section 5.8.4.

5.7 Passing Arguments to the main Function

Previously, we have written the main function header like this:

```
int main(void);
```

This form is also acceptable:

```
void main();
```

The void or empty parameter list informs C that the main function requires no input values.

However, it is possible to give the main function a parameter list. In computing environments that use a *command-line interface*

command-line interface

to execute programs, such as UNIX and MS-DOS, it is possible to pass arguments from the command line when the program is executed. In fact, C provides some predefined variables for this purpose. Consider this problem:

Write a program that accepts three command-line inputs: two integer values and a character flag that tells the program to determine and display the larger or smaller of the two numbers.

P-5.11 solves this problem.

P-5.11 [larger.c]

```
#include <stdio.h>
#include <stdlib.h>

int main(int argc,char *argv[])
{
  int n1,n2,display;
  if (argc < 4) {
    printf("Please enter two integers on the command line,\n");
    printf("then -s or -l to return smaller or larger value.\n");
    printf("Separate input by spaces.\n");
```

```
      return -1;
   }
   else {
    n1=atoi(argv[1]);
    n2=atoi(argv[2]);
    printf("%i %i\n",n1,n2);
    printf("%c\n",argv[3][1]);
    switch (argv[3][1]) {
      case 's':
      case 'S':
        if (n1 <= n2) printf("%i\n",n1);
        else printf("%i\n",n2);
        break;
      case 'l':
      case 'L':
        if (n1 >=n2) printf("%i\n",n1);
        else printf("%i\n",n2);
        break;
      default:
        printf("Unknown command line option.\n");
        return -2;
    }
    return 0;
   }
}
```

To run P-5.11 after it has been compiled, type, for example:

```
larger.exe 2 3 -s
```

The program will display the result 2, the smaller of 2 and 3. The -s is treated as a command-line option. On UNIX systems, for example, options are typically preceded by a hypen, although there is no reason why this *must* be so; that is, you could write the program so that the command line would be `larger.exe 2 3 s`.

How does C read this command-line input into the program? First, consider the main function header:

```
int main(int argc, char *argv[]);
```

The parameter list contains two variables: an integer variable, `argc`, and an array of pointers to characters, `argv`. Both of these names are predefined in C. They can, in fact, be given other names, but these names are generally accepted by convention.

To interpret `argc` and `argv`, it is first necessary to understand that C treats values entered on the command line as strings, even if they *look* like numbers, as in this example. The integer variable `argc` contains the number of command-line strings, *including the name of the executable file*. In P-5.11, the program expects that `argc` will have a value of 4: a string for the executable file name, two integers, and the -s or -l option.

The variable `argv` is an array of pointers to the first character in each of these strings. Thus in P-5.11 `argv[1]` points to the first integer, `argv[2]` to the second integer, and `argv[3]` to the option flag. Numbers entered in this way can be interpreted by using standard intrinsic ASCII-to-number conversion functions, as described in Table 5.1.

Table 5.1. ASCII-to-number conversion functions

Function Name	Description
atoi(char *string)	Converts string to a type integer value. Include stdlib.h.
atof(char *string)	Converts string to a type double value. Include stdlib.h or math.h.

Both functions require as arguments pointers to the first character in a string. In P-5.10, `atoi` is used because the string must be converted to an integer.

In order to interpret the command line flag `-s` or `-l`, or its uppercase equivalent `-S` or `-L`, the program looks at the second character of `argv[3]`, `argv[3][1]`, and uses this value to control a `switch` construct. If the command-line input can be intepreted as expected, the program displays the smaller of the two integer values.

If the user doesn't enter enough information on the command line, an explanatory message is displayed and the program terminates. If the user enters enough information but doesn't enter an appropriate flag, the program is again terminated. In principle, the system on which the program is being executed could make use of the different `return` values, -1 or -2, but we won't deal with that problem here.

The technique of passing arguments from the command line is best applied when the input requirements are not complicated. This is because there is no user prompt for input, but only, at most, a message describing what was wrong if the user did not provide the expected information. A typical use involves passing the name of a file to a program. For example, data may be collected for each month of the year and stored in files with names that identify the months. As long as files for different months are formatted identically, the program can process any of those monthly files, and the desired file can be specified when the program is executed.

5.8 Applications

5.8.1 The Quadratic Equation Revisited

1 Define the problem.

Recall from the discussion of the application in Section 4.5.1 of Chapter 4 that the quadratic equation $ax^2 + bx + c = 0$ has two, one, or no real roots, depending on the value of the discriminant $b^2 - 4ac$. In P-4.9, the calculations for the real root(s) were made and a value of 0 was assigned to one or more roots that didn't exist, so as not to leave the variable unassigned. Write a function that determines how many real roots a quadratic equation has, calculates the real roots as appropriate, and then returns a "status" flag equal to 0, 1, or 2, depending on how many real roots were found.

2 Outline a solution.

Refer to the application Section 4.5.1 for a discussion of the quadratic equation and conditions for finding real roots.

3 Design an algorithm.

It is typical C programming style for a function to return multiple output values indirectly through pointers. However, instead of giving such a function a data type of `void`, it is given type `int` and an output flag is returned directly so the calling program can interpret the values produced by the function. For this problem, the output flag will return a value of 0, 1, or 2.

4 Convert the algorithm into a program.

P-5.12 [quadrat2.c]

```
#include <stdio.h>
#include <math.h>

int GetRoots(double a,double b,double c,double *r1,double *r2);

int main(void)
```

```
{
  double a,b,c,root1,root2;
  int n_roots;

  printf("Enter coefficients for ax^2+bx+c: ");
  scanf("%lf %lf %lf",&a,&b,&c);
  n_roots=GetRoots(a,b,c,&root1,&root2);
  printf("%i\n",n_roots);
  switch(n_roots) {
    case 2:
      printf("The 2 real roots are: %lf %lf\n",root1,root2);
      break;
    case 1:
      printf("The 1 real root is: %lf %lf\n",root1);
    case 0:
      printf("There are no real roots.\n");
  }
  return 0;
}

int GetRoots(double a,double b,double c,double *r1,double *r2) {
/* Returns single root in r1, assigns non-existent roots
   a value of 0. */
  double discriminant;
  int n_roots;

  discriminant=b*b-4.0*a*c;
  printf("discriminant = %lf\n",discriminant);
  if (discriminant > 0.0 ) {
    *r1=(-b+sqrt(discriminant))/2.0/a;
    *r2=(-b-sqrt(discriminant))/2.0/a;
    n_roots=2;
  }
  else if (discriminant == 0.0) {
    *r1=-b/2.0/a;
    *r2=0.;
    n_roots=1;
  }

  else {
    *r1=0.;*r2=0.;
    n_roots=0;
  }
  return n_roots;
}
```

Running P-5.12

```
Enter coefficients for ax^2+bx+c: 1 2 -3
discriminant = 16.000000
2
The 2 real roots are: 1.000000 -3.000000
```

5 *Verify the operation of the program.*

Use a calculator to evaluate the determinant and find the real root(s).

5.8.2 Finding Prime Numbers

1 *Define the problem.*

Write and test a function that determines whether a specified integer is prime.

2 *Outline a solution.*

An integer is prime if it can be divided evenly only by itself and 1. To design an algorithm for finding prime numbers, we can make use of these facts:

1. The numbers 1, 2, and 3 are prime.
2. Any even number greater than 2 cannot be prime.
3. Every number that is not prime has at least one divisor less than or equal to its square root. (For example, 49 is divisible only by its square root, 7.)

The third fact is especially useful because it tells us how to limit the range of possible divisors that must be tested.

3 *Design an algorithm.*

An algorithm that expresses the facts given in Step 2 looks like this:

IF $n \leq 3$, *n is prime.*
ELSE IF remainder from integer division n/2 equals 0, n is not prime.
ELSE IF remainder from integer division n/divisor equals 0, n is not prime.
ELSE IF divisor > $\sqrt{n}$, n is prime.
ELSE try divisor + 2 (a recursive call).

4 *Convert the algorithm into a program.*

P-5.13 [prime.c]

```c
#include <stdio.h>
#include <math.h>
#define TRUE 1

int IsPrime(int n, int trial);

int main()
{
  int prime,n;
  do {
    printf("Give an integer, 0 to quit: ");
    scanf("%i",&n);
    if (n == 0) break;
    prime=IsPrime(n,3);
    if (prime == TRUE)
      printf("%i is prime.\n",n);
    else
      printf("%i isn't prime.\n",n);
  } while (n != 0);

  return 0;
}

int IsPrime(int n, int trial)
{
  if (n <= 3)
    return 1;
  else if (n%trial == 0)
    return 0;
  else if (trial >= (int)sqrt((double)n) )
    return 1;
  else
    return IsPrime(n,trial+2);
}
```

Running P-5.13

```
Give an integer, 0 to quit: 37
37 is prime.
Give an integer, 0 to quit: 49
49 isn't prime.
Give an integer, 0 to quit: 0
```

5 *Verify the operation of the program.*

There is no simple general solution to determine whether an integer is prime—otherwise this program should use that solution—but this program can be tested with several numbers that are known to be prime or not prime. If it works for these, there is no reason to think that it won't work for other numbers.

Problem Discussion

The function in P-5.13 suffers only from the fact that a test divisor must be included in the parameter list and hence must be provided when the function is called. The smallest divisor that must be tried is 3. Therefore, the function call must be IsPrime(n,3) rather than the more natural call IsPrime(n). This can easily be avoided by making IsPrime a "dummy" function whose parameter list includes only n and which then calls a second function to do the actual work of determining whether n is prime, including the first test divisor.

5.8.3 The Towers of Hanoi

1 *Define the problem.*

The Towers of Hanoi problem is a famous programming exercise that provides a striking demonstration of the power of recursive algorithms. Suppose ten rings are stacked on a pole and are graduated in size from the largest on the bottom to the smallest on top. Nearby are two other poles. The object is to move the stack of ten rings from their original pole to one of the other poles, using the third pole as a working space during the transfer. There are only two rules governing how the rings can be moved:

(1) The rings are moved one at a time.
(2) At no time can a larger ring be moved onto a smaller ring.

Write a program that solves the Towers of Hanoi problem by printing a list of all steps required to move the rings from one pole to another.

2 Outline a solution.

It takes some thought and planning to figure out how the transfers should be made. Consider the problem with only four rings. The original pole is labelled A, the destination pole is C, and the intermediate pole is B. Table 5.2 shows the required transfers, which can easily be worked out with a little trial and error. This transfer requires 15 moves. In general, moving n rings from one pole to another requires $2^n - 1$ moves.

3 Design an algorithm.

Although it might not be obvious how to instruct a program to make a large number of moves in what seems like a complicated pattern, it is actually easy to write an algorithm for moving n rings in a programming language that supports recursion. Consider this statement of the problem of moving n rings from A to C:

1. Move $n - 1$ rings from A to B.
2. Move the nth ring from A to C.
3. Move $n - 1$ rings from B to C.

This solution takes a typical recursive approach of defining one level of a problem's solution in terms of a previous level. Specifically, the problem of moving n rings is stated in terms of the problem of moving $n - 1$ rings in the same sense that the recursive algorithm for n! defined n! in terms of n and $(n - 1)!$. By making successive recursive calls with argument n-1, the problem of moving n rings can be reduced to the point that eventually the only problem the algorithm needs to solve directly is the trivial problem of moving one ring. The algorithm design looks like this:

DEFINE *(n as initial number of rings, start, aux, and final as strings)*
INITIALIZE   *start = 1, aux = 2, final = 3*
CALL *MoveRings(n, 1, 3, 2)*

SUBPROGRAM *MoveRings(n, start, final, aux)*
IF *n_rings > 0* **THEN**
        CALL *MoveRings(n_rings – 1, start, aux, final)*
        WRITE *("Transfer ring ",n_rings," from ",start," to ",final)*
        CALL *MoveRings(n_rings – 1,aux,final,start)*
(end IF)

Table 5.2. Transfers for the Towers of Hanoi problem when n = 4

Move	A	B	C
(Start)			
1 from A to B			
2 from A to C			
1 from B to C			
3 from A to B			
1 from C to A			
2 from C to B			
1 from A to B			
4 from A to C			
1 from B to C			
2 from B to A			
1 from C to A			
3 from B to C			
1 from A to B			
2 from A to C			
1 from B to C			

Convert the algorithm into a program.

The algorithm in Step 3 is easy to convert into a very short C program.

P-5.14 [towers.c]

```c
#include <stdio.h>

void MoveRings(int n_rings, int start, int finish, int aux);

main()
{
  int n_rings;

  printf("Give number of rings to move: ");
  scanf("%i",&n_rings);
  MoveRings(n_rings,1,3,2);
  return(0);
}

void MoveRings(int n, int start,int finish,int aux)
{
  if (n > 0)
  {
    MoveRings(n-1,start,aux,finish);
    printf("Move ring %i from %i to %i\n",n,start,finish);
    MoveRings(n-1,aux,finish,start);
  }
}
```

Running P-5.14

```
Give number of rings to move: 4
Move ring 1 from 1 to 2
Move ring 2 from 1 to 3
Move ring 1 from 2 to 3
Move ring 3 from 1 to 2
Move ring 1 from 3 to 1
Move ring 2 from 3 to 2
Move ring 1 from 1 to 2
Move ring 4 from 1 to 3
Move ring 1 from 2 to 3
Move ring 2 from 2 to 1
Move ring 1 from 3 to 1
Move ring 3 from 2 to 3
Move ring 1 from 1 to 2
Move ring 2 from 1 to 3
Move ring 1 from 2 to 3
```

5

Verify the operation of the program.

If P-5.14 works for four rings and reproduces the steps shown in Table 5.2, there is no reason to think it will not work for other values of n. If n is too large, a particular programming environment may not be able to handle the large number of recursive calls, but this is not a fault of the algorithm. Certainly your programming environment should handle values of n as large as 10.

Problem Discussion

You may find it hard to believe that such an apparently difficult problem can be solved with so little code, because the algorithm doesn't actually contain a solution in terms of specifying directly how the rings must be moved. However, the solution implemented in P-5.14 is typical of recursive algorithms, which work because of the way calls to subprograms keep track of the local values of their parameters.[2] The variables `start`, `aux`, and `final` are initially given the values 1, 2, and 3, but their local values change when the recursive calls are made. It is possible to write an iterative version of the Towers of Hanoi algorithm (because, as noted previously, this is possible for all recursive algorithms), but it requires a more specific set of instructions from the programmer, and it is certainly more trouble than it's worth!

5.8.4 Trapezoidal Rule Integration

1

Define the problem.

Write a program that uses Trapezoidal Rule numerical integration to evaluate the normal probability density function.

2

Outline a solution.

As previously noted, the normal probability density function does not have an analytic integral, so numerical methods are required. In this discussion, we will

---

[2]The information is maintained on the run-time stack. To find out more about this, consult a computer science text on programming or data structures.

simply present the formula for Trapezoidal Rule integration; this and other related techniques will be discussed more fully in Chapter 9. Assuming that the range $[x_a, x_b]$ is divided into n equal intervals of size Δx, the integral of f(x) over that range can be approximated by

$$\int_{x_a}^{x_b} f(x)\,dx \approx \left(\sum_{i=0}^{n-1} [f(x_i) + f(x_i + \Delta x)]\right)\frac{\Delta x}{2} = \frac{[f(x_a) + f(x_b)]\Delta x}{2} + \Delta x \sum_{i=1}^{n-1} f(x_i)$$

where $x_i = xa + i \cdot \Delta x$.

3 Design an algorithm.

The algorithm for the Trapezoidal Rule integration function is trivial—it involves no more than a direct translation of the formula into C. The main function should serve as a simple driver program to test the operation of the Trapezoidal Rule integration.

4 Convert the algorithm into a program.

P-5.15 [trapezoi.c]

```
#include <stdio.h>
#include <math.h>

double pdf(double x);
double Trapezoidal_Rule(double x1,double x2,double (*f)(double));
double t(double x1,double x2,double (*f)(double)) {
   int i,n=100;
   double sum=0.,dx;
   dx=(x1+x2)/n;
   for (i=1; i<=n; i++)
     sum+=f(x1+(i-1)*dx)+f(x1+i*dx);
   return sum*dx/2.;
}

int main(void)
{
   double z;

   printf("Give value of standard normal variable, >0: ");
   scanf("%lf",&z);
   printf("%lf\n",Trapezoidal_Rule(0.,z,pdf));
   printf("%lf\n",t(0.,z,pdf));
```

```
   return 0;
}

double pdf(double x) {
   return exp(-x*x/2.)/sqrt(8.*atan(1.));
}

double Trapezoidal_Rule(double x1,double x2,double (*f)(double)) {
   int i,n=100;
   double sum=0.,dx;

   dx=(x2-x1)/n;
   for (i=1; i<n; i++)
     sum+=f(x1+i*dx);
   return (f(x1)+f(x2))*dx/2.+sum*dx;
}
```

Running P-5.15

```
Give value of standard normal variable, >0: .5
0.191462
```

5 Verify the operation of the program.

Tabulated values for the integral of the standard normal probability density function (pdf) can be found in any book on statistics. These tables often give the integral from 0 to z rather than from $-\infty$ to z. For z = 0.5, the integral of the pdf from 0 to 0.5 is 0.1915. Note that the integral of the pdf from $-\infty$ to z, which is the value usually required in statistics applications, is 0.5 plus the integral from 0 to z, so that the integral from $-\infty$ to 0.5 is 0.5 + 0.1915 = 0.6915.

Problem Discussion

The primary point of this application is to illustrate how to pass a function through the parameter list of another function. The program defines the normal probability density function in pdf and the name of this function is given as the argument corresponding to the parameter double (*f)(double) in the Trapezoidal_Rule function. In generalizing this application to other problems, it is important to realize that the driver program can pass *any* appropriate function to Trapezoidal_Rule. The only requirement is that the function must require a single type double argument and must return a type double result.

5.9 Debugging Your Programs

5.9.1 Passing Multiple Outputs Through Parameter Lists

The C syntax for using pointers to pass multiple output values through the parameter list of a function can be confusing. At the design level, it is important to be clear about which parameters are Input and which are Output. When you implement an algorithm design, it is essential to keep track of which names refer to variables and which to pointers. It may be helpful to develop the habit of using a _ptr suffix with pointer names. Within functions that have Output values, you must use the dereferencing operator (*) when you assign a value because you need to assign values not to the parameter (pointer) name itself but to the memory location to which the pointer points. Also, when you use scanf, fscanf, or sscanf to read a value for an Output variable, remember *not* to use the address-of operator, again because the name is a pointer and hence is already an address.

   When you call a function with pointers in its parameter list, remember that the corresponding variable names in the argument list must be preceded by an address-of operator. Failure to do so will not produce a compile-time error but may generate a run-time error and in any case will not produce the desired results.

5.9.2 Recursive Functions

C's implementation of recursive functions is straightforward, but the algorithm development for such functions is sometimes challenging. The trick for such algorithms is not to worry about the details of how the programming environment keeps track of the values of local variables during the recursive calls; such manual tracking of calculations can be a difficult task for an algorithm that generates multiple recursive paths. If your algorithm correctly states the recursive relationship that you wish to implement, the programming environment will do the rest. Although it is possible in principle to exhaust your programming environment's resources for managing multiple recursive calls, this is rarely a problem in practice.

   Remember that every recursive algorithm must have both a terminating branch and at least one branch that generates the recursive call. These branches are typically defined with **IF...THEN...** or **CHOOSE** pseudocode statements. Recursive algorithms generally replace count-controlled or conditional loops. Rather than having a terminating condition coded as part of a loop structure, the terminating branch of the **IF...THEN...** or **CHOOSE** statement is responsible for terminating the recursive calls. If your recursive algorithm contains a loop structure, it is probably wrong. A recursive algorithm is typically very short; if yours is not, it probably needs to be redesigned. If your recursive algorithm isn't properly terminated, your program will continue to generate recursive calls until the programming environment space reserved for such calls is exhausted. Then your program will crash.

5.9.3 Reusable Code

This chapter has outlined briefly how to incorporate previously written code modules into your programs. In a course based on this text, you are generally responsible for all your own code, but this is certainly not true for the professional application of programming languages in science and engineering. You can practice creating your own libraries of source code and object code files.

Remember that the #include statement is used only for uncompiled source code files and not for object code files, which have already been compiled. Don't forget to specify a complete path reference for #include files; that reference usually is not the same as the one in which the standard header files reside.

5.10 Exercises

For each of these exercises, write one or more functions to perform the required calculations. Where reasonable, use functions with multiple outputs returned indirectly through pointers. The purpose of your main function should be to get user input, call the function(s), and display results.

1. (a) Write a program that asks the user to enter a currency amount and then calculates how many dollar bills, quarters, dimes, nickels, and pennies are required to return this amount in change. Assume that the minimum total number of dollar bills and coins should be returned. This means that your program should return first the maximum number of bills, then the maximum number of quarters, then the maximum number of dimes, and so forth. That is, even though you obviously could return $0.66 in change as, for example, six dimes and six pennies, the program should tell you to return this change as two quarters, one dime, one nickel, and one penny. This restriction actually makes the problem easier to solve. Do the calculations in a function that returns the number of each coin required to make change. (For comparison, see Exercise 2 in Chapter 3.) [change.c]

(b) Modify the program from part (a) so that the currency amount is entered directly from the command line. [change2.c]

2. Write a program that asks the user to supply the mass and velocity of an object and then calculates and prints the kinetic energy and linear momentum of that object. The kinetic energy is $mv^2/2$, and the momentum is mv. Use metric units (mass in kilograms, velocity in meters per second, energy in joules). Use a single function to return both values. (For comparison, see Exercise 5 in Chapter 3.) [kinetic2.c]

Extra Credit:
    Include code for functions that will convert the kinetic energy and momentum into their British system equivalents. The British unit of energy is ft-lb, and the unit of momentum is slug-ft/s. 1 ft-lb = 1.356 joule; 1 slug = 14.59 kg; 1 ft/s = 0.3048 m/s.

3. Given the (x,y) coordinates of two points in a plane, write a program that calculates (a) the shortest distance between the two points, and (b) the (x,y) coordinates of a point halfway between the two points lying on a straight line joining the points. (Refer to Figure 3.8.) Use a single function to return all three values. (For comparison, see Exercise 10 in Chapter 3.) [points.c]

Extra Credit:
    Modify your program so it also calculates the slope of the line joining two points in a plane. What restriction will this calculation impose on the location of the two points?

4. An incompressible fluid such as water flows at speed v_1 through a cylindrical pipe with diameter d_1. The pipe then narrows gradually to diameter d_2. The mass flowing through the tube must remain constant, so the velocity v_2 of the fluid in the smaller pipe is given by the equation of continuity:

$$A_1v_1 = A_2v_2$$

where A_1 and A_2 are the cross-sectional areas of pipes with diameters d_1 and d_2. The mass flux through the pipe is

$$\text{mass flux} = \rho Av$$

where ρ is the fluid density of kg/m^3 and either A_1 and v_1 or A_2 and v_2 may be used.
    Write a program that asks the user to supply the two pipe diameters and speed v_1 and then calculates v_2 and the mass flux flowing through the pipe, assuming the fluid is water with a density of 1000 kg/m^3. [fluid.c]

5. The root-mean-square (rms) speed of gas molecules v_{rms} is given by

$$v_{rms} = \sqrt{\frac{3kT}{m}}$$

where k is Boltzmann's constant, 1.38×10^{-23} J/K, T is temperature in Kelvins, and mass is in kg. Express mass in terms of the atomic weight of the gas times the mass of one atomic mass unit, 1.660×10^{-27} kg.

The average speed v_{avg} for gas molecules is approximately related to rms speed by

$$v_{rms} \approx 1.09 \, v_{avg}$$

Write a program that calculates v_{rms} and v_{avg} for a specified gas and temperature; for example, oxygen molecules at 25°C. An oxygen molecule (O_2) has a mass of 32 atomic mass units. Don't forget to convert °C to K, where 0°C = 273.15 K. [gas_spd.c]

6. A text file contains real numbers in this format:

```
7.7
6.6
5.5
8.8
5.5
```
(and so forth)

Write a program that calculates the average value (mean) and the standard deviation of all values in the file according to the formulas:

$$\text{mean} = \frac{\sum_{i=1}^{n} x_i}{n} \qquad \text{standard deviation} = \sqrt{\frac{\sum_{i=1}^{n} x_i^2 - \left(\sum_{i=1}^{n} x_i\right)^2 / n}{n-1}}$$

where n is the total number of points in the file.

For comparison, see Exercise 9 in Chapter 4. The difference here is that you should write a separate function to calculate the mean and standard deviation, given $\sum x_i^2$, $(\sum x_i)^2$, and n as inputs. [stats2.c]

7. Recall Exercise 12 in Chapter 4, in which you were asked to write a function that estimates the square root of a number using Newton's algorithm. Rewrite that function as a recursive function.

8. A special set of functions called Legendre polynomials are sometimes required in science and engineering applications. Table 5.3 gives the Legendre polynomials $P_n(x)$ for $0 \leq n \leq 7$.

Table 5.3. The first eight Legendre polynomials

n	$P_n(x)$
0	1
1	x
2	$(3x^2 - 1)/2$
3	$(5x^3 - 3x)/2$
4	$(35x^4 - 30x^2 + 3)/8$
5	$(63x^5 - 70x^3 + 15x)/8$
6	$(231x^6 - 315x^4 + 105x^2 - 5)/16$
7	$(429x^7 - 693x^5 + 315x^3 - 35x)/16$

By making use of the fact that $R_0(x) = 1$ and $R_1(x) = x$, Legendre polynomials of order $n \geq 2$ can be generated through a recursion relation:

$$R_n(x) = \frac{2n-1}{n} x R_{n-1}(x) - \frac{n-1}{n} R_{n-2}(x)$$

Write a recursive function to evaluate the Legendre polynomial for any value of n and x, where $n \geq 0$. [legendre.c]

9. Bessel functions are sometimes encountered in advanced engineering and science mathematics (for example, to describe electric charge configurations in cylindrical coordinates). Bessel functions of the first kind, $J_n(x)$, for nonnegative integer values of n and any real number x, can be defined in terms of an infinite series:

$$J_n(x) = \sum_{s=0}^{\infty} \frac{(-1)^s}{s!\,(n+s)!}\left(\frac{x}{2}\right)^{n+2s} = \sum_{s=0}^{\infty} G_s(n.x)$$

where

$$G_o(n,x) = \frac{x^n}{2^n n!}$$

and

$$G_s(n,x) = G_{s-1}(n,x)\frac{(-1)}{s\,(n+s)}\left(\frac{x}{2}\right)^2$$

Figure 5.4 illustrates these functions for n = 0 and n = 1.

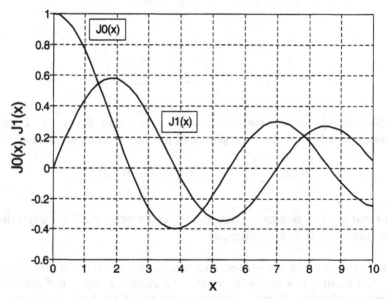

Figure 5.4. Bessel functions of order 0 and 1.

Write and test a function to evaluate Bessel functions for specified values of n and x, using the first 10 terms in the infinite series expansion. When you test this function, you should print out the values of the individual terms in the series to make sure that evaluating only the first 10 terms is reasonable.

Note that the function $G_s(n,x)$ is defined recursively. However, you might wish to consider if using a recursive function is the best way to evaluate Bessel functions. Do not let your decision be based just on the fact that recursive functions is a topic covered in this chapter. [bessel.c]

Extra Credit:

Bessel functions of the first kind for n > 1 may be obtained from the recursive relation

$$J_{n+1}(x) = \frac{2n}{x} J_n(x) - J_{n-1}(x)$$

Write a recursive function that calculates higher order Bessel functions in this way and compare your results with calculating the functions directly from the series expansion.

10. A standard problem in numerical analysis is to find the roots of the equation $f(x) = 0$. One well-known approach is called the bisection method.

How can we tell whether there are any roots over the closed interval $[x_a, x_b]$? Suppose that the sign of $f(x_a)$ is different from the sign of $f(x_b)$. The obvious interpretation of this fact is that the function has crossed the x-axis at least once in the range $[x_a, x_b]$. It is also possible that the function crossed the x-axis more than once, in which case the total number of crossings must be odd. This means that $f(x)$ must have at least one real root in the range $[x_a, x_b]$.

A second possibility is that the sign of $f(x_a)$ is the same as the sign of $f(x_b)$. This means that there may be no roots or that the function has crossed the x-axis an even number of times, so that $f(x)$ must have either no roots or an even number of roots in the range $[x_a, x_b]$.

A third possibility is that $f(x)$ just touches the x-axis without crossing it. For example, this is true for the function

$$f(x) = x^2 - 6x + 9 = (x - 3)(x - 3)$$

This function, which never crosses the x-axis, has two identical real roots, thereby complicating the search for a generally applicable root-finding algorithm. Figure 5.5 illustrates these three possibilities.

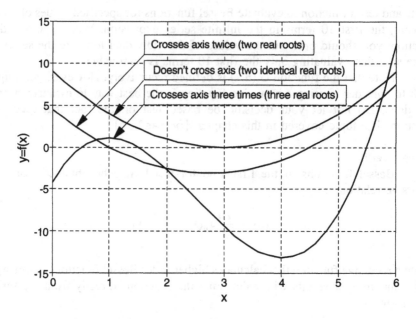

Figure 5.5. Polynomials with one or more real roots.

For the purpose of this exercise, we will proceed on the assumption that roots can be found by identifying the places where a function crosses the x-axis. (That is, we will ignore the third possibility mentioned above.) Assume that the interval $[x_a, x_b]$ is divided into subintervals $[x_L, x_R]$ sufficiently small that each subinterval contains either one root or no roots. However, we shouldn't overlook the possibility that we may select the subintervals so that either $f(x_L) = 0$ or $f(x_R) = 0$, or both may equal zero in the case where $f(x)$ can have more than one root. In that case, either x_L or x_R, or both x_L and x_R, are roots.

If neither of the subinterval endpoints is a root, continue the search for the root in the open interval (x_L, x_R). Find the midpoint in the interval $[x_L, x_R]$. There are then three possibilities, which take into account the fact that if the product $f(x_L) \cdot f(x_R)$ is less than zero, the function crosses the x-axis somewhere in the interval (x_L, x_R):

(1) $f(x_{mid}) = 0$
(2) $f(x_L) \cdot f(x_{mid}) < 0$
(3) $f(x_{mid}) \cdot f(x_R) < 0$

If (1) is true, then x_{mid} is a root. In general, it is unlikely that $f(x_{mid})$ will ever be exactly zero, so this condition needs to be implemented as $|f(x_{mid})| < \varepsilon$, where ε is some appropriately small user-supplied value.

If (2) is true, then the root must lie in the interval $[x_L, x_{mid}]$. Let $x_R = x_{mid}$ and try again with this new interval. If (3) is true, then the root must lie in the interval $[x_{mid}, x_R]$. Let $x_L = x_{mid}$ and try again. As a result of repeatedly halving the interval in this way, x_{mid} will eventually satisfy the inequality $|f(x_{mid})| < \varepsilon$, based on the assumption that the original interval (x_L, x_R) contains one root. It is also possible to terminate the algorithm when the interval becomes sufficiently small: $x_R - x_L < \varepsilon'$, where ε' is some other user-supplied small value. In that case, we can also assume that $f(x_{mid})$ is sufficiently small.

This description of the bisection algorithm is easy to implement recursively. Divide the search interval in half and look again in the appropriate half. These repeated searches on a new interval half the size of the current interval generate the recursive calls. The other possibilities, such as $|f(x_{mid}) < \varepsilon|$, provide multiple terminating conditions for the recursive function.

Using this discussion of the bisection algorithm, write a program that finds one or more roots of a function over a specified interval. Test your program by defining a function that contains at least two roots, such as $x^2 - 2$, and by specifying an initial interval that includes those roots. Use a count-controlled loop to divide the initial interval into 10 equal subintervals. Each such subinterval defines one of the intervals $[x_L, x_R]$ discussed above. Search recursively for a root within each of those subintervals and display the results of each search. [bisect2.c]

11. Recall Exercise 13 in Chapter 3, in which you were asked to write a polynomial function that approximated the integral of the normal probability density function (pdf). In this exercise you will write a program to compare that approximation with a numerical integration of the pdf, as was done in this chapter in Section 5.8.4. Your main function should not do any calculations itself; rather, it should simply call functions to do the two calculations.

For this exercise, functions to do the calculations should be written in another source code file that will be compiled separately and then linked to the main function. Give the main function access to the functions by #includeing an appropriate header file. The code for numerically integrating a function of one variable using Simpson's Rule is given below.

```
double F(double z)
{
  return exp(-z*z/2.0)/sqrt(8.0*atan(1.0));
}
double Simpson(double x1,double x2,int n_segs,double (*F)())
{
  int i;
  double dx,sum_odd,sum_even;

  dx=(x2-x1)/n_segs;
  sum_odd=0.0;  sum_even=0.0;
  for (i=1; i<=n_segs-1; i+=2)
    sum_odd+=F(x1+(double)i*dx);
```

```
for (i=2; i<=n_segs-2; i+=2)
    sum_even+=F(x1+(double)i*dx);
return (F(x1)+F(x2)+4.*sum_odd+2.*sum_even)*dx/3.;
}
```

Note that the numerical integration function Simpson requires four parameters: the lower integration limit, which is 0 for this problem; the upper limit, which is the standard normal variable z; the number of integration steps, which could be given a value of 100; and a reference to a function that evaluates the normal probability density function. Also, Simpson integrates the function from 0 to z rather than from −∞ to z. Although Simpson could be called directly to evaluate the integral, a cleaner information interface involves creating another function that requires only the standard normal variable z as its single argument and which returns the value returned from Simpson plus 0.5 (because the integral of the pdf from −∞ to 0 is 0.5). With such a function, your main program code will look something like this:

```
printf("Give value of standard normal variable z: ");
scanf("%lf",&z);
printf("From Simpson's rule integration: %lf\n",
       normal_int(z));
printf("   From polynomial approximation: %lf\n",
       normal_poly(z));
```

When you write the header file, it should contain references only to those functions needed directly by your main function:

```
extern normal_poly(double z);
extern normal_int(double z);
```

As they should, these function prototypes hide the details of implementing the calculations, especially for the numerical integration. [normal3.c]

12. The Julian day system is used in astronomical calculations to overcome the complexities inherent in the civil calendar system. These problems occur because the length of a solar year is not an even number of calendar days. (One solar year is *approximately* 365.25 days.) Every day is assigned a unique, consecutively numbered Julian day starting with the January 1, -4712. Julian days begin at Greenwich noon; that is, noon at the Greenwich Observatory near London. For example, midnight at the start of Greenwich calendar day January 1, 1998, (or January 1.0, 1998) is Julian day 2450814.5, and Greenwich noon on January 1, 1998, (or January 1.5, 1998) is Julian day 2450815.0. Note that days are allowed to include fractional parts. Thus days should be represented as real numbers rather than integers.

It is possible to write algorithms for converting back and forth between dates given in the Gregorian calendar (the modern civil calendar) and Julian days, although they are certainly not obvious.[3] For a specified month m, day d, and year y, the Julian day JD is given by the following algorithm:

1. If m > 2, leave y and m unchanged. If m equals 1 or 2, replace y by y − 1 and m by m + 12.

2. Calculate A = ⟨y/100⟩ and B = 2 − A + ⟨A/4⟩, where ⟨...⟩ indicates that a division is truncated to a whole number. That is, ⟨7/4⟩ = 1.

3. The Julian Day is then

$$JD = \langle 365.25(y + 4716)\rangle + \langle 30.6001(m + 1)\rangle + d + B - 1524.5$$

where JD can include a fractional part, as noted above. The number 30.6001, rather than 30.6, is required to prevent inappropriate truncations due to inaccuracies in handling real arithmetic. For example, 5 times 30.6 gives 153 exactly, but this calculation done in real arithmetic might give a result of 152.999999, a value that will then be truncated to 152.

The conversion from the older Julian calendar to the modern Gregorian calendar took place in many parts of Europe in 1582. The day following October 4 on the Julian calendar became October 15 on the Gregorian calendar. However, because the change was mandated by the Pope in Catholic countries, some non-Catholic countries resisted or delayed the change. In Great Britain, the change wasn't made uniformly until 1752. Thus, caution is required when converting historical calendar dates to Julian dates.

The inverse operation, to convert a Julian day to its corresponding Gregorian calendar day, is:

1. Add 0.5 to the Julian day. Let z be the integer part and f the decimal part of the result. If z < 2299161, let A = z. If z ≥ 2299161,

$$\alpha = \langle(z - 1867216.25)/36524.25\rangle$$
$$A = z + 1 + \alpha - \langle\alpha/4\rangle$$

2. Calculate

$$B = A + 1524$$
$$C = \langle(B - 122.1)/365.25\rangle$$
$$D = \langle 365.25C\rangle$$
$$E = \langle(B - D)/30.6001\rangle$$

---

[3]The algorithms given here are from Jean Meeus, *Astronomical Algorithms*, Willmann-Bell, Inc., Richmond, VA, 1991. (www.willbell.com)

3. Calculate

$$d = B - D - \langle 30.6001E \rangle + f \quad \text{(day including decimal part)}$$
$$m = E - 1 \text{ if } E < 14, \text{ or } E - 13 \text{ if } E = 14 \text{ or } 15$$
$$y = C - 4716 \text{ if } m > 2 \text{ or } C - 4715 \text{ if } m = 1 \text{ or } 2$$

Do *not* replace 30.6001 with 30.6. Note that d can include a fractional part.

Implement these algorithms in two functions. Test the functions in a program that asks the user to provide a calendar date, calculates the Julian day, and converts that Julian day back to its calendar date. [julcal.c]

13. Certain kinds of atmospheric measurements are made with a sun photometer, an instrument consisting of a detector that views a narrow beam of sunlight and responds only to a narrow range of frequencies. In order to interpret such measurements, the position of the sun must be known relative to the observer and relative to a horizontal plane at the earth's surface. Although it is possible in principle to measure directly the solar elevation angle (the angular distance of the sun above the horizontal plane) or its zenith angle (90° degrees minus the elevation angle), it is usually more accurate to calculate the solar position from astronomical equations. Such equations, based on astronomical theory and observations, are complicated because the geometry of the earth's rotation around the sun and about its own axis is complicated.[4]

The terminology in these equations is probably unfamiliar and the equations are probably obscure. However, your task is to write a program that implements the equations, not to derive them or even to understand their derivation. For the most part, you will not be able to determine independently whether your program produces the correct answer. Consequently, you must be extremely careful when you translate these algorithms into C.

Julian centuries from 2000:

$$T = (JD - 2451545.0)/36525.0$$

(Use the Julian day calculation from the previous exercise to get JD.)

Solar position in ecliptic coordinates:

geometric mean longitude of the sun:
$$L_0 = 280.46645 + 36000.76983T + 0.0003032T^2$$

mean anomaly of the sun:
$$M = 357.52910 + 35999.05030T - 0.0001559T^2 - 0.00000048T^3$$

---

[4]See, for example, Jean Meeus, *Astronomical Algorithms*, Willmann-Bell, Inc., Richmond, VA, 1991. (www.willbell.com)

eccentricity of the earth's orbit:

$$e = 0.016708617 - 0.000042037T - 0.0000001236T^2$$

equation of the sun's center:

$$C = (1.914600 - 0.004817T - 0.000014T^2)\sin(M)$$
$$+ (0.019993 - 0.000101T)\sin(2M) + 0.000290\sin(3M);$$

true longitude of the sun:

$$L_{true} = (L_0 + C) \text{ modulus } 360. \text{ If } L_{true} < 0°, \text{ add } 360°.$$

true anomaly of the sun:

$$f = M + C$$

earth-sun distance:

$$R = 1.000001018(1 - e^2)/[1 + e \bullet \cos(f)]$$

Angular position of the Greenwich meridian:

sidereal time:

$$\theta_0 = 280.46061837 + 360.98564736629(JD - 2451545) + 0.000387933T^2$$
$$- T^3/38710000$$
Replace θ_0 with θ_0 modulus 360. If $\theta_0 < 0°$, add 360°.

Obliquity of the ecliptic:

$$\varepsilon = 23 + 26/60 + 21.448/3600 - 46.8150/3600T - (0.00059/3600)T^2$$
$$+ (0.001813/3600)T^3$$

Conversion of solar coordinates to equatorial (earth-centered) and observer coordinates:

right ascension:

$$\tan(\alpha) = \tan(L_{true})\cos(\varepsilon)$$

declination:

$$\sin(\delta) = \sin(\varepsilon)\sin(L_{true})$$

hour angle of the sun with respect to the observer's longitude (L_{obs}):

$$H = \theta_0 + L_{obs} - \alpha$$

azimuth angle of sun at the observer's longitude and latitude (λ_{obs}), relative to south:

$$\tan(\zeta) = \sin(H)/[\cos(H)\sin(L_{obs}) - \tan(\delta)\cos(\lambda_{obs})]$$

elevation angle of sun above a horizontal plane at the observer's position:

$$\sin(\varepsilon) = \sin(\lambda_{obs})\sin(\delta) + \cos(\lambda_{obs})\cos(\delta)\cos(H)$$

The equations giving angular quantities as a function of time T—L_0 and M, for example—assume angles specified in degrees. When you use these angular quantities as arguments in trigonometric functions—sin(H), for example—be careful to convert the angles from degrees to radians. You must also be careful to use real arithmetic when appropriate. In the equation for the obliquity of the ecliptic, for example, the quantity 26/60 translated into source code as the integer division `26/60` will give a value of 0!

For the right ascension and azimuth, use the `atan2` function to obtain an angle in the proper quadrant. To do this for the right ascension, replace tan(L_{true}) with sin(L_{true})/cos(L_{true}).

14. Equations of the form

$$e^{at} - at - b = 0$$

are sometimes encountered in heat transfer problems. This is an equation that cannot be solved analytically, but it can easily be solved numerically. If the equation is rewritten as

$$e^{at} = at + b$$

then an obvious graphical solution is to plot each side of the equation separately, as shown in Figure 5.6 for a = 0.5 and b = 10. Any point where the two curves intersect is a root of the original equation.

A standard numerical approach to solving this kind of equation involves rewriting the original equation in the form t = g(t). For this equation, there are two obvious possibilities:

$$t = (e^{at} - b)/a$$
$$t = \ell n(at + b)/a$$

To find t, first make an initial guess; any reasonable value should work. Then evaluate the right side of the equation to get a new value of t. Substitute this new value and evaluate the expression again. Repeat the procedure of reevaluating t in this way until the difference between the new and old values of t becomes less than some specified small number. Although such an approach is not guaranteed to work, it is often the case that this iterative algorithm will converge to a value of t that is a root of the original equation.

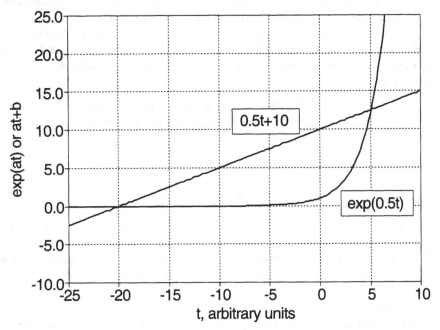

Figure 5.6. Graphical solution to $e^{at} - at - b = 0$.

For the coefficients used here (a = 0.5, b = 10), Figure 5.6 shows that there are two real roots—one at about t = −20, and another at about t = 5. If the independent variable t represents time in a heat transfer problem, for example, only the positive root has physical significance. Which root will the iterative solution find? It is interesting that, for this equation, one formulation of t = g(t) will find the positive root and the other will find the negative root.

Write a program that will solve this equation iteratively. Implement a function that will iterate on a function passed through its parameter list. Define two functions, g1 and g2, one for each formulation of t = g(t) given above, and call the iterating function twice, once with each of these functions as an argument. What are the roots and which definition of g(t) gives the physically significant positive root?

Hint: This algorithm can be implemented either iteratively or recursively. It would be good practice to do it both ways. [heat_xfr.c]

15. In astronomy, the so-called equation of time is used to account for the fact that standard time (clock time) is based on a fictitious mean sun that rotates around the earth at a constant rate. The motion of the real sun around the earth is complicated by two facts: (1) the earth's equator is tilted with respect to the

ecliptic plane (the plane in which the earth rotates around the sun); (2) the earth's orbit around the sun is slightly elliptical rather than circular.

Thus, true solar time is different from clock time. For an observer at the Greenwich meridian (0° longitude) whose clock reads standard time, the difference between clock time and true solar time (clock time − solar time) E is given in minutes by

$$E = (0.000075 + 0.001868\cos\Gamma - 0.032077\sin\Gamma \\ - 0.014615\cos2\Gamma - 0.04089\sin2\Gamma)(229.18)$$

where Γ is the day angle. In radians, and ignoring leap years:

$$\Gamma = 2\pi(\text{day} - 1)/365$$

Note that this value may be positive or negative. The maximum time correction is about 16 minutes, with a maximum error of a little more than 0.5 minute.[5]

Write a program that asks a user to supply a day number and then calculates and displays the equation of time correction. [sol_time.c]

Extra Credit:

(1) Write a function that calculates the day number from the calendar date (month, day, and year). This function should account for leap years. Modify the equation for Γ so that the denominator is 365 or 366 depending on whether the year is a leap year. Include a function that will convert the day of the year back to the calendar date, correctly accounting for leap years. Meeus[6] gives the following equation for day number n:

$$n = \text{INT}\left(\frac{275\,m}{9}\right) - k\cdot\text{INT}\left(\frac{m+9}{12}\right) + d - 30$$

where k is 1 for a leap year and 2 for a common year. The reverse calculation is:

If n < 32, then m = 1 and d = n. Otherwise,

---

[5]See Chapter 1 of Muhammad Iqbal: *An Introduction to Solar Radiation*, Academic Press, 1983.

[6]See Jean Meeus, *Astronomical Algorithms*, Willmann-Bell, Inc., Richmond, VA, 1991. (www.willbell.com)

$$m = \text{INT}\left[\frac{9(k+n)}{275} + 0.98\right]$$

$$d = n - \text{INT}\left(\frac{275\,m}{9}\right) + k \bullet \text{INT}\left(\frac{m+9}{12}\right) + 30$$

(See also Exercise 15 in Chapter 3.)

(2) In the original problem statement, the time correction is calculated relative to Greenwich Mean Time, at a standard time longitude of 0°. At other longitudes, an additional correction must be made: 4 minutes per degree of longitude difference between the observer's standard time longitude L_s and the observer's actual longitude L_a:

$$\text{true solar time} = 4(L_s - L_a) + E$$

The standard longitudes for time zones in North America and Hawaii are given in Table 5.4.

Table 5.4. Standard time zones for North America

Time Zone Name	Zone Time (hours)	Standard Longitude
Atlantic	4	60°W
Eastern	5	75°W
Central	6	90°W
Mountain	7	105°W
Pacific	8	120°W
Alaska	9	135°W
Hawaii	10	150°W

(3) Write a function based on these equations that calculates the time of true solar noon, i.e., the clock time at which true solar time is 12:00 noon, for a specified day and longitude.

16. Write and test a recursive function that calculates x^n, where x is any real number (positive or negative) and n is any integer (positive or neegative). Define

$0^n = 0$ and $x^n = x \cdot x^{n-1}$. If n is negative, then $x^n = 1/x^{-n}$. Note that for the intrinsic function pow, the exponent is type double rather than int. As a result the pow function will produce errors if the base is negative and the exponent is not a whole number.

17. Write and test a recursive function that finds the greatest common divisor of two integers m and n, using Euclid's algorithm:

1. Find the integer remainder of m/n (m mod n).
2. If the remainder is 0, then n is the largest integer divisor of both m and n.
3. If the remainder is not 0, replace m with n and n with the integer remainder from the original division. Repeat the steps until the remainder is 0.

For example, what is the greatest common divisor of 30 and 12?

1. The integer remainder of 30/12 is 6.
2. The remainder is not 0.
3. The integer remainder of 12/6 is 0. Therefore, 6 is the largest integer divisor of both m and n.

This algorithm implies that m is greater than n, but this is not a requirement, as you can see by trying 12 and 30 rather than 30 and 12.

18. Write and test a recursive function that returns 1 if an integer is prime and 0 if it is not. You can take advantage of the following facts:

1. The integers 1, 2, and 3 are prime.
2. Any even integer greater than 2 is not prime.
3. If an integer has no divisor less than or equal to its square root, it must be prime. That is, if an integer has a divisor greater than or equal to its square root, it must also have a divisor less than or equal to its square root. Odd integers that are perfect squares, such as 49, have two divisors, each of which is equal to the square root.

To implement this algorithm, it is helpful the use two separate functions, one of which has a single parameter associated with the integer to be tested. The prototypes should look like this:

```
int Is_Prime(int n);
int Get_Prime(int n,int m);
```

where n is the integer to be tested and m is a trial divisor. Only the function Is_Prime is called directly. Then Is_Prime conducts some preliminary tests on n and calls `Get_Prime` only if the other tests cannot determine whether n is prime. Of these two functions, only `Get_Prime` is called recursively.

6.1 Arrays in Structured Programming

Up to now, we have discussed only *data objects* for which a variable name corresponds to a single value and a single memory location consisting of one or more bytes, as appropriate for the data type of the variable. In this chapter, we will

> data object
> array

develop a new model for data representation which allows us to manage many pieces of related information. This important user-defined data object, called an *array*, is a collection of related values organized under a single name. Although arrays can be implemented as purely abstract entities, in science and engineering they more often serve as implementations for vectors or representations for tabulated data. In this section, we will develop the basic concepts of arrays by posing a specific data management problem and describing a way of organizing the information required to solve that problem.

Suppose you are conducting an experiment to monitor the concentration of tropospheric ozone, the levels of which are subject to federal regulation. You have in place equipment that produces one measurement per hour for 24 hours. You would like to store these measurements and then write a program to analyze the data. How should your program handle this task? One way would be to associate a unique variable name with each ozone measurement:

```
ozone1
ozone2
ozone3
ozone4
...
ozone23
ozone24
```

This already seems a little awkward, and it will quickly become unworkable if you decide that what you really need is hourly measurements for an entire month. Suddenly you're faced with creating up to 744 variable names!

Fortunately, there's an easier way: define a single name—ozone—and an indexing system that can be used to access all the ozone measurements under this single variable name. Symbolically, each measurement could be addressed like this:

```
ozone(1)
ozone(2)
...
ozone(24)
```

The interpretation of this system is the obvious one: ozone(1) is the measurement at the first hour, ozone(2) is the measurement at the second hour, and so forth. If you need more measurements, all you have to do is increase the value of the largest index from 24 to 744 for an entire month:

```
ozone(1)
ozone(2)
...
ozone(743)
ozone(744)
```

At the algorithm design level for this problem, the information is awkward to manage even conceptually without some kind of indexing scheme. Also, as we will see, it is difficult and impractical to implement solutions to some kinds of programming problems without an array-based approach. Thus when you implement this conceptual model for representing data in a programming language, you will use an array.

One-dimensional arrays are often associated with vectors in the physical and mathematical sense, or with *vector data* in a more generalized sense, as opposed to *scalar data*. This is a distinction that should be familiar from an introductory physics course. To cite some examples, the speed of a moving object is represented by a single number and is a scalar quantity, but the velocity of a moving object is a vector quantity that describes both speed and direction with components in each of three coordinates in physical space. Mass is a scalar quantity, but weight as a consequence of the gravitational force acting on mass is a vector quantity.

vector data
scalar data

The association of arrays with vectors is especially relevant to problems in mathematics, science, and engineering, but the use of arrays in programs isn't restricted to applications that can be physically associated with vectors. In programming, arrays are organizational tools for managing large amounts of related information. You should use array notation any time you need to manipulate collections of related values, regardless of whether that use is associated with some kind of physical vector operation. For example, the problem of managing ozone measurements has no physical vector significance, but it is nonetheless a natural candidate for an array representation. You can think of the ozone data as a vector in "data space" rather than in physical space.

It is easy to misinterpret the meaning of dimension when that word is applied to arrays. In physics, a three-dimensional vector might refer to the position or velocity of an object in space because space has three dimensions.[1] However, such a vector is represented by a *rank* one (one-dimensional) array in

rank
dimension
extent
shape

---

[1]Note to physics students: This statement refers to the properties of space as described by Newtonian mechanics.

programming. To put it another way, the **dimension** of an array, in the programming use of that term, does not describe the size or **extent** of an array—the number of values stored in the array—but is related along with the extent to its **shape**. A vector describing position or velocity or, more abstractly, a stream of measurements, has shape one, regardless of how many components it contains, but a table organized into several rows and columns is most naturally represented as an array of shape (rank) two, regardless of how many rows and columns it has.

You *could* represent monthly ozone data with a one-dimensional array of size 744. However, in terms of organizing this kind of information, it makes more sense to define a rank two array—essentially, a table of values. One index—from an implementation point of view, it won't matter which one—will represent a day of the month and the other will represent an hour in the day. The entire array still requires 31x24 = 744 values, but each dimension has its own extent; 31 for the first dimension and 24 for the second. Assume the first index represents the day and the second the hour. Then a two-dimensional (rank two) representation in an array called `ozone` will look like this:

```
On day 1:     ozone( 1, 1)
              ozone( 1, 2)
              . . .
              ozone( 1,24)
On day 2:     ozone( 2, 1)
              ozone( 2, 2)
              . . .
              ozone( 2,24)
. . .
On day 31:    ozone(31, 1)
              ozone(31, 2)
              . . .
              ozone(31,24)
```

As you can see from this example, the dimensionality of an array is associated with the *number* of array indices required to access values in the array. A rank two array requires two indices. Organizing the rank two `ozone` array so that its first dimension represents days and its second dimension represents hours is an arbitrary but reasonable choice. The next section will describe the implementation of rank one arrays. We will return later to the problem of representing ozone in a two-dimensional table with a rank two array.

6.2 One-Dimensional Array Implementation in C

In this section, we will discuss the C implementation of array concepts. Consider the implementation of a one-dimensional array to hold 24 ozone values. Like any other data object, an array must be declared before it can be used in a program:

```
float ozone[24];
```

What can we learn from this single statement? First, as a matter of good programming style,

---
The name of an array corresponding to a physical quantity should be descriptive.

For the ozone example, a name such as `ozone` makes sense both for algorithm design and for the implementation. There is no justification for using an abbreviated or meaningless name for a physical quantity, although we will often use a short name such as A when we are discussing or using arrays in the abstract.

The number in brackets following the array name defines its size, or extent.

The declared extent of an array represents the maximum number of values that array can hold.

The extent of an array can be declared with the aid of a `#define` directive:

```
#define MAX 24
float ozone[MAX];
```

In general, this is better programming style than the previous declaration, as it makes references to the maximum number of values an array can hold, which often appear in several places in a program, easy to modify.

A value in an array is called an ***array element***. The array elements are related in the organizational sense. In addition, as a matter of implementation,

| array element |

Every element in an array must have the same data type.

As indicated in the declaration statement, each of the 24 elements of the `ozone` array is a type `float` number. Array elements can have any defined data type, including any of C's intrinsic types and, as we will see in Chapter 7, user-defined data types.

Previously in this text, we have generally associated the values of physical quantities with type `double` real numbers. We will sometimes make exceptions to this choice when we use arrays. Why? Because arrays can occupy a lot of space in memory, and it is sometimes reasonable to conserve that space by using a data type that requires no more bytes per element than necessary.

It is important to realize that the declared extent of an array represents the *maximum* number of values an array can hold. It is not necessary to use all of the elements. When arrays are used in programs that process data from external sources, is it often true that the actual number of values that must be processed is unknown at the time the code is written. Thus, the working size of an array may be significantly smaller than its declared size.

Elements in an array must be given values one at a time; there are no operations in C that apply to an array object as a whole.[2] Usually, it is a good idea to initialize all the elements in an array because it is a mistake, at least as a matter of programming style, to use an uninitialized array element on the right side of an assignment operator, just as this is a mistake for scalar variables. Again, it is possible to distinguish between the declared extent of an array and its working size. Unused elements can simply be ignored and need never be given a value; it is of no consequence that declared space is wasted if the working size of the array is smaller than its extent.

Later in this chapter, there are several examples showing how to assign values to array elements. However, we will demonstrate here how to initialize an array's elements as part of its declaration:

```
float a[]={1.1,3.7,4.4};
```

In this statement, the square brackets that specify the extent of the array are empty, and its size is inferred from the number of values appearing within curly brackets. Although this is not a very practical strategy for large arrays, it can be useful in some circumstances—for example, in programs that process three-dimensional physical vectors with only three components.

Now let's see how to access the values in an array. Assume we have already given a value to each element in a one-dimensional array of extent 10, and that we now wish to display those values.

```
int i;
float A[10];
...
for (i=0; i<10; i++)
  printf("%f\n",A[i]);
```

The loop counter variable i serves as an **array index** for accessing the values in A. Note that i takes values in the range 0–9 rather than 1–10. This is because

array index

> In C, the first array index must always be 0. For an array of extent n, the array indices must be in the range 0 to (n-1) and NOT 1 to n.

---

[2]There is no inherent reason why a programming language cannot implement operations that can be applied to entire arrays. Fortran 90, for example, contains many such operations.

In terms of this important rule, C differs from other languages such as Fortran and Pascal, in which you may select values for both the upper and lower value of an array index. In the ozone example discussed earlier in this chapter, the natural mathematical notation for the fourth measurement in the day is ozone(4), or $ozone_4$. In C, however, the fourth measurement in a one-dimensional array holding ozone measurements would be accessed as `ozone[3]` because the array index values for the first four measurements are 0, 1, 2, and 3, rather than 1, 2, 3, and 4.

Another difference between C's array notation and a mathematical notation that might use parentheses or subscripts is that

Array indices in C are always enclosed in brackets, with one pair of brackets for each dimension.

Thus, the mathematical notation A(i) or A_i is implemented in C as `A[i]`, or `A[i-1]` if you consider the mathematical index as starting at 1 rather than 0 (so $i - 1 = 0$ when $i = 1$). In a two-dimensional representation of ozone measurements, the second measurement on the second day is accessed in C by `ozone[1][1]` and not `ozone[2][2]`. Note that the notation `ozone[1,1]` is meaningless to C and will generate a syntax error because each dimension needs its own pair of brackets.

The differences between how arrays are usually notated in mathematics, or how you express positions in a one- or two-dimensional table, and C's array notation are easy to forget; consequently, a great deal of care is required when you write C programs that use arrays. Using parentheses rather than brackets for array indices and forgetting to enclose a reference to each dimension in its own pair of brackets are common mistakes that generate syntax errors. These mistakes are relatively easy to detect and fix.

On the other hand, using an inappropriate array element in a program will cause problems with your program that can be very difficult to detect because

The C language standard does not provide a means of checking for the use of inappropriate array indices.

Attempts to access values in an array which lie outside the declared limits are called *array boundary violations*. An array boundary violation

array boundary violation

will go undetected at compile time and may not produce an obvious error at run time. The results of such violations range from the obvious, such as crashing your computer system, to the subtle and mostly undetectable. The former is the best kind of violation with respect to the integrity of your computer program and the latter is the worst. There is no strategy for avoiding array boundary violations other than being careful when you write code. The inability to detect array boundary violations is a serious deficiency in the design of C that sets it apart from other languages such as Fortran and Pascal.[3]

When you are using arrays, it is important to distinguish between the data type of the values held in the array and the data type of the array indices used to access those values. The elements of an array can have any data type—they are type float real numbers in the ozone array—but

---

The indices of C array elements must be ordinal.

It is important to remember that the data type of an array index and the data type of its elements need not be, and generally are not, related.

In a more general sense, array indices must be ordinal because the indices must provide a means of one-to-one labelling for the elements of an array. Hence it makes no sense to consider a real number index for an array. However, in C, the restriction to integer indices has one not-so-obvious exception: you can use characters for array indices because C will perform an implicit type cast. Thus, as long as x has a declared size of at least 66, the references x['A'] and x[65] are equivalent because the uppercase letter A occupies position 65 in the ASCII collating sequence; that is, its value typecast to int is 65.

Especially in science and engineering, arrays are often used to process data from an external source. Here is a simple generic data processing problem that will illustrate the basics of using arrays in C:

> Read measurements from a file. Calculate the average of all measurements. Display all measurements greater than or equal to the average.

In designing a solution to this problem, it's important to realize that only the requirement to display values greater than or equal to the average of all measurements suggests the use of an array. The average can be calculated on the fly, as your program reads through the data file. However, the code to display only some measurements requires that *all* the measurements be accessed again; your program can't decide which measurements to display until all of them have been processed.

---

[3]One could argue that this deficiency in C renders it unsuitable for use in scientific and engineering programming. Obviously, this is an argument that has fallen on deaf ears.

One solution to this problem is to close and reopen the original file, or rewind the file back to the beginning[4] and read through it again. This is an unappealing solution because file I/O is slow compared to operations that take place in memory. A better idea is to store the values in an array so they can be manipulated in memory. In general, this is a much more flexible approach because it removes some restrictions that apply to sequential access (text) files. When data are stored in an array, you can access values in any order and alter them simply by reassigning them. In the text file implementation we have used so far in this text, values are accessible only in sequence, and you cannot read and write values in the file at the same time because sequential access text files are opened as either read-only or write-only.

Program P-6.1 shows how to use an array to implement a solution to the problem of displaying measurements greater than or equal to the average of all measurements. It uses data file arrays.dat.

P-6.1 [averages.c]

```
/* A typical array-based problem. */
#include <stdio.h>
#define FILENAME "arrays.dat"
#define MAX_SIZE 20

int main(void)
{
   float x[MAX_SIZE],avg;
   int n=0,status,i;
   FILE *infile;

   infile=fopen(FILENAME,"r");
   while (1) {
      status=fscanf(infile,"%f",&x[n]);
      if (status == EOF) break;
      avg+=x[n];
      printf("%i %f\n",n,x[n]);
      n++;
   }
   fclose(infile);
   printf("There are %i values.\n",n);
   avg/=(double)n;
   printf("The average value is %f\n",avg);
   printf("Values >= average:\n");
   for (i=0; i<n; i++)
      if (x[i] >= avg) printf("%i %f\n",i+1,x[i]);
   return 0;
}
```

---

[4]We haven't discussed how to rewind a file, but you can look up the rewind function in a C reference manual. The word is related to earlier computers in which information was stored on magnetic tapes that literally had to be rewound to return to the beginning of a file.

Running P-6.1

```
0 5.500000
1 -2.200000
2 -3.300000
3 6.600000
4 7.100000
5 8.800000
6 9.200000
7 11.400000
8 -5.300000
9 1.100000
There are 10 values.
The average value is 3.890000
Values >= average:
1 5.500000
4 6.600000
5 7.100000
6 8.800000
7 9.200000
8 11.400000
```

Remember that in C, there is no special keyword to use in a data declaration for an array. Space for the array is allocated by including it in a declaration statement with the data type of its elements and specifying the maximum number of elements in brackets. Because problem specifications can change, it is often convenient, but not required as a matter of syntax, to define the maximum number of elements as a constant, as has been done in P-6.1 with MAX_SIZE. Then, if the maximum size of the array needs to be changed, the change can be made in just one place in the source code.

A crucial point about C arrays is that they use *static allocation*. This means that the maximum number of elements in an array is set at the time the source code is compiled. As a consequence,

| *static allocation* |

The maximum number of elements in a statically allocated array cannot be changed while a program is running.

In P-6.1, this means that the data file averages.dat must contain no more than 20 values. Actually, the file should contain no more than 19 values. Why? Consider the operation of the while... loop when MAX_SIZE equals 20 and averages.dat contains 20 values. Suppose the loop has processed all 20 values. When the fscanf function tries to read another value, it encounters an end-of-file mark. At that time, the current value of n is 20, so fscanf will be trying to read a value for x[20]. However, the element x[20] doesn't exist because the array x has been allocated only 20 locations, for indices 0 through 19. Even though, in this example, the program encounters an end-of-file mark and never actually tries to write a value into element x[20], it is better programming style in general to assume that

> An array that will hold data read from an external file of unknown length should be declared with an extent that is larger than, rather than only as large as, the maximum number of values the file will ever be expected to contain.

In P-6.1, the array elements are declared as type float, rather than double, which we have usually preferred for physical quantities. This isn't essential, but it takes into account the fact that the space set aside for arrays in C implementations is limited, and type float variables may take less space than type double variables.

It's important to understand the statement

```
for (i=0; i<n; i++)
```

used to display values at the end of P-6.1. When the while... loop terminates after encountering an end-of-file mark, n has a value equal to the total number of values found in the file. This value is the working size of the array, and it must never be larger than the declared array extent. The for... loop initializes i to 0, and it executes only as long as i is *less than* n. That is, the value of the array index takes values in the range 0–(n − 1), as is appropriate.

It is very easy to make indexing errors when you're manipulating arrays. For example, replacing the for... loop statement in P-6.1 with

```
for (i=1; i <= n; i++);
```

probably doesn't look unreasonable, and it certainly won't generate a compile-time or run-time error message. However, this loop will start with the second array element (index 1), and it will attempt to display element x[n]. In P-6.1, element x[n] has not been assigned a value. If n equals MAX_SIZE, the element x[n] doesn't even exist. The former situation is an algorithm design error. The latter situation is an implementation error that results in an array boundary violation because the array reference lies outside the allowed range of indices, which must be in the range 0–(MAX_SIZE − 1).

The code in P-6.1 is important because it serves as a template for how to avoid logical errors and array boundary violations in this very common data processing situation. Remember that an array boundary violation does not automatically or immediately cause your program to crash. It simply forces your program to access memory locations that lie outside the memory space allocated for the array. Your program will certainly be willing to read from an unintended location, with unknown consequences. If you try to *write* information in such a forbidden location, by assigning a value to a nonexistent array element, the consequences can include crashing your computer system.

Finally, note that when values are read into the elements of arrays containing numerical or character (as opposed to string) elements, as in the statement

```
fscanf(infile,"%f",&x[i]);
```

the address-of operator must be used to reference the address of that element, just as this operator is required when scalar values are read. This makes sense because each element of an array is, in fact, just a scalar quantity. It is only the array entity itself that is no longer a scalar quantity.

Of course, there are ways to assign array elements other than by reading them directly from a data file. Array elements can appear on the left side of an assignment operator just as scalar variables can. The statements

```
x[4]=x[1];
x[2]=3;
x[(n+2)/2]=0;
x[c-65]+=1;
```

are all reasonable, assuming appropriate declarations. Variable n is probably an integer rather than a character. Variable c could be either an integer or a character that will be type cast to an integer; if c has the value 'A', the statement would reference element x[0].

As noted earlier in this chapter, one thing you can't do in C is assign a value to an *entire* array with a single statement. It is often required to initialize all the elements of an array before that array is used in a program. This code, which appears to be a temptingly simple way to initialize array elements, makes no sense and will generate a compilation error:

```
float x[10];
x=0.; /* Makes no sense! */
```

6.3 Using Arrays in Function Calls

Arrays can appear in function argument and parameter lists, but there are some important new rules to learn. It is straightforward to use array *elements* as arguments in calls to functions, as opposed to an entire array, because array elements are treated just like scalar variables. Indeed, when an array element is passed by value as an argument in a function call, the function has no way of distinguishing between that value and a scalar variable because the value of the array element is copied into a temporary location. Similarly, when a function performs calculations on output quantities by modifying their memory locations through pointers, as discussed in Chapter 5, the function has no way of knowing whether the location it is asked to modify is associated with a scalar variable or an array element.

The new rules apply to including an *entire* array in a function's parameter list. The syntax for an array parameter is

```
data_type array_name[]
```

The empty brackets, which are required, are used to indicate that the parameter is an entire array and not just a simple variable. The extent of the array is not given in the parameter list. This is because

> **A C function does not reallocate space for an array appearing in its parameter list because space allocation for that array has already been made in the main program.**

This is an important difference between the treatment of arrays and simple variables when they are passed to functions. When a scalar variable is passed as an input argument to a function, it is passed by value. That is, the function allocates new memory space and copies the value of the argument into this newly allocated space. Thus the function works with its own local copy of the variable and not with the value in the original memory location.

However, this information flow model does not apply to arrays passed as arguments. Instead,

> **When an entire array is passed to a function through its parameter list, it is passed by reference, and what is actually transmitted to the function is the address of the initial array element.**

This is true regardless of whether, in the algorithm design sense, you think of the array as input or output. The significant consequence of how C treats arrays passed to functions is:

> **When a function manipulates the contents of an array, it operates on the *original* array because it directly accesses the array's memory locations.**

This treatment of arrays, as pass-by-reference parameters, isn't at all obvious at the source code level, where the symbolic names used to identify arrays make them look just like scalar variables.

The fact that an array isn't treated strictly as input to a C function raises the possibility that unwanted changes can be made to the contents of an array. It is basically up to the programmer to make sure this doesn't happen. One way is to include the `const` keyword prior to the array type declaration in the parameter list: `const int A[]` rather than `int A[]`. Using this keyword doesn't alter the fact that arrays are passed by reference (that is, that the function still has access to the original memory locations in the array), but it does allow the compiler to produce executable code that will prevent changes to the contents of the array.

P-6.2 shows how to pass an array to a function. It uses the same data file, `arrays.dat`, as P-6.1. The function `ArrayModify` modifies the array elements by multiplying each array element by –1.

P-6.2 [arrays2.c]

```
/* Passing arrays to functions. */
#include <stdio.h>
#define MAX_SIZE 10

void ArrayModify(double a[]);

void main()
{
        int i;
        double x[MAX_SIZE];
        FILE *infile;

        infile=fopen("arrays.dat","r");

        for (i=0;i<MAX_SIZE;i+=1)
        {
          fscanf(infile,"%lf",&x[i]);
          printf("%d   %lf\n",i,x[i]);
        }
        fclose(infile);
        ArrayModify(x);
        for (i=0; i<MAX_SIZE; i+=1)
                printf("%d   %lf\n",i,x[i]);
}

void ArrayModify(double a[])
{
        int i;

        for (i=0; i < MAX_SIZE; i+=1)
        {
                a[i]=-a[i];
                printf("%d   %lf\n",i,a[i]);
        }
}
```

Because of the way C treats arrays, it is also possible to call `ArrayModify` like this:

```
ArrayModify(&x[0]);
```

This use of the address-of operator is equivalent to passing the entire array because

> **The name of an array is associated with the location of its first element.**

To put it another way, what the function gets is a pointer to the first element in the array, which is equivalent to a pointer to the entire array. We will avoid using this address-of syntax in order not to confuse passing an entire array with passing just one element of an array to be treated as output from a function, which we may also wish to do.

Program P-6.3 gives another example of using arrays. In this case, the program must read the following external data file (planets.dat) containing data about the sun and the planets:

```
Name      Dia (km) Distance(10^6 km)
Sun       1302000     0
Mercury      4878    57.9
Venus       12102   108
Earth       12760   150
Mars         6786   228
Jupiter    142800   778
Saturn     120660  1427
Uranus      52400  2870
Neptune     50460  4500
Pluto        2200  5900
```

These data will be stored in three *parallel arrays*, which means that a particular index in each array must always be associated with the same planet. For example, the third element (index 2 in C) of the name, diameter, and distance arrays must refer to the planet Venus.

parallel arrays

Even though it is easy to determine just by inspection that this file contains 10 data records, the code will treat it as a file of unknown length and must therefore look for the end-of-file mark. This kind of code is applicable to many programming problems, and it should be studied carefully. The program first uses fgets to read the header line in the data file and then, inside the loop, uses fscanf to read the data records. It uses status, the return value from fscanf, to look for the end-of-file mark.

P-6.3 [planets2.c]

```
#include <stdio.h>
#define NAME_LENGTH 8

void main()
```

```
{
  FILE *InFile;
  double distance[11],diameter[11];
  char name[NAME_LENGTH][11], one_line[81];
  char *line_ptr;
  int index,status;

  if( (InFile=fopen("planets.dat","rt")) != NULL)
  {
    printf("Opening file...\n");
    line_ptr=fgets(one_line,sizeof(one_line),InFile);
    index=0;
    while(1)
    {
      status=fscanf(InFile,"%s %lf %lf",name[index],
                    &distance[index],&diameter[index]);
      if (status == EOF) break;
      printf("(%2i) %-8s %10.0lf %10.1lf\n",index,name[index],
             distance[index],diameter[index]);
      index+=1;

    }
    printf("done...\n");
  }
  else printf("Trouble opening file...\n");
  fclose(InFile);
}
```

Running P-6.3

```
Opening file...
( 0) Sun        1302000        0.0
( 1) Mercury       4878       57.9
( 2) Venus        12102      108.0
( 3) Earth        12760      150.0
( 4) Mars          6786      228.0
( 5) Jupiter     142800      778.0
( 6) Saturn      120660     1427.0
( 7) Uranus       52400     2870.0
( 8) Neptune      50460     4500.0
( 9) Pluto         2200     5900.0
done...
```

Here's another example. Consider the basic statistics required to describe a set of measurements, the average m and standard deviation s, defined as

$$
m = \frac{\sum_{i=1}^{n} x_i}{n} \qquad s = \sqrt{\frac{\sum_{i=1}^{n} x_i^2 - \left(\sum_{i=1}^{n} x_i\right)^2 / n}{n-1}}
$$

The n − 1 (rather than n) in the denominator of the expression for s indicates that the statistics are for a sample taken from a presumably normal population whose true statistics, usually represented by μ and σ, are unknown. That is, these are "sample statistics" rather than "population statistics," and they are normally the correct ones to use in experimental work. The sample standard deviation is greater than the population standard deviation and takes into account the fact that, when taking measurements of a physical quantity, the population statistics for that quantity are not known because they require an infinite number of measurements.

In P-6.4, C's random number generator is used to create an array of uniformly distributed numbers in the range [0,1]. It then calculates the mean and standard deviation as though the number were normally distributed. (For comparison, see Exercise 11 in Chapter 4, in which a pair of uniformly distributed numbers is converted to a pair of normally distributed numbers.)

P-6.4 [statistc.c]

```
#include <stdio.h>
#include <stdlib.h> /* for random number generator */
#include <math.h>
#include <time.h> /* for seeding random number generator */
#define N_SAMPLES 100

/* function prototypes */
void get_data(double array[]);

void main()
{
  double data_array[N_SAMPLES];
  double sum_x=0.0, sum_x2=0.0;
  double average, std_dev;
  int i;

  get_data(data_array);
  for (i=0; i < N_SAMPLES; ++i)
  {
    printf("%lf\n",data_array[i]);
    sum_x=sum_x+data_array[i];
    sum_x2=sum_x2+data_array[i]*data_array[i];
  }
/*  printf("%lf  %lf  %lf\n",sum_x,sum_x2,(double)N_SAMPLES); */
  std_dev=sqrt((sum_x2-sum_x*sum_x/(double)N_SAMPLES)/
          ((double)N_SAMPLES-1.0));
  average=sum_x/(double)N_SAMPLES;
  printf(
      "average = %lf, standard deviation = %lf\n",std_dev,average);
}

void get_data(double data_array[])
{
  int i;
/* Reinitialize rand each time, using
   seed from system clock.
   Use 1 to get the same values every time. */
  srand((unsigned)time(NULL));
```

```
    for (i=0; i < N_SAMPLES; ++i)
        data_array[i]=(double)rand()/(double)RAND_MAX;
}
```

Running P-6.4

```
0.731132
0.499252
0.565935
0.986633
0.543277
...
0.716993
0.381603
0.071841
0.635365
0.338359
average = 0.495047, standard deviation = 0.282844
```

Problem Discussion

Program P-6.4 is a straightforward application of arrays. It is of particular interest because it shows how to use C's rand function to generate an array of pseudorandom real numbers uniformly distributed in the range [0,1]. If you have forgotten how the random number generator works, refer to the application in Chapter 4, Section 4.5.5. Don't forget to use an explicit type cast for either the numerator or denominator, or both, in this calculation. Otherwise, the integer division will be truncated to 0.

Typically for random number generators implemented as part of a programming language, the algorithm must be initialized (seeded) with a single random value that serves as the starting point in order to avoid producing the same sequence of pseudorandom numbers every time the program runs. In this code, the time library provides access to the system clock. A "tick" from this clock, extracted while the program is running, is essentially a random integer that can be used as the argument for srand, the function that seeds rand. Not all random number generating algorithms perform adequately in the statistical sense, so it may be necessary to test the randomness of the resulting sequence for certain kinds of applications. However, for any program encountered in an introductory programming course, you may assume that rand produces integers that really are random.

As noted in the comments in P-6.4, you should include the stdlib.h header file to use C's random number generator and the time.h header file to access the system clock.

6.4 Multidimensional Arrays

For the ozone problem discussed in Section 6.1, it was suggested that the natural way to represent the ozone data was with a rank two array in which one dimension represented days and the other represented hours. The declaration of multidimensional arrays is straightforward:

```
data_type array_name[first extent][second extent][...]
```

The dimension for each rank is enclosed in brackets. The ANSI C standard requires that a compiler support at least rank six arrays. However, it is unlikely that you will need to use more than rank three arrays; one reason is that multidimensional arrays can occupy a *lot* of memory. For example, the array A[10][10][10][10] requires 10,000 memory locations. Some C compilers will not support arrays of this size, even if they seem necessary for the algorithm.

For the ozone problem, the array could be declared like this:

```
#define MAX_DAYS 31
#define MAX_HOURS 24
...
int ozone[MAX_DAYS][MAX_HOURS];
```

It is always acceptable, and usually better programming style, to give the extent value for each array dimension in a #define directive so that changes in the extent for each array dimension are easy to modify later. In this case, you might argue that these particular extents—the maximum number of days in a month and the number of hours in the day—are unlikely to change. However, it is sometimes useful to test a program that manipulates a relatively large set of data with a smaller subset of those data, in which case it might be desirable to limit the extent of the array dimensions to smaller values during program development.

Remember that each array dimension has its own set of brackets, so that a reference to row 3, column 4 in array ozone must be written ozone[2][3]. It is a common mistake to write something like ozone[row,col], especially if you have written programs in some other language, but at least this mistake will generate a syntax error.

Once you have learned how to define multidimensional arrays, you need to know how to enter data into the elements of such arrays. In typical science and engineering problems, as noted previously, data for the kinds of problems that require the use of multidimensional arrays are often contained in external text files that must be accessed by a program for processing. We will examine this problem and its solution first by writing a simple demonstration program, P-6.5, to read data into a two-dimensional array, and then by writing a program to process data for the monthly ozone data problem discussed in Section 6.1.

P-6.5 expects a data file containing 12 numbers, which will be stored in a two-dimensional array representing a matrix of data containing three rows and four columns. What should the data file look like? First of all, we will assume that the data file contains *just* numbers. That is, there are no header lines or other text information in the file.

The obvious way to arrange the data file is in three rows containing four numbers each. Then the layout of the data will mirror their organization in the program. This choice, in turn, presumably mirrors the problem the program is intended to solve. However, it is not obvious that the nested for... loop in P-6.5 will read such a file successfully. In a Fortran program, for example, the corresponding loop structure and "read" command would imply that the data file contained only one value per line. Potential problems arise because each line of a text file contains an end-of-line mark. In Fortran, the READ statement (only approximately the equivalent of C's fscanf function) always reads past an end-of-line mark, so the Fortran equivalent of the code in P-6.5 would read only one value on a line regardless of how many values were actually present. In Pascal, to cite another example, there are different functions (read and readln) that can be used depending on whether you wish to read all the values on a line or just one value. However, in C, *the code in P-6.5 will work regardless of whether the values in the data file are arranged on one or more lines.* As a practical matter, the end-of-line mark is treated by C simply as "white space" separating the last number on one line from the first number on the next line. You can see this for yourself by trying P-6.5 first with the file readaray.da1, which contains one value per line, and then replacing readaray.da1 with readaray.da2, which contains the same values arranged in three lines containing four numbers each.

```
readaray.da1          readaray.da2
1.1                   1.1 1.2 1.3 1.4
1.2                   2.1 2.2 2.3 2.4
1.3                   3.1 3.2 3.3 3.4
1.4
2.1
2.2
2.3
2.4
3.1
3.2
3.3
3.4
```

P-6.5 [readaray.c]

```c
/* Demonstrate reading data into 2-D array. */
/* The data can be either one value per line (readaray.da1) or */
/* row-by-row (3 rows of 4 values each, see readaray.da2). */
#include <stdio.h>
#define N_ROWS 3
```

```
#define N_COLS 4
void main()
{
   FILE *infile;
   float data_array[3][4];
   int row,col;

   infile = fopen("readaray.da1","r");
   for (row=0; row < N_ROWS; row+=1)
   {
      for (col=0; col < N_COLS; col+=1)
         {
         fscanf(infile,"%f",&data_array[row][col]);
         printf("%5.1f",data_array[row][col]);
         }
      printf("\n");
   }
   fclose(infile);
}
```

Running P-6.5

```
1.1  1.2  1.3  1.4
2.1  2.2  2.3  2.4
3.1  3.2  3.3  3.4
```

Program P-6.5 operates identically in either case. Note that the code in P-6.5 assumes that the total number of values in the file is known ahead of time. If this weren't true, it would be necessary to include code to test for the end-of-file, as was done in P-6.3.

Finally, note how the new-line character (\n) is printed in a separate statement outside the inner loop in P-6.5. Thus the data are displayed row-by-row regardless of how they are arranged in the original data file.

Now we will return to the ozone problem. The data are contained in file ozone.dat. The file contains two header lines that describe the contents of the file and a third line that contains the number of days in the month. These three lines are then followed by hourly measurements for each day in the month. We will make two important assumptions about the records containing the hourly data:

(1) There are no missing data.
(2) The numerical values are separated by spaces only and not, for example, by commas.

Program P-6.6(a) shows how to read a file containing ozone measurements and store the values in a two-dimensional array for processing.

P-6.6(a) [ozone.c]

```c
/* Process ozone data. */
#include <stdio.h>
#define MAX_DAYS 31
#define MAX_HOURS 24
#define FILE_NAME "ozone.dat"

void main()
{
   char one_line[100];
   int day, hour, n_days;
   static int ozone[MAX_DAYS][MAX_HOURS];
   FILE *infile;

   infile=fopen(FILE_NAME,"r");
/* Read and print two header lines. */
   (void)fgets(one_line,sizeof(one_line),infile);
   printf("%s\n",one_line);
   (void)fgets(one_line,sizeof(one_line),infile);
   printf("%s\n",one_line);
/* Get days in month. */
   fscanf(infile,"%d",&n_days);
   printf("There are %d days in this month.\n",n_days);
/* Read ozone data. */
   for (day=0; day < n_days; ++day)
     for (hour=0; hour < MAX_HOURS; ++hour)
       fscanf(infile,"%i",&ozone[day][hour]);
   fclose(infile);
/* Display ozone data. */
   for (day=0; day < n_days; ++day)
   {
     printf(" (%2i)",day+1);
     for (hour=0; hour < MAX_HOURS; ++hour)
       printf("%3i",ozone[day][hour]);
     printf("\n");
   }
}
```

Running P-6.6(a)

```
Units: parts per billion

JULY 1990

There are 31 days in this month.
( 1) 48 55 47 43 42 39 38 38 40 43 50 59 65 62 56 55 48 45 40 39 31 28 28 25
( 2) 23 23 23 23 23 23 23 19 19 16 23 27 28 33 41 45 47 46 35 40 48 51 42 41 43
( 3) 43 42 41 33 26 18  9 19 34 41 42 56 71 67 70 79 85 88 82 67 69 63 43 45
( 4) 46 41 37 34 26 21 21 24 37 49 61 76 92111105113118118108 84 74 65 54 53
( 5) 40 26 27 31 25 19 29 40 48 56 78 93 95 98 97 89 49 41 32 32 19 19 14 10
( 6) 16 13 16 17 12  8  6  9 11 17 21 31 43 54 74 85 89 92 67 52 49 47 43 34
( 7) 13 16 15 20 20 17 16 17 18 20 24 32 44 57 68 73 80 65 61 58 47 42 40 39
( 8) 43 46 47 45 37 30 28 25 30 40 58 69 72 69 70 67 62 56 52 47 37 33 31 29
( 9) 27 23 23 28 26 23 21 19 22 25 35 50 65 98125138135109 61 42 21 25 25 14
(10) 10  4 15 20  8  2  5 13 21 35 39 36 44 58 65 70 82 73 67 65 45 29 38 30
(11) 13 16 17  7 10  9 14 16 12 12  9 14 18 18 22 27 32 29 28 33 36 30 27 19
(12) 17 10 15 12 26 15 18 10  8  5  6 10 15 19 23 10  8  9  3 16  7  1  2  3
(13)  7  4  1  9 14 12 10  7  4  4  3  3  6  6 11 17 18 12 11 21 20 19 17 10
(14)  8 19 15 17 14 18 15 17 20 19 20 24 26 30 30 30 32 29 26 15  8  7  8  9
(15) 12 12 13 12 10 12 15 18 22 25 26 27 31 30 33 28 29 31 30 35 34 30 35 31
(16) 35 30 30 28 24 18 10 12 19 26 35 50 61 67 68 69 63 58 56 56 46 45 47 49
(17) 45 39 31  5 24 13  4 16 33 46 68 78 84 78 92 79 82 77 75 72 61 44 49 35
(18) 24 17 19 15  5  3  3  9 20 37 64 78 81 96 99 95 88 82 81 77 68 58 49 38
(19) 32 28 30 32 17 21 16 20 26 44 67 88108110 97110102106107 97 84 69 54 54
(20) 76 64 56 43 34 26 21 23 26 30 37 52 76 82 85 78 75 96 92 67 52 54 46 45
(21) 41 34 36 36 31 26 25 25 32 40 47 59 66 75 74 74 64 54 45 46 52 39 35 27
(22) 15  4  4  7 10 10 11 17 25 32 43 52 80110111 98 80 56 72 72 66 58 54 46
(23) 44 44 42 38 40 38 32 28 34 47 43 54 68 66 48 45 48 48 48 52 45 43 31 19
(24) 22 25 27 25 26 20 16 13 16 25 30 39 42 54 64 69 71 69 64 59 49 50 44 41
(25) 43 21  2  2  4  4  8 14 24 32 41 40 49 59 68 75 79 75 71 59 27  6  5 10
(26) 20 33 36 35 32 29 26 32 33 35 45 53 62 67 74 88 92 85 85 65 64 67 54 41
(27) 31 26 22 13 14 11  8 12 16 15 20 23 22 17 26 36 36 23 24 42 34 26 14
(28) 17 10  7  5  3  4  6  8 11 13 16 17 26 28 31 37 36 26 20 20 21 21 17
(29) 20 15 20 15 12  9  9  5  8 17 22 22 27 33 39 49 51 47 48 42 34 32 37 44
(30) 36 39 33 33 23 18 11 13  8 18 29 45 54 69 77 81 89 96115112 98 62 37 15
(31) 12  9  7 10 11 12  8  5  7  9 15 27 29 55 64 72 52 31 33 25 19 20 26 28
```

Remember that the indices for a C representation of these data have values 0–30 and 0–23 rather than 1–31 and 1–24. Also, note that each dimension has its own set of brackets. This is different from the notation that you would probably use in algorithm design. For example, you might write (30,23) to represent data for 11pm on the 30th day of the month. However, neither (29,22) nor [29,22] will work in C; the array indices [29][22] represent 11pm on the 30th of the month.

For the compiler used to write P-6.6(a), an array of size 31 × 24 is too large to be stored with the usual declaration. The addition of the static keyword as part of the declaration causes the array to be stored in a different (and presumably larger) part of memory. You can include this reserved word with any array declaration.

The two header lines in ozone.dat are treated as strings. However, because there are spaces in the text of the header lines, fscanf won't work properly because, as pointed out in the discussion of P-6.5, fscanf doesn't read past the end-of-line mark. Consequently, P-6.6(a) uses fgets to read the header into the string variable one_line. This function *will* read the end-of-line mark and will also insert a new-line character (\n) as the last character in one_line. (That's why there is a blank line in the output of this program following the display of each of the first two header lines.) The (void) type cast in the fgets statements tells the compiler to ignore the return value from fgets, as we don't need it in this program.

The third line, which contains a single numerical value (the number of days in the month), is read with fscanf. Finally, the nested for... loop and fscanf are used to read and store the ozone data. The success of this approach depends on the two assumptions we made about the contents of the data file. If data were missing, or if the program had to check for extraneous characters in the file, the code to read the file would be *much* more complicated!

There is an important restriction that applies to using multidimensional arrays as parameters in functions. Consider P-6.6(b), which illustrates a modification of P-6.6(a) in which the code required to display the ozone data is given in a function.

P-6.6(b) [part of ozone_f.c]

```
void Display(int O[][24],int n);
...

/* Display ozone data. */
  Display(ozone,n_days);
  ...
}
void Display(int O[][24],int n) {
  int day,hour;

  for (day=0; day < n; ++day)
  {
    printf("(%2i)",day+1);
    for (hour=0; hour < MAX_HOURS; ++hour)
      printf("%3i",O[day][hour]);
    printf("\n");
  }
}
```

Only the *first* dimension can be left blank when a multidimensional array appears in a function's parameter list. In the ozone problem, this means there is really no choice about using an array in which days is the first dimension and hours is the second. If this order is used, the first dimension is "variable" in the sense that it is possible in principle to rewrite the source code to expand, or even to shrink, the ozone array to handle as many days as required to process the available data. However, the extent of the second dimension is fixed because *every* day will have 24 hours. In general, this restriction means that arrays have to be constructed so that the potentially variable dimension comes first. This requires careful planning when you design your algorithm.

6.5 Accessing Arrays With Pointers

Section 6.3 explained that when an array is passed to a function, the function actually gets the address of the location of the first element of the array. Or, to put it another way, what is passed is a pointer to the first element of the array. Although it's possible to write programs that don't explicitly acknowledge this special relationship between arrays and pointers, as the programs presented so far in this chapter have done, typical C programming style makes heavy use of pointers. A pointer-based approach to accessing arrays is illustrated in program P-6.7. This is a version of P-6.2 in which the name of the array (x) doesn't appear at all in any of the statements that assign values to the elements of the array or display those values. Instead, the elements of the array are accessed by manipulating the value of a pointer to the array. The pointer is declared and initialized so that it points to the first element:

```
double x[MAX_SIZE];
double *ptr=x;
```

The initialization of `ptr` along with its declaration is optional. The statements

```
double *ptr;
...
ptr=x;
```

would have the same effect. In fact, `ptr` is reset to x in an assignment statement twice later in the program. The operation of the assignment statement itself is a little different. Previously, an assignment meant, "Evaluate the expression on the right of the assignment operator and store it in the memory cell associated with the variable name on the left of the assignment operator." However, this assignment statement means, "Give the pointer on the left of the assignment operator a value equal to the memory location at which the array on the right of the assignment statement starts."

P-6.7 [arrays3.c]

```
#include <stdio.h>
#define MAX_SIZE 10

void ArrayModify(double a[]);

void main()
{
    int i;
    double x[MAX_SIZE];
    double *ptr=x; /* Initialize to beginning of array. */
    FILE *infile;

    infile=fopen("arrays.dat","r");
```

```
      for (i=1;i <= MAX_SIZE;i+=1)
      {
        fscanf(infile,"%lf",ptr++);
      }
      fclose(infile);
      ptr=x; /* Point to beginning of array. */
      for (i=1; i <= MAX_SIZE; i+=1)
        printf("%d %d %lf\n",i,ptr,*ptr++);
      ArrayModify(x);
      ptr=x;
      for (i=1; i <= MAX_SIZE; i+=1)
            printf("%d  %lf\n",i,*ptr++);
}

void ArrayModify(double *ptr)
{
      int i;

      for (i=1; i <= MAX_SIZE; i+=1)
      {
        *ptr=-(*ptr); /* The parentheses are optional. */
        ptr+=1;
      }
}
```

As a result of the declaration statement for `ptr` in P-6.7, in which a pointer is bound to the array x, it is now possible to access the elements of x by manipulating the pointer. A critical difference between P-6.7 and P-6.2 can be seen in the loop that fills the array with values from the `arrays.dat` file. In P-6.2, the loop looked like this:

```
for (i=0;i<MAX_SIZE;i+=1)
{
  fscanf(infile,"%lf",&x[i]);
}
```

In P-6.7, the loop looks like this:

```
for (i=1;i <= MAX_SIZE;i+=1)
{
  fscanf(infile,"%lf",ptr++);
}
```

In P-6.2, the loop counter starts at 0 and ends at `MAX_SIZE-1`. In P-6.7, the counter starts at 1 and ends at `MAX_SIZE`, which is incorrect when usual array notation is being used. The loop in P-6.7 has been written in this way (it wouldn't have to be different from the loop in P-6.2) to emphasize the fact that the individual array elements aren't mentioned by name in the loop and the loop counter is used *just* as a counter and not as an index. Instead, the pointer variable `ptr`, which has been initialized to point to the first element of x, is incremented inside the `fscanf` statement.

The statement executed inside the loop could also be written (perhaps a little more clearly) as

```
fscanf(infile,"%lf",ptr);
ptr+=1;
```

It's important to note that the & operator does *not* appear in front of ptr in fscanf because ptr is itself an address, not a value.

It might seem curious that incrementing operators can be used in statements like ptr++ or ptr+=1 that involve pointers. What does it mean to increment a pointer (using the ++ or += operators)? Up to now, incrementing operations have been applied only to scalar variables. However, when these operations are applied to a pointer, they increment (or decrement) the pointer by moving to the next (or previous) memory location appropriate to a particular data type. That is, the 1 appearing directly in the statement ptr+=1; or by implication in the statement ptr++; is interpreted not as the numerical value 1, but as "advance one memory location for the data type to which the pointer is bound." (The number of bytes in memory by which the pointer is advanced depends on the data type of the array elements.) Although you can do this as a matter of syntax with pointers to simple variables, the next or previous memory location wouldn't normally have any useful significance. Thus these operations make sense only when they are applied to pointers bound to arrays. In P-6.7, for example, incrementing (or decrementing) ptr results in ptr pointing to the next (or previous) element of x. The number of bytes by which ptr actually changes depends on the data type of the elements of x.

As you can see from the statement

```
printf("%d %d %lf\n",i,ptr,*ptr++);
```

it is possible to print the value of a pointer in C. This value is the address of the first byte in memory occupied by the current array element to which ptr is pointing. If the value of ptr is printed directly after it is initialized to x, it points to the first memory location occupied by the array. If you run this program on your own system, you can see that incrementing ptr increases its value by (probably) eight bytes, indicating that a type double variable occupies eight bytes in memory. This output also demonstrates that C stores elements in an array in contiguous memory locations, as you would expect. For the most part, information about the actual location of an array and its elements in memory falls into the "interesting, but..." category.

Finally, examine the header statement and prototype for function ArrayModify. In the prototype, the declaration is given as double a[], which indicates that the parameter represents an array. Also, when ArrayModify is called, the argument is the name of the array x. However, the parameter in the function implementation is a pointer to a quantity of type double. Although the declarations for this parameter may appear to be inconsistent, they are not. This is because C *automatically* interprets the name of an array in a function parameter list as a pointer to the first element of that array.

Regardless of the notation used, function ArrayModify expects as input a pointer bound to a value of type double. As long as this pointer contains the location of the first element of the array, ArrayModify can access all the other elements just by incrementing that pointer. Note that ArrayModify in P-6.7 contains no explicit array notation at all.

The warnings about array boundary violations apply when you're using pointers to access arrays just as they do when you're using explicit array notation. C does not include any mechanism for checking for such violations, regardless of the notation you're using. If you're not careful, your program can produce results that may look okay even though they're wrong, or you can crash your computer system. (Some operating systems are more vulnerable to crashes than others.)

It may seem awkward and unintuitive to access arrays by using pointers, but this notation is more descriptive of how C actually handles arrays. In fact, it is fair to say that array notation is simply a high-level translation of array operations that makes C a little easier to use as a procedural language because array notation is closer to the mathematical representation of arrays. It is common C programming practice to make use of pointers when dealing with arrays, and sometimes there are good reasons to do so. In Chapter 7, we will discuss more complex (and larger) data structures and arrays of those structures. If, for example, an array containing large data structures as its elements must be sorted, it may be more efficient to sort pointers to array elements rather than to sort the array elements themselves. However, for straightforward problems in which arrays are used to organize information, array notation remains the simpler and more desirable choice.

6.6 More About Strings

6.6.1 Strings as Arrays

A chapter on arrays may seem an odd place to discuss the string data type. Why here? Previously, we used strings of characters as a natural and very useful extension of the char data type. Now, however, we are in a position to develop a better understanding of strings because the notation for declaring a string implies that C treats strings as arrays of characters. For example, the declaration

```
char name[15];
```

means that the variable name is associated with an array of characters. That is, name is a pointer to the location containing the first character in the string. It should be clear now why, when a character string is read as input, the & operator is not used, as in this example:

```
printf("Enter your Social Security number (xxx-xx-xxxx) and age: ");
scanf("%s %i",ssn,&age);
```

The reason is that variable ssn is *already* an address because it is the name of an array of characters.

Because character strings are arrays, it is possible to apply array-like operations to their elements, but you must be careful. Consider P-6.8.

P-6.8 [strings.c]

```
/* STRINGS.C */

#include <stdio.h>
#include <string.h>

int main(void)
{
  char name[15];
  int i;

  printf("Enter your first and last name: ");
  scanf("%s",name);
  printf("length: %i\n",strlen(name));
  for (i=0; i<strlen(name); i++)
    printf("%c",name[i]);
  printf("\n");
  for (i=0; i<15; i++)
    printf("%4i",(int)name[i]);
  printf("\n");
  printf("Enter your first and last name: ");
  fflush(stdin);
  fgets(name,sizeof(name),stdin);
  printf("%s %i\n",name,strlen(name));
  return 0;
}
```

With the &s conversion specifier, the scanf function reads characters typed at the keyboard up to the first blank or end-of-line character (created by pressing the Enter key). Thus if you type David Brooks, the string saved by scanf will be just David. The first for... loop in P-6.8 displays this string one character at a time. The loop terminating condition is obtained from an intrinsic function, strlen, that counts the number of characters in the string—five, because David contains five letters. (String-handling functions will be discussed further in Section 6.6.2.) The second loop attempts to look at all 15 characters in the character array, based on the fact that the array has been declared as having extent 15. However, everything following the last letter before a blank space entered at the keyboard is "garbage;" the Brooks part of the typed input is nowhere to be found.

On the other hand, the fgets reads *everything* up to and including the end-of-line character, whether from the keyboard (the stdin input device) or from some other data source, and then automatically adds a null character (' \0 ') to the end of those characters. Thus strlen returns a value of 13 if David Brooks is entered for the name—12 characters, including the space between the first and last name, plus the character generated by pressing the Enter or Return key. The differences between scanf and fscanf can be important (and frustrating if you forget them) when you use these functions in your programs.

6.6.2 String Functions

In order to use strings successfully, you must become familiar with the several intrinsic functions for dealing with strings. These are sometimes required in unexpected places because of the way C treats strings. For example, suppose you wish to compare two strings for equality. The obvious code is

```
if (string1 == string2)...; /* won't work! */
```

However, this won't work because the names string1 and string2 are *addresses* (pointers to the first character in the string), and not *values*. Although it would certainly be possible to write a compiler that understood this expression in context, the C language typically does not make this kind of concession to programmers. Instead, there is a separate intrinsic function for comparing two strings; it is included in Table 6.1, which describes several functions for manipulating strings. All functions in Table 6.1 require inclusion of the <string.h> header file. There are often different or additional functions in a particular implementation of C, so if you have problems using these functions or wish to make use of additional string manipulation capabilities, you must consult the documentation for your version of C.

Table 6.1. Some intrinsic functions for manipulating strings

Function Name and Parameters	Description
strcat(S1,S2)	For null-terminated strings, appends S2 to the end of S1, adds a null character, and returns modified S1.
strcmp(S1,S2)	For null-terminated strings, compares S1 to S2. Returns 0 if S1 and S2 are identical, a negative value if S1 is less than S2, and a positive value if S1 is greater than S2.
strcpy(S1,S2)	For null-terminated strings, copies S2 to S1 and returns modified S1.
strlen(S1)	Returns length of S1, not counting null termination character.
strncat(S1,S2)	For null-terminated strings, appends at most n characters of S2 to S1, adds a null character, and returns modified S1.
strncmp(S1,S2,n)	Compares at most the first n characters of S1 and S2, with return values identical to strcmp.
strncpy(S1,S2,n)	For null-terminated strings, copies n characters of S2 to S1 and returns modified S1. If n is less than length of S2, a null character is not automatically appended to end of S1. If n is greater than length of S2, S1 is padded with null characters.

6.7 Applications

6.7.1 Cellular Automata and Sierpinski Triangles

1 *Define the problem.*

A topic of great interest in biology and engineering is the study of artificial organisms called automata. These can be thought of as artificial life forms that, with the aid of a set of rules for reproducing themselves and dying, appear to be self-organizing. When rules are incorporated into a computer program, they can lead to surprising patterns, some of which can also be derived from fractal theory. One interesting pattern is the Sierpinski triangle, illustrated in Figure 6.1.

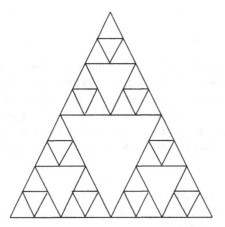

Figure 6.1. A Sierpinski triangle.

When a single cell—represented by an asterisk—is given an appropriate set of organizing rules, it will propagate into multiple cells in a pattern that resembles a Sierpinski triangle. The rules are:

> For cell i, if cell i − 1 is occupied and cells i and i + 1 are not, or if cell i − 1 is empty and cell i + 1 is occupied, then an organism will appear in cell i in the next generation. Otherwise the cell will be empty.

Write a program that uses these rules to produce a pattern that looks like a Sierpinski triangle.

2 *Outline a solution.*

1. Consider an array of cells. The contents of each cell are represented by a single character. When a cell is alive, it will contain an asterisk; when it's not, it will contain a blank space. Start with an initial population that consists of a single live cell somewhere near the middle of the array. Display this state by printing the contents of the array as a single line of output.
2. Now apply the organizing rules, encoded as boolean expressions, to get from this initial state to the next state.
3. Display this new state.
4. Repeat steps 2 and 3 for a specified number of generations.

3 Design an algorithm.

There is one tricky part to implementing this algorithm: The tests to determine the contents of a cell in the next generation must be applied to a *copy* of the current generation. Otherwise, a cell that will not be occupied until the next generation may be modified so that it will already appear to be populated in the current generation, or a cell that will be empty in the next generation will no longer be occupied in the current generation, thereby affecting the evaluation of adjacent cells.

```
DEFINE (logical arrays cell(40), old_cell(40); character array ch(40);
        # of generations; i and j as loop counters)
INITIALIZE arrays cell = false
ASSIGN cell(20) = true (Put an organism in the middle.)
WRITE (0 and ch) (Display generation 0.)
 ASSIGN  n = 15 (number of generations)
LOOP (for j = 1 to n)
        (Apply the propagation rules.)
        ASSIGN old_cell = cell (Make temp copy.)
        LOOP (for i = 2 to 39 ) (Stay away from ends of array.)
                (Apply rules...)
                IF (old_cell(i-1) & not(old_cell(i)) & not(old_cell(i+1)))
                        OR (not(old_cell(i-1)) & old_cell(i+1))
                THEN
                        cell(i) = true
                ELSE
                        cell(i) = false
        END LOOP
        (Display new generation.)
        LOOP (for i = 1 to 40)
                IF (cell(i) = true) THEN WRITE("*")
                ELSE WRITE(' ')
        END LOOP
END LOOP
```

4 Convert the algorithm into a program.

P-6.9 [sierpins.c]

```c
/* One-dimensional cellular automata with rule that generates
   a Sierpinski triangle. */

#include <stdio.h>
#define SIZE 40
#define N_CYCLES 15

void Display(int a[],int size);
void Update(int a[],int size);

int main(void)
{
  int a[SIZE],i;

  for (i=0; i<SIZE; i++)
    a[i]=0;
  a[SIZE/2]=1;
  printf("Generation  0:  ");
  Display(a,SIZE);
  for (i=1; i<= N_CYCLES; i++) {
    Update(a,SIZE);
    printf("Generation %2i:  ",i);
    Display(a,SIZE);
  }
  return 0;
}
void Update(int a[], int size)
{
  int old_a[SIZE],a_1,a0,a1,i;

  for (i=0; i<size; i++)
    old_a[i]=a[i];
  for (i=1; i<size-1; i++)
    a[i]=(old_a[i-1] && !old_a[i] && !old_a[i+1])
      || (!old_a[i-1] && old_a[i+1]);
}

void Display(int a[],int size)
{
  int i;
  for (i=0; i<size; i++)
    if (a[i] == 1) printf("*");
    else printf(" ");
  printf("\n");
}
```

Running P-6.9

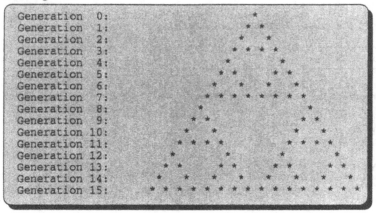

```
Generation  0:                              *
Generation  1:                           *  *
Generation  2:                        *     *
Generation  3:                     *  *  *  *
Generation  4:                  *        *
Generation  5:               *  *     *  *
Generation  6:            *     *     *     *
Generation  7:         *  *  *  *  *  *  *  *
Generation  8:      *                          *
Generation  9:   *  *                       *  *
Generation 10:   *     *                 *     *
Generation 11:   *  *  *  *           *  *  *  *
Generation 12:   *        *        *        *
Generation 13:   *  *     *  *     *  *     *  *
Generation 14:   *     *     *     *     *     *     *
Generation 15:   *  *  *  *  *  *  *  *  *  *  *  *  *  *  *  *
```

5 *Verify the operation of the program.*

The printed output of P-6.9 either will look like a Sierpinski triangle or it won't. An incorrect implementation of the propagation rules will yield some other perhaps equally interesting pattern.

Problem Discussion

This problem presents an ideal opportunity to use boolean (logical) data types because there are only two possible states for a cell—occupied or empty. However, because C lacks a separate boolean data type, such a representation must be simulated; P-6.9 uses 1s and 0s.

Note how the relational and logical operators are used in P-6.9. In keeping with the suggestion made in Chapter 3 that learning the precedence rules for these operators is a thankless task, you might feel compelled to add some parentheses. Alternatively, you can simply try writing the expression with a minimum of parentheses and see what happens; the worst outcome is that you will get an unintended result, in which case you can simply rewrite the code.

It may seem amazing that such a well-organized pattern can result from following a few simple rules. It would be interesting to apply these rules to different starting configurations containing more than one organism, or to change the propagation rules.

6.7.2 Probability Analysis for Quality Control of Manufacturing Processes

This application makes specific use of how C treats strings of characters as arrays of characters.

1 Define the problem.

A manufacturer's experience has shown that 10 percent of all integrated circuits (ICs) will be defective. Because of this high failure rate, a quality control engineer monitors the manufacturing process by testing random samples every day. What is the probability that:

(a) Exactly two ICs in a sample of 10 will be defective?
(b) At least two will be defective?
(c) No more than two will be defective?

2 Outline a solution.

You are not expected to know how to solve this problem, even in principle, unless you have had a probability and statistics course. However, you should be able to write the source code once you know what the solution is.

(a) The probability that, for example, the first two ICs in a sample of 10 will be defective is $(0.1)^2(0.9)^8 = 0.004305$. However, there are $_{10}C_2 = 45$ possible combinations of two defective and eight good ICs. From probability theory, the number of combinations of n things taken k at a time is

$$_nC_k = n!/[k!(n - k)!]$$

where ! indicates the factorial function. Therefore, the probability that any two ICs in a sample of 10 will be defective is

$$P(=2) = {}_{10}C_2(0.1)^2(0.9)^8 = (45)(0.004305) = 0.1937$$

(b) The probability of finding at least two defective ICs is equal to 1 minus the probability of finding 0 defective ICs minus the probability of finding 1 defective IC:

$$P(\geq 2) = 1 - {}_{10}C_0(0.1)^0(0.9)^{10} - {}_{10}C_1(0.1)^1(0.9)^9 = 0.2639$$

(Remember that $0!=1$ by definition.)

(c) The probability of finding no more than two defective ICs is

$$P(\leq 2) = {}_{10}C_0(0.1)^0(0.9)^{10} + {}_{10}C_1(0.1)^1(0.9)^9 + {}_{10}C_2(0.1)^2(0.9)^8 = 0.9298$$

There are several approaches that could be taken to writing a program to solve this problem. One solution would be simply to "hard code" the required calculations. This program would need to include, as a minimum, a user-defined function to calculate the factorial function.

However, in the context of C's string manipulation capabilities discussed in this chapter, there is a more elegant solution. The program described here will include user-defined functions for calculating combinations *and* a function for calculating factorials. Then, the user will type a character string that can be parsed to yield values to use as arguments for function calls and for the other calculations that are required. For example, for part (b) of the problem, the user could type

```
1-c(10,0,.1)-c(10,1,.1)
```

This character string would result in the evaluation of the expression $P(\geq 2)$, as shown above. The first two values inside the parentheses will be used as arguments for a function to calculate the combinations of n things taken k at a time. The third value is the probability of a defective IC. The probability of a good IC (0.9) is just 1 minus this value.

The key to the program is to enclose the desired numerical values inside parentheses. If your program then searches for a left parenthesis and its matching right parenthesis, the characters inside that set of parentheses can be copied into a string and read with sscanf. This probably sounds more difficult than it actually is. (As you will see, the C code to do this isn't really very hard to write.)

Note that such a program doesn't know how to solve probability problems. It just performs the required calculations based on user input. Also, because the magnitude of n! grows rapidly with n, there may be some restrictions on the size of the sample if default int data types are used for n and k.

3 *Design an algorithm.*

DEFINE *(character string (a); integers: length of string, loop counter (i),*
n and k, sign (+1 or -1), location of a left parenthesis;
probability, prob_a (real numbers).
(NOTE: prob_a is the probability that a single unit will be defective.
"probability" is the probability that the event defined by the string will
occur.)
WRITE *(Prompt user for string. Give "syntax" example.)*
READ *(a)*
INITIALIZE *probability = 0*
sign = 1
(Values in parentheses after string variable refer to character position,
not to C array indices.)
IF *a(1:1) = '1'* **THEN ASSIGN** *probability = 1*
LOOP *(through the string, one character at a time)*
NOTE:
a(i:j) means a substring consisting of j characters starting at position i.
    CHOOSE *(based on value of a(i:1)*
      '+' **ASSIGN** *sign = 1*
      '−' **ASSIGN** *sign = -1*
      '(' **ASSIGN** *left = i*
      ')' *process substring:*
         READ(a(left+1:i-1),*)n,k,prob_a
         INCREMENT *probability = probability+sign•C(n,k)•prob_a^k •*
                                (1 − prob_a)^{(n-k)}
        WRITE *(n,k,C(n,k) (optional)*
    (end IF...)
END LOOP
WRITE *(probability)*

4 *Convert the algorithm into a program.*

P-6.10 [`prob.c`]

```
/* Evaluate probabilities by parsing a string expression and
   performing the implied calculations. */

#include <stdio.h>
```

```
#include <string.h>
#include <math.h>

double ParseString(char a[]);
void SubString(char a[],int left,int right,char sub_a[]);

long unsigned Fact(int n) {
  long unsigned prod=(long unsigned)1;
  int i;

  if (n>1) for (i=2; i<=n; i++) prod*=(long unsigned)i;
  return prod;
}
int C(int n,int k) {
  int c;
  c=(int)(Fact(n)/Fact(k)/Fact(n-k));
  printf("C(%3i,%3i) = %3i\n",n,k,c);
  return c;
}

int main(void)
{
  char a[80];
  double probability;

  printf(
      "Enter expression to be evaluated (no syntax checking).\n");
  printf("Example: 1-c(10,0,.2)-c(10,1,.2)\n");
  printf("----> ");
  scanf("%s",a);
  probability=ParseString(a);
  printf("probability = %lf\n",probability);
  return 0;
}


double ParseString(char a[])
{
  int sign,left,right,i,n,k;
  char b[10];
  double probability=0.,prob_a;

  if (a[0] == '1') probability=1.;
  sign=1;
  for (i=0; i<strlen(a); i++) {
    switch(a[i]) {
      case '+':
      sign=1;
      break;
      case '-':
      sign=-1;
      break;
      case '(':
      left=i;
      break;
      case ')':
      SubString(a,left+1,i-1,b);
      sscanf(b,"%i,%i,%lf",&n,&k,&prob_a);
      probability+=sign*(double)C(n,k)*pow(prob_a,(double)k)*
                   pow(1.-prob_a,(double)(n-k));
```

```
        break;
        default:; /* Ignore everything else. */
    }
  }
  return probability;
}
void SubString(char a[],int left,int right, char b[])
/*Create substring of a starting at "left" and ending at "right."*/
{
  int i,i_b=-1;
  for (i=left; i<=right; i++) {
    i_b++;
    b[i_b]=a[i];
  }
  b[i_b+1]='\0';
}
```

Running P-6.10

```
Enter expression to be evaluated (no syntax checking).
Example: 1-c(10,0,.2)-c(10,1,.2)
----> 1-c(10,0,.1)-c(10,1,.1)
C( 10,  0) =   1
C( 10,  1) =  10
probability = 0.263901
```

5 *Verify the operation of the program.*

This program needs to be checked carefully by hand to ensure both that the user-defined functions work properly and that the character string is interpreted correctly. It's easy to be confused by probability calculations, which sometimes produce counterintuitive results, so it takes some time to achieve a high level of confidence in the answers produced by this program.

Problem Discussion

P-6.10 allows you to do each of the probability calculations specified in the problem statement, as well as others. Both the required values and the algebraic form of the calculations are given as user input, which makes the program versatile. By forcing the user to specify how the user-defined combination function C is to be used, the program is actually simplified. Instead of having to know a lot about probability calculations, all the program has to do is use the general-purpose functions in a user-specified way. Note that, although the c's in the suggested user response string (as in c(10,1,.1)) make the input look more algebraic, they are optional. Only the balanced left and right parentheses are required for the program to work.

The program doesn't perform any syntax checking on the user's input. In particular, it assumes that every left parenthesis is matched by a right parenthesis and that the characters inside a set of parentheses can be read as three numerical values with the specified format conversion. This means that the values must be separated by commas and a comma must directly follow each of the first two numbers, with no intervening blanks.

Choosing appropriate data types and using type casting are extremely important in P-6.10. The factorial function has type long unsigned because even 8! may be too big for an int variable in some C implementations. However, the number of combinations resulting from dividing possibly large factorials is unlikely to be too large for an int variable, so the C function is type int.

6.7.3 Parsing a String Containing an Unknown Number of Numerical Values

In this application, we will return to the problem discussed in Section 2.3, in which we wrote a program to do some simple processing on a file of "station reports" using this data file:

```
1001 14 17.7 13.3 12.9 19.9 11 9 20
1002 17.7
1003 14 15 16 17 18 19 20
1001 4.4 5.5 6.6
1004 14 15 17.1 18.1
1004 11.1 12.1 13.3 4.4 8.8
1005 39 38 37 36 35 34 33 32
```

The integer value is interpreted as a station ID, and the real numbers are interpreted as measurements reported by that station. In Section 2.3, a restriction placed on this file was that a report could contain no more than eight measurements. This restriction made it easy to read each report using fscanf (see P-2.8 in Section 2.3):

```
in=fopen("stations.dat","r");
while(1) {
  line_ptr=fgets(one_line,sizeof(one_line),in);
  if (line_ptr == NULL) break;
  one_line[strlen(one_line)-1]='\0';
  printf("%s\n",one_line);
  status=sscanf(one_line,"%i %f %f %f %f %f %f %f %f",
    &ID,&x,&x,&x,&x,&x,&x,&x,&x);
  n_reports=n_reports+1;
  n_measurements=n_measurements+(status-1);
}
fclose(in);
```

The variable status returned from sscanf tells the program how many measurements (status-1) were actually found in each report. With this restriction, it is also easy to save each measurement value simply by using an array containing no more than eight values:

```
float x[8];
...
    status=sscanf(one_line,"%i %f %f %f %f %f %f %f %f",
              &ID,&x[0],&x[1],&x[2],&x[3],&x[4],&x[5],&x[6],&x[7]);
```

However, it is not so easy to process the station reports if your program does not know ahead of time the maximum number of measurements in each report. Because there is no limit on the number of measurements in a report, it is no longer feasible to write an appropriate format for sscanf. To solve this problem, we will make use of some relatively obscure string manipulation functions—strcspn and strspn. Program P-6.11 reads the stations.dat data file and extracts numerical values when it is unknown ahead of time how many numerical values there will be in the string. The only requirement imposed on the string is that the numerical values be separated by one or more spaces. (Compare this code to that of P-2.8.)

P-6.11 [extract.c]

```
#include <stdio.h>
#include <string.h>
int main(void) {
  char a[80],separators[]=" ",*p;
  int ID;
  float x;
  FILE *in;
  in=fopen("stations.dat","r");
  while (1) {
    p=fgets(a,sizeof(a),in);
    if (p == NULL) break;
    sscanf(p,"%i",&ID);
    printf("%i",ID);
    p+=strspn(p,separators);

    while (1) {
      p+=strcspn(p,separators);
      if (*p == 0) break;
      sscanf(p,"%f",&x);
      printf(" %5.1f",x);
      p+=strspn(p,separators);
    }
    printf("\n");
  }
  fclose(in);
  return 0;
}
```

The intrinsic functions strspn and strcspn allow C to search for a user-specified set of characters within a null-terminated string (in this case, just one character—a blank space—is involved) and position a pointer within the string at the first matching (strcspn) or nonmatching (strspn) character. Then the program can locate the beginning of a numerical value (with strcspn), read that value using sscanf, reposition the pointer to the end of the numerical value (with strspn), read another value, and so forth.

This problem has a somewhat obscure relationship to arrays. However, note how P-6.11 makes use of the fact that the name of the character array a is equivalent to a pointer to that array. This equivalence is established in the calls to fgets. (The call to fgets also appends the control character '\0' to the end of the array to create a properly terminated character string.) Thereafter, access to the character elements of the array is through the pointer p rather than through an index notation. The pointer is easy to manipulate and C does not care where in the character string the pointer is positioned. Advancing the pointer loses the characters positioned to the left of the pointer. In general, it's certainly not a good idea to lose part of an array in this way, but it is okay in this code because when it occurs, all the values to the left of the pointer have already been processed.

6.8 Debugging Your Programs

There are many pitfalls in using arrays. Many of these are syntax errors that will be detected by your compiler and can easily be fixed. These errors are most likely to involve inappropriate references to array elements, and they can be a nagging problem if you have done any programming in some other language. The references A(1,1), A[1,1], A(1)(1) will all generate syntax errors, assuming that A[1][1] is what you meant to write.

The major hidden problem with C arrays is array boundary violations. As noted in this chapter, the C standard does not provide a way to check for such violations, which can have serious consequences in a program. It is not uncommon for programs to appear to work even though they produce incorrect answers. Hence, the responsibility for using arrays falls directly on the programmer.

With multidimensional arrays, a major source of problems is incorrect use of array indices in the logical sense—interchanging row and column indices, for example. No programming language can detect this kind of error because interchanging a row and column index might be precisely what a programmer intends to do. Again, because of C's lack of array boundary checking, certain index interchanges that generate undefined array element references, and which might be detectable in some other language, will go unreported in C. The best way to avoid such logical errors is to use meaningful names for the indices of multidimensional arrays—row and col rather than i and j, for example.

Loop structures, and especially count-controlled loops, go hand in hand with arrays. The nested loop structures required to access multidimensional arrays can be confusing to write and debug. It is important always to use unique variable names for counter variables in each level of the loop and never to reassign loop counter variables within their loops. On the other hand, it is good style to reuse loop counters in order to avoid a proliferation of unnecessary variable declarations for *sequential* (rather than nested) loop structures.

Finally, it is tempting to use arrays even when a problem does not require them. This should be done sparingly. The programming overhead required to manage arrays in a program, and the potential for errors, argue for using scalar variables whenever possible. For example, if a problem can be solved simply by reading values from a file and performing some kind of one-time processing of those values, then it is unnecessary and somewhat misleading to store the values in an array. However, if the problem requires multiple uses of data values or if it is likely that the problem statement may change so that additional access to the values will be needed, then it makes sense to define array structures for storing values as they are being read from a file.

6.9 Exercises

1. Referring to Section 2.3 and the problem addressed by program P-2.8, use a two-dimensional array to modify P-2.8 so the output includes the total number of reports from each station and the total number of measurements for each station. Assume that there will be no more than 11 stations with IDs 1000 through 1010 and, as before, no more than 8 measurements per report. (Alternatively, you can use the approach to reading reports demonstrated in P-6.11 from the application in Section 6.7.3.) Make use of the ID numbers to generate appropriate array element references. [station2.c]

2. A bored postal employee is playing with a row of mailboxes. Initially, all the boxes are closed. Then, starting with the second box, the employee opens every second box. Then, starting with the third box, the employee opens every third box if it's closed and closes it if it's open. Then, starting with the fourth box,... and so forth. When the employee gets to the end of the line of mailboxes, which ones are still closed?
Hint: Use an array of 1s and 0s to represent the state of the boxes, with 1 representing a closed box; 40 or so elements are sufficient to see the pattern. [mailbox.c]

3. A table contains two columns of numerical values. The first column gives values of an independent variable and the second column gives values of the corresponding dependent variable. In engineering applications, it is often required to interpolate between tabulated values. You can hold a table of such values in two arrays. Suppose array X holds n values of an independent variable and array Y holds n values of a tabulated dependent variable. Write a program that accepts a value of an independent variable x, where $X(1) \leq x \leq X(n)$, and then interpolates a value of y for that value of x.

The formula for calculating y by linearly interpolating between values y_1 and y_2 for a value of x that lies between corresponding values of the independent variable x_1 and x_2 is

$$y = y_1 + (y_2 - y_1)\frac{(x - x_1)}{(x_2 - x_1)}$$

Use these values to test your program:

x	y
5.0	5.9
10.0	6.6
15.0	7.1
20.0	8.3
25.0	10.0
30.0	12.2

In your program, make sure that when the user provides a value of x, it lies within the limits of the tabulated values of the independent variable; that is, it is not allowed to extrapolate past the tabulated values in either direction. Make sure to test your program for values of x at each end of the table. That is, for the data shown here, test the program when x = 5 and when x = 30, as well as at intermediate values of x.

Hint: Separate this problem into two parts. First, determine the two positions in the table between which the interpolation will be done. Then do the interpolation. [interp2.c]

4. When a time sequence of measurements is made on a noisy system, it is often desired to smooth the data so that trends are easier to spot. One simple smoothing technique is a so-called unweighted moving average. Suppose a data set consists of n values. These data can be smoothed by taking a moving average of m points, where m is some number significantly less than n. The average is unweighted because old values count just as much as newer values. The formula for calculating the ith smoothed value S_i is

$$S_i = (\sum_{j=i-m+1}^{i} x_j)/m , \quad i \geq m$$

Figure 6.2 shows an unweighted moving average with m = 0 for a data set of 100 random numbers in the range [0,200]. A moving average does smooth these data, but because the data are random, by definition there shouldn't be any trend to spot.

The algorithm for calculating a moving average over m values for a data set containing n values is:

1. Calculate the sum of the first m points. The first average is sum/m.

2. For i = m + 1 to n, add the ith value to the sum and subtract the $(i-m)^{th}$ value. Then calculate the average for this new sum.

3. Repeat Step 2 until i = n. If the data set contains n points, there will be n – m + 1 moving average calculations.

Write a subroutine that calculates and displays a moving average over a specified number of points for a one-dimensional array of specified size. Store the results in a second array of the same size. For a moving average over m points, the first m-1 elements of the second array should be set to 0. Test the subroutine in a program that generates an array of random numbers and smoothes that array with the moving average subroutine. [move_avg.c]

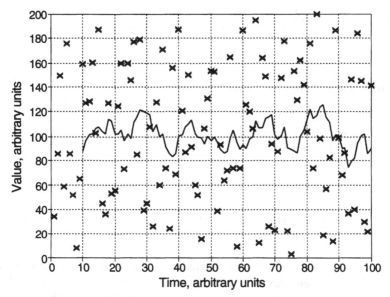

Figure 6.2. Unweighted moving average with m=10 for 100 random values.

5. Simulation problems often require that values be selected randomly from a predefined set. This is a trivial problem if the same value can be used more than once. More care is required if each value in a set of n values can be used only once, or to put it another way, if it is required that after n values have been used, every value in the set has been used once. The latter problem is analogous to dealing cards randomly from a deck.

Suppose a deck of cards is represented by the integer values 1–52. One way to shuffle this deck is to use a loop to swap every card in the deck with another randomly chosen card. It is of no concern that cards can be swapped more than once and that a card can be swapped with itself. Here is an algorithm to swap a pair of cards:

ASSIGN temp = card(i)
          index = random #, 0-51
          card(i) = card(index)
          card(index) = temp

Note that the array *elements* have values from 1 to 52, but the array *indices* have values from 0 to 51. Incorporate this algorithm into a complete program that will deal four random hands of 13 cards each. [`carddeck.c`]

6. Consider the following main function that tests a user-defined function for finding the largest element in an array:

```
#include <stdio.h>
int get_max(int a[],int n);

int main(void)
{
   int a[]={1,2,3,15,4,6};
   printf("%i\n",get_max(a,5));
   return 0;
}
int get_max(int a[],int n) {
   static int max=-1000000;
/* Put your code here. */


}
```

(a) Write a function that returns the position of the largest element in array a. Use a `for...` loop.

(b) Write a *recursive* function that returns the position of the largest element in array a. To implement this code, you need to use the `static` reserved word when a variable is declared in a function that is called more than once. For example, the statement

```
static int max=0;
```

in a function results in the initialization of variable max to 0 only *once*, the first time the function is called. The variable will *not* be reinitialized on subsequent calls to the function. Specifically, the variable will not be reinitialized on subsequent recursive calls to the function. [arraymax.c]

7. Consider the following program, the purpose of which is to linearly interpolate values in a one-dimensional array.

```
/* Interpolate values along a one-dimensional array. */
#include <stdio.h>
#include <math.h>
#define N 10

void interpolate(float a[],int n);

int main(void)
{
   float a[N];
   int i;

   for (i=0; i<N; i++) a[i]=0.;
   a[0]=10.;
   a[9]=100.;
   for (i=0; i<N; i++) printf("%6.1f",a[i]);
   printf("\n");
   interpolate(a,N);
   for (i=0; i<N; i++) printf("%6.1f",a[i]);
   printf("\n");

   return 0;
}

void interpolate(float a[],int n) {



}
```

The program specifies the values at each end of the array, which are fixed. Then it calls function interpolate. For this example, with an array of size 10, the program should print

```
  10.0   0.0   0.0   0.0   0.0   0.0   0.0   0.0   0.0 100.0
  10.0  20.0  30.0  40.0  50.0  60.0  70.0  80.0  90.0 100.0
```

You must implement an iterative solution with a do... while loop. For each trip through this loop, use a for... loop to recalculate the inner elements of the array (in this case, elements with indices 1 through 8) according to this algorithm:

(1) Set each inner element equal to the average of the preceding and following elements.

(2) Exit the do... while loop when the new value of the middle element in the array differs from its previous value by less than some small specified amount. Regardless of whether the value of n passed as an argument is even or odd, you can define the middle element as having the index mid=n/2, where mid is a variable defined locally inside function interpolate.

Note, however, that the specified terminating condition for the do... while loop will not work if array element 0 has a value of 0. This is because the middle element will keep its original initial value of 0 through the first iteration and will therefore terminate the loop after only one iteration.

Physically, you can think of this program as estimating the steadystate temperature distribution along a slender uniform rod, each end of which is held at a fixed temperature. Clearly, there are simpler ways to do linear interpolation. However, this algorithm is relatively simple to modify for other than linear interpolation. and for problems involving two-dimensional interpolations. (See Exercise 13 below.) [interpol.c]

8. The intrinsic function strncpy copies a specified number of characters from one string into another string, starting at the beginning of the "from" string. (See Table 6.1.) Write a function that copies n characters from string a into string b, starting at any specified character. The prototype for such a function could look like this:

```
void sub_string(char a[],char b[],start,n);
```

The variable start should refer to an array index. That is, to start copying at the first character of string a, start should have a value of 0, not 1.

This function prototype is different from strncpy's because the arguments are reversed—string a is the "from" string and string b is the "to" string—and because sub_string does not have a return value. String b should always include a terminating character ('\0') even though the string returned by strncpy may not. If you like, you can make the prototype for this function more like that of strncpy, even though it seems more useful for the copied string to include a null terminating character.[5] Be sure to write a short program to test and verify your function. [substrng.c]

9. Write a program that declares a type double two-dimensional array with extents [SIZE][SIZE+1], where SIZE is a #define constant. Fill the array,

---

[5]Author's note: the prototype of sub_string is the way it is simply because that's the way I prefer it; the strncpy syntax seems backwards to me.

except for the righthand column, with random numbers. Use the righthand column to hold the average of the numbers in the each row. Display the entire array, including the column that holds the row averages. You can assume SIZE is small enough that each row of the array can be stored on a single line.

10. Consider file tempphil.dat, which contains average monthly temperatures from Philadelphia for the years 1960-1990.

```
Average Temperature (deg F)
60    34.2 35.4 32.7 56.7 61.2 70.6 73.3 74.5 67.3 54.8 45.5 27.6
61    25.0 34.0 43.1 49.8 58.6 69.9 75.6 73.5 71.5 55.7 45.2 31.0
62    30.0 30.4 40.5 52.0 64.1 71.7 72.0 72.0 63.1 56.3 42.1 31.0
63    27.5 26.5 42.9 52.5 60.2 70.4 76.0 71.2 62.8 57.1 48.0 27.9
64    33.0 31.8 42.7 50.8 65.1 72.4 76.6 72.2 67.2 52.6 47.1 37.5
65    29.2 33.3 37.6 49.0 65.5 70.0 74.1 73.1 69.2 53.7 44.2 37.0
66    29.1 31.5 42.5 47.8 59.5 72.1 77.9 74.8 65.2 53.1 46.8 35.5
67    36.0 29.0 38.5 51.7 55.9 72.1 76.6 75.1 67.0 56.8 42.8 38.5
68    28.9 30.4 44.4 54.6 59.7 71.2 77.1 77.8 69.4 58.1 45.6 32.3
69    29.8 32.0 39.7 55.3 64.6 73.4 75.1 75.2 67.2 55.0 44.4 33.5
70    24.5 33.1 38.3 51.5 64.9 71.6 76.9 76.7 72.0 60.1 48.2 35.8
71    27.8 36.1 40.7 51.6 60.9 74.3 77.4 75.3 71.6 63.5 46.1 41.6
72    35.1 32.4 40.7 49.7 63.6 68.7 77.1 76.0 69.2 52.7 43.6 39.9
73    34.4 33.6 47.2 53.4 60.3 74.6 77.9 78.8 70.7 59.2 48.0 38.6
74    35.9 31.7 43.3 55.8 62.4 70.3 76.9 76.8 68.1 54.8 48.5 39.4
75    37.3 35.8 41.2 48.7 66.6 72.2 76.6 77.1 66.6 61.2 52.7 36.9
76    28.7 40.9 46.3 56.6 62.7 75.2 75.3 74.8 67.3 52.5 39.9 30.3
77    20.2 33.6 48.8 57.2 65.8 68.6 77.8 76.2 69.9 54.3 46.4 32.6
78    28.0 24.7 39.0 50.6 61.4 72.6 75.6 79.2 68.5 55.5 47.9 38.6
79    32.5 23.0 47.0 52.3 66.4 69.1 76.2 75.5 68.5 54.9 50.1 38.2
80    31.8 29.7 40.2 54.7 65.4 70.6 78.5 80.0 72.2 54.9 43.2 32.5
81    25.3 37.9 40.0 54.7 62.6 72.0 76.9 74.9 66.8 53.1 45.6 34.6
82    24.7 34.4 41.7 50.2 65.9 68.7 76.9 73.5 67.6 56.9 48.4 41.3
83    34.1 34.0 43.7 51.0 62.1 72.0 77.9 77.1 69.0 56.6 46.7 33.2
84    26.2 38.7 35.5 50.2 60.2 73.0 73.9 75.2 64.7 61.2 44.4 41.9
85    27.3 35.3 44.6 55.5 64.5 68.8 75.4 74.1 69.1 59.3 51.3 33.3
86    32.8 32.1 44.5 53.3 66.8 73.8 78.1 74.0 68.3 57.8 44.5 37.9
87    31.9 32.5 45.7 53.1 63.9 74.6 79.5 75.4 68.8 52.5 48.0 39.2
88    27.3 34.6 44.7 51.3 63.6 72.3 80.7 78.3 66.7 51.8 47.7 35.4
89    36.5 34.8 42.3 52.4 62.4 74.7 76.3 75.6 69.7 58.3 44.9 25.5
90    40.3 41.2 46.1 53.3 61.3 72.2 78.0 75.8 68.0 61.9 49.7 42.1
```

Write a program that uses these values to calculate the average temperature for each year and the average of the monthly average temperature for all years in the file; that is, calculate the averages across each row and down each column. Your program's output should reproduce all the values in the file, as shown. Display the yearly average temperature at the end of each line. When all data have been processed, add an additional line of output that displays the average of all the monthly average temperatures.

In terms of design and implemention for this kind of problem, it may be helpful first to design and write code that does nothing but reproduce the contents of the data file, as shown. It is convenient in terms of reading data from the file to store the monthly average temperatures in an array that is overwritten with new values as you process each year.

After you have succeeded in reading and displaying the file, you can then add data definitions and code to do the required calculations. Note that the yearly average temperatures don't need to be held in an array because each yearly average can be calculated on the fly and displayed as it is calculated.

It is possible, and acceptable as a matter of style, to implement this problem using one-dimensional arrays. However, you may find it easier to store all the temperature measurements in a two-dimensional array whose second dimension is 12. [tempphil.c]

11. The game of Life provides a simple two-dimensional model of how organisms are born, survive, and die. It is played on a two-dimensional board with m rows and n columns. The game is started by establishing an initial distribution of organisms in a small region of the board. The distribution of the next generation of the population is calculated according to three rules:

(1) A new organism will appear in the next generation in any empty square with exactly three living neighbors.

(2) An organism in a square surrounded by less than two neighbors will die from loneliness in the next generation, and an organism in a square surrounded by more than three neighbors will die from overcrowding in the next generation.

(3) An organism with two or three neighbors will survive into the next generation.

Write a program that plays this game. A 20 × 20 board is certainly large enough. You should produce output for several generations using at least the following initial population distributions, where an X indicates that an organism occupies that square:

```
(1)     -------            ---X--
        --XXX--            ----X-
        ---X---            --XXX-
```

Some initial configurations die out, some form patterns that grow, oscillate, or become stable, and others form patterns that reproduce themselves and move across the board. The second of the two initial configurations shown above is called the glider, for reasons that are apparent from following it through four generations:

```
(2)     --X-        ----         ----        -----        -----
        ---X        -X-X         ---X        --X--        ---X-
        -XXX  -->   --XX   -->   -X-X  -->   ---XX  -->   ----X
        ----        --X-         --XX         --XX-        --XXX
```

Question: What happens to two gliders that start from opposite sides of the board and "collide" in the middle?

Hint: You can simplify the code by assuming that any organism occupying a row or column at the edge of the game board simply disappears in the next generation. This means that the rules for the game apply only to $(m - 1) \times (n - 1)$ squares on the board. One way to apply the rules is to create an intermediate board configuration that marks births and deaths for the next generation. This is necessary because organisms don't die immediately when you detect that they have less than two or more than three neighbors. They stay there until all the rules have been applied to all squares on the board for the current generation. Similarly, new organisms aren't born until the start of the next generation, so they can't count as neighbors during the current generation. [life.c]

12. A terrain map is stored in digital form as integers in a two-dimensional array. Write a program to examine the array and find high and low spots in the terrain. The criterion for a high or low spot will be a user-specified amount above or below the average of the eight surrounding values.

For the purposes of this program, you can assume that the values are in the range 0–9. Print the original array and, next to it, an array that has high and low spots marked with the letters H and L. A 20×20 array is large enough. You can either use a random number generator to create the original array or manually create some more meaningful pattern such as a "mountain range" or "valley." Some sample output for a random configuration is shown in Figure 6.3.

```
          Look for differences >     4.0000000
  80049726420096732609     +-------------------+
  98993765555866751665     | H                 |
  92963649758076007267     |L            L    H |
  42656156372985104461     |L    L             |
  69703872560985655139     |H  L        LH     |
  06873874745619060247     |            L L L  |
  56372675111978597581     |          L LH   H |
  82801839947613638148     |  L  L      L     L |
  37453949894019191082     |            L H H LH|
  05868892687760244491     |        L         H |
  32891669863529244108     |    L        H   LL |
  87356395794731439382     |                 H H|
  54575719084038623368     |        L L   H    |
  74996174932405620873     |         H   L   L |
  77624904068377508883     |    HL L           |
  22254284728657164754     |    H H      L     |
  90601530345986559496     |L L             H H|
  89647213209988943141     |         L   H  L  |
  66029884073921148437     | L     L           |
  42958575844660457699     +-------------------+
```

Figure 6.3. Sample output from the terrain map program.

Hint: You can't look for high and low spots in the rows and columns at the edges of the map because you must look at all eight surrounding values. [terrain.c]

13. A computer engineer designing a new computer chip is concerned about operating temperatures within the chip. Tests show that passive heat sinks attached to each side of the rectangular chip can maintain each edge of the chip at a specified temperature. The four edges can be at different temperatures, which allows the engineer to design the component layout so that the most temperature-sensitive components can be located near the coolest edge. Write a program to determine the temperature distribution within the chip.

One way to solve this problem is to divide the rectangular area into a two-dimensional grid, as shown in Figure 6.4. Initialize the nodes at each edge of the chip to the specified temperatures. Initialize the interior nodes to some other value; a good choice would be the average of all the edge temperatures. Then, using an iterative loop, recalculate the temperature of each interior node as the average of the temperatures of the four surrounding nodes. Terminate the iteration when the difference between the current and recalculated temperature for *every* node is less than some specified small amount.

Hint: The conditional loop to conduct the iteration could be in the main function. It should call a function whose purpose is to recalculate the node temperatures and return a flag value that indicates whether the terminating conditions for the iteration have been met.

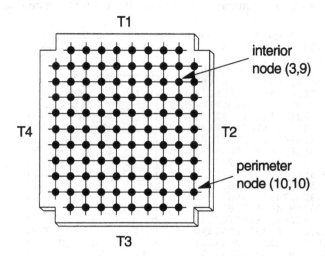

*Figure 6.4. Nodes on a circuit board for determining
interior temperature distribution.*

One obvious verification for your program is to set all four edges to the same temperature. Then a successful iteration should result in all the interior nodes reaching this temperature. In this case, it would not be helpful to initialize the interior temperatures to the average of the edge temperatures because then no iteration would be necessary. Try a different initial value, such as zero or half the edge temperature. [circt_bd.c]

14. Write a series of functions that perform the following operations on vectors having type double components:

1. addition of two n-component vectors

$$A + B = \sum_{i=1}^{n} (A_i + B_i)$$

2. subtraction of two n-component vectors

$$A - B = \sum_{i=1}^{n} (A_i - B_i)$$

3. scalar (dot) product of two n-component vectors

$$A \bullet B = \sum_{i=1}^{n} A_i B_i$$

4. vector (cross) product of two three-component vectors

$$A \times B = (A_y B_z - B_y A_z,\ A_z B_x - B_z A_x,\ A_x B_y - Y_x A_y)$$

Each function should accept as input two vectors and return as output through its parameter list either a third vector or, in the case of the dot product, a single number.

When you have tested all your functions, create a header file and save the function implementations in a separate library file. You can also compile the function implementations into an object file for use by other programs. [vector1.c]

15. Write a program that reads a text file one character at a time and counts the number of times each letter appears in the file. Store the results in an array of integers of size 26—one element for each letter in the alphabet—and display the contents of the array after reading the file.

Your program must take into account the fact that letters can be either uppercase or lowercase. Write your own function to convert uppercase letters to lowercase, or vice versa, or use the intrinsic function isupper or islower. (Consult a C reference manual or the documentation for your compiler.) The uppercase alphabet starts at position 65 in the ASCII collating sequence and the lowercase alphabet starts at 97. [cnt_alph.c]

16. Write and test a *recursive* function that accepts as input a string and the length of the string and prints the string backwards, one character at a time. [backward.c]

17. Write and test a function that converts the day of the year (an integer in the range 1–366) into the month and day of the month. Your function should store the number of days in each month in an array declared like this:

```
int month[]={31,28,31,30,31,30,31,31,30,31,30,31};
```

The function should then modify the number of days in February depending on whether the year is a leap year. Be sure to account for the fact that century years not evenly divisible by 400 are not leap years—for example, 2000 is a leap year, but 2100 isn't. [day_conv.c]

User-Defined Data Objects

7.1 Creating User-Defined Data Objects

The array, discussed in Chapter 6, is a simple example of a user-defined data object that is implemented in C and other high-level languages. It is also possible to construct other kinds of user-defined data objects within a program. The purpose of doing so is to simplify the representation and management of related pieces of information. As an example, think of a card file that contains information about chemicals—their names, symbols, molecular weights, etc. Each card contains information for a specific chemical, so all the information on each card is related. It doesn't make sense to store each fact about each chemical on separate sets of cards—all the names on one set, all the symbols on another set, and so forth. For this problem, the basic conceptual storage unit is a single card containing all the information about a single chemical, not each value on the card.

In C, this card file model can be implemented by defining a data object that exists just while the program containing that definition is executing. There are two syntax forms:

```
struct structure_name {
   one or more data field declarations
}
typedef struct structure_name data_type;

   or

typedef struct {
   one or more data field declarations
}data_type;
```

The reserved word `struct` is used to define the data object, the *data fields* of which appear in a statement block enclosed with curly braces. Especially in the context of object-oriented programming, the fields defined in a `struct` are also called *data members*. In the first syntax form, the structure definition is followed by a `typedef` statement in which the user-supplied *structure_name* is given a user-supplied *alias*—`data_type` in the syntax example—by which the structure will be known within a program. It is okay for this new name to be the same as the structure name; hence the syntax

data field
data member
alias

```
typedef struct structure_name structure_name
```

is allowed.

In the second syntax form, the definition of a new data type is contained within a single statement. We will usually use this syntax because it is simpler. In either case, *data_type* becomes the name for the object's data type definition and it can be used to declare variables in the same way that variables are associated with any of C's intrinsic data types.

Within a data structure, one or more various fields are defined. In the chemical data card file example, these fields will correspond to the name, symbol, and so forth, for each chemical. Often, the fields consist of one or more intrinsic data types or character arrays (character strings), as appropriate for the problem at hand. However, the fields can also be arrays of numbers, other structs, or even arrays of other structs. If a field is declared as having a data type associated with a structure, that structure must already have been defined in the source code.

Once a variable is declared as having the data type of a structure, that variable name can be used with the names of fields in the structure to access and manipulate information. With this syntax, it is easy to become confused about the difference between a data *type* and a variable *name* declared as having that data type. Thus it may be helpful to be consistent about using a _type suffix (for example, when you create structs).

Program P-7.1 shows how to define a data object, declare a variable as having that data type, read values for the fields of the variable from an external file of unknown length, and display the results. Each record consists of four numbers—the time, in hours, minutes, and seconds, and a measurement of some physical quantity. The first few records of the file might look like this:

```
01 15 45 19.9
10 07 05 20.1
12 33 59 33.3
```
(and so forth)

P-7.1 [structur.c]

```c
/* Demonstrate use of structures. */

#include <stdio.h>
#define FILE_NAME "structur.dat"

int main(void)
{
    typedef struct {
        int hr,min,sec;
        float measurement;
    }data_record_type;
```

```
/*   struct data_record {
   int hr,min,sec;
   float measurement;
};
typedef struct data_record data_record_type; */

FILE *Infile;
int count=0;
int status=0;
data_record_type measurements;

Infile=fopen(FILE_NAME,"r");
while (status != EOF) {
   status=fscanf(Infile,"%d %d %d %f",&measurements.hr,
              &measurements.min,&measurements.sec,
              &measurements.measurement);
   if (status != EOF) {
     printf("%d %d %d %f\n",measurements.hr,measurements.min,
            measurements.sec,measurements.measurement);
     count++;
   }
}
printf("There are %d records.",count);
fclose(Infile);
return 0;
}
```

In P-7.1, the two equivalent syntax possibilities for defining a data object are shown. The first, which we will usually use in this text, is printed in bold italics, and the second is commented out. The remaining statement in bold italics declares the variable `measurements` as having data type `data_record_type`. It is this declaration statement that causes C to set aside enough memory to hold all the fields defined in the `struct` block.

P-7.1 answers some important questions about accessing the fields within a stuctured variable. In this | **dot operator** |
program, each "value" of the variable `measurements` actually consists of four values—the four numerical fields declared in the `struct` definition. Each field of the record must always be referred to in association with the name of its structured variable. The syntax uses the **dot operator** (.) to separate a field name from its variable name:

> `structured_variable_name.field_name`

The dot operator is also called the **component access operator** or **member access operator**. Examples of this syntax are found in | **component access operator** |
   | **member access operator** |
the `fscanf` and `printf` statements in P-7.1.
Values are read into the fields `hr`, `min`, `sec`, and `measurement` with the

fscanf statement; the & operator is required for any field that would otherwise require it based on its data type.

More than one variable can be declared as having the same type. For example, in P-7.1, you could write

```
data_record measurements,m2;
```

so that both measurements and m2 have data type data_record. Then you could assign either individual fields or an entire record. Both these statements are allowed:

```
m2.measurement=measurements.measurement;
m2=measurements;
```

As you might expect, the second statement results in all the fields in measurements being copied into the fields of m2; this is an important and very useful syntax feature.

It might occasionally be useful to know that it is possible to declare variable names in a program which have the same name as fields in a struct definition. Thus in P-7.1, it would be possible to define variables named hr, min, and sec that are completely independent of the fields of the same name in structure data_record_type. However, this can be confusing. Even if these duplicate names seem like a reasonable idea at the time you write a program, if you ever need to modify the code or examine it to try to understand why the program works as it does, you will probably wish you had used different names.

Although it may seem like a lot of trouble to define and use structured data types in this way, the aggravation of the extra typing associated with the dot operator is more than compensated by the self-documenting nature of the resulting statements and by the flexibility the syntax offers in the management of information. Also, as we will see later in the chapter, structs can be used to simplify considerably the writing of functions.

7.2 Arrays of Structures

In scientific and engineering programming, structs are often used to hold collections of measurements. Hence it is important to consider how to use arrays of structs. Recall from Chapter 6 that one requirement imposed on arrays is that every element in an array must hold the same type of data. In the card file model illustrated in Figure 7.1, the box holding the cards becomes the array, the cards—through their definition within a struct—become the array elements, and the various pieces of information written on each card become the fields of the struct.

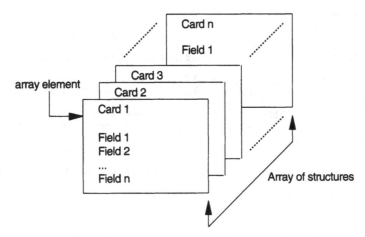

Figure 7.1. A card file model for arrays of structures.

In Chapter 6, program P-6.3 showed how to store information about the planets in three parallel arrays—one each for the name, diameter, and distance from the sun. Parallel arrays can be awkward when large amounts of related information must be manipulated. For example, suppose more information about each planet must be added to a database. A new array for each quantity will have to be created. It will be even more inconvenient if the planetary data need to be sorted—by the planet's diameter, for example—because then the contents of all the parallel arrays need to be rearranged at the same time.

The `struct` data type can alleviate this problem by collecting all the information about a planet in a single user-defined data object. Then it is easy to define an array whose elements have this data type. With this approach, it is as easy to add new information about planets as it is to add new planets. Program P-7.2 produces the same results as P-6.3, but it uses an array of structures to hold the values.

P-7.2 [`planets4.c`]

```c
#include <stdio.h>
#define NAME_LENGTH 8

typedef struct {
  char name[NAME_LENGTH];
  double diameter, distance;
} planet_type;

void main()
{
  FILE *InFile;
  int status=0;
  int index=0;
```

```
planet_type planets[11];
char header_line[81];

if( (InFile=fopen("planets.dat","rt")) != NULL) {
  printf("Opening file...\n");
  (void)fgets(header_line,sizeof(header_line),InFile);
  while (1) {
    status=fscanf(InFile,"%s %lf %lf",planets[index].name,
              &planets[index].distance,&planets[index].diameter);
    if (status == EOF) break;
    printf("%-8s %10.01f %10.11f\n",planets[index].name,
          planets[index].distance,planets[index].diameter);
    index++;
  }
  printf("done...\n");
  /* Note that "index" is number of records, not last accessible
     array element, which is index-1. */
  printf("Found %i records.\n",index);
}
else printf("Trouble opening file...\n");
fclose(InFile);
}
```

The first essential task for any program that uses external data is to read, store, and play back the stored information. Often, setting up an appropriate data structure and echoing the data after they have been stored is the hardest part of writing a program. In P-7.2, the return value from the fopen function is used to determine whether the file has been opened successfully. This shouldn't be necessary for programs and data files you write yourself, because presumably you are certain that the files really do exist. Nonetheless, because C is notoriously unhelpful about reporting problems with finding files, it certainly doesn't hurt to add this extra code.

As usual, P-7.2 uses the return value from fscanf to control the loop. The string fields in each array element don't need the & operator (because the string fields are, themselves, arrays of characters), but the numerical fields do, just as though they were simple variables. As usual in code to store data in an array, the final value of index after the loop terminates is the total number of records found (10, including the sun and its nine planets), and not the index of the last array element used (9). It is important to remember what index contains to avoid problems if you extend this program to access the array elements.

There is another consequence of how the conditional loop is written in P-7.2. The final call to fscanf, which results in status being assigned the value EOF, contains references to array element 10. Nothing is placed in this array element, because the fscanf function fails to find more data. However, the potential reference to the out-of-bounds array element 10 is the reason the size of the array has been set to 11 rather than 10. If you rewrite the conditional loop to use fgets, which reads each record into a string rather than directly into the array elements, you could test for the end-of-file *before* incrementing the array index and parsing the string into its component fields. This would allow the size of the array to be set to its natural value of 10.

7.3 Functions With Structures as Parameters and Data Types

We have previously considered several implementations of code to calculate the area and circumference of a circle of specified radius. These included

(a) using two functions, one which returns the area, and the other which returns the circumference:

```
double circle_area(double radius);
double circle_circumference(double radius);
```

(b) using one function that returns both area and circumference indirectly through pointers:

```
void circle_stuff(double radius,double *area,double *circumference);
```

There is yet another choice: use a `typedef` to create a structure `circle_type` that includes as its fields the radius, area, and circumference. In the `main` function, ask the user to provide the radius field. Then call a function with this prototype:

```
circle_type circle_stuff(circle_type c);
```

The function should calculate the area and circumference fields and return the variable `c`, which will now contain the desired values in its fields.

This implementation is possible because not only can a function include user-defined data types in its parameter list, it can also have a user-defined structure as its data type. In effect, this allows functions to return multiple values directly through the fields of that structure, thereby circumventing one of the limitations of using the `return` statement in a function. Program P-7.3 shows how to do this.

P-7.3 [`circle_s.c`]

```
/* Calculate the area and circumference of a circle
    of specified radius, using a structure to hold all values. */
#include <stdio.h>
#define PI 3.14159

typedef struct {
  double radius, area, circumference;
} circle_type;
```

```
circle_type circle_stuff(circle_type c);

int main(void)
{
  circle_type circle;

  printf("Give radius: ");
  scanf("%lf",&circle.radius);

  /* Calculate the area and circumference. */

  circle=circle_stuff(circle);

  printf("The area is %.2f\n",circle.area);
  printf("The circumference is %.2f\n",circle.circumference);

  return (0);
}
circle_type circle_stuff(circle_type c) {
  c.area=PI*c.radius*c.radius;
  c.circumference=PI*2.*c.radius;
  return c;
}
```

The critical code for this program is printed in bold italics. The first block of code uses a typedef to define a data object containing the radius (the input) and the area and circumference (the output) for this problem. As in other approaches to managing the flow of information within a program, the designation of a quantity as input or output has significance only at the algorithm design level; it makes no difference from C's point of view what significance a programmer attaches to a particular field in a structure. In particular, it is okay in P-7.3 for the struct to contain fields for both the input to (radius) and the output from (circumference) the function.

Function circle_stuff has as its single parameter a data object with type circle_type. Inside the function, the area and circumference fields are calculated based on the values of the radius field, and the entire data object is returned to main. In main, the statement

```
circle=circle_stuff(circle);
```

passes the object circle as input to circle_stuff and replaces circle with its updated value returned as output from circle_stuff.

Although defining and using structs may seem more trouble than it is worth because of the extra programming overhead they impose, the judicious use of structs can simplify code by making functions easier to write and existing programs easier to modify. Using data objects in parameter lists shortens those lists because the multiple parameters that may be required when only intrinsic data types are used can be replaced by a single parameter having a user-defined data type. Also, using a data object as the type for the returned value from a function can eliminate the need for pointers to return multiple outputs through a function's parameter list.

7.4 Applications

7.4.1 Finding the Perimeter and Area of a Plot of Land

1 *Define the problem.*

The boundaries of a plot of land are defined by three or more straight line segments. The coordinates for three or more corner points, in the form of (x,y) pairs, are stored in a data file. Write a program that accesses this file and calculates the length of each line that defines the boundary, the perimeter of the plot of land, and its area. A sample set of coordinates for the plot shown in Figure 7.2, in arbitrary units, is

```
1 1
2 0
3 0
3 2
2 2
```

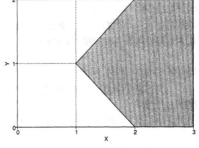

Figure 7.2. Sample land boundaries.

For the sample illustrated in Figure 7.2, the perimeter of this plot is 6.828, and its area is 3.000.

2 *Outline a solution.*

The length of segment i is

$$length_i = \sqrt{(x_i - x_{i-1})^2 + (y_i - y_{i-1})^2}$$

for i > 1 and

$$length_1 = \sqrt{(x_1 - x_n)^2 + (y_1 - y_n)^2}$$

for i = 1. The area is

$$\text{area} = |x_1y_2 + x_2y_3 + \ldots + x_{n-1}y_n + x_ny_1 - y_1x_2 - y_2x_3 - \ldots - y_{n-1}x_n - y_n x_1|/2$$

3 *Design an algorithm.*

Here is an algorithm for the loop that calculates segment length (L), perimeter, and area.

INITIALIZE perimeter = 0
                         area = 0
LOOP (from 2 to n)
        ASSIGN $L_i = [(x_i - x_{i-1})^2 + (y_i - y_{i-1})^2]^{1/2}$
        INCREMENT perimeter by L_i
END LOOP
ASSIGN $L_1 = [(x_1 - x_n)^2 + (y_1 - y_n)^2]^{1/2}$
INCREMENT perimeter by L_1

LOOP (from 1 to n-1)
        INCREMENT area by $x_i \cdot y_{i+1} - y_i \cdot x_{i+1}$
END LOOP
INCREMENT area by $(x_n \cdot y_1 - y_n \cdot x_1)/2$

4 *Convert the algorithm into a program.*

Represent each coordinate pair and its associated boundary length segment in an array of structures. Each plot of land has only one perimeter and area, so these values will be defined separately.

P-7.4 [boundary.c]

```
#include <stdio.h>
#include <math.h>
#define FILENAME "boundary.dat"
#define MAX 15

typedef struct {
   double x,y,L;
} land_type;
```

```c
void ReadData(char filename[],land_type a[],int *n);
void Calculate(land_type a[],int n,double *perimeter,double *area);
void DisplayData(land_type a[],int n);

int main()
{
  land_type a[MAX];
  int n;
  double perimeter,area;

  ReadData(FILENAME,a,&n);
  Calculate(a,n,&perimeter,&area);
  printf("%i coordinate pairs\n",n);
  DisplayData(a,n);
  printf("perimeter and area: %lf %lf\n",perimeter,area);

  return 0;
}
void Calculate(land_type a[],int n, double *perimeter,double *area)
{
  int i;
  *perimeter=0.;
  *area=0.;
  for (i=1; i<n; i++) {
    a[i].L=sqrt((a[i].x-a[i-1].x)*(a[i].x-a[i-1].x)+
         (a[i].y-a[i-1].y)*(a[i].y-a[i-1].y));
    *perimeter+=a[i].L;
  }

  a[0].L=sqrt((a[n-1].x-a[0].x)*(a[n-1].x-a[0].x)+
              (a[n-1].y-a[0].y)*(a[n-1].y-a[0].y));
  *perimeter+=a[0].L;
  for (i=0; i<(n-1); i++)
    *area+=a[i].x*a[i+1].y-a[i].y*a[i+1].x;
  *area=(*area+a[n-1].x*a[0].y-a[n-1].y*a[0].x)/2.;
}
void ReadData(char filename[],land_type a[],int *n) {
  FILE *in;
  int status=0;

  in=fopen(filename,"r");
  *n=-1;
  while (1) {
    (*n)+=1;
    status=fscanf(in,"%lf %lf",&a[*n].x,&a[*n].y);
    if (status == EOF) break;
    /* printf("%lf %lf\n",a[*n].x,a[*n].y); */
  }
  fclose(in);
}
void DisplayData(land_type a[],int n)
{
  int i;
  for (i=0; i<n; i++)
    printf("%8.4lf %8.4lf %8.4lf\n",a[i].x,a[i].y,a[i].L);
}
```

Running P-7.4

```
5 coordinate pairs
   1.0000    1.0000    1.4142
   2.0000    0.0000    1.4142
   3.0000    0.0000    1.0000
   3.0000    2.0000    2.0000
   2.0000    2.0000    1.0000
perimeter and area: 6.828427 3.000000
```

5 Verify the operation of the program.

The results shown in the sample output from P-7.4 are easy to verify by hand. If the program works for these simple data, there is no reason to expect that it won't work for larger files.

7.4.2 A Set of Functions to Perform Operations on Complex Numbers

1 Define the problem.

The C language doesn't directly support a complex number data type. However, computations involving complex numbers are important in many science and engineering disciplines. The goal of this application is to create a set of functions that will perform the following operations:

1. Add, subtract, multiply, and divide two complex numbers.

2. Find the polar coordinates (radius and angle with respect to the x-axis) of a complex number "vector."

2 Outline a solution.

For calculations with two complex numbers $c_1 = a_1 + b_1 i$ and $c_2 = a_2 + b_2 i$ which produce a third complex number c:

addition: $\qquad c = (a_1 + a_2) + (b_1 + b_2)i$

subtraction: $\qquad c = (a_1 - a_2) + (b_1 - b_2)i$

multiplication: $\qquad c = (a_1a_2 - b_1b_2) + (a_1b_2 + a_2b_1)i$

division: $\qquad c = \left(\dfrac{a_1a_2 + b_1b_2}{a_2^2 + b_2^2} \right) + \left(\dfrac{a_2b_1 - a_1b_2}{a_2^2 + b_2^2} \right)i$

For operations on a single complex number:

$$\text{magnitude} = \sqrt{a^2 + b^2}$$

$$\text{angle} = \tan^{-1}(b/a)$$

Design an algorithm.

Create a separate function for each of the above operations. In addition, create one function to accept the real and imaginary components of a single complex number from the keyboard and another to display a single complex number. The design of these algorithms is straightforward and need not be given in explicit detail here.

There are some implementation decisions concerning how to display a complex number when one of its components is 0. We will choose to display the number in the format a + bi even when a or b is 0. The input function will work somewhat analogously to the `scanf` function in the sense that it will return a status flag of 1 when the read operation is successful and a 0 if it is not; usually this flag can be ignored. The components of the complex number will be returned indirectly through a pointer to a structure containing the components.

The division operation cannot be carried out if both a_2 and b_2 are 0. You may wish to add code to take this fact into account.

Convert the algorithm into a program.

P-7.5 [`complex.c`]

```
#include <stdio.h>
#include <math.h>

typedef struct{
  double a,b;
} complex_t;
```

```c
int scan_c(complex_t *c) {
  int status=0;
  printf("Give components of complex number a+bi in format a b: ");
  status=scanf("%lf %lf",&(*c).a,&(*c).b);
  if (status == 2) return 1;
  else return 0;
}
void print_c(complex_t c) {
  printf("%+lf%+lfi\n",c.a,c.b);
}
complex_t add_c(complex_t c1,complex_t c2) {
  complex_t c;
  c.a=c1.a+c2.a;
  c.b=c1.b+c2.b;
  return c;
}
complex_t subtract_c(complex_t c1,complex_t c2) {
  complex_t c;
  c.a=c1.a-c2.a;
  c.b=c1.b-c2.b;
  return c;
}
complex_t multiply_c(complex_t c1,complex_t c2) {
  complex_t c;
  c.a=c1.a*c2.a-c1.b*c2.b;
  c.b=c1.a*c2.b+c2.a*c1.b;
  return c;
}
complex_t divide_c(complex_t c1,complex_t c2) {
  complex_t c;
  double d;
  d=c2.a*c2.a+c2.b*c2.b;
  c.a=(c1.a*c2.a+c1.b*c2.b)/d;
  c.b=(c2.a*c1.b-c1.a*c2.b)/d;
  return c;
}
double mag_c(complex_t c) {
  return sqrt(c.a*c.a+c.b*c.b);
}
double angle_c(complex_t c) {
  return atan2(c.b,c.a);
}
int main(void)
{
  complex_t c1,c2,c;
  (void)scan_c(&c1); (void)scan_c(&c2);
  print_c(c1); print_c(c2);
  printf("addition and subtraction:\n");
  print_c(add_c(c1,c2));
  print_c(subtract_c(c1,c2));
  printf("multiplication and division:\n");
  print_c(multiply_c(c1,c2));
  print_c(divide_c(c1,c2));
  printf("polar coordinates (length, radians):\n");
  printf("%lf %lf\n",mag_c(c1),angle_c(c1));
  printf("%lf %lf\n",mag_c(c2),angle_c(c2));
  return 0;
}
```

Running P-7.5

```
Give components of complex number a+bi in format a b: 2 3
Give components of complex number a+bi in format a b: 4 5
+2.000000+3.0000001
+4.000000+5.0000001
addition and subtraction:
+6.000000+8.0000001
-2.000000-2.0000001
multiplication and division:
-7.000000+22.0000001
+0.560976+0.0487801
polar coordinates (length, radians):
3.605551 0.982794
6.403124 0.896055
```

5 *Verify the operation of the program.*

It is essential to test the results from each function against a hand-worked example.

Problem Discussion

Most of the code in P-7.5 is straightforward. The main function serves simply as a driver program for testing all the other functions. The code for the complex number functions is given prior to the main function rather than using function prototypes with the function code following the main function. This facilitates saving just the functions as a separate file that can be #included in other programs.

One important feature of P-7.5 is the atan2 function, which is used to return the angle between the real and complex components; this function, but not atan, returns an angle in the appropriate quadrant, based on the signs of the real and imaginary components of a complex number. It would be a serious program design error, which might be invisible at the algorithm design stage, to use the atan function instead.

A possible source of confusion concerns the syntax for scanf as it is used inside the scan_c function:

```
status=scanf("%lf %lf",&(*c).a,&(*c).b);
```

The expression &(*c).a means "the address of the field in a complex_t structure pointed to by the pointer c." The parentheses are required because of the relative precedence of the & and * operators.

A final detail concerns the %+lf format specifier in print_c. This forces display of a + or − sign along with a number.

7.4.3 Analyzing Data From a Datalogger

1 *Define the problem.*

The computer revolution has profoundly influenced how scientific data are collected. Analog instruments can be connected to a datalogger that performs analog-to-digital (A-D) conversions and uses its own onboard memory to store thousands of measurements in digital form along with a date and time stamp. Such devices typically can be programmed to collect data at specified intervals.

For the purposes of this application, we will consider data collected with a simple datalogger that samples, at intervals of one minute, a single analog voltage input in the range from 0 to 2.5 V. It converts the analog signal to a digital value in the range from 0 to 255—that is, the datalogger performs an eight-bit A-D conversion. Data from the datalogger can be downloaded to a computer and exported as an ASCII text file containing the date and time, to the nearest second, the converted digital count, and the analog voltage corresponding to that count. Because of the relatively coarse (eight-bit) A-D conversion, this device has an analog resolution of only 10 mV for a full-scale signal of 2.5 V.

Write a program that reads an exported file from the datalogger and saves the average, minimum, and maximum voltages over 30-minute periods, where each period starts with minute 1 or 31 and ends at minute 30 or 60 (or 0). The data collection can start and end at any time relative to the start of a half hour, but you can assume that there are never any missing data once the datalogger starts collecting data. Ignore incomplete sequences of data that don't include 30 values, which may occur only at the beginning or end of the file. Round off minutes and seconds to the nearest minute; that is, 30m 58s is minute 31 and 30m 12s is minute 30. A sample file, apr06.dat, the first few lines of which are shown here, can be found on the Web site given in Section 6 of the Preface. Note that the file contains one header line. The first six values are the month, day, year, hour, minute, and second of the measurement. The eighth value is the digital count resulting from the A-D conversion of the analog input signal, and the seventh value is the analog voltage corresponding to that digital count, based on a 2.5 V full-scale analog signal.

```
Date     Time       V      A-D
 4  5 97 13 56 58 0.000 1
 4  5 97 13 57 58 0.000 1
 4  5 97 13 58 58 0.000 1
 4  5 97 13 59 58 0.725 75
 4  5 97 14  0 58 0.598 62
 4  5 97 14  1 58 0.618 64
. . .
```

2 *Outline a solution.*

The most compact way to represent data for this program is in terms of a structure defining all the numerical data in each record. Although it might seem that an array is required to store the groups of 30 measurements, this is *not* true, as all the data can be processed on the fly. The required calculations for obtaining the average, minimum, and maximum values are not difficult. The most challenging part of the program involves grouping the measurements properly in sets of 30, starting with minute 1 or 31, as specified.

Each time the program reads a record from the data file, calculate the rounded minute from the minute and second fields. Increment a counter and update a variable that contains the sum of all measurements within a 30-minute period. Update the minimum or maximum if required, by comparing the current values against the current measurement. Then there are two possibilities:

(1) The rounded minute has a value other than 30, 60, or 0.
   Continue to the next record.
(2) The rounded minute has a value of 30, 60 or 0.
   Check the counter to see if it has a value of 30. If it does, divide the sum by 30 to get the average during this 30-minute period. When the rounded minute has a value of 60 or 0, this represents the end of an hour. If the rounded minute has a value of 0, set it to 60 and decrement the hour by 1. Thus a time of 2hr 0m 17s will be displayed as 1h 60m. This makes sense because this calculated time represents the time at the end of a 30-minute averaging period, so the time that represents this period is the ending time minus 15 minutes. Thus for 1h 60m, the average time for the interval from 1h 30min to 1h 60m will be 1h 45m.

Display the average, minimum, and maximum. Regardless of the value of the counter, reset both the variable containing the sum of all measurements and the counter variable to 0. Then continue to the next record.

3 *Design an algorithm.*

Here is an algorithm for the data processing loop in the main program.

OPEN *(data file)*
READ *(header line)*
INITIALIZE *average = 0, counter = 0*

LOOP *(until end of file)*
    READ *(one record)*
    INCREMENT *counter by 1*
                    average = average plus new measurement
    IF *(voltage > max)* **THEN ASSIGN** *max = voltage*
    IF *(voltage < min)* **THEN ASSIGN** *min = voltage*
    ASSIGN *min_round = Round(min + sec/60)*
    (optional, during program development) **WRITE** *(all fields)*
    IF *(min_round = 30, 60, or 0)* **THEN**
           CALL *DumpData(IN: data record, min_round;*
                          IN/OUT: average, max, min, counter)
END LOOP
CLOSE*(data file)*

Here is a subprogram to process and display the 30-minute averages. The decision has been made to display a rounded minute of 0 as 60. The **WRITE** command can be interpreted as directing output to the monitor during program development and to a file when the program development is complete.

SUBPROGRAM *DumpData(IN: data record, min_round;*
                          IN/OUT: average, max, min, counter)
IF *(counter = 30)* **THEN** *(this is a complete 30-minute sequence)*
    IF *(min_round = 0)* **THEN ASSIGN** *min_round = 60 (for display)*
    ASSIGN *average = average/30*
    WRITE *(month, day, year, hour, minute, average, min, max)*
(end **IF***)*
ASSIGN *counter= 0*
    average = 0
    min = large number
    max = small number
(end **SUBPROGRAM***)*

 Convert the algorithm into a program.

P-7.6 [datalog8.c]

```
/* DATALOG8.C */

#include <stdio.h>
#include <math.h>
#define N_MEAS 30
#define FILENAME "apr06.dat"
#define OUTFILE "apr06.out"
```

```
typedef struct {
  int mon,day,yr,hr,min,sec;
  float V;
  int d;
} data_type;

void DumpData(FILE *out,data_type m,int min_rnd,
              float *avg,float *min,float *max,int *kount);

int main(void)
{
  int n_pts=0,min_rnd,kount=0,status=0;
  float avg=0.,min=500.,max=-500.;
  FILE *in,*out;
  char one_line[80];
  data_type m;

  in=fopen(FILENAME,"r");
  out=fopen(OUTFILE,"w");
  (void)fgets(one_line,sizeof(one_line),in);
  /* printf("%s",one_line); */
  while (1) {
    status=fscanf(in,"%i %i %i %i %i %i %f %i",
                  &m.mon,&m.day,&m.yr,&m.hr,&m.min,&m.sec,&m.V,&m.d);
    if (status == EOF) break;
    n_pts++;
    kount++;
    avg+=m.V;
    if (m.V > max) max=m.V;
    if (m.V < min) min=m.V;
    min_rnd=(int)floor(m.min+m.sec/60.+.5);
    /* printf("%5i %2i %2i %2i %2i %2i %2i %6.3f %3i (%2i)\n",
      n_pts,m.mon,m.day,m.yr,m.hr,m.min,m.sec,m.V,m.d,min_rnd); */
    if ( (min_rnd == 30) || (min_rnd == 60) || (min_rnd == 0) )
      DumpData(out,m,min_rnd,&avg,&min,&max,&kount);
    /* fflush(stdin); scanf(); */
  }
  fclose(in);
  fclose(out);
  printf("There are %i records in this file.\n",n_pts);
  return 0;
}
void DumpData(FILE *out,data_type m,int min_rnd,
              float *avg,float *min,float *max,int *kount) {
              printf("kount = %i\n",*kount);
  if (*kount == N_MEAS) {
    if (min_rnd == 0) {
      min_rnd=60;
      m.hr--;
    }
    printf("%2i %2i %2i %2i %2i %6.3f %6.3f %6.3f\n",
 m.mon,m.day,m.yr,m.hr,min_rnd,*avg/(float)N_MEAS,*min,*max);
    fprintf(out,"%2i %2i %2i %2i %2i %6.3f %6.3f %6.3f\n",
 m.mon,m.day,m.yr,m.hr,min_rnd,*avg/(float)N_MEAS,*min,*max);
  }
  *kount=0;
  *avg=0; *min=500.; *max=-500.;
}
```

Running P-7.6 (These are the contents of the APR06.OUT file produced by the program.)

```
4  5 97 14 30  0.445  0.323  0.686
4  5 97 14 60  0.423  0.353  0.510
4  5 97 15 30  0.575  0.412  0.765
4  5 97 15 60  0.396  0.235  0.608
4  5 97 16 30  0.337  0.196  0.441
4  5 97 16 60  0.115  0.068  0.176
4  5 97 17 30  0.109  0.059  0.137
4  5 97 17 60  0.034  0.019  0.059
4  5 97 18 30  0.007  0.000  0.019
4  5 97 18 60  0.000  0.000  0.000
4  5 97 19 30  0.000  0.000  0.000
4  5 97 19 60  0.000  0.000  0.000
4  5 97 20 30  0.000  0.000  0.000
4  5 97 20 60  0.000  0.000  0.000
4  5 97 21 30  0.000  0.000  0.000
4  5 97 21 60  0.000  0.000  0.000
4  5 97 22 30  0.000  0.000  0.000
4  5 97 22 60  0.000  0.000  0.000
4  5 97 23 30  0.000  0.000  0.000
4  5 97 23 60  0.000  0.000  0.000
4  6 97  0 30  0.000  0.000  0.000
4  6 97  0 60  0.000  0.000  0.000
4  6 97  1 30  0.000  0.000  0.000
4  6 97  1 60  0.000  0.000  0.000
4  6 97  2 30  0.000  0.000  0.000
4  6 97  2 60  0.000  0.000  0.000
4  6 97  3 30  0.000  0.000  0.000
4  6 97  3 60  0.000  0.000  0.000
4  6 97  4 30  0.000  0.000  0.000
4  6 97  4 60  0.000  0.000  0.000
4  6 97  5 30  0.000  0.000  0.000
4  6 97  5 60  0.000  0.000  0.000
4  6 97  6 30  0.003  0.000  0.010
4  6 97  6 60  0.025  0.010  0.049
4  6 97  7 30  0.096  0.059  0.117
4  6 97  7 60  0.146  0.098  0.216
4  6 97  8 30  0.211  0.176  0.284
4  6 97  8 60  0.272  0.206  0.412
4  6 97  9 30  0.317  0.225  0.421
4  6 97  9 60  0.404  0.314  0.568
4  6 97 10 30  0.289  0.147  0.549
4  6 97 10 60  0.132  0.068  0.196
4  6 97 11 30  0.243  0.108  0.490
4  6 97 11 60  0.577  0.402  1.461
4  6 97 12 30  0.563  0.333  1.127
4  6 97 12 60  0.789  0.333  1.441
4  6 97 13 30  0.899  0.274  1.137
4  6 97 13 60  0.350  0.245  0.568
4  6 97 14 30  0.198  0.108  0.314
4  6 97 14 60  0.086  0.059  0.147
4  6 97 15 30  0.070  0.039  0.108
4  6 97 15 60  0.026  0.019  0.039
```

5 *Verify the operation of the program.*

During the development of P-7.6, it was important to verify that the measurement groups were formed correctly at half-hour time boundaries. This verification step is the reason for the #define N_MEAS 30 statement in the code. The algorithm is written so that it looks for half-hour groups based on the value of the rounded minute in each record. However, the algorithm doesn't "know," except through the value of N_MEAS, that there are supposed to be 30 measurements in each such group. Therefore, a small test file was created with only five measurements in each 30-minute interval. For processing that file, N_MEAS was given a value of 5 rather than 30. The results of processing this small test file were then compared with hand calculations, which would have been much more tedious with data from the original file.

7.5 Debugging Your Programs

Often the most difficult part of writing a program is defining an appropriate data object and writing code to reference the various parts of that object. Therefore, it is important to give careful consideration to these preliminary parts of a program. No matter what the nature of a problem that involves storing and processing data, your first programming goal should always be to write code that defines an appropriate structure and then reads and displays the input data fields in that structure. Often, this includes writing code that will read at least some of the data fields from an external file.

As a matter of programming style, don't forget that data objects can have arrays as fields. This is often a better implementation choice than a two-dimensional array because of the ease with which additional information can be added to a struct.

When you need arrays of structs, it is important in the interests of conserving memory not to "over-type" the data fields. Thus, you may wish to consider abandoning the practice followed throughout this text of defining physical quantities as type double variables in favor of using more memory-efficient float variables wherever possible.

The syntax problems involved in using structs are minor and center around field references. It is particularly easy to get confused about the syntax of referencing fields in elements of arrays of structs. For example, given an array of structs A, the proper way to reference the data1 field in the 10th element of A is A[9].data1, not A.data1[9]. If data1 is itself an array, an appropriate reference might be A[9].data1[1].

Finally, it is easy to become confused about the difference between a user-defined data type and a variable name declared as having that data type. It may be helpful to establish for yourself a naming convention for structures; for example, always including the suffix _type in the name of a `struct`.

7.6 Exercises

In each of these exercises, your program *must* use `structs` even if you believe there are reasonable alternatives.

1. Referring to Exercise 10 in Chapter 6, modify that program so that it uses a `struct` to store the year, monthly temperature data, and yearly average temperature. [tempphi2.c]

Extra Credit:
Use a one-dimensional array of structures to hold all the input and calculated values for this problem. (Successful allocation of space for this array may require that the array declaration be preceded by the `static` keyword.)

2. Referring to Section 2.3 and the problem addressed by program P-2.8, use an array of `structs` to modify P-2.8 so the output includes the total number of reports from each station and the total number of measurements at each station. Assume that there will be no more than 11 stations with IDs 1000 through 1010 and, as before, no more than eight measurements per report. Use the ID numbers to generate appropriate array element references. Compare this exercise to Exercise 1 in Chapter 6. [station2.c]

3. Consider the file hi_lo.dat, containing the date and the high and low temperature for that date. The first 10 records for Philadelphia in 1997 look like this:

```
01/01/97   30   16
01/02/97   46   31
01/03/97   60   43
01/04/97   59   44
01/05/97   66   45
01/06/97   56   36
01/07/97   37   28
01/08/97   39   26
01/09/97   31   26
01/10/97   41   33
```

The term "heating degrees" is defined as 65° F minus the daily average temperature in degrees Fahrenheit. Suppose you can approximate the daily average temperature by taking the average of the high and low temperature for the day.

Then the heating degrees on January 1, 1997, are $65 - (30 + 16)/2 = 42$. These calculations, or more accurate ones obtained by averaging hourly temperatures, can be used by energy companies to monitor and, based on projected high and low temperatures, to predict the demand for energy. In the summer, a negative value for heating degrees may be interpreted as "cooling degrees."

Write a program that uses an appropriate array of `structure`s to store the data in this file and also the calculated heating degrees for each day. Your program should display all the information in the file, plus the heating degrees. Note that even though this exercise asks you to store information in an array, the required calculations *could* be done one record at a time, without using an array. [`deg_day.c`]

4. See Exercise 5 in Chapter 6. Modify that problem so the deck is represented by card values 1-13 in each of four suits: clubs, diamonds, hearts, and spades. Aces have value 1 and the face cards—jacks, queens, and kings—have values 11, 12, and 13. Define an appropriate structure for this card representation. Hold the deck in an array of structures and shuffle the array using the algorithm shown. [`carddec2.c`]

Extra Credit:
Modify the structure so the values of cards can be represented by both numerical values and words. Then the 11 of spades can be printed as the jack of spades. Number cards can be printed as either the 2 of clubs or the two of clubs. [`carddeck.c`]

5. Consider the file `metals.dat`, which contains the name, chemical symbol, and density in gm/cm^3 of several metals:

```
aluminum Al 2.7
cobalt Co 8.9
copper Cu 8.9
gold Au 19.1
silver Ag 9.4
```

Write a program that performs the following tasks:

1. Stores data about the metals in an appropriate structure.
It is *not* allowed simply to store the data as a one-dimensional array of strings.

2. Prompts the user enter part or all of the name of a metal, starting from the beginning of the name.
This means that the program must compare what the user enters against the corresponding number of characters in the metal name field and display all

matches. For example, the program will respond to the user entering co by finding matches with cobalt and copper. However, no matches will be found if the user types o, because no metal name in the list begins with the letter o.

3. Displays all fields for each match.

If no matches are found, the program should print an appropriate message.

4. Gives the user a chance to quit the program or enter another name.

Hint: It may not be obvious how to compare part or all of two strings in C. The statement

```
if (test_string == from_unit) ...
```

will not work, even though it doesn't produce a syntax error. Why not? Because C treats strings as arrays of characters, rather than as single entities, and there is no "built-in" way in C to compare an entire array with a single statement. (Because the name of a string is equivalent to the address of the first character in the string, the statement will never be true because the strings reside in different memory locations even if all the characters are the same.) However, such comparisons can be made by using the standard C functions strcmp, for comparing two entire strings, and strncmp, for comparing the first n characters of a string; see Table 6.1 in Chapter 6. If you did Exercise 8 in Chapter 6, you can avoid potential incompatibilities among different C implementations by using the function you were asked to write in that exercise to extract substrings to be compared with the standard C function strcmp. [metals.c]

6. In Section 7.1 at the beginning of this chapter, the discussion of why and how to create data objects used a chemical database as an example. Write a program similar to the one in Exercise 5 that allows a user to search for a particular chemical name in a record that includes name, symbol, and density or some other relevant numerical quantity. Be sure to take into account the fact that a chemical name may consist of more than one word, unlike the names of metals for the problem posed in Exercise 5.

Hint: You will not be able to use scanf to get keyboard input for a name that contains more than one word, because scanf treats blanks as separators between values, not as part of a value. Instead, you must use gets or fgets to extract an entire string from the keyboard buffer. We haven't used the intrinsic function gets in this text, but fgets will work perfectly well. See, for example, P-2.6 in Chapter 2. To substitute the keyboard for an external file, simply replace the file name with stdin, the standard "file name" for the keyboard buffer.

Remember that the string returned by `fgets` includes the end-of-line character, which you will need to remove as shown in P-2.6. Also, you should make sure the keyboard buffer is empty before you read from it; include a `fflush(stdin);` statement before each `fgets` statement in your program. [chemical.c]

7. As any science or engineering student knows, it's easy to make mistakes when converting physical quantities from one system of units to another. One way to minimize such errors is to develop your own database of unit conversions. Here is a short database of conversions. The first column contains the "from" unit, the second column contains the "to" unit, and the third column contains the number by which a quantity expressed in the "from" unit must be multiplied to get the corresponding quantity expressed in the "to" unit.

```
fathoms         feet              6.0
feet            inches            12.0
feet            yards             0.33333333
inches          centimeters       2.54
miles per hour  feet per second   1.4666667
miles per hour  meters per second 0.4470408
```

Write a program that stores the contents of this or a similar file in an appropriate array of `structs`. The program should prompt the user to enter part or all of the first word in the name of a "from" unit. The program should then display all "from" unit matches and ask the user to choose the desired one.

Here are some specifications your program must meet.

1. The user must start typing the name of the "from" unit from the beginning, but not all of the name needs to be entered.

This means that the program must compare what the user enters against the corresponding number of characters in the "from" unit name and display all matches. For example, the program will respond to the user entering `f` by displaying the first three conversions, but it won't display anything if the user enters `ee` because no "from" unit name begins with the letters `ee`.

2. The "from" unit response from the user must not contain any spaces.

This restriction means that the user should enter no more than a single word even if the "from" unit name consists of several words. If you use `scanf` to read user input of the "from" unit, which is the simplest code to write, your program will think that the keyboard entry `miles per hour` represents *three* separate character strings and not just one. Thus C will assign only the first word of these three, `miles`, to the "from" unit, and ignore the other two. It is important to use a `flush(stdin);` statement prior to each `scanf`, in order to clear the keyboard buffer before reading each new unit name.

3. When your program displays one or more matches, it must number them and ask the user to select one. Your program must also contain some protection against an inappropriate choice.

4. Once an appropriate conversion is selected, your program can either simply display the requested conversion or prompt the user to enter a numerical value to be converted. Although it's certainly true that this last step is the whole point of the program, its implementation is trivial compared to the code required to get to this point. However, if you choose simply to display the conversion as text, it is *not* allowed to store information about the conversion simply as part of a single string. That is, your program must store separately in appropriate structure fields the matching "to" unit name as well as the numerical conversion constant.

Hints:

1. See Exercise 5 for comments about how to compare two strings.

2. The restriction in specification 2 can easily be removed by using fgets to read a string from the keyboard. See Exercise 5 for comments about how to handle strings with embedded blanks.

Extra Credit:

Remove the restriction that the user's keyboard input must not contain any embedded blank spaces in the name of the "from" unit. [units.c]

8. Any real number n (positive or negative) can be expressed in scientific notation in the format

$$n = \text{mantissa} \times 10^{\text{exponent}}$$

where $0.1 \le \text{mantissa} < 1.0$. Write a program that includes functions to extract the mantissa and exponent for a real number and to find the mantissa and exponent for the sum, difference, product, and quotient of two real numbers. A call to a function to do mathematical operations could look like this:

```
c = sci_note(a,'+',b)
```

where a, b, and c are variables declared as structs having a mantissa and exponent as their two fields. [sci_note.c]

Searching and Sorting Algorithms

8.1 Introduction

There are many algorithms that are basic to computing in any technical discipline. Some of these are routinely included as part of an introductory computer science course. Some are of interest to particular areas of science and engineering. Others fall under the general category of numerical analysis algorithms; these will be covered separately in Chapter 9.

It is important for every programmer to have some sense of these widely applicable algorithms to avoid wasting large amounts of time whenever certain common programming problems arise. In this chapter *searching algorithm* *sorting algorithm* we will discuss *searching algorithms* and *sorting algorithms*. These are important because in many computer applications, a great deal of time is spent looking for particular things in a collection of related things. Admittedly, "things" is a vague and untechnical word, but it is chosen to convey the sense that searching algorithms should be applicable regardless of the nature of what is being sought.

As we will see later in this chapter, the efficiency of searching algorithms can be improved dramatically by performing the search on a list of things that are in order. For a collection of numbers, "in order" means that the numbers appear in either ascending or descending order. For a list of words, "in order" means that the words are alphabetized as they would be in a dictionary, either with or without case sensitivity.

Sorting algorithms are therefore of great practical interest because it is so often necessary to reorganize lists of things so they are in a useful order. We will discuss three different sorting algorithms in this chapter. They vary greatly in their efficiency when they're applied to lists originally in random order, but each of them may be a reasonable choice in certain circumstances.

Before we begin the process of designing and implementing searching and sorting algorithms, note that we will often refer to a *list* collection of values as a *list* and we will often use the words list and array as if they were equivalent. However, there is a significant difference between these two terms. A list is an abstract entity for which certain operations such as searching and sorting can be defined. An array is a specific implementation of a list, although by no means the only possible one. (In fact, we will examine an alternative implementation for lists in Chapter 10.) In this chapter, lists of things to be searched or sorted will be implemented as arrays. Except for the inevitable C-specific implementation details, the material in this chapter isn't as much about C per se as it is about the applying a high-level programming language and the concept of arrays to solving some important computing problems.

A specific goal of this chapter is to develop a library of functions that perform searching and sorting operations. You should be able to use these functions in your own programs even if you don't spend a great deal of time understanding the details of their operation. Consider, for example, an algorithm to search for all occurrences of a specified value in a list. That algorithm will be implemented as a C function that will then be incorporated into a driver program to test its operation. In order to use that function in your own programs, you need only understand how it is used in the driver program. Then you can either copy the source code for the function into your own source code or link a precompiled library in which the desired function resides.

Ideally, such a library of functions should operate with a high level of *data abstraction*; that is, the code inside the functions should be *independent* of the contents of the list the function is intended to

| *data abstraction* |
| *data-aware function* |

manipulate. Assuming the list is implemented as an array, then the function can be used with *any* array of values, including arrays of structures, as discussed in Chapter 7. In practice, a small amount of code will typically be required to accommodate the contents of a specific array of values. However, this additional code can be restricted to one or more *data-aware functions* that will be provided separately from the library functions. In order to achieve the desired level of data abstraction, we will use an alias for the data type of an array when it appears as a parameter in functions that implement searching and sorting algorithms, as described in Chapter 7. This alias will be given a specific global data type, either an intrinsic data type or a `struct`, whenever the library functions are used.

8.2 Searching Algorithms

We will begin our discussion of searching algorithms with a specific example. However, the goal of data abstraction will never be far from our thoughts as we implement this example. Suppose you are asked to write a program to find information in a database of chemicals. The database may or may not be sorted by chemical name. In either case, the program will contain a menu of options that include:

1. Find any occurrence of a specified chemical name or string of characters.
2. Find all occurrences of a specified chemical name or string of characters.

Each of these requests is reasonable and may even appear equivalent from a program user's point of view, but each imposes different requirements on algorithm design. Suppose, for the first option, that there are multiple occurrences of the same name or more than one chemical that contains a specified string of characters. Do you wish your program to find the *first* occurrence or will you be satisfied with *any* occurrence? The second option may force you to search through the entire database because it specifically asks for *all* occurrences of a specified string of characters.

For either of these options, as long as you cannot | **linear search** |
assume that the list of chemicals is sorted in some useful order, there is no generally applicable approach other than to search through the list, starting at the beginning. An appropriate algorithm, called a *linear search*, is conceptually very simple and is the topic of Section 8.2.1. Section 8.2.2 will deal with the possibility that you may wish to find an item in a *sorted* list. In this case a more efficient algorithm is available.

8.2.1 Linear Searches

An algorithm that searches for a single occurrence of a specified value in a list is simple, as long as we are satisfied to find only the first such occurrence in the list.

SUBPROGRAM *FindOne(IN: list, size, search_value;*
OUT: integer position of first occurrence, "found")
INITIALIZE *"found" to value that can't be an array element (–1 in C)*
LOOP *(through list with index i until search_value is found or to end of list)*
  IF *(current item in list matches search_value)* **THEN**
    ASSIGN *"found" = i*
END LOOP

Note the double terminating condition for the **LOOP** structure. The loop terminates when the desired value is found *or* the end of the list is reached; this condition is required to handle the case in which the desired item is not found in the list.

An algorithm for finding all occurrences of a specified value is also simple: look through the entire list and save the position of each list value that matches.

SUBPROGRAM *FindAll(IN: list, size, search_value;*
OUT: integer array of positions, "found")
DEFINE *integer index*
INITIALIZE *elements of found to values that can't be array elements*
  (–1 in C)
  index to 0 (current element of "found" array)

LOOP (through list with index variable i)
    IF (list[i] = search_value) **THEN**
        ASSIGN found[index] = i
        INCREMENT index by 1
END LOOP

In this pseudocode implementation, it is assumed that the *found* array has the same size as the original list. Each of its elements is initialized to −1, a value that cannot represent an index to any array element. Inside the loop, whenever a match is found, the current *found* array element is given the value of the list index, and the *found* array index is incremented by 1. When the subprogram terminates, *found* contains the positions of all matches in the list.

Both these algorithms are called linear searches because the search starts at the beginning of the list and continues sequentially either to the end of the list (*FindAll*) or until the first occurrence of the specified value is found (*FindOne*). Program P-8.1(a) gives the C implementation of these two algorithms. The source code file srchsort.c contains code for other functions, too, but only the relevant functions are shown. P-8.1(b) shows how to use the functions to search through an array of integers.

P-8.1(a) [srchsort.c (partial listing)]

```c
void FindAll(data_type a[],int lo,int hi,data_type what,int found[],
             int (*compare)(data_type a,data_type b)) {
  int i,index=0,n_items;

  n_items=hi-lo+1;
  for (i=0; i<n_items; i++)
    found[i]=-1;
  for (i=lo; i<=hi; i++)
    if (compare(a[i],what) == 0) {
      found[index]=i;
      index++;
    }
}

void FindOne(data_type a[],int lo,int hi,data_type what,int *found,
             int (*compare)(data_type a,data_type b)) {
  int i=0;

  *found=-1;
  do {
    if (compare(a[i],what) == 0) *found=i;
    i++;
  } while ( (*found == -1) && (i<=hi) );
}
```

P-8.1(b) [srchtest.c]

```c
#include <stdio.h>
#define N 10

typedef int data_type;

#include "srchsort.h"
#include "srchsort.c"

void MakeArray(data_type a[],int n);
int SearchCompare(data_type a,data_type b);

int main(void)
{
  data_type a[N],what;
  int found[N],found_one,i;
  char yes_no;

  srand(3);
  MakeArray(a,N);
/* Test linear sort routine. */
  while (1) {
    printf("Look for what? ");
    fflush(stdin);scanf("%i",&what);
    FindOne(a,0,N-1,what,&found_one,SearchCompare);
    if (found_one != -1)
      printf("Found one match at (%i) %i\n",found_one,a[found_one]);
    else
      printf("Didn't find any match.\n");
    FindAll(a,0,N-1,what,found,SearchCompare);
    printf("Found matches at:\n");
    for (i=0; i<N; i++)
      if (found[i] != -1) printf("(%i) %i\n",found[i],a[found[i]]);
    printf("More (y/n)? ");
    fflush(stdin);scanf("%c",&yes_no);
    if (yes_no == 'n') break;
  }
  return 0;
}

void MakeArray(data_type a[],int n) {
  int i;

  for (i=0; i<n; i++) {
    a[i]=rand()%20;
    printf("(%2i) %i\n",i,a[i]);
  }
}

int SearchCompare(data_type a,data_type b) {
  if (a == b) return 0;
  else if (a < b) return -1;
  else return 1;
}
```

Problem Discussion

Note that as an implementation detail, low and high indices (lo and hi) are passed to the functions in P-8.1(a), rather than just the size of the array, as was done in the pseudocode. This allows part or all of a list to be searched. Remember that lo and hi must be array indices in the range from 0 to n − 1 and not from 1 to n. The found array returned as output from FindAll is assumed to have a declared size of at least (hi − lo + 1).

Program P-8.1(b) tests each of the linear search algorithms using an array of integers, as defined by the typedef statement printed in bold italics. The files srchsort.h and srchsort.c contain function protypes and implementations for a library of several searching and sorting functions. These files are #included in P-8.1(b) even though only the two functions described in P-8.1(a) are needed to implement the algorithms discussed in this section. While it may appear "wasteful" to copy these files in their entirety into a program that needs only some of the code, it is no more wasteful than including the stdio.h header file and linking to its associated I/O functions. The presence of unnecessary files can slow compilation and create executable files that are larger than necessary. However, this is rarely a significant problem in practice.

The header file srchsort.h contains all the information a programmer needs to use srchsort.c. It should *not* be necessary for the programmer to examine the code in srchsort.c in order to use the functions. Here is a partial listing of srchsort.h., with documentation and prototypes for FindAll and FindOne.

```
/* FindAll searches elements "lo" through "hi" of the array "a" for
   occurrences of "what." The values of "lo" and "hi" must be
   array element references, from 0 to n-1, where n is the declared
   size of "a," and not "position" references 1 to n. The integer
   array "found" is initialized to -1 and, on return, contains the
   positions of matching elements in array "a."
      The data_type of the elements of "a" must be specified prior to
   a call to FindAll, typically prior to the main function, through
   an appropriate typedef statement.
      FindAll requires access to a user-supplied function "compare"
   that compares two quantities of type data_type and returns a
   0 if they are equal.
*/
extern void FindAll(data_type a[],int lo,int hi,data_type what,
               int found[],int (*compare)(data_type a,data_type b));

/* FindOne searches elements "lo" through "hi" of the array "a" for
   the first occurrence of "what." It returns a pointer to the index
   for which the match was found and a pointer to the value -1
   otherwise. See also the documentation for FindAll.
*/
extern void FindOne(data_type a[],int lo,int hi,data_type what,
               int *found,int (*compare)(data_type a,data_type b));
```

It is important to understand how the data abstraction discussed in Section 8.1 has been achieved in P-8.1(a) and P-8.1(b). The parameter lists of the functions shown in P-8.1(a) use the alias `data_type` for the array and for values that must have the same data type as elements of the array. The `typedef` statement in P-8.1(b), printed in bold italics, associates this alias with a specific data type—integers in this case.

P-8.1(b) contains code for two other functions, `MakeArray` and `SearchCompare`, that are data-aware. `MakeArray` is of no general interest, as its only purpose in this program is to generate an array of values to test the search functions. The `SearchCompare` function is needed whenever the search functions are applied to a specific array of data; this function must be tailored to the actual data type of the array elements used in `srchtest.c`. Function `SearchCompare` is made available to `FindOne` and `FindAll` by the inclusion of a pointer to the function in the parameter list of these two functions, using the syntax discussed in Section 5.6.

Function `SearchCompare` returns three possible results, −1, 0, or 1, depending on whether the first parameter is less than, equal to, or greater than the second parameter. As used by the functions in P-8.1(a), the first parameter corresponds to an array element argument and the second parameter corresponds to the value being searched for. Remember that only the `returned` data type and parameter list of the comparison function, and not its name, must agree with the function given in the function prototype and implementation. For the linear search algorithms, it is necessary only to have an "equal to" or "not equal to" response, as noted in the documentation in `srchsort.h`. However, the sorting algorithms discussed in the next section will require "less than" and "greater than" responses, as well.

The value returned indirectly through `FindOne`'s parameter list is −1 if no match is found and the location of the array element if a match is found. In `FindAll`, the array `found` is initialized to −1 and, on return, contains the indices for all matching elements in array a.

As noted, `data_type` in P-8.1(b) has been defined as having type `int`. It is this alias data type definition, along with a user-supplied function for comparing values, which allows the search algorithms to work with *any* kind of array. Suppose the list contains character strings or real numbers rather than integers. Then the criterion for defining and implementing a match will change. For example, we know that we cannot compare two strings with a statement like

```
if (stringA == stringB)...; /* won't work */
```

(We must use the intrinsic function `strcmp` instead.) Also, we know it is generally undesirable to compare real numbers for equality, so we might choose to write something like

```
if (fabs(a-b) < LIMIT)...;
```

The effort to write a data-aware comparison function is more than compensated by the increased flexibility to search lists regardless of their contents. For example, it is easy to use the search functions to match a specified field in an array of `structures`. The changes necessary to accommodate such a search are made not in the search functions themselves, but in the user-supplied `compare` function.

To see how this might work, consider again the simple problem addressed by program P-7.1: read and display a list of measurements from a file with format

```
01  02  03  66.6
04  03  16  17.7
11  12  56  3.3
```
(and so forth)

where the first three values in each record are the hour, minute, and second at which a measurement is made, and the fourth value in each record is the measurement itself. Suppose you are required to find all measurements taken during a user-specified hour. This search criterion is easy to accommodate with the functions included in `srchsort.c`. Program P-8.2 is an extension of P-7.1 which stores the measurements in an array of `structs` and adds the required capability to compare values.

P-8.2 [`structu2.c`]

```c
#include <stdio.h>
#define FILE_NAME "structur.dat"
#define MAX 20

typedef struct {
  int hr,min,sec;
  float measurement;
}data_type;

#include "srchsort.h"
#include "srchsort.c"

int SearchTime(data_type a,data_type b);

void main()
{

  FILE *Infile;
  int status=0,count=0,found[MAX],i;
  data_type measurements[MAX],time_rec;
  char yes_no;

  Infile=fopen(FILE_NAME,"r");
  while (1)
  {
    status=fscanf(Infile,"%d %d %d %f",
                &measurements[count].hr,
                &measurements[count].min,
```

```
                    &measurements[count].sec,
                    &measurements[count].measurement);
  if (status == EOF) break;
  {
    printf("%2d %2d %2d %f\n",measurements[count].hr,
                      measurements[count].min,
                      measurements[count].sec,
                      measurements[count].measurement);
    count++;
  }
}
printf("There are %d records.\n",count);
fclose(Infile);
/* Get search hour. */
  while (1) {
    printf("Which hour (0-24)? ");
    fflush(stdin); scanf("%i",&time_rec.hr);
    FindAll(measurements,0,count-1,time_rec,found,SearchTime);
    for (i=0; i<count; i++)
      if (found[i] != -1)
        printf("%2d %2d %2d %f\n",measurements[found[i]].hr,
                          measurements[found[i]].min,
                          measurements[found[i]].sec,
                          measurements[found[i]].measurement);

    printf("More (y/n)? ");
    fflush(stdin); scanf("%c",&yes_no);
    if (yes_no != 'y') break;
  }
}

int SearchTime(data_type a,data_type b) {
  if (a.hr == b.hr) return 0;
  else return 1;
}
```

In P-8.2, it has been necessary to declare time_rec, another variable with type data_type, in order to have a place to hold the specified hour for use in SearchTime, even though only the hr field is used. You might be tempted to read the hour into an int variable and pass just that value to SearchTime. However, this would generate a compilation error because the data type of the arguments for the compare function in FindAll must be the same as that of the elements of the array being searched. It does not matter that the other fields in time_rec have not been assigned values, because they are not used anywhere in the program.

8.2.2 Binary Search

Recalling the options discussed earlier in the chapter for a program that searches a list of chemical names, consider how to implement a request to find a certain chemical name. If the names are in random order, the linear search algorithms from Section 8.2.1 must be applied. This is okay for small lists, but it seems inefficient for large lists. Is there any way to construct a more efficient algorithm? If the list is sorted in order—alphabetically by chemical name, in this case—then, in fact, a much more efficient algorithm exists for finding a single occurrence of a specified name.

Let's investigate the possibilities by playing a simple game:

1. You will pick an integer between 1 and 100.
2. I will guess the number.
3. You will tell me whether the number I have guessed is too big or too small relative to the number you've picked.

How many tries will I need to guess your number?

Here's one way to play the game: you pick 33.

My guess	Your response
50	too big
25	too small
37	too big
31	too small
34	too big
32	too small
33	you guessed it!

Obviously, another way to play the game is to use a linear search of the numbers from 1 to 100: "Is the number 1? Is it 2? Is it 3?... On the average, if you pick a number randomly from this range, it will take 50 tries to guess the number. For the above example, it will take 33 tries. However, the solution here requires only seven guesses! In fact, it should never require more than seven guesses to find a number in the range 1-100.

This solution requires that guesses be chosen in a particular way. My first guess of 50 is in the middle of the range of possible numbers. When you reply that 50 is too big, then I know that the number must be in the range 1-49. Therefore, my next guess is 25—the number in the middle of the range 1-49. When you tell me that 25 is too small, I select 37, a number in the middle of the range 26-49. At each step I discard half the possible range of numbers, and by continuing in this way I must eventually arrive at the number you have selected.

This algorithm is called a **binary search**. By selecting a value that is at the midpoint of the remaining range at each step and discarding half the list after each unsuccessful guess, this algorithm guarantees that I can find any value in an *ordered* list of size n (or determine that the value doesn't exist in the list) in no more than $\log_2(n)$ guesses. For finding a value in a list of 100 numbers, no more than seven guesses should ever be required because $2^7 \approx 100$. (To put it another way, a range of

binary search

numbers as large as 128 can be divided in half no more than seven times—64, 32, 16, 8, 4, 2, 1.) This is a significant improvement over a linear search. Suppose you have to find a value in a list containing 1,000,000 values. A linear search will require an average of 500,000 comparisons. However, a binary search on an ordered list of 1,000,000 values will require no more than 20 comparisons because $2^{20} \approx 1,000,000$.

The number guessing game is a simplified version of the general binary search problem because if everybody follows the rules of the game, the number to be guessed is guaranteed to exist within the range of numbers 1–100. In order to generalize the binary search algorithm, the problem must be formulated properly. First of all, the list must be in order; it makes no conceptual sense to attempt a binary search on a randomly ordered list. Second, a binary search will find only one occurrence of a specified value. If that value appears more than once in the list, you have no way of knowing which occurrence the binary search will locate. (However, because the list must be in order, you could use a binary search to find one occurrence and then look forward and backward in the list to find additional occurrences.) These restrictions must be compatible with the problem the binary search is being used to solve. Third, a binary search must account for the possibility that the specified value doesn't exist in the list of available values.

The outline of a solution follows the steps used in the number guessing game:

1. Select a value in the middle of the possible range.
2. If that value is the desired value, stop.
3. If the value is smaller than the desired value, reset the lower boundary of the possible range to the middle position plus 1, and search the upper half of the range.
4. If the value is larger than the desired value, reset the upper boundary of the possible range to the middle position minus 1, and search the lower half of the range.
5. Repeat steps 1–4 until the desired value is found or until the lower boundary is larger than the upper boundary.

It should be clear from the way steps 3 and 4 are worded that this is a solution that lends itself to a recursive algorithm. P-8.3(a) is a function that performs a recursive binary search on a sorted array; it is included in the srchsort.c file. P-8.3(b) is a test program that finds a specified value in a hard-coded array of integers. As before, the code is written so that the BinarySearch function can be applied to part or all of any array. The header file srchsort.h contains documentation for BinarySearch, which from the perspective of a program that uses the function, should behave exactly like FindOne from P-8.1.

P-8.3(a) [srchsort.c (partial listing)]

```
void BinarySearch(data_type a[], int lo, int hi,
                  data_type what,int *found,
                  int (*compare)(data_type a,data_type b)) {
    int mid;

    if (lo > hi) *found=-1;
    else
        {
        mid=(lo+hi)/2;
        if (compare(a[mid],what) == 0)
        *found=mid;
        else if (compare(what,a[mid]) < 0)
        BinarySearch(a,lo,mid-1,what,found,compare);
        else
        BinarySearch(a,mid+1,hi,what,found,compare);
        }
}
```

P-8.3(b) [bintest.c]

```
#include <stdio.h>
#define N 10

typedef int data_type;

#include "srchsort.h"
#include "srchsort.c"

int SearchCompare(data_type a,data_type b);

int main(void)
{
    data_type a[]={-17,-3,0,1,4,6,7,18,29,30};
    data_type what;
    int found_one,i;
    char yes_no;

    srand(3);
/* Test binary sort routine. */
    for (i=0; i<N; i++) printf("%i\n",a[i]);
    while (1) {
      printf("Look for what? ");
      fflush(stdin);scanf("%i",&what);
      BinarySearch(a,0,N-1,what,&found_one,SearchCompare);
      if (found_one != -1)
        printf("Found one match at (%i) %i\n",
          found_one,a[found_one]);
      else
        printf("Didn't find any match.\n");
      printf("More (y/n)? ");
      fflush(stdin);scanf("%c",&yes_no);
      if (yes_no == 'n') break;
    }
    return 0;
}
```

```
int SearchCompare(data_type a,data_type b) {
  if (a == b) return 0;
  else if (a < b) return -1;
  else return 1;
}
```

Problem Discussion

The binary search algorithm is deceptively simple. It's easy to write code that looks okay and works *most* of the time. Clearly, this is unacceptable; therefore, all such algorithms must be tested in a driver program. Search algorithms should be tested with a list whose contents you know. Be sure to search for values at the beginning and end of the list, as well as for values that don't exist in the list.

As a demonstration of how to modify the binary test program to search for a different kind of value, consider a program whose task is to search a list of names that are in alphabetical order, as shown in Table 8.1.

Table 8.1. Data file for use with binary search algorithm

```
Alice
Allen
Bob
Carla
David
Evelyn
Frank
Frank
Grace
Grace
Grace
Hal
Laura
Susan
Ted
Wanda
```

This file is in alphabetical order, but it contains duplicate names, so we know that a binary search will find one occurrence of a duplicate name but not necessarily the first one.

How should data_type be defined? A name needs to be represented as an array of characters, so the obvious representation of a list of names is as a two-dimensional array of characters. However, BinarySearch expects a one-dimensional array of type data_type. A simple solution that is easily extended to accommodate more complicated data structures is to define a name as a struct whose single field is an array of characters:

```
typedef struct {
  char name[20];
} data_type;
```

Program P-8.4 shows how to use this definition.

P-8.4 [namefind.c]

```c
#include <stdio.h>
#include <string.h>
#define N 20

typedef struct {
  char name[20];
} data_type;

#include "srchsort.h"
#include "srchsort.c"

int SearchCompare(data_type a,data_type b);
void GetData(data_type a[],int *n_rec);

int main(void)
{
  data_type a[N],what;
  int found_one,i,n_recs;
  char yes_no;

  GetData(a,&n_recs);
  for (i=0; i<n_recs; i++) printf("%s\n",a[i].name);
  while (1) {
    printf("Look for what? ");
    fflush(stdin);scanf("%s",what.name);
    BinarySearch(a,0,n_recs-1,what,&found_one,SearchCompare);
    if (found_one != -1)
      printf("Found one match at (%i) %s\n",
                found_one,a[found_one].name);
    else
      printf("Didn't find any match.\n");

    printf("More (y/n)? ");
    fflush(stdin);scanf("%c",&yes_no);
    if (yes_no == 'n') break;
  }
  return 0;
}

void GetData(data_type a[],int *n) {
  FILE *in;
  int i=0,status=0;

  in=fopen("names.dat","r");
  while (1) {
    status=fscanf(in,"%s",a[i].name);
    if (status == EOF) break;
    printf("%s\n",a[i].name);
    i++;
  }
```

```
    fclose(in);
}

int SearchCompare(data_type a,data_type b) {
    if (strcmp(a.name,b.name) == 0) return 0;
    else if (strcmp(a.name,b.name) < 0) return -1;
    else return 1;
}
```

8.2.3 Choosing a Searching Algorithm

As indicated earlier in the chapter, linear searching algorithms are required under some circumstances. In particular, if a list isn't sorted in any useful order, then a linear search is required. Linear searching algorithms are referred to as order N algorithms. They are often represented in what is known as *big O notation* as *O(N) algorithms*. For any O(N) algorithm, the number of operations required to complete the algorithm is directly proportional to N. Because operations on your computer translate directly into time, doubling the size of the list means that the search will take twice as long with an O(N) algorithm.

> big O notation
> O(N) algorithm

On the other hand, as noted in Section 8.2.2, a binary search is an *O(log₂N) algorithm*, which means that the number of operations is proportional to the log to the base 2 of N. As noted above, this represents a tremendous increase in efficiency for large lists, with a binary search taking no more than 20 comparisons to find a value in a list of 1,000,000 items, rather than the average of 500,000 comparisons required by a linear search.

> $O(log_2 N)$ algorithm

The savings represented by a binary search are so significant that it is often worth the extra effort to devise algorithms that combine binary and linear searching techniques. For example, you know that a binary search finds only one occurrence of a specified value even if that value occurs several times (sequentially) in a sorted list. In the list of names used by P-8.4, the name Grace appears three times. You can use a binary search to locate one occurrence of Grace, but you won't know whether it's the first, second, or third. Therefore, once you have found one occurrence of Grace, you can do a linear search forward and backward to find additional occurrences. Since the list is in order, you can stop the search in either direction when you find a name other than Grace. A hybrid algorithm might seem like a waste of time for a short list, but it makes sense as an efficient way to search a large list. Note that the prototype and output for such a hybrid function should be identical to those of function FindAll previously given in P-8.1(a).

8.3 Sorting Algorithms

The discussion of searching algorithms in Section 8.2 makes clear the importance of putting lists in sorted order so that an efficient binary search algorithm can be used. In this section, we will develop three different algorithms for sorting lists. As in the previous section, we will implement lists as arrays, and we will design algorithms so they can be applied easily to different kinds of data, including arrays of structures. The first two algorithms are somewhat intuitive in nature, but the third, and generally best, method is much less obvious.

Regardless of the algorithm used, the problem statement for developing the algorithms is the same: start with a list represented as an array of values and sort the list into ascending or descending order.

8.3.1 Selection Sort

In order to develop this sorting algorithm, it will help to work with a specific example. Suppose this list of seven integers is stored in an array A:

$$17 \quad 4 \quad 11 \quad 9 \quad 13 \quad 3 \quad 5$$

1. Assume the value in the first element of the array is the smallest value in the entire list.

Assume smallest = $A(1) = 17$.

2. Starting at the second element, compare all the remaining elements with the first element. If you find a smaller one, mark it as the smallest element.

Assign new smallest = $A(6) = 3$.

3. When you have found the position of the smallest remaining element, exchange this element with the first element. Now the smallest element is where it belongs.

These operations look like this:

In this and following steps, the integers in bold type indicate values that have been put in their proper place in the array.

4. Repeat steps 1-3 starting at the second, third, etc., position, up to the $(n-1)^{st}$

position.

After each of five repetitions of steps 1-3, the array looks like this:

(2nd repetition)   3   4   11   9 13 17   5 (no exchange required)

(3rd repetition)   3   4 |11| 9 13 17 | 5 |
                            └─▲─┘   └─▲─┘
                              └────────────────┘

                     3   4   5   9 13 17 11

(4th repetition)   3   4   5   9 13 17 11 (no exchange required)

(5th repetition)   3   4   5   9 |13| 17 |11|
                                   └─▲─┘   └─▲─┘
                                     └──────────┘

                     3   4   5   9 11   17   13

(6th repetition)   3   4   5   9 11 |17| |13|
                                        └─▲─┘└─▲─┘
                                          └────┘

                     3   4   5   9 11   13   17

Note that in some cases, the element initially chosen as the smallest remains the smallest. Then it's not necessary to exchange a pair of elements.

An algorithm to implement these steps looks like this.

SUBPROGRAM *Selection(IN/OUT: array A of type data_type; IN: size)*
DEFINE *(current, test, smallest, as integers)*
LOOP *(current = 1 to size – 1)*
    ASSIGN *smallest = current*
    LOOP *(test = current + 1 to size)*
        IF *(A(test) < A(smallest))* **THEN**
            ASSIGN *smallest = test*
    END LOOP
    IF *(A(current) <> A(smallest))* **THEN**
        CALL *Swap(A(current),A(smallest))*
END LOOP
(end of subprogram)

SUBPROGRAM *Swap(IN/OUT: a, b of type data_type)*

DEFINE *(temp as data_type)*
ASSIGN *temp = a*
      a = b
      b = temp
(end of subprogram)

We will reuse the *Swap* subprogram in subsequent algorithms.

    P-8.5(a) contains the source code for a function that implements the Selection Sort algorithm.

P-8.5(a) [`srchsort.c`** (partial listing)]**

```
void Swap(data_type *x,data_type *y) {
  data_type temp;
  temp=*x;
  *x=*y;
  *y=temp;
}
void SelectionSort(data_type a[],int lo,int hi,
   int (*compare)(data_type a,data_type b))
{
      int i,j,min;

      for (i=lo; i<hi; i++) {
        min=i;
        for (j=i+1; j <=hi ; j++)
           if (compare(a[j],a[min]) == -1) min=j;
        Swap(&a[i],&a[min]);
      }
}
```

    Similar to the implementations of searching algorithms in Section 8.2, the code implementation of the Selection Sort algorithm requires both a lower and an upper limit on the elements of the array to be sorted, rather than just the size of the array. Remember, however, that for a list containing n items, these values are array indices in the range 0 to n − 1 and not list positions in the range 1 to n. The header file `srchsort.h` contains a prototype for `SelectionSort` but not for `Swap`, which is local to `srchsort.c`:

```
/* SelectionSort sorts elements "lo" through "hi" of array "a." The
   data_type of the elements of "a" must be specified by the main
   program through an appropriate typedef statement.
      SelectionSort requires access to the same user-supplied compare
   function as FindAll.
*/
extern void SelectionSort(data_type a[],int lo,int hi,
   int (*compare)(data_type a,data_type b));
```

Program P-8.5(b) shows how to use `SelectionSort`.

P-8.5(b) [sorttest.c]

```c
#include <stdio.h>
#include <math.h>
#define MAX_SIZE 20

typedef float data_type;

#include "srchsort.h"
#include "srchsort.c"
void GetData(data_type a[],int *n);
int SortCompare(data_type a,data_type b);

int main(void)
{

  int i,n_recs;
  float a[MAX_SIZE];

  GetData(a,&n_recs);
  SelectionSort(a,0,n_recs-1,SortCompare);
  printf("After sorting:\n");
  for (i=0; i<n_recs; i++)
    printf("%d  %lf\n",i,a[i]);

  return 0;
}

void GetData(data_type a[],int *n) {
  FILE *infile;
  int i=0,status=0;

  infile=fopen("arrays.dat","r");
  while (1) {
    status=fscanf(infile,"%f",&a[i]);
    if (status == EOF) break;
    printf("%d  %f\n",i,a[i]);
    i++;
  }
  fclose(infile);
  *n=i;
}

int SortCompare(data_type a,data_type b) {
  if (fabs(a-b) < 1e-5) return 0;
  else if (a < b) return -1;
  else return 1;
}
```

It is easy to verify the operation of such an algorithm for a particular list, but it's not so easy to be confident that it will work correctly for *every* list. Thus P-8.5(b) should be expanded to test SelectionSort not only for lists originally in random order, but also for lists already in order, lists that are backwards, and lists whose contents are all the same value.

Problem Discussion

Because of the nested `for...` loops appearing in the code, the Selection Sort algorithm is an *O(N²) algorithm*. That is, the number of operations required to

| $O(N^2)$ *algorithm* |

sort a list is proportional to the square of the number of items in the list. However, Selection Sort has the advantage that elements in a list are exchanged only when the final location of an element is known. It performs the same number of comparisons regardless of the initial order of values in the array. This isn't necessarily a disadvantage in most circumstances. However, if the list is initially almost in order, Selection Sort performs a lot of unnecessary comparisons. The next section describes an algorithm that performs substantially better than Selection Sort if a list is already almost in order.

Also, note that the code in `SelectionSort` *always* swaps two elements at the end of the interior loop, even if `i` is equal to `min`, in which case there is no reason to swap the elements. This makes the code a little shorter, but it would certainly be reasonable to modify the code so that `Swap` is called *only* if `i` and `min` are different.

8.3.2 Insertion Sort

Insertion Sort is another intuitive sorting algorithm. Suppose you're being dealt a hand in a card game such as bridge. Every time you're given a new card, you sort the hand by automatically inserting the new card into its proper place. The same process can apply to sorting a list. Again, it will help to use a specific example. Suppose the list contains these values:

17   4 11 9 13 3 5

Start with the second value. If it is greater than or equal to the first element, leave it alone. Otherwise, put the second value in its proper place by moving the first value up one position and putting the second value where the first value used to be.

| 17 | | 4 | 11 | 9 | 13 | 3 | 5 |

4 **17** 11 9 13 3 5

The values in bold type represent a subset of the list that is sorted.

Repeat this step until you get to the end of the list.

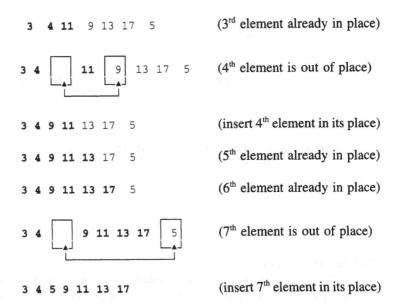

3   4 11   9 13 17   5   (3rd element already in place)

3 4 [   ] 11 [9] 13 17   5   (4th element is out of place)

3 4 9 11 13 17   5   (insert 4th element in its place)

3 4 9 11 13 17   5   (5th element already in place)

3 4 9 11 13 17   5   (6th element already in place)

3 4 [   ] 9 11 13 17 [5]   (7th element is out of place)

3 4 5 9 11 13 17   (insert 7th element in its place)

We can implement this easily in pseudocode.

LOOP *(for i from 2 to n)*
    Insert the list[i] item in its proper place if it isn't where it belongs.
END LOOP

It is perhaps not obvious how to move elements to their proper positions if they are out of position. Here is the pseudocode.

ASSIGN *temp = list[i]*
LOOP *(as long as temp < list[i-1] and i > 1)*
        ASSIGN *list[i] = list[i – 1]*
        DECREMENT *i by 1*
END LOOP
ASSIGN *list[i] = temp*

Program P-8.6 gives source code for the InsertionSort function from srchsort.c. To test this function, it is necessary only to substitute a call to InsertionSort for a call to SelectionSort in P-8.5(b). The header file srchsort.h contains a prototype for InsertionSort; its documentation is identical to that for SelectionSort.

P-8.6 [srchsort.c (partial listing)]

```
void InsertOne(data_type a[],int i) {
  data_type temp;

  temp=a[i];
  while ( (compare(temp,a[i-1]) == -1) && (i > 0) ) {
    a[i]=a[i-1];
    i--;
  }
  a[i]=temp;
}
void InsertionSort(data_type a[],int lo,int hi,
              int (*compare)data_type a,data_type b)) {
  int i;
  for (i=lo+1; i<=hi; i++)
    InsertOne(a,i);
}
```

Problem Discussion

The algorithm has been implemented as two separate functions. Although this may make the code easier to understand, the primary reason is that function `InsertOne` can be used separately from function `InsertionSort`. For example, it can be used to insert into its proper place a new item in a list that is already sorted. For this reason, the header file `srchsort.h` contains function prototypes for both these functions.

The Insertion Sort is still an $O(N^2)$ algorithm; its nested loop comes from the fact that `InsertOne`, which contains its own loop, is called from within a loop in `InsertionSort`. However, this algorithm is more efficient than the Selection Sort algorithm for lists that are already almost in order.

8.3.3 The Recursive Quicksort Algorithm

Because of their nested loop structures, the Selection Sort and Insertion Sort algorithms discussed in Sections 8.3.1 and 8.3.2 are both $O(N^2)$ algorithms, which means that if you double the length of the list to be sorted, the sorting time increases by a factor of four rather than two. Thus sorting operations performed on large lists can take a very long time. (This will be discussed in more detail in Section 8.3.4.) Fortunately, it is possible to design a sorting algorithm that is more efficient, but this is *not* an intuitive approach you are expected to discover on your own.

First, consider Table 8.2, which shows the number of operations required to sort a list containing 128 items and then the number of operations to sort that list if it can be subdivided into two or more sublists. The initial size of 128 is significant only because it can be evenly divided by 2 down to size 1. The effort required to sort the original and subdivided lists is an arbitrary measure of computer operations or elapsed time. If $O(N^2)$ algorithms are assumed, this effort is proportional to N^2, and for the purposes of this discussion this value will simply be set to N^2. On modern computers, the actual time required to sort even large lists may be small, so whether the fact that an algorithm is $O(N^2)$ is of any practical concern depends on the application. For the sake of this discussion, we will assume that the performance of the algorithm is at least potentially significant.

Listing the time required to sort 128 lists of size 1, as shown in Table 8.2, might appear to be pointless because no sorting actually has to be done. However, as we shall soon see, this limiting case isn't as irrelevant as it seems.

Table 8.2. Effort to sort lists with an $O(N^2)$ algorithm, relative units

Number of Lists	Effort Required to Sort List(s)
1	$1 \cdot 128^2 = 16,384$
2	$2 \cdot 64^2 = 8,192$
4	$4 \cdot 32^2 = 4,096$
8	$8 \cdot 16^2 = 2,048$
16	$16 \cdot 8^2 = 1,024$
32	$32 \cdot 4^2 = 512$
64	$64 \cdot 2^2 = 256$
128	$128 \cdot 1^2 = 128$

The message of Table 8.2 is that it should take only half as long to sort two lists of size N/2 as it does to sort one list of length N, one quarter as long to sort four lists of size N/4, etc. Is there some way to take advantage of these savings? Suppose we arbitrarily divide a list of length N into two sublists or *partitions* of length N/2; this is an operation that can be done for free in the sense that the small computational effort required is the same no matter how large the list. Can we save time or operations simply by sorting these two lists? No, because the two individually sorted lists have to be merged back together again, and this operation carries its own computational cost that offsets the savings achieved by sorting two shorter lists.

However, suppose we could subdivide a list into two parts so that one partition contains small values and the other contains large values. To do this, select one value in the original list, called the *pivot value*, and use this value to subdivide the list into two partitions, one that contains values less than or equal to the pivot value and the other that contains values greater than or equal to the pivot value:

`<= pivot value`	`>= pivot value`

Although the "less than or equal to" and "greater than or equal to" phrases appear to create overlapping lists, this definition is required to account for the special situation in which all values in the list are the same.

If we now sort these two partitions, the result is equivalent to sorting the entire list. The algorithm can be stated in three steps:

(1) Divide a list into two partitions, one containing small values and the other containing large values.
(2) Sort the lefthand partition if it contains more than one value.
(3) Sort the righthand partition if it contains more than one value.

If we can construct the partitions with no computational cost, it's obvious that even if we use an $O(N^2)$ sorting algorithm, we have devised a more efficient approach to sorting a list. Of course, it should be clear that the partitioning can't be done for free. However, once we have written a partitioning algorithm, we don't actually have to worry about selecting a sorting algorithm. All we have to do is continue to subdivide the partitions. Eventually, every partition will contain no more than one value. When this occurs, the entire list will be sorted. In effect, the apparently trivial final entry in Table 8.2, sorting 128 lists of size 1, will become a reality. Essentially, we have traded partitioning effort for sorting effort. As it turns out, this will be an excellent trade!

The three-step sorting algorithm above involves repeatedly performing the same operations until a terminating condition is reached. Not surprisingly, such an algorithm can easily be implemented recursively:

SUBPROGRAM *Quicksort(IN/OUT: array; IN: lower,upper)*
DEFINE *left,right*
CALL *Partition(array,lower,upper,left,right)*
IF *first < right* **THEN CALL** *Quicksort(array,lower,right)*
IF *left < last* **THEN CALL** *Quicksort(array,left,upper)*

This is called a Quicksort algorithm. The values *lower* and *upper* are the boundaries of the original list or, during recursive calls, the boundaries of the subset of the list currently being sorted. In the original call to the subprogram, *lower* and *upper* would typically be 1 and n for a list containing n values (0 and n – 1 in a C implementation). The values *left* and *right* are the lower and upper boundaries of the lefthand and righthand partitions returned from the *Partition* subprogram:

(original list)

lower		upper

(partitioned list)

lower	right	left		upper

As noted above, partitioning requires computational resources. The first step is to select the pivot value. Table 8.2 implies that the best results will be achieved if each partitioning operation divides a list into equal halves—plus or minus one, depending on whether the list contains an odd or even number of values. Ideally, then, the pivot value should be the median value in the list. However, the median can't be found without sorting the list first!

If the list is originally almost in order, or in reverse order, a good approximation to the median is the element in the middle of the list. If the list is originally in random order, then there is no computation-free way to find the median and, in fact, there is no way to pick a pivot value that is better than a randomly chosen value without performing time-consuming operations on the list. Thus, an element in the middle of the list is still as reasonable a choice as any other. The middle element between two specified limits *lower* and *upper* is simply the element (*lower* + *upper*)/2, assuming integer division.

To illustrate the partitioning process, consider this list of seven random integers:

$$10 \quad -1 \quad 14 \quad \mathbf{9} \quad 3 \quad 11 \quad 13$$

The pivot value 9, element (1 + 7)/2 = 4, is printed in bold type. Our task is to create two partitions, one that contains elements less than or equal to 9 and the other that contains values no less than 9. How can we produce these two partitions "in place," using the memory locations occupied by the original list?

The solution may not be immediately obvious. Start at the left end of the list and move a "list pointer," which will become an array index in the code implementation, to the right as long as the element is less than 9. Save its location. Now start at the right end of the list and move to the left as long as 9 is less than the element. Save its location. For this example, the left pointer doesn't move at all because the first element, 10, must be moved to the upper partition. Moving down from the right, the first element that is out of place in the upper partition is 3.

```
  L           R
  ↓           ↓
┌─────────────────────────┐
│ 10  -1  14  9  3  11  13 │
└─────────────────────────┘
```

Now exchange these two elements. Increment the left pointer by one position and decrement the right pointer by one position.

```
    L     R
    ↓     ↓
┌─────────────────────────┐
│ 3  -1  14  9  10  11  13 │
└─────────────────────────┘
```

Move the left pointer to the right as long as the element is less than 9 and move the right pointer to the left as long as 9 is less than the element. Save the locations. For this example, the right pointer doesn't move at all.

```
      L R
      ↓ ↓
┌─────────────────────────┐
│ 3  -1  14  9  10  11  13 │
└─────────────────────────┘
```

Exchange the elements and advance the pointers:

```
    R   L
    ↓   ↓
┌─────────────────────────┐
│ 3  -1  9  14  10  11  13 │
└─────────────────────────┘
```

At this point, the right pointer is less than the left pointer, and this condition defines the first two partitions:

```
┌──────────┐  ┌──────────────┐
│ 3  -1  9 │  │ 14  10  11  13 │
└──────────┘  └──────────────┘
```

Note that the two partitions haven't been sorted because that's not the purpose of creating the partitions. All that has happened is that they are divided into small and large values. Continue to apply this algorithm on the new partitions. In each case, the pivot value is printed in bold type.

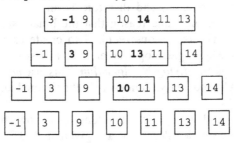

The translation of this process into a complete algorithm requires a great deal of care to ensure that it will produce the appropriate partitions regardless of the size or contents of the sublist being partitioned. There are several problems that can occur when the left and right pointers meet in the interior of the list, and it is *very* easy to come up with an algorithm that looks reasonable but that won't work under all conditions. Here is the complete pseudocode for a partitioning algorithm:

```
SUBPROGRAM Partition(IN: array, lower, upper; OUT: left, right)
DEFINE (pivot)
ASSIGN left = lower
       right=upper
       pivot = a[(lower + upper)/2] (use integer division)
LOOP (until right ≤ left)
  (Move up from the left as long as the element is less than pivot.)
     LOOP (while a(left) < pivot)
          INCREMENT left = left + 1
     END LOOP
  (Move down from the right as long as pivot is less than the element.)
     LOOP (while pivot < a(right))
          INCREMENT right = right – 1
     END LOOP
  (Swap if required and increment/decrement pointers.)
     IF (left <= right) THEN
          IF (left ≠ right) THEN CALL Swap(a(left),a(right))
          INCREMENT left = left + 1
                    right = right – 1
     (end IF...)
END LOOP
```

The partitioning part of the Quicksort algorithm is a binary process (because it repeatedly divides the list into two parts) and therefore is an

$O(Nlog_2N)$ *algorithm*

$O(\log_2 N)$ algorithm for the same reason that the binary search algorithm is an $O(\log_2 N)$ algorithm. The operations required to create each partition are $O(N)$ because they involve a single loop (rather than a nested loop). Therefore, the Quicksort algorithm is an *$O(Nlog_2N)$ algorithm*. This is a *major* improvement over $O(N^2)$ algorithms. Consequently, Quicksort is the favored algorithm for general-purpose sorting tasks.

Partitioning and Quicksort functions can now be included in the srchsort.c source code file. They are given in P-8.7. The srchsort.h header file will contain the prototype for the QuickSort function but not for the partitioning function, which is not accessed directly by a program that needs to call a sorting algorithm. Again, the code is written so that this algorithm can be applied to any kind of array, including an array of structures. The Quicksort function can be tested in P-8.5(b) by substituting its name for SelectionSort. Indeed, an important feature of all these sorting algorithms is that the information interface is the same for each of them, so they can be used interchangeably in a program.

P-8.7 [srchsort.c (partial listing)]

```
void MakePartition(data_type a[],
                   int lower, int upper, int *right, int *left,
                   int (*compare)(data_type a,data_type b))
{
  int mid,flag;

  mid=(lower+upper)/2;
  *left=lower;
  *right=upper;
  while (compare(a[*left],a[mid]) < 0) *left+=1;
  while (compare(a[mid],a[*right]) < 0) *right-=1;
  while (*left < (*right-1))
  {
    Swap(&a[*right],&a[*left]);
    (*left)+=1;
    (*right)-=1;
    while (compare(a[*left],a[mid]) < 0) (*left)+=1;
    while (compare(a[mid],a[*right]) < 0) (*right)-=1;
  }
  if (*left <= *right)
  {
    if (compare(a[*left],a[*right]) < 0) Swap(&a[*right],&a[*left]);
    (*left)+=1;
    (*right)-=1;
  }
}
```

```
void QuickSort(data_type a[], int lower, int upper,
        int (*compare)(data_type a,data_type b)) {
    int upper_left, lower_right;

    if (lower < upper)
    {
        MakePartition(a,lower,upper,&upper_left,&lower_right,compare);
        if (lower < upper_left) QuickSort(a,lower,upper_left,compare);
        if (upper > lower_right) QuickSort(a,lower_right,upper,compare);
    }
}
```

Problem Discussion

The success of the Quicksort algorithm in producing $O(N\log_2 N)$ behavior rests on the assumption that partitions will be consistently of approximately equal size. If this assumption is not justified in practice, then Quicksort can deteriorate into an $O(N^2)$ algorithm. Even though Quicksort *could* be implemented as an iterative algorithm, as all recursive algorithms can, this is more trouble than it's worth.[1]

8.3.4 Efficiency of Sorting Algorithms

Recall that in Section 8.2.3, we identified linear and binary search algorithms as $O(N)$ and $O(\log_2 N)$ algorithms. We can characterize sorting algorithms in the same way, to determine the relationship between the number of operations required to sort a list and the size of the list being sorted.

Consider the Selection Sort algorithm, which contains nested for... loops. For an array of size N, the statements inside the outer loop are executed approximately N times and the statements inside the inner loop are executed, on average, approximately N/2 times each time the inner loop is executed. Altogether, then, each operation inside the inner loop is executed approximately (N)(N/2) times. If N = 100, the if... statement is executed roughly 10,000/2 = 5,000 times. If N = 200, the if... statement is executed roughly 20,000 times, a factor of four increase. In general, if the size of the array increases, the number of operations required to sort the array with a Selection Sort algorithm increases as the square of the factor by which the array size increases.

This relationship between array size and performance characterizes an $O(N^2)$ algorithm. An N^2 dependence on array size represents a severe performance penalty for large values of N, with the result that the Selection Sort and Insertion

---

[1]Versions of Fortran prior to Fortran 90 did not support recursion. As a result, older Fortran programming texts generally did not discuss the Quicksort algorithm because of the difficulty of writing a nonrecursive version of the algorithm.

Sort algorithms are not very efficient for large arrays. Although computer scientists and programmers may not be happy with a theoretically inefficient algorithm, acceptable performance is largely a matter of perception, depending on your own definition of a severe performance penalty for a particular problem.

The Selection Sort algorithm requires the same number of comparison operations regardless of the original state of the list being sorted. On the other hand, the performance of the Insertion Sort depends strongly on the original state of the list. If the list is backwards, for example, the Insertion Sort is very inefficient. However, if the list is originally almost in order, the Insertion Sort is very efficient (because it makes only about N comparisons and no exchanges if the list is already in order). If the list is in random order, the Insertion Sort is still an $O(N^2)$ algorithm. In this case, a conditional loop is nested inside a `for...` loop.

In summary, the Selection Sort is a reasonable choice for small lists that are originally in random order, but the Insertion Sort is better if the list is originally almost in sorted order. As noted above, the Quicksort algorithm is always the appropriate choice for large lists that are believed to be originally in random order.

8.5 Application: Merging Sorted Lists

Even though this application doesn't make direct use of the material in this chapter, it belongs to the same family of algorithms for manipulating the contents of lists.

1 *Define the problem.*

A common data management problem involves merging two sorted lists of data. Write a program that will merge two lists of numbers.

In a practical science or engineering problem, this problem might involve two sets of measurements made with two different instruments over the same period. If the data include the time of each measurement, it might be desirable to merge the two sets into a single set of measurements in chronological order.

It is certainly possible simply to append one set of sorted measurements to another and then sort the resulting combined set of measurements. If the two lists are not already individually sorted by time, the most reasonable choice is to append one list to the other and sort the entire list at once. Algorithms for doing this have been discussed earlier in this chapter. However, assuming that each list of measurements is already arranged in time sequence, it is more efficient to merge the two lists than to sort the combined list. This is especially true if the combined list of measurements is very large; for example, too large to be stored in memory in an array.

Even though we can easily imagine real applications of a merging algorithm, such as combining lists of measurements sorted by time, the abstract merging process requires careful thought and meticulous algorithm design outside the context of a particular practical application. Therefore we will consider the simple problem of merging two lists of integers, assuming that each list is already sorted in ascending order. In order to make this problem more easily applicable to a practical situation, we will store the lists of integers in two files, and we will operate directly on the contents of the files rather than storing their contents in arrays within the program. This will allow us to apply the solution to lists that are too large to be stored in arrays. We will use the files lista.dat and listb.dat, as shown in Table 8.3.

Table 8.3. Data for testing a list-merging algorithm

list a	list b
1	3
3	5
5	5
7	6
7	6
9	7
11	7
17	8
21	9
21	11
22	12
22	13
	14
	15
	16
	17
	18
	22
	24
	25
	26
	27

These two lists have several characteristics that are important for developing and testing a merging algorithm: they are of different lengths, each list contains some duplicate values, and the lists have some values in common.

2 Outline a solution.

It's easy to see how to start the process of merging the two lists, but you will have to be especially careful toward the end of each list. You can assume that each list contains at least one value, as there is no point trying to merge two lists if one of them is empty.

Also, you can assume that a pseudocode instruction to print a value will initially mean nothing more than displaying that value on your monitor screen. Once you're convinced that the algorithm is working properly, you can replace this instruction with an instruction that writes a value into a new file.

With these assumptions in mind, here is an algorithm.

1. Read one value from each list.

2. Compare the values. If one value is smaller than the other, print the smaller value and read another number from the same list. If both values are the same, print both values and read another number from each list.

3. Eventually, you will come to the end of one of the lists. Be sure the last value from that list is printed. If there are still numbers in the other list, they will be larger than all the numbers printed so far. Read the remaining numbers and print them all. Note that you will not necessarily reach the end of the shorter list first; when you reach the end of a list is determined not by its length, but by its contents.

This solution outline doesn't include the details of what to do when you reach the end of a list. The best way to develop a complete algorithm is to work through the sample lists given above:

```
Operation              Value:       Compare      Output
                       a     b
-----------------------------------------------------
read a                 1
read b                       3
(now we are inside a loop)
                                    a<b (1<3)
print a                                          1
read a                 3
                                    a=b (3=3)
print a and b                                    3
                                                 3
read a and b           5     5
                                    a=b (5=5)
print a and b                                    5
                                                 5
read a and b           7     5
                                    a>b (7>5)
print b                                          5
read b                       6
                                    a>b (7>6)
print b                                          6
read b                       6
                                    a>b (7>6)
print b                                          6
read b                       7
                                    a=b (7=7)
print a and b                                    7
                                                 7
read a and b           7     7
                                    a=b (7=7)
print a and b                                    7
                                                 7
```

```
read a and b          9      8
                              a>b  (9>8)
print b                                      8

.
.
.
                      22     22
                              a=b  (22=22)
print a and b                                22
                                             22
read a and b          22     24
                              a<b  (22<24)
print a                                      22
(end of "a" list and end of loop)
```

Now that the algorithm has reached the end of the a list, what remains to be done? The current value of b (24) hasn't yet been printed. Therefore, the algorithm must print that value and then read and print the rest of the b list.

As you know from previous discussions, it is not allowed to try to read past the end of a file. You will have to incorporate a test for the end-of-file when you design the merging algorithm.

3 Design an algorithm.

DEFINE *("a" and "b" lists; a and b values;*
        end_a and end_b as logical variables)
OPEN *("a" and "b" lists)*
READ *(a and b from "a" and "b" lists)*
LOOP *(as long as there are data in both lists)*
    IF *(a < b)* **THEN**
            WRITE *(a)*
            IF *(NOT end_a)* **CALL** *ReadOne(from "a",a,end_a)*
            IF *(end_b)* **WRITE** *(b)*
    ELSE IF *(a = b)* **THEN**
            WRITE *(a,b)*
            IF *(NOT end_a)* **CALL** *ReadOne(from "a",a,end_a)*
            IF *(NOT end_b)* **CALL** *ReadOne(from "b",b,end_b)*
    ELSE
            WRITE *(b)*
            IF *(NOT end_b)* **CALL** *ReadOne(from "b",b,end_b)*
            IF *(end_a)* **WRITE** *(a)*
    (end IF...)
END LOOP

IF (NOT end_a) THEN
    WRITE (a)

    LOOP (to end of "a")
        READ (from "a",a)
        WRITE (a)
    END LOOP
(end IF...)
IF (NOT end_b) THEN
    WRITE (b)
    LOOP (to end of "b")
        READ (from "b",b)
        WRITE (b)
    END LOOP
(end IF...)

4

Convert the algorithm into a program.

P-8.8 [merge.c]

```c
#include <stdio.h>
typedef int list_type;
int ReadOne(FILE *in_a,list_type *a);
void ReadAll(FILE *in);

int main(void)
{
  FILE *in_a, *in_b;
  int status_a,status_b;
  list_type a,b;

  in_a=fopen("lista.dat","r");
  if (in_a != NULL) printf("List a is open.\n");
  in_b=fopen("listb.dat","r");
  if (in_b != NULL) printf("List b is open.\n");
  status_a=ReadOne(in_a,&a);
  status_b=ReadOne(in_b,&b);
  while ( (status_a == 0) && (status_b == 0) ) {
    if (a < b) {
      printf("%i\n",a);
      if (status_a == 0) status_a=ReadOne(in_a,&a);
      if (status_b != 0) printf("%i\n",b);
    }
    else if (a == b) {
      printf("%i\n%i\n",a,b);
      if (status_a == 0) status_a=ReadOne(in_a,&a);
      if (status_b == 0) status_b=ReadOne(in_b,&b);
    }
    else {
      printf("%i\n",b);
```

```
    if (status_b == 0) status_b=ReadOne(in_b,&b);
    if (status_a != 0) printf("%i\n",a);
  }
}
if (status_a == 0) {
  printf("%i\n",a);
  ReadAll(in_a);
}
if (status_b == 0) {
  printf("%i\n",b);
  ReadAll(in_b);

}
fclose(in_a);
fclose(in_b);
return 0;
}
int ReadOne(FILE *in,list_type *x) {
  int status=0;
  list_type a;

  (void)fscanf(in,"%i",&a);
  *x=a;
  status=feof(in);
  return status;
}
void ReadAll(FILE *in) {
  list_type x;
  int status=0;

  while (1) {
    status=fscanf(in,"%i",&x);
    if (status == EOF) break;
    printf("%i\n",x);
  }
}
```

Running P-8.8

```
List a is open.
List b is open.
1 3 3 5 5 5 6 6 7 7 7 7 8 9 9 9 11 11 12 13 14 15 16 17 17 18
21 21 22 22 22 24 25 26 27
```

(To save space, the output values are listed horizontally across the output box. In the actual program output, the values are listed one per row.)

5 *Verify the operation of the program.*

It is not a trivial matter to verify the operation of this program under *all* possible input conditions! As a minimum, you need to test situations for which the "a" or "b" list has only one value, the values in one or both lists are all the same, and all the values in one list are larger (or smaller) than all the values in the other list. If you use the program on real data of your own, be sure to test it with a subset of the data that is small enough to verify by hand.

Problem Discussion

Although P-8.8 prints a message when each file is successfully opened, it assumes that this will be true and does not take action if either file isn't found. This is consistent with our usual goal of keeping code simple and focused on the specific problem at hand. It is easy to add code to check for the successful opening of both files if you think it is necessary.

The major implementation challenge in P-8.8 is keeping track of the end-of-file status of each file. This is accomplished by using the intrinsic feof function, which returns a nonzero value when the end-of-file mark is the next character in the file and 0 otherwise. Function ReadOne reads one value from an open file and returns the end-of-file status after reading that value. The arguments used in a call to this function determine whether the "a" or "b" list is read. Once the end of the shorter list has been found, then function ReadAll is used to read to the end of the remaining list.

8.6 Debugging Your Programs

The code presented in this chapter is meant to be incorporated into other programs that need searching and sorting capabilities. Assuming that the functions work as intended, their application is straightforward. You should create your own library of source code and compile it on your own computer system. If you study the header file and driver programs, it should be clear in each case what is required to use each function. Remember that you must tailor the data-aware compare function, which can have whatever local name you choose for it, to meet the needs of your program.

The fact that a program uses library functions that have have been tested under a range of conditions does not mean it is a good idea to assume those functions will always work. It is still important to test *your* program with *your* data.

8.7 Exercises

1. Recalling Exercise 5 in Chapter 7, modify that program to use the search functions given in P-8.1.

2. Write a function whose prototype and output are identical to function FindAll, as described in P-8.1(a). This function should use a binary search to find one occurrence of a name in an array. Then it should search linearly in both directions to find all the remaining occurrences of that name in the array. Add this function to your library of searching and sorting functions and also to the header file. Include appropriate documentation.

3. Write a version of the Insertion Sort algorithm that can be used to maintain the order of a sorted list when new values are added to the list. First add the new value to the end of an array. Then use function `InsertOne` as given in P-8.6 to insert this new value in its proper place.

4. A database of drugs contains the name of the drug, the recommended maximum daily dose, and the recommended maximum cumulative dose. In some cases, both the daily and cumulative maximums are assumed to be proportional to body weight and are given in the database for a 150-pound individual of either gender. In some cases, drugs may be approved for only men or only women. The maximum dose for a drug that is not approved is given as 0.

Proposed treatments for patients are also available in a database. The information includes the proposed drug, the gender and weight of the patient, the proposed daily dose, and the number of days the treatment will last.

Write a program that will read and store drug information in an array and will then read and process a file containing information about proposed treatments. Search through the drug file for the drug name given in a proposed treatment. If the proposed treatment exceeds either the maximum daily or the cumulative dose, print an appropriate message. Assume that the daily dose remains constant throughout the treatment. Account for the possibility that one or more proposed treatments will include drugs that are not yet entered into the drug database.

Sample data files, which can be downloaded from the Web site mentioned in Section 6 of the Preface, include `drugbase.dat` (the drug database) and `drugbase.in` (the treatment database). You should add records to `drugbase.in` to ensure that all program branches are tested. (That is not currently the case.) [`drugbase.c`]

`drugbase.dat`

| Drug Name | Maximum dose: P = weight-dependent, with value for 150 lb | | | |
	Daily (M)	Cum (M)	Daily (F)	Cum (F)
abracap	P2.3	100	3.0	100
betalit	0.5	10	0.5	100
deproved	P0.01	0.05	0	0
ethicoo	P0	0	500	5000
gonagain	1.5	15	1.5	10
heptez	0.001	0.05	0.0005	0.025

```
drugbase.in

drug        wt.   daily, mg  days
--------------------------------
abracap   M 300     900        10
gonagain  F 120      .1       200
newdrug   F 135     100        20
```

5. In Section 8.2.3, it was suggested that a binary search could be combined with a linear search to find all the occurrences of a specified value in the list. Using a sorted list that contains some duplicate values (the data type of items in the list can be whatever you like), write and test a function that uses a binary search to find one occurrence of a value and then searches backward and forward in the list to find all occurrences of that value. Add this function to your library of searching and sorting functions. Its information interface should be identical to function FindAll, as listed in P-8.1(a). [hybrid.c]

6. Especially if a large sorted list contains many duplicate values, it may make sense to construct an index to values in the array. An index array will hold this kind of information in a structure:

```
value   first location   number of values
17      1                10
19      11               41
22      52               13
33      65               17
(and so forth)
```

For the value 19, for example, the index array indicates that the first 19 is in element 11 and that there are 41 values of 19 altogether.

    Create a data file based on these and a few additional values. Then write a program that generates an index array and uses the array to search for and display all occurrences of a specified value. When you test your program, be sure to include a test for a value that doesn't exist in the array. The assumption is that the index array is small compared to the array being searched. If so, you could justify using a linear search of the index array. However, as long as the indexed values (the lefthand column in the example) are sorted, you can also apply a binary search to this array. [index_to.c]

7. Under special conditions, it's possible to devise an O(N) sorting algorithm. Suppose you wish to sort a large list of lowercase letters initially in random order and stored in an array A. There are only 26 possible values, a number that is assumed to be much smaller than the number of letters to be sorted. The Counting Sort algorithm takes advantage of this situation. Here is an outline.

1. Define an index array with 26 elements, one for each letter of the alphabet.

2. Read through an array A of lowercase letters. Convert each character to an integer in the range 0 through 25 and increment the corresponding element of the index array by one. When you're done, the index array will contain the number of a's, b's, and so on.

3. Read through the index array from positions 0 through 25 and set each element equal to itself plus the previous element. When you're done, the index array will contain the last position occupied by each letter in a new sorted array. For example, if the original list contains 23 a's, 33 b's, and 41 c's, the first three elements of the index array will be 23, 56, and 97.

4. Read through the original array of letters again. Convert each letter to an integer in the range 0 through 25 and use this value to access the corresponding element in the index array. Put the letter into its indicated position in a new array B, which will hold the sorted data. Then decrement the value in the index array by 1. Consider the example in step 3. Here's what will happen in this loop:

```
Letter in A   Letter in B   1st 3 Components of Index Array
                            23   56   97  (original contents)
a             B(23)=a       22   56   97
a             B(22)=a       21   56   97
b             B(56)=b       21   55   97
b             B(55)=b       21   54   97
b             B(54)=b       21   53   97
c             B(97)=c       21   53   96
```

The first letter in the A array is an a. It goes in element 23 of the B array. The first element in the index array is decremented by 1, from 23 to 22. The next letter in A is also an a. It goes in element 22 of the B array, and the first element in the index array is decremented again. The third letter in the A array is a b. It goes in element 56 of the B array, and the second element of the index array is decremented by 1. This continues until all the letters have been placed in the B array.

5. Print the list of sorted letters.

Note that this algorithm doesn't contain any nested loops; that's why it's an O(N) algorithm. Also, it should be clear that the B array isn't actually required to sort letters because a sorted array of letters can easily be created just by overwriting the original A array with the appropriate number of a's, b's, and so on. However, the algorithm has been written this way, with two arrays, in order to make possible the Extra Credit part of this problem, in which all the original values in the A array must be saved.

Extra Credit:
Create an array of words in random order. (The words could be just random combinations of letters.) Use a Counting Sort to put all words starting with a together, all words starting with b together, and so forth. You can use the index array to determine the first and last positions for words beginning with a, b, and so on. Then use Quicksort to sort groups of words beginning with the same letter. This is an efficient way to sort a large list of words. [knt_sort.c]

8. As director of a wildlife tracking project, one of your jobs is to collect field reports of radio tracking data and enter them in a database. Each report consists of a tracking number for each animal, the date, and two location coordinates. For the purposes of this problem, the coordinates are arbitrary real numbers. A small sample set of reports might look like this (see file wildlife.dat):

```
101    05/05/97    55.3    44.8
101    05/06/97    57.1    43.4
102    05/05/97    66.0    13.3
102    06/01/97    66.8    22.1
102    06/05/97    69.0    25.7
101    06/01/97    50.0    50.9
```

Note that the tracking reports for a particular animal aren't necessarily consecutive, but you can assume that all reports for each animal are in chronological order.
Write a program that will perform these three functions:

1. Add new reports to the database, entered from the keyboard.
2. Print out all the tracking reports for a specified animal.
3. Print all reports for a specified date.

One way to solve this problem is to store the data in an array of structures and use the searching algorithms described earlier in this chapter. However, for this exercise we will take a different approach. Although we will still use arrays, this approach can easily be generalized to the case where there are too many reports to store in an array.
What you need to do is create a data structure that provides links from one data object to the next:

```
struct TrackType {
    int ID;
    char date[9];
    float x,y;
    int SameAnimal,SameDate;
}
```

The variables SameAnimal and SameDate are pointers,[2] in the form of array indices, to the next report on the same animal and the next report on the same date. For example, in the above example, the first mention of animal 101 is in the first record of a file. Hence the array index of the first mention of animal 101 is 0. The SameAnimal field in the structure should contain a value of 1, which points to the next element containing a reference to animal 101. That element should "point" to element 5. Finally, the SameAnimal field in element 5 should contain a −1 or some other value that cannot be interpreted as an array index.

If we wish to access the reports for animal 101, we need to know where the first report is stored in the array. If we need to add another report for animal 101, we need to know where the last report is stored. We will save this kind of information in two additional arrays that provide an index to the first and last locations of each animal and date. The complete access and storage scheme is illustrated in Figure 8.1.

Animal Index Array

100	-1	-1
101	0	5
102	2	4
103	-1	-1

Date Index Array

05/05/97	0	2
05/06/97	1	1
06/01/97	3	5
06/05/97	4	4
	-1	-1

Data Array

101	05/05/97	55.3	44.8	1	2
101	05/06/97	57.1	43.4	5	-1
102	05/05/97	66.0	13.3	3	-1
102	06/01/97	66.8	22.1	4	5
102	06/05/97	69.0	25.7	-1	-1
101	06/01/97	50.0	50.9	-1	-1

Figure 8.1. Storage scheme for the wildlife tracking problem.

Although you might reasonably argue that this approach is a lot of work, especially for such a small data set, it does make sense for accessing very large collections of data. Once the index and data arrays are set up, the data array is essentially self-searching because each array element contains all the information needed to find the next occurrence of either the animal ID or the report date. The

---

[2]Although the concept is similar, this use of the word pointer is not the same as the programming implementation of this term as we have used it throughout this text.

major justification for this approach is not yet evident because we have not yet discussed random access files. (We will discuss this topic in Chapter 10.) However, if you imagine large amounts of data being stored in a file structure that can be accessed randomly, then the index arrays, which can be stored permanently as text files, can be used to access information in this large data file without applying any searching or sorting algorithms.

To create the index arrays, define an appropriate structure for the fields as shown. Initialize the first pointer and last pointer fields to −1. Read the report file and, one at a time, store new reports. Set the SameAnimal and SameDate fields in the new element to −1. Then:

(a) If an animal or ID doesn't yet exist in its index array, add it and save the data array index in the first pointer and last pointer fields of the index array.

(b) If an ID and/or date already exists in its index array, set the SameAnimal and SameDate field(s) in the current last pointer element for the corresponding ID or date report to point to the new report. Then replace the last pointer value in the index array(s) to point to the newly added report.

To print all reports for a specified animal or date, first search for the animal code or date in its index array. Then use the first pointer value to locate the first report. Thereafter, use the pointer from the SameAnimal or SameDate field in the record to locate the next record. When the SameAnimal or SameDate field contains a −1, then you are at the end of the list of reports for that animal. Follow the same procedure to print all reports for a specified date.

Hints:
1. For a shorter version of this exercise, construct just the index array for finding animals by their ID.
2. The animal IDs are defined so that you don't actually have to search for a particular animal in the animal index array. Use the remainder of dividing its ID by 100 to find it in the index array; for example, 107%100 equals 7 .
3. As shown in Figure 8.1, the pointer fields give your program access to animals and dates from the oldest to the newest. It is equally easy to build links that work the other way around. [wildlife.c]

Basic Statistics and Numerical Analysis

9.1 Introduction

Statistical and numerical analysis are among the most important applications in scientific and engineering programming. This chapter describes algorithms for basic descriptive statistics and for some standard problems in numerical analysis, including:

- mean, standard deviation, and linear regression (Section 9.2)
- numerical differentiation and integration (Sections 9.3 and 9.4)
- solving systems of linear equations (Section 9.5)
- finding the roots of an equation (Section 9.6)
- numerical solutions to differential equations (Section 9.7)

The topics in this chapter require a greater degree of mathematical sophistication than earlier material. Although the text does not presume to provide all the necessary background, the discussion of each topic includes at least a sketchy mathematical introduction. It is an understatement to say that there are several possible approaches to most of the problems discussed in this chapter, which are quite properly the subject of entire texts and courses. For each of these problems, this text will discuss just one simple approach and will present a complete solution in the form of an algorithm, an implementation using one or more functions, and a simple driver program to test the functions.

In contrast to earlier chapters, applications are included with each section of the chapter rather than at the end. In this way, each section is independent of the others. For example, if you understand algebraic equations, you should be able to understand the section that deals with solving systems of linear equations, which does not rely on calculus, even if you bypass the sections on numerical differentiation and integration, which do require some understanding of calculus. To further underscore the independence of each section, equations are numbered starting with (1) within each section.

Although the algorithms discussed in this chapter will work satisfactorily for a wide range of problems, it is a mistake to apply them blindly. For many kinds of realistic problems, more robust algorithms will be needed to minimize computational problems.[1] It's important to remember that *all* numerical methods

---

[1]There is an entire software industry built around the development of C function libraries for professional use in solving difficult problems in numerical analysis.

have inherent limitations. Quantification of those limitations is largely absent from the discussions in this chapter not because it is unimportant, but because an appropriate treatment lies well beyond the scope of this text. With this caveat, however, it is equally true that it never hurts to try the relatively simple algorithms presented here as long as you are willing to retain a healthy skepticism about the results.

9.2 Basic Descriptive Statistics

Statistical characterization of data is essential in all areas of science and engineering. Hence, some basic algorithms for this task are essential tools for any programmer. This section is restricted to the statistics of normal distributions and linear regression. The results will not be derived, but will simply be stated in a way that facilitates their computation.

9.2.1 The Sample Mean and Standard Deviation

Consider a collection of measurements x that are *assumed* to be drawn from a normally distributed population. These measurements can be characterized by two quantities: their **arithmetic mean** and **standard deviation**. The arithmetic mean (what is commonly called the average) m of n such measurements is defined as

arithmetic mean
standard deviation
variance

$$m = \frac{\sum_{i=1}^{n} x_i}{n} \tag{1}$$

The standard deviation s is a measure of the variability in the data. It is defined as the square root of the **variance** s^2:

$$s^2 = \frac{\sum_{i=1}^{n} (x_i - m)^2}{n - 1} \tag{2}$$

This definition can be put into a form that is easy to calculate on the fly from a list of measurements because the calculation doesn't require that the mean be obtained ahead of time:

$$s^2 = \frac{\sum_{i=1}^{n} x_i^2 - \left(\sum_{i=1}^{n} x_i\right)^2 / n}{n - 1} \tag{3}$$

The standard deviation has the property that approximately 68 percent of all normally distributed measurements of a quantity will be within ± s, 95 percent within ±2 s, and 99.7 percent within ±3 s. The "plus or minus three standard deviations" rule is sometimes used as a basis for discarding measurements outside these limits; this may or may not be a good idea, depending on the application and the nature of the quantity being measured.[2]

Because tables of cumulative probabilities are based on the standardized normal variable z, having a mean of 0 and a standard deviation of 1, it is often desirable to transform the mean and standard deviation of a set of measurements into the corresponding standardized normal variable. For any measurement x,

$$z = \frac{x - m}{s} \tag{4}$$

Figure 9.1 illustrates the standard normal distribution which, for obvious reasons, is referred to as the bell curve.

Especially for small sets of data, it is important to distinguish between the sample mean and standard deviation m and s and the population mean and standard deviation μ and σ. The former are available from direct observation, but the latter are usually unknown; it is often assumed that statistics derived from a large sample are the same as population statistics. The n − 1 in the denominator of the formula for standard deviation is there specifically because s is the sample standard deviation and not the population standard deviation. For small data sets, this has the effect of increasing the sample standard deviation compared to the population standard deviation. To put it another way, the smaller the sample, the greater the uncertainty about the properties of the entire population from which the sample is drawn.

---

[2] The existence of the Antarctic ozone hole was confirmed in the 1980s only after scientists rewrote satellite data analysis algorithms to accept measurements that had previously been rejected by such a statistical test.

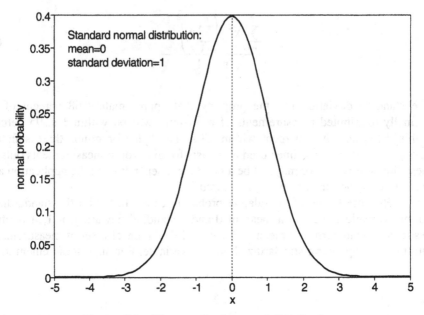

Figure 9.1. The standard normal distribution.

9.2.2 Linear Regression and the Linear Correlation Coefficient

Assume that a collection of measurements has been taken of a quantity y that is a function of an independent variable x. Further assume that these data can be represented by an equation of form

$$y(x) = a + bx \tag{5}$$

where a and b are the intercept and slope of a straight line called the **linear regression line**. In general, this linear relationship will be an imperfect representation of both the observed and the actual relationship between x and y, either because there is noise in the system or because the relationship is not really linear. Linear regression attempts to determine the values of a and b that *best* represent the data, assuming that a linear relationship is a reasonable choice for the data being examined.

    The usual definition of the best representation uses the **sum of squares of the residuals**, defined as the sum of the squares of the differences between measured and modeled values of y:

$$\text{sum of squares} = \sum_{i=1}^{n} (y_i - y_{model})^2 \tag{6}$$

The method of least squares asserts that the best values of a and b are those that minimize the sum of squares for a particular set of measurements. These parameters are given by

$$a = \frac{(\sum y_i)(\sum x_i^2) - (\sum x_i)(\sum x_i y_i)}{n\sum x_i^2 - (\sum x_i)^2}$$

$$b = \frac{n\sum x_i y_i - (\sum x_i)(\sum y_i)}{n\sum x_i^2 - (\sum x_i)^2} \tag{7}$$

The **standard error of estimate** of y on x is a measure of the variability about the regression line. It is obtained from

standard error of estimate

$$s_{y,x}^2 = \frac{\sum y_i^2 - a\sum y_i - b\sum x_i y_i}{n - 2} \tag{8}$$

The value n − 2 in the denominator once again reflects the fact that this statistic is calculated from a sample of measurements rather than from an entire population. The standard error of estimate of y on x has properties similar to the standard deviation. If lines are drawn parallel to and at vertical distances $s_{y,x}$, $2s_{y,x}$, and $3s_{y,x}$ above and below the best-fit regression line, 68, 95, and 99.7 percent of the measurements will fall within these lines.

A quantitative measure of the applicability of a linear regression model is given by the **correlation coefficient**. This is a dimensionless quantity in the range [−1,+1], which is equal to the ratio of the explained variation in a set of data to the total variation, with respect to the best-fit regression line:

correlation coefficient

$$r = \pm\sqrt{\frac{\text{explained variation}}{\text{total variation}}} = \pm\sqrt{1 - s_{y,x}^2/s_y^2} \tag{9}$$

The explained variation is equal to the total variance s_y^2 of all the measurements calculated using equation (2) or (3) from Section 9.2.1, minus the square of the standard error of estimate $s_{y,x}$. When r is +1, all the data lie exactly along the regression line, with positive slope. A negative value of r denotes a regression line with negative slope. When r equals 0, y and x are totally unrelated to each other; that is, a value of x provides *no* information about what the corresponding value of y might be. Intermediate values of r indicate that a linear relationship is only partially successful as a model to explain the behavior of y as a function of x. Note that a linear model for data with a strong random component (as opposed to an inherently nonlinear relationship) can still be reasonable even if the correlation coefficient isn't close to 1.

When, as is often the case, a regression line is forced to pass through the coordinates (0,0) (i.e., it is required that y = 0 when x = 0), the slope is the only coefficient required for the model:

$$b = \frac{\sum y_i}{\sum x_i} \tag{10}$$

and the standard error of estimate of y on x is given by

$$s_{y,x}^2 = \frac{\sum y_i^2 - 2b\sum x_i y_i + b^2 \sum x_i^2}{n - 2} \tag{11}$$

We can now develop and implement algorithms for two functions—one for calculating mean and standard deviation and another for performing linear regression on a set of data. In each case, the data will be held in one or more appropriate arrays. In the first algorithm, we will include a test on the variance as a precaution to make sure it is non-negative before taking the square root to calculate the standard deviation. However, the variance should never be less than 0. If the data have a standard deviation of 0 (which requires all the measurements to be the same), then it is possible for arithmetic roundoff errors to produce a very small negative value for the variance.

We will also include in the first algorithm a provision for calculating either the population or the sample standard deviation, as specified by a user-supplied character flag. For experimental data, as noted above, the sample statistic is generally accepted as the appropriate choice.

SUBPROGRAM *NormalStats(IN: A (array of real numbers),*
n (# of elements), flag (character);
OUT: avg, std_dev)
DEFINE *sum, sum_sq, variance, i (loop counter)*
ASSIGN *sum = (sum of A_i's)*
sum_sq = (sum of A_i^2's)

CHOOSE (between flag= 'p' for population stats and 's' for sample stats)
      'p': **ASSIGN** variance = $(sum\_sq + sum^2/n)/n$
      's': **ASSIGN** variance = $(sum\_sq + sum^2/n)/(n-1)$
IF variance $\geq$ 0 **THEN**
      ASSIGN std_dev = $\sqrt{variance}$
ELSE
      WRITE (appropriate message?)
      ASSIGN std_dev = some "error" value (optional?)
(end IF...)
ASSIGN avg = sum/n

For the linear regression analysis, there are two choices to be made: one for population or sample statistics and the other for a regression line that either is or isn't forced through x-y coordinates (0,0). This function requires *NormalStats* as part of the calculations for the correlation coefficient. Note that the intercept parameter *a* is declared as an *IN/OUT* variable. This is because its value on input is used to determine whether the regression should be forced through (0,0); if that value is other than 0, a full regression is assumed. Note that the standard error of estimate is also included in the output. Several sums over the components of data vectors, as defined in equations (7), (8), (10), and (11), are required in this algorithm. These sums are represented with shorthand **ASSIGN** statements in the algorithm.

SUBPROGRAM LinearRegression(IN: x, y (arrays), n, flag (character);
                                  IN/OUT: a; OUT: b, s_yx, r)
DEFINE sum_x, sum_y, sum_xy, sum_xx, sum_yy, temp, avg, std_dev
        i (loop counter)
ASSIGN sum_x = (sum elements of x)
      sum_y = (sum elements of y)
      sum_xy = (sum elements of x•y)
      sum_yy = (sum elements of y•y)
(Get regression parameters.)
IF (a $\neq$ 0) **THEN** (calculate full regression)
      ASSIGN temp = n•sum_xx - sum_x^2
          a = (sum_y•sum_xx-sum_x•sum_xy)/temp
          b = (n•sum_xy – sum_x•sum_y)/temp
          s_yx = $\sqrt{sum\_yy - 2b\,sum\_xy + b^2 sum\_xx}/n$
ELSE (just calculate slope)
      ASSIGN b = sum_y/sum_x
          s_yx = $\sqrt{(sum\_yy - 2b\,sum\_xy + b^2 sum\_xx)/n}$
IF (flag = 's') **THEN ASSIGN** s_yx = $s\_yx \sqrt{n/(n-2)}$ (for sample stats)

(Get correlation coefficient.)
CALL *NormalStats(y,n,flag,avg,std_dev)*
ASSIGN $r = \sqrt{1 - (s\_yx/std\_dev)^2}$ *(assume std_dev is OK)*

P-9.1 implements these algorithms and tests them by calculating a regression line for linear data upon which a random "noise signal" is superimposed.

P-9.1 [stats.c]

```c
#include <stdio.h>
#include <math.h>
#include <stdlib.h>
#include <time.h>
#define SIZE 50

int NormalStats(double a[],int n,char flag,
              double *avg,double *std_dev);
void NormalArray(double a[],int n);
void LinearRegression(double x[],double y[],int n,char flag,
                  double *a,double *b,double *s_yx,double *r);
int main(void)
{
  double x[SIZE],y[SIZE],avg,std_dev;
  double a,b ; /* intercept and slope for linear regression */
  double s_yx; /* standard error of estimate of y on x */
  double corr; /* correlation coefficient */
  int n=SIZE,i;

  NormalArray(x,n);
  printf("array generated\n");
  NormalStats(x,n,'p',&avg,&std_dev);
  printf("population mean and std dev: %lf %lf\n",avg,std_dev);
  NormalStats(x,n,'s',&avg,&std_dev);
  printf("    sample mean and std dev: %lf %lf\n",avg,std_dev);
  NormalArray(y,n);
  for (i=0; i<n; i++) {
    x[i]=(double)i;
    y[i]=2.*i+10.*y[i];
    printf("%8.3lf %8.3lf\n",x[i],y[i]);
  }
  a=1.; /* Set a != 0 for full regression analysis. */
  LinearRegression(x,y,n,'s',&a,&b,&s_yx,&corr);
  printf("FOR FULL REGRESSION...\n");
  printf("regression coefficients: %lf %lf\n",a,b);
  printf("standard error of estimate of y on x : %lf\n",s_yx);
  printf("correlation coefficient: %lf\n",corr);
  a=0.; /* Set a=0 for regression forced through (0,0). */
  LinearRegression(x,y,n,'s',&a,&b,&s_yx,&corr);
  printf("FOR REGRESSION FORCED THROUGH (0,0)...\n");
  printf("regression coefficients: %lf %lf\n",a,b);
  printf("standard error of estimate of y on x : %lf\n",s_yx);
  printf("correlation coefficient: %lf\n",corr);
  return 0;
}
```

```
int NormalStats(double a[],int n,char flag,
            double *avg,double *std_dev) {
  double sum=0.,sum_sq=0.,variance;
  int i,return_value=1;

  for (i=0; i<n; i++) {
    sum+=a[i];
    sum_sq+=a[i]*a[i];
  }
  switch (flag) {
    case 'p':
      printf("variance for population statistics\n");
      variance=(sum_sq-sum*sum/n)/n;
      break;
    case 's':
      printf("variance for sample statistics\n");
      variance=(sum_sq-sum*sum/n)/(n-1.);
      break;
    default :
      printf("From NormalStats: FLAG ERROR, 's' assumed.\n");
      variance=(sum_sq-sum*sum/n)/(n-1.);
      return_value=0;
  }
  if (variance < 0.) {
    printf("From NormalStats: NEGATIVE VARIANCE %lf\n",variance);
    *std_dev=-1.;
    return_value=-1;
  }
  else
    *std_dev=sqrt(variance);
  *avg=sum/n;
  return return_value;
}
void LinearRegression(double x[],double y[],int n,char flag,
                double *a,double *b,double *s_yx,double *r) {
  double avg,std_dev;
  double sum_x=0.,sum_y=0.,sum_xy=0.,sum_xx=0.,sum_yy=0.,temp;
  int i;

  for (i=0; i<n; i++) {
    sum_x+=x[i];
    sum_y+=y[i];
    sum_xy+=x[i]*y[i];
    sum_xx+=x[i]*x[i];
    sum_yy+=y[i]*y[i];
  }
  if ((*a) != 0.) { /* calculate full regression */
    temp=n*sum_xx-sum_x*sum_x;
    *a=(sum_y*sum_xx-sum_x*sum_xy)/temp;
    *b=(n*sum_xy-sum_x*sum_y)/temp;
    *s_yx=sqrt((sum_yy-(*a)*sum_y-(*b)*sum_xy)/n);
  }
  else { /* just calculate slope */
    *b=sum_y/sum_x;
    *s_yx=sqrt((sum_yy-2.*(*b)*sum_xy+(*b)*(*b)*sum_xx)/n);
  }
  switch (flag) {
    case 'p':
      printf("Linear regression for population statistics\n");\
      break;
```

```
      case 's':
        printf("Linear regression for sample statistics\n");
        *s_yx=(*s_yx)*sqrt((double)n/(n-2.));
        break;
      default:
        printf("FROM LinearRegression: FLAG ERROR, 'p' assumed\n");
  }
/*  Use NormalStats to get standard deviation of y. */
  NormalStats(y,n,flag,&avg,&std_dev);
  if (std_dev > 0.) {
      temp=1.-(*s_yx)*(*s_yx)/std_dev/std_dev;
      if (temp >= 0.)
        *r=sqrt(temp);
      else { /* an error condition exists */
        *r=0.;
        printf("FROM LinearRegression: ERROR CONDITION %lf\n",temp);
      }
    }
  else { /* an error condition exists */
    printf("FROM LinearRegression: ERROR CONDITION %lf\n",std_dev);
    *r=0.;
    }
}
void NormalArray(double a[],int n) {
  int i;
  double two_pi=8.*atan(1.),u1,u2;

  srand((unsigned)time(NULL));
  for (i=0; i<n; i+=2) {
    u1=(double)rand()/RAND_MAX;
    u2=(double)rand()/RAND_MAX;
    if (u1 == 0.) u1=1e-15; /* u1 must not be 0 */
    a[i]   =sqrt(-2.*log(u1))*cos(two_pi*u2);
    a[i+1]=sqrt(-2.*log(u1))*sin(two_pi*u2);
    printf("%lf %lf\n",u1,u2);
  }
  if (n%2 == 1) { /* create one more value */
    u1=(double)rand()/RAND_MAX;
    u2=(double)rand()/RAND_MAX;
    if (u1 == 0.) u1=1e-15;
    a[n-1]=sqrt(-2.*log(u1))*cos(two_pi*u2);
  }
}
```

Running P-9.1 (partial output)

```
Linear regression for sample statistics
variance for sample statistics
FOR FULL REGRESSION...
regression coefficients: -2.226585 2.098195
standard error of estimate of y on x : 10.532472
correlation coefficient: 0.945389
Linear regression for sample statistics
variance for sample statistics
FOR REGRESSION FORCED THROUGH (0,0)...
regression coefficients: 0.000000 2.007314
standard error of estimate of y on x : 10.617187
correlation coefficient: 0.944481
```

Figure 9.2 shows the data and the full linear regression for this sample output.

Problem Discussion

The code in P-9.1 contains some safeguards against potential problems with the calculations—primarily taking the square root of a negative number. However, these safeguards don't test the code itself. The only way to verify the accuracy of all the code is to check it carefully and compare results against an example worked through by hand. Even though normal statistics aren't intended to be applied to very small samples, the calculations themselves can be checked adequately with a data set of only three or four measurements.[3]

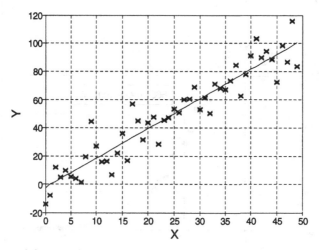

Figure 9.2. Randomized linear data with linear regression line.

---

[3]If you have access to a spreadsheet, it should include built-in functions for performing these calculations. Make sure you understand whether your spreadsheet calculates population or sample statistics; some spreadsheets have separate functions for each.

9.2.3 Application: Analyzing Wind Speed Data

1 Define the problem.

Because of the straightforward implementation and interpretation of normal statistics, it is tempting to apply them even when their use may not be justified. Consider an instrument that records wind speed. The measurements are averaged over an hour, and these hourly averages are collected for an entire year. Figure 9.3 shows a count histogram of 8697 wind measurements in 0.5 mile per hour increments. The data are from data file windspd.dat. The entire file is too large to list here.[4] The data presented in Figure 9.3 are calculated from the program developed in this application.

These wind speed data are not normally distributed, and the physical reason is clear. The average wind speed (about 6.2 mph) is small, and therefore relatively close to 0, compared to the upper range of observed wind speeds, but the lower limit must be 0. Thus the distribution of wind speeds is strongly skewed from the bell shape of a normal distribution.

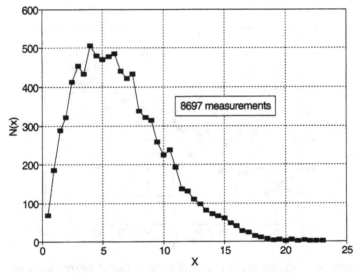

Figure 9.3. Count histogram of wind speed in increments of 0.5 mph.

---

[4]The file windspd.dat contains real wind speed data from a state-maintained air quality monitoring station near Philadelphia, Pennsylvania.

Is it possible to transform such data into a normal distribution? One common approach is to calculate the statistics of the logarithms of the measurements. If the logarithms are normally distributed, they create a so-called lognormal distribution.[5] In this application, we will write a program that assumes wind speed is lognormally distributed.

2 Outline a solution.

The solution is straightforward: Read the data file and accumulate the sums $\Sigma \ell n(x)$ and $\Sigma [\ell n(x)]^2$.

3 Design an algorithm.

The algorithm design is straightforward.

4 Convert the algorithm into a program.

P-9.2 [`windspd.c`]

```
#include <stdio.h>
#include <math.h>
#define FILENAME "windspd.dat"
#define N_HIST 50

void ReadFile(char filename[],
              double *sum_ln,double *sum_ln_sq,int *n,int hist[]);

int main(void)
{
    int hist[N_HIST];
    double sum_ln,sum_ln_sq;
    double mean,std_dev;

    int i,n;
    FILE *out;

    ReadFile(FILENAME,&sum_ln,&sum_ln_sq,&n,hist);
    mean=sum_ln/n;
    std_dev=sqrt((sum_ln_sq-sum_ln*sum_ln/n)/(n-1.0));
```

---

[5]Brief discussions of the lognormal distribution can be found in statistics texts. The classic work on this topic is Aitchison, J., and J. A. C. Brown, *The Lognormal Distribution*, Cambridge University Press, NY, 1957.

```
   printf("            Number of hourly values: %1i\n",n);
   printf("     Mean and std. dev. of ln(data): %10.3lf %10.3lf\n",
         mean,std_dev);

   for (i=0; i<N_HIST; i++) {
     printf("%4.1lf %i\n",i/2.,hist[i]);
   }
   return 0;
}

void ReadFile(char filename[],
            double *sum_ln,double *sum_ln_sq,int *n, int hist[]) {
   int mon,day,hr;
   int m,yr,n_days,index;
   FILE *infile;
   int status=0;
   double ln_x,x;

   infile=fopen(filename,"r");
   for (index=0; index<N_HIST; index++)
     hist[index]=0.0;
   *sum_ln=0.0; *sum_ln_sq=0.0; *n=0;
   for (mon=0; mon<12; mon++) {
     status=fscanf(infile,"%i %i %i",&m,&yr,&n_days);
/*     printf("%i %i %i\n",m,yr,n_days); */
     for (day=0; day<n_days; day++) {
       for (hr=0; hr<24; hr++) {
       status=fscanf(infile,"%lf,",&x);
       /* printf("%5.1f",x); */
       if (x >= 0.0) {
/* Accumulate data for statistics. */
         (*n)++;
         if (x == 0.0) x=1e-6;
         ln_x=log(x);
         *sum_ln+=ln_x;
         *sum_ln_sq+=ln_x*ln_x;
/* Generate histogram data. */
         index=x*2.0;
         hist[index]+=1;
       }
       }
       /* printf("\n"); */
     }
   }
   fclose(infile);
}
```

Running P-9.2

```
                Number of hourly values: 8697
        Mean and std. dev. of ln(data):      1.600      0.923
 0.0  68
 0.5  185
 1.0  287
 1.5  321
 2.0  413
 2.5  454
 3.0  432
 3.5  505
 4.0  479
 4.5  470
 5.0  478
 5.5  485
 6.0  441
 6.5  422
 7.0  433
 7.5  337
 8.0  322
 8.5  313
 9.0  257
 9.5  225
10.0  237
10.5  192
11.0  136
11.5  131
12.0  111
12.5  97
13.0  82
13.5  71
14.0  66
14.5  59
15.0  47
15.5  41
16.0  26
16.5  23
17.0  14
17.5  9
18.0  7
18.5  3
19.0  5
19.5  1
20.0  5
20.5  1
21.0  3
21.5  1
22.0  1
22.5  1
23.0  0
23.5  0
24.0  0
24.5  0
```

5 *Verify the operation of the program.*

These calculations are straightforward—it makes no difference that the mean and standard deviation are being calculated for the logarithm of the measurements. The real question is whether the calculations make sense for these data.

Problem Discussion

An unknown for coding this problem is the size of the histogram array, as it is not known ahead of time what the maximum wind speed is. In this case, it seemed reasonable to assume that the maximum hourly averaged wind speed would not exceed 25 mph. This turned out to be a good guess.

It is clear that the calculations can be done for this problem without difficulty. However, it is an entirely different matter to demonstrate that the primary assumption made for the problem—that the natural logarithm of wind speeds is normally distributed—is justified. Figure 9.4 shows the count histogram for the logarithm of the wind speed.

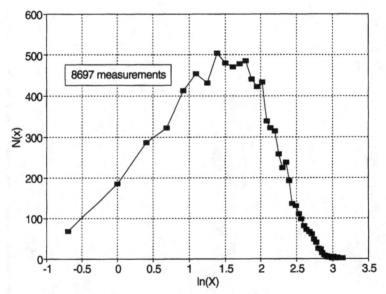

Figure 9.4. Count histogram of the logarithm of wind speed in increments of 0.5 mph.

The distribution of ℓn(wind speed) is certainly "more normal" than the distribution of wind speed itself, and it seems reasonable that such data *might* be lognormally distributed. Air pollution data often have distributions similar to these wind speed data. Lognormal statistics are often applied to such data in spite of the fact that they are not really lognormally distributed, simply because the calculations are easy to do and the interpretation of the resulting numbers within the context of a normal distribution is straightforward. It is beyond the scope of this application either to investigate the lack of lognormality or to decide whether assuming lognormality is a useful thing to do just because the numbers are easy to obtain.

9.3 Numerical Differentiation

9.3.1 Newton's and Stirling's Formulas

Consider the function $f(x)$. The derivative $f'(x)$ is the rate of change of $f(x)$ with respect to x. Although the derivatives of analytic functions are usually available without much difficulty,[6] rates of change are often required for experimental data that are not expressed in analytic form. For example, you might collect data as a function of time and then require an estimate of rates of change with respect to time based on those data. In either case, an estimate of a function's rate of change can be obtained by calculating the slope between two evaluations of the function at two closely spaced values of x. Here are three intuitive formulas based on a simple graphical interpretation of the derivative as the slope of a function:

$$f'(x) \approx [f(x+\Delta x) - f(x)]/\Delta x \qquad \text{(Newton's forward formula)} \qquad (1)$$

$$f'(x) \approx [f(x+\Delta x) - f(x-\Delta x)/]/(2\Delta x) \quad \text{(Stirling's formula)} \qquad (2)$$

$$f'(x) \approx [f(x) - f(x-\Delta x)]/\Delta x \qquad \text{(Newton's backward formula)} \qquad (3)$$

where Δx is a small interval. The second of these formulas averages the calculation in the forward and backward direction and seems generally the best choice. Note that it does not matter whether a function has been evaluated analytically at $x \pm \Delta x$ or whether the Δx's correspond to some interval between experimental data.

These formulas are trivial to implement in C. However, there are reasons to be cautious in their application. They (and similar higher order versions) are

---

[6]The availability of symbolic algebra software such as Maple V means that even difficult analytic derivatives can be obtained with little effort.

basically polynomial approximations. Even if the difference between f(x) and its polynomial approximation is small, there is no guarantee that the same is true of the difference between an analytic derivative and the polynomial approximation to that derivative. Additionally, for functions whose derivatives can become large (in absolute magnitude), it is important to select appropriately small values of Δx; the criteria for defining "small" may not always be obvious.

If the formulas are used to approximate rates of change for experimental data, the dominant error source is most likely the data themselves, through the independent or dependent variable or some combination of the two. Suppose measurements are taken as a function of time so that the interval Δx becomes Δt. In general, you would expect that the best approximation to the derivative would be obtained when Δt is small. However, because Δt appears in the denominator, small errors in measuring time intervals can produce approximations to the derivative that are wildly in error.

In some experimental situations, therefore, it might be preferable to approximate the data with a well-behaved analytic function whose derivative can be calculated analytically; this is a tradeoff between representing accurately all measurements of a dependent variable and "smoothing" the numerically generated rates of change of that variable. In other situations, a numerical derivative is actually the desired result. Suppose production cost data are available monthly for a manufacturing facility. A backward formula using this month's and last month's costs gives the true rate of change in sales from last month to this month; there is no reason to think of this value as an approximation.

9.3.2 Application: Estimating the Speed of a Falling Object

1 *Define the problem.*

Table 9.1 gives time, distance, and speed for an object accelerating under the influence of gravity (9.8 m/s^2), ignoring air resistance. (See the file falling.dat.) Suppose time and distance are measured. Distance is measured accurately, but time is measured with an error in the range ± 0.2 s. Write a program that simulates such measurements and uses them to estimate the speed as a function of time using an appropriate approximation formula.

Table 9.1. Distance and speed as a function of time

time	distance	speed
0	0.00	0
1	4.90	9.80
2	19.60	19.60
3	44.10	29.40
4	78.40	39.20
5	122.50	49.00
6	176.40	58.80
7	240.10	68.60
8	313.60	78.40
9	396.90	88.20
10	490.00	98.00
11	592.90	107.80
12	705.60	117.60
13	828.10	127.40
14	960.40	137.20
15	1102.50	147.00
16	1254.40	156.80
17	1416.10	166.60
18	1587.60	176.40
19	1768.90	186.20
20	1960.00	196.00

2 Outline a solution.

When an object is accelerating, a backward approximation formula will underestimate the true speed. For example, using the values for distance at t = 0 and t = 1, the estimated speed is 4.9/ = 4.9 m/s—half the true value. For the same reason, a forward formula will overestimate the speed. Therefore, Stirling's formula is the best choice from the three possibilities previously discussed. If the acceleration is constant and if there are no errors in any of the measurements, this formula will yield the actual speed.

The solution to this problem should include a general-purpose subprogram that approximates the derivative using Stirling's formula. (See Equation (2) above.) Its implementation is straightforward. However, note that the original definition of Stirling's formula assumes that the interval Δx between f(x) and its forward and backward values is the same. This is an unnecessary assumption and one that may not be true when experimental data are being used. (In this problem, the true time intervals are equal, but because of the random component, the measured time intervals will not be equal, in general.) Therefore, replace the definition of Stirling's formula with:

$$f'(x_2) = \frac{[f(x_2) - f(x_1)]/(x_2 - x_1) + [f(x_3) - f(x_2)]/(x_3 - x_2)}{2} \qquad (4)$$

The main program should read the data file and use the subprogram to calculate the speed, assuming there is a random error in the time measurement. It will be adequate for this problem to assume that time errors are linearly distributed over the range ±0.2 s.

3 Design an algorithm.

The design of a subprogram to implement this version of Stirling's formula is trivial.

SUBPROGRAM Stirling(IN: $x_1, x_2, x_3, y_1, y_2, y_3$; OUT: derivative)
ASSIGN derivative=$[(y_2 - y_1)/(x_2 - x_1)+(y_3 - y_2)/(x_3 - x_2)]/2$

The design of the driver program is straightforward, and no algorithm design should be required.

Convert the algorithm into a program.

P-9.3 [falling.c]

```c
#include <stdio.h>
#include <stdlib.h>
#include <time.h>

#define G 9.8  /* m/s^2 (gravitational acceleration) */
#define DT 0.2 /* range for time error, s */
#define N 21
#define FILENAME "falling.dat"

typedef struct {
  float true_time,measured_time,
      true_distance,true_speed,measured_speed;
} fall_data;

float Stirling(float x1,float x2,float x3,
               float y1,float y2,float y3) {
  return ((y2-y1)/(x2-x1)+(y3-y2)/(x3-x2))/2.;
}

int main(void) {
  fall_data fall[N];
  float g,x,speed;
  int i,n,status;
  FILE *in;
  char one_line[80];

  in=fopen(FILENAME,"r");

  /* Get data. */
  fgets(one_line,sizeof(one_line),in); /* Read past header line. */
  srand((unsigned)time(NULL));
  n=0;
  while (1) {
    status=fscanf(in,"%f %f %f",
                  &fall[n].true_time,&fall[n].true_distance,
      &fall[n].true_speed);
    if (status == EOF) break;
    fall[n].measured_time=fall[n].true_time+(rand()%5-2.)*DT;
  /*  printf("%6.2f %8.2f %6.2f\n",
fall[n].true_time,fall[n].true_distance,fall[n].measured_time); */
    n++;
  }
  fclose(in);
  printf("  true      true measured      true measured\n");
  printf("  time distance      time     speed     speed\n");
  for (i=0; i<n; i++) {
    fall[i].true_speed=fall[i].true_time*G;
```

```
if ((i > 0) && (i < (n-1))) {
  fall[i].measured_speed=Stirling(fall[i-1].measured_time,
                        fall[i  ].measured_time,
                        fall[i+1].measured_time,
           fall[i-1].measured_time*fall[i-1].measured_time*G/2.,
           fall[i  ].measured_time*fall[i  ].measured_time*G/2.,
           fall[i+1].measured_time*fall[i+1].measured_time*G/2.);
  printf("%6.2f %8.2f %8.2f %8.2f %8.2f\n",fall[i].true_time,
         fall[i].true_distance,fall[i].measured_time,
         fall[i].true_speed,fall[i].measured_speed);
}
else
  printf("%6.2f %8.2f %8.2f %8.2f\n",fall[i].true_time,
         fall[i].true_distance,fall[i].measured_time,
         fall[i].true_speed);
}
}
```

Running P-9.3

true time	true distance	measured time	true speed	measured speed
0.00	0.00	0.40	0.00	
1.00	4.90	1.20	9.80	11.27
2.00	19.60	1.80	19.60	18.13
3.00	44.10	2.60	29.40	27.93
4.00	78.40	4.40	39.20	40.18
5.00	122.50	5.00	49.00	50.47
6.00	176.40	6.20	58.80	59.78
7.00	240.10	7.00	68.60	68.60
8.00	313.60	7.80	78.40	77.42
9.00	396.90	9.00	88.20	87.22
10.00	490.00	9.80	98.00	98.00
11.00	592.90	11.40	107.80	109.27
12.00	705.60	12.00	117.60	118.09
13.00	828.10	12.80	127.40	125.44
14.00	960.40	13.60	137.20	135.24
15.00	1102.50	15.20	147.00	147.98
16.00	1254.40	16.40	156.80	158.27
17.00	1416.10	16.60	166.60	165.13
18.00	1587.60	17.80	176.40	173.46
19.00	1768.90	18.60	186.20	184.73
20.00	1960.00	20.40	196.00	

5 *Verify the operation of the program.*

These calculations are easy to verify with a calculator.

Problem Discussion

Because Stirling's formula requires values from one step backward and one step forward, the loop to calculate and display speed starts at i = 1 and ends at n − 1. There is no loss of information at t = 0 because the speed is zero. However, the speed at the final time step cannot be calculated using this method.

The code in P-9.3 applies to experimental data taken at discrete values of an independent variable, even though the data for this particular problem have been generated with an analytic function so that results from the numerical procedure can be evaluated. In general, experimental data may not correspond to an analytic function, so there may not even *be* an analytic derivative for comparison.

However, suppose you wish to estimate the derivative of an analytic function—one whose value exists and can be calculated *everywhere* over a range of interest. (You may additionally wish to require that the analytic derivative of the function also exists and that it can be calculated everywhere over the range, even though you don't know what it is.) Then a function that implements Stirling's formula can take a slightly different form:

```
double Stirling_f(double (*f)(double x),double dx);
```

where f is the name of a function passed from the calling program and dx is the interval over which the backward and forward values are to be calculated. The implementation of Stirling_f is left as an end-of-chapter exercise.

9.4 Numerical Integration

9.4.1 Polynomial Approximation Methods

It is often the case that functions cannot be integrated analytically. Such functions don't even have to be very complicated. (See the application in this section.) In such a situation, numerical integration techniques must be used. There are several widely used methods, including those that use polynomials to piece together an approximation of a function $y = f(x)$. We will present equations for three closely related polynomial approximation methods: the Rectangular Rule, the Trapezoidal Rule, and Simpson's Rule. These all have in common the fact that the integration range of the independent variable is divided into many intervals of equal size.

The Rectangular Rule is the easiest algorithm to understand because it has a simple graphical interpretation. Assume that the value of $y = f(x)$ is known for any value of x in the range $[x_a, x_b]$. The integral of $f(x)$ over the range x_a to x_b can be approximated by dividing the range into n equal segments of length Δx and taking the sums of the function evaluated at the midpoints of each segment:

$$\int_{x_a}^{x_b} f(x)\, dx \;\approx\; \left(\sum_{i=1}^{n} f(x_i - \Delta x/2) \right) \Delta x \tag{1}$$

where $x_i = x_1 + i \cdot \Delta x$. This process is illustrated in Figure 9.5, although in practice many more than eight subdivisions of the integration interval would be used.

Trapezoidal Rule integration also has a simple graphical interpretation. The integral of a function $y = f(x)$ between two closely spaced points x and $x + \Delta x$ can be approximated by the area of the trapezoid formed by the points $(x,0)$, $(x,f(x))$, $(x + \Delta x, f(x + \Delta x))$, and $(x + \Delta x, 0)$. To put it another way, the integral can be approximated by the average of $f(x)$ evaluated at x and $x + \Delta x$, multiplied by Δx:

$$\int_{x}^{x+\Delta x} f(x)\, dx \;\approx\; \frac{[f(x) + f(x + \Delta x)]\Delta x}{2} \tag{2}$$

Hence, assuming the range $[x_a, x_b]$ is divided into n equal intervals of size Δx, the integral of $f(x)$ over that range can be approximated by

$$\int_{x_a}^{x_b} f(x)\, dx \approx \left(\sum_{i=0}^{n-1} [f(x_i) + f(x_i + \Delta x)] \right) \frac{\Delta x}{2} = \frac{[f(x_a) + f(x_b)]\Delta x}{2} + \Delta x \sum_{i=1}^{n-1} f(x_i) \tag{3}$$

where $x_i = x_a + i \cdot \Delta x$.

Simpson's Rule is similar in principle to the other two; it approximates the integral of $f(x)$ over the range from $x - \Delta x$ to $x + \Delta x$ by a second-order polynomial. For the range x_1 to x_2 divided into n equal intervals of size Δx, where n must be an even number, and where $x_i = x_a + i \cdot \Delta x$, it can be shown that

$$\int_{x_a}^{x_b} f(x)\, dx \;\approx\; \left(\sum_{i=2,4,6,\dots}^{n} [f(x_{i-2}) + 4f(x_{i-1}) + f(x_i)] \right) \frac{\Delta x}{3}$$

$$= \left(f(x_a) + f(x_b) + 4 \sum_{i=1,3,5,\dots}^{n-1} f(x_i) + 2 \sum_{i=2,4,6,\dots}^{n-2} f(x_i) \right) \frac{\Delta x}{3} \tag{4}$$

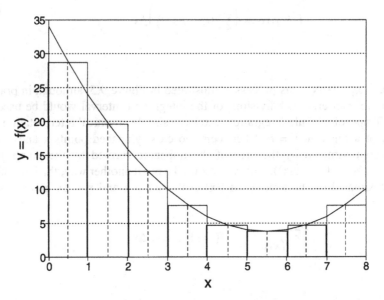

Figure 9.5. Rectangular Rule integration.

In this section we will develop an algorithm for Simpson's Rule integration, and we will write and test a function that implements this algorithm. (A corresponding implementation for Rectangular Rule integration is left for end-of-chapter exercises. Trapezoidal Rule integration has been implemented as an application in Chapter 5.) Here is an algorithm to be implemented as a C function.

SUBPROGRAM *(IN: F, x_a, x_b, n_steps; OUT: integral)*
DEFINE *(odd sum, even sum, i)*
ASSIGN *$\Delta x = (x_b - x_a)/$n_steps*
INITIALIZE *odd sum = 0*
       even sum = 0
LOOP *(for i = 1 to n_steps-1, steps of 2)*
    INCREMENT *odd sum = odd sum + F(x_a + i•Δx)*
END LOOP
LOOP *(for i = 2 to n_steps-2, steps of 2)*
    INCREMENT *even sum = even sum + F(x_a + i•Δx)*
END LOOP
ASSIGN *integral = [F(x_a) + F(x_b) + 4•(odd sum) + 2•(even sum)]•Δx/3*

P-9.4 contains code for a function that implements this algorithm.

P-9.4 [`simpson.c`]

```c
#include <stdio.h>
#include <math.h>
#define N 100

double simpson(double a,double b,int n,double (*f)());
double f_of_x(double x);
double pdf(double x);

int main(void)
{
  printf("Integral of x^2 from 1 to 5: %lf\n",
         simpson(1.,5.,N,f_of_x));
  printf("Integral of pdf from 0 to 2: %lf\n",simpson(0.,2.,N,pdf));
  return 0;
}
double simpson(double a,double b,int n,double (*f)()) {
  double h,odd,even;
  int i;
  odd=0.;even=0.;
  h=(b-a)/(double)n;
  for (i=2; i<=n; i+=2)
    odd+=f(a+(i-1)*h);
  for (i=2; i<=n-2; i+=2)
    even+=f(a+i*h);
  return h/3.*(f(a)+f(b)+4.*odd+2.*even);
}
double f_of_x(double x) {
  return x*x;
}
double pdf(double z) {
  return exp(-z*z/2.)/sqrt(8.*atan(1.));
}
```

Running P-9.4

```
Integral of x^2 from 1 to 5: 41.333333
Integral of pdf from 0 to 2: 0.477250
```

Problem Discussion

In program `simpson.c`, the numerical integration function is used to integrate x^2 from 1 to 5 and the standard normal probability distribution function

$$\text{pdf} = \frac{e^{-z^2/2}}{2\pi}$$

from 0 to 2. The first example can be integrated analytically: $\int x^2 dx = x^3/3$. The second example cannot be integrated analytically, but a table of values can be found in any statistics text.

As implemented, the number of integration steps is provided as input to the function. It would certainly be okay to replace this parameter with a hardcoded value defined inside function `simpson`.

9.4.2 Application: Evaluating the Gamma Function

Once you have developed a computer algorithm and satisfied yourself that it works for several cases of interest, you are likely to trust it in the future. That trust is easily misplaced, in this application, which is full of traps for the mathematically unsophisticated programmer. The mathematical details of this application won't make much sense if you haven't had a course in integral calculus, but the code itself isn't very difficult to follow.

1   Define the problem.

The gamma function appears in physics problems involving wave functions and probabilities; it is defined for positive values of n in terms of an integral:

$$\Gamma(n) = \int_0^\infty e^{-x} x^{n-1} dx \tag{5}$$

When n is an integer,

$$\Gamma(n) = (n - 1)! \tag{6}$$

That is, the gamma function is just a generalization of the factorial function to noninteger numbers. Gamma functions for noninteger values of n are defined through a recursion relationship:

$$\Gamma(n + 1) = n\Gamma(n) \tag{7}$$

The integral that defines the gamma function can't be evaluated analytically except in special cases, so numerical integration is required to calculate the gamma function for noninteger values of n. Write a program that will evaluate the gamma function for any positive value of n.

2 Outline a solution.

At first, this problem might appear hopeless because one of the limits on the integral is infinity. Fortunately, the integrand (the function being integrated) decreases rapidly toward zero as x increases. Figure 9.6 shows the integrand as a function of x for n = 0.5, 1.5, and 2.5, for x from 0 to 5. At x = 20, the value of the integrand for n = 2.5 is about 1.8×10^{-7}. This suggests that it should be possible to obtain a useful approximation to $\Gamma(n)$ by limiting the range over which a numerical integration is done.

Furthermore, once the integral has been evaluated for $0 \leq n \leq 1$, the recursion relationship can be used to evaluate the gamma function for all other values of n. It will be helpful to know that, as a special case, the integral for $\Gamma(1/2)$ can be evaluated analytically; it yields a value of $\sqrt{\pi}$.

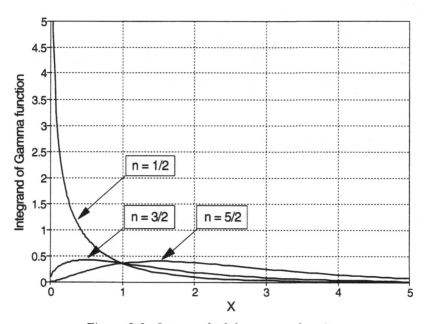

Figure 9.6. Integrand of the gamma function.

3 Design an algorithm.

The algorithm is straightforward: Incorporate Simpsons's Rule into a subprogram and include it in a driver program that evaluates the integral of $e^{-x}x^{n-1}$.

4 Convert the algorithm into a program.

In P-9.5, the driver program tests the algorithm for the hard-coded values n = 0.5 and n = 1.5.

P-9.5 [gamma.c]

```c
#include <stdio.h>
#include <math.h>

double gamma_integrand(double x,double z);
double gamma(double z);

int main(void) {
  double g;

  g=gamma(0.5);
  printf("gamma(0.5) = %lf\n",g);
  g=gamma(1.5);
  printf("gamma(1.5) = %lf %lf %lf\n",g,g*2.,sqrt(4.*atan(1.)));
}
double gamma_integrand(double x,double z) {
  return exp(-x)*pow(x,z-1.);
}
double gamma(double z) {
  int n=20000,i;
  double dx,sum=0.,x_max=20.;

  dx=x_max/n;
  for (i=2; i<=(n-2); i+=2)
    sum+=2.*gamma_integrand(i*dx,z);
  for (i=1; i<=(n-1); i+=2)
    sum+=4.*gamma_integrand(i*dx,z);
  sum=(sum+gamma_integrand(x_max,z))*dx/3.;
  return sum;
}
```

Running P-9.5

```
gamma(0.5) = 1.732652
gamma(1.5) = 0.886224 1.772449 1.772454
```

5

Verify the operation of the program.

One test of the operation of P-9.5 is to compare its direct calculation of $\Gamma(0.5)$, given in the first line of output as 1.732652, with the known value of $\sqrt{\pi}$ = 1.772454. Even though the intervals used in the Simpson's Rule calculation seem very small (there are 20,000 steps over the range [0,20]), the numerical result is not very close to the right answer. Why not? Can the accuracy be improved by increasing the number of steps? In fact, the accuracy will improve somewhat for a step size of 0.0001. However, examine Figure 9.6 again and note that for n = 0.5, the integrand approaches infinity as x approaches 0; to put it in mathematical terminology, the integrand has a singularity at x = 0 for any n in the range $0 \leq n < 1$.

The significance of this application should now be clear. Even though the numerical integration algorithm *appears* to work and even produces an answer that isn't too far from the correct one, the process is fatally flawed because of the nature of the function we have tried to evaluate.

Fortunately, because of the recursion relationship that applies to the gamma function, we can salvage the situation. Whereas in the integrand, $x^{1/2-1} = x^{-1/2} = 1/x^{1/2}$ has a singularity at x = 0, $x^{3/2-1} = x^{1/2}$ does not. This means that we can evaluate $\Gamma(1/2)$ by first evaluating $\Gamma(3/2)$ and then applying the recursion relationship given in equation (7). This strategy will work for any value of n in the range $0 \leq n < 1$. When $\Gamma(1.5)$ is evaluated and used to obtain $\Gamma(0.5)$, the result of 1.772449 is very close to the correct value of $\sqrt{\pi}$.

Even though the recursion relationship apparently allows us to circumvent a problem with this application of numerical integration, it is still prudent to be concerned about the behavior of the gamma function. For reasons that are beyond the scope of this text, some functions are better candidates for Simpson's Rule integration than others, and you should be wary of applying any numerical integration algorithm unless you can develop confidence in the results by referring to independent sources.

Problem Discussion

In P-9.5, the step size used in the Simpson's Rule algorithm has been hard-coded within the function. If you wish, you can require this value to be provided as input by the user or by the calling program. It might be a good idea to do this while you're testing the function. However, in the same sense that a programmer shouldn't have to worry about the details of how C evaluates the `sin` function, you shouldn't have to ask the user of this function to provide values that are relevant only to the internal details of how the gamma function will be evaluated.

9.5 Solving Systems of Linear Equations

9.5.1 Linear Equations and Gaussian Elimination

The behavior of many physical systems can be represented, or at least approximated, by a system of linear equations. This section presents one technique for solving such a system.

1   Define the problem.

Consider the following system of three equations, linear in x:

$$
\begin{aligned}
x_1 a_{11} + x_2 a_{12} + x_3 a_{13} &= c_1 \\
x_1 a_{21} + x_2 a_{22} + x_3 a_{23} &= c_2 \\
x_1 a_{31} + x_2 a_{32} + x_3 a_{33} &= c_3
\end{aligned}
\tag{1}
$$

In vector notation, this system is expressed as $\mathbf{AX} = \mathbf{C}$. Implement an algorithm that will solve this system of equations for x_1, x_2, and x_3. The method should be easy to generalize to larger systems.

2   Outline a solution.

One widely used technique for solving a system of linear equations is Gaussian elimination. Suppose system (1) could be replaced with the following system:

$$
\begin{aligned}
x_1 + x_2 a'_{12} + x_3 a'_{13} &= c'_1 \\
x_2 + x_3 a'_{23} &= c'_2 \\
x_3 &= c'_3
\end{aligned}
\tag{2}
$$

The matrix formed by the terms to the left of the equal sign in system (2) is called an **upper triangular matrix**, in which all the coefficients

upper triangular matrix

below the left-to-right, top-to-bottom diagonal are 0. (We will henceforth refer to this particular diagonal simply as the diagonal.) The coefficients along the diagonal are 1. We now claim, without proof or additional discussion, that a solution for system (2) is equivalent to a solution for system (1). We further claim that, for many systems of equations related to properly formulated problems of physical interest, it is possible to convert a set of system (1) equations into a set of system (2) equations. This process is called triangularizing the matrix.[7]

If such a triangularized system can be found, it is straightforward to solve for all the x's, using a process called **backsubstitution**:

$$
\begin{aligned}
x_3 &= c'_3 \\
x_2 &= c'_2 - x_3 a'_{23} \\
x_1 &= c'_1 - x_2 a'_{12} - x_3 a'_{13}
\end{aligned}
\tag{3}
$$

We will now work through the calculations required to convert system (1) into the upper triangular form (2). It will be easier to follow the calculations if we use a numerical example with coefficients that can be expressed as rational numbers. (Rational coefficients are used only for demonstration purposes and do *not* affect the general applicability of the method.) Consider this system of equations:

$$
\begin{aligned}
x_1 \bullet (1/3) + x_2 \bullet (1/2) + x_3 \bullet (1/4) &= 6 \\
x_1 \bullet (2) + x_2 \bullet (1/3) - x_3 \bullet (1/4) &= 6 \\
x_1 \bullet (1/4) - x_2 \bullet (1/8) + x_3 \bullet (1) &= 8
\end{aligned}
\tag{4}
$$

The coefficients along the diagonal are called the pivot values. The first step in the solution is to find the row with the pivot value (in absolute magnitude) in the first column and interchange that row with the top row in system (4). In this example, the largest coefficient in the first column occurs in the second row. Therefore, interchange the first and second rows:

$$
\begin{aligned}
x_1 \bullet (2) + x_2 \bullet (1/3) - x_3 \bullet (1/4) &= 6 \\
x_1 \bullet (1/3) + x_2 \bullet (1/2) + x_3 \bullet (1/4) &= 6 \\
x_1 \bullet (1/4) - x_2 \bullet (1/8) + x_3 \bullet (1) &= 8
\end{aligned}
\tag{5}
$$

The next step is to divide row 1 by the coefficient in the first column. The result is that the first pivot will have a coefficient of 1:

$$
\begin{aligned}
x_1 \bullet (1) + x_2 \bullet (1/6) + x_3 \bullet (-1/8) &= 3 \\
x_1 \bullet (1/3) + x_2 \bullet (1/2) + x_3 \bullet (1/4) &= 6 \\
x_1 \bullet (1/4) + x_2 \bullet (-1/8) + x_3 \bullet (1) &= 8
\end{aligned}
\tag{6}
$$

---

[7]For additional discussion, see any text on numerical analysis.

The next step is to multiply the first row by the coefficient in column 1 of the second row and subtract row 1 from row 2. Then multiply the (original) first row by the coefficient in column 1 of the third row and subtract row 1 from row 3. This produces a reduced system of equations:

$$
\begin{array}{llll}
x_1 \bullet (1) & + \; x_2 \bullet (1/6) & + \; x_3 \bullet (-1/8) & = 3 \\
& x_2 \bullet (1/2 - 1/18) & + \; x_3 \bullet (1/4 + 1/24) & = 5 \\
& x_2 \bullet (-1/8 - 1/24) & + \; x_3 \bullet (1 + 1/32) & = 29/4
\end{array} \tag{7}
$$

$$
\begin{array}{llll}
x_1 \bullet (1) & + \; x_2 \bullet (1/6) & + \; x_3 \bullet (-1/8) & = 3 \\
& x_2 \bullet (8/18) & + \; x_3 \bullet (7/24) & = 5 \\
& x_2 \bullet (-4/24) & + \; x_3 \bullet (33/32) & = 29/4
\end{array}
$$

Of the remaining coefficients in column 2 of rows 2 and 3, 8/18 is larger in magnitude than -4/24, so these rows don't need to be interchanged. Divide row 2 by the coefficient of the second pivot:

$$
\begin{array}{llll}
x_1 \bullet (1) & + \; x_2 \bullet (1/6) & + \; x_3 \bullet (-1/8) & = 3 \\
& x_2 \bullet (1) & + \; x_3 \bullet (21/32) & = 45/4 \\
& x_2 \bullet (-4/24) & + \; x_3 \bullet (33/32) & = 29/4
\end{array} \tag{8}
$$

Now, multiply row 2 by -4/24 and subtract row 2 from row 3:

$$
\begin{array}{llll}
x_1 \bullet (1) & + \; x_2 \bullet (1/6) & + \; x_3 \bullet (-1/8) & = 3 \\
& x_2 \bullet (1) & + \; x_3 \bullet (21/32) & = 45/4 \\
& & x_3 \bullet (73/64) & = 219/24
\end{array} \tag{9}
$$

Finally, divide row 3 by the coefficient of x_3:

$$
\begin{array}{llll}
x_1 \bullet (1) & + \; x_2 \bullet (1/6) & + \; x_3 \bullet (-1/8) & = 3 \\
& x_2 \bullet (1) & + \; x_3 \bullet (21/32) & = 45/4 \\
& & x_3 \bullet (1) & = (219/24) \bullet (64/73) = 8
\end{array} \tag{10}
$$

This immediately gives $x_3 = 8$ for one of the solutions. Now substitute x_3 into row 2:

$$
x_2 = 45/4 - (21/32) \bullet 8 = 6 \tag{11}
$$

and x_3 and x_2 into row 1:

$$
x_1 = 3 - 6/6 + 8/8 = 3 \tag{12}
$$

It is easy to verify that these values satisfy the original equations. For example, $3(1/3) + 6(1/2) + 8(1/4) = 6$.

3

Design an algorithm.

Based on the example from Step 2, we can design an algorithm. The sequence of operations is sufficiently involved that it is worth designing the algorithm first in outline form and then in more detail.

1. Define an array to hold the coefficients (a) and the constants (c):

2. Read a data file containing a value for n and the $(n) \cdot (n+1)$ elements of A.

3. Triangularize the matrix.

LOOP *(through each row)*
    a. For each row below current row, look for a coefficient A(row,current_row) that is larger in absolute magnitude than the coefficient A(current_row, current_row).
    b. If a larger coefficient exists, exchange that row with current_row.
    c. Divide all columns in the current row of A by A(current_row,current_row)
    d. For all rows below current_row, multiply the coefficients in (original) current_row by the first coefficient in the row and subtract from the corresponding coefficient in row.
END LOOP

4. Backsubstitute to find solutions.

    a. Solve directly for last root.
    b. Substitute in previous row, continuing to first row.

Here is the algorithm in more detail.

DEFINE *(array of real numbers A with n rows and n+1*
           columns and array of size n to hold roots)
OPEN *(data file)*
READ *(n)*
READ *(n•(n+1) elements of A)*
(Triangularize the matrix.)
LOOP *(for row = 1 to n_rows)*
    (Search for row with larger pivot.)
    IF *(row < n_rows)* **THEN ASSIGN** *PivotRow=row*

```
        LOOP (for i = row+1 to n_rows)
                    IF /A(i,row)/>/A(PivotRow,PivotRow)/
                    THEN ASSIGN PivotRow=i
        END LOOP
            {Swap rows if required.)
        IF (PivotRow ≠ row) THEN
                LOOP (for col = row to n_cols)
                        ASSIGN temp = A(PivotRow,col)
                                A(PivotRow,col) = A(row,col)
                                A)row,col) = temp
                END LOOP
                (end IF...)
        (end IF...)
        (Divide all coefficients in row by pivot.)
        ASSIGN DivideBy = A(row,row)
        LOOP (for col  = row to n_cols)
         ASSIGN A(row,col) = A(row,col)/DivideBy
        END LOOP
        (Reduce the (row)th column to 0.)
        IF (row < n_rows) THEN
                LOOP (for i = row+1 to n_rows)
                        LOOP (for col = row+1 to n_cols)
                                ASSIGN A(i,col) = A(i,col - A(row,col)•A(i,row)
                        END LOOP
                        ASSIGN A(i,row) = 0
                END LOOP
        (end IF...)
        (optional for testing: print reduced matrix)
END LOOP
(Backsolve for roots.)
ASSIGN roots(n_rows) = A(n_rows,n_cols)
LOOP (for row = n_rows-1 (down) to 1)
        ASSIGN roots(row) = A(row,n_cols)
        LOOP (for i = row+1 to n_rows)
                ASSIGN roots(row) = roots(row) - A(row,i)•roots(i)
        END LOOP
END LOOP
```

4 *Convert the algorithm into a program.*

Program P-9.6 uses the data file `gauss.dat`.

P-9.6 [gauss.c]

```
#include <stdio.h>
#include <math.h>
#define MAX_ROWS 4
#define MAX_COLS 5
#define FILENAME "gauss.dat"

void GaussianElimination(double a[][MAX_COLS],int n_rows,
                 int n_cols, double solutions[]);
void PrintMatrix(double a[][MAX_COLS],int n_rows,int n_cols);

int main()
{
   double a[MAX_ROWS][MAX_COLS],solutions[MAX_COLS];
   int n_rows,n_cols,rows,cols;
   FILE *in;

   in=fopen(FILENAME,"r");
   (void)fscanf(in,"%i",&n_rows);
   n_cols=n_rows+1;
   for (rows=0; rows < n_rows; rows++)
      for (cols=0; cols < n_cols; cols++)
         fscanf(in,"%lf",&a[rows][cols]);
   PrintMatrix(a,n_rows,n_cols);
   GaussianElimination(a,n_rows,n_cols,solutions);
   printf("solutions: ");
   for (rows=0; rows < n_rows; rows++)
      printf("%8.2lf",solutions[rows]);
   printf("%\n");
}

void GaussianElimination(double a[][MAX_COLS],int n_rows,
                 int n_cols, double solutions[])
{
/* Solve system of linear equations using Gaussian
   elimination with partial (row) pivoting. */

   int row,col,pivot_row,i,j;
   double divide_by,temp;

   for (row=0; row < n_rows; row++) {
/* Search for pivot row. */
      if (row < n_rows-1) {
         pivot_row=row;
         for (i=row+1; i < n_rows; i++)
            if (fabs(a[i][row]) > fabs(a[pivot_row][pivot_row]))
               pivot_row=i;

/* Swap pivot row if required. */
         if (pivot_row != row) {
         for (col=row; col < n_cols; col++) {
            temp=a[pivot_row][col];
            a[pivot_row][col]=a[row][col];
            a[row][col]=temp;
         } /* for... */
         } /* if... */
      } /* if... */
```

```
/* Divide by pivot. */
    divide_by=a[row][row];
    for (i=row; i < n_cols; i++)
      a[row][i]=a[row][i]/divide_by;

/* Reduce the (row)th column to 0. */
    if (row < (n_rows-1)) {
      for (i=row+1; i < n_rows; i++) {
        for (j=row+1; j < n_cols; j++)
        a[i][j]=a[i][j]-a[row][j]*a[i][row];
        a[i][row]=0.0;
        }
      }

/* Print reduced matrix. */
    PrintMatrix(a,n_rows,n_cols);
  } /* end for... */

/* Backsolve for solutions. */
  solutions[n_rows-1]=a[n_rows-1][n_cols-1];
  for (row=n_rows-2; row >= 0; row--) {
    solutions[row]=a[row][n_cols-1];
    for (i=row+1; i < n_rows; i++)
      solutions[row]=solutions[row]-a[row][i]*solutions[i];
  }
}

void PrintMatrix(double a[][MAX_COLS],int n_rows,int n_cols)
{
  int rows,cols;

  printf("From PrintMatrix\n");
  for (rows=0; rows < n_rows; rows++) {
    for (cols=0; cols < n_cols; cols++)
      printf("%8.2lf",a[rows][cols]);
    printf("\n");
  }
}
```

Running P-9.6

```
From PrintMatrix
      0.33      0.50      0.25      6.00
      2.00      0.33     -0.25      6.00
      0.25     -0.13      1.00      8.00
From PrintMatrix
      1.00      0.17     -0.13      3.00
      0.00      0.44      0.29      5.00
      0.00     -0.17      1.03      7.25
From PrintMatrix
      1.00      0.17     -0.13      3.00
      0.00      1.00      0.66     11.25
      0.00      0.00      1.14      9.12
From PrintMatrix
      1.00      0.17     -0.13      3.00
      0.00      1.00      0.66     11.25
      0.00      0.00      1.00      8.00
solutions:      3.00      6.00      8.00
```

5 Verify the operation of the program.

For the example used to develop the algorithm, the intermediate calculations with fractions all cancel out to give exact solutions in terms of integer values. However, in general, the potential loss of accuracy as a result of cumulative errors involving real arithmetic on computers is always a concern in any algorithm that involves many calculations. For reasons that aren't obvious, the algorithm we have used seeks to minimize arithmetic errors by searching for the row with the largest coefficient in the pivot column and interchanging it with the current row.[8] However, there is still no guarantee that unacceptable errors won't accumulate. If the physical problem represented by the equations is poorly defined, it is possible that the algorithm will give answers that look okay but, in fact, are wrong. (This can happen with so-called ill-conditioned matrices. A famous example is presented in Exercise 11 at the end of this chapter.) In extreme cases, divisions by zero can occur, and the program will crash. This might be distressing, but it is a better result than obtaining wrong answers with a program that doesn't crash.

In any algorithm involving many calculations with real numbers, you should *never* assume that the results are correct until you have checked them thoroughly. This is not always easy to do! One test you can perform is to substitute the x values into the original equations. In Exercise 7 at the end of this chapter, you are asked to modify P-9.6 to include calculation of a residual vector. Each component of the residual vector should be very close to zero for a good solution. However, this is what mathematicians call a necessary but insufficient condition to guarantee a good solution. Ill-conditioned matrices can result in solutions for which the residuals are small even though the solution is not correct. Such matrices may not even have a good solution.

---

[8]It is also possible to interchange both columns and rows to move the absolutely largest coefficient in the reduced system to the pivot position. However, it can be shown that this results in relatively small improvements to the overall accuracy of the method. Such a solution is called "Gaussian elimination with full pivoting." The solution described here is called "Gaussian elimination with partial pivoting."

9.5.2 Application: Current Flow in a DC Circuit With Multiple Resistive Branches

1 Define the problem.

Consider the DC circuit shown in Figure 9.7. It consists of a voltage source connected to several resistive branches. Kirchoff's Laws state that the voltage drop around any closed branch of such a network of resistances must be zero. This fact leads directly to a series of linear equations that describe the current flow in the three branches of this circuit:

$$(R_1 + R_2)I_1 \qquad\qquad\qquad - R_2I_3 = 0$$
$$(R_3 + R_4)I_2 \qquad\qquad - R_4I_3 = E$$
$$-R_2I_1 \qquad - R_4I_2 + (R_2 + R_4 + R_5)I_3 = 0$$

Solve this equation for these values:

R1 = 100 Ω   R4 = 250 Ω
R2 = 200 Ω   R5 = 150 Ω
R3 = 300 Ω   E = 6 V

2 Outline a solution.

In a physics course, you would probably be asked to derive the equations yourself, which is the only difficult part of this problem. Note that the direction of current flow is normally considered positive in the direction from the positive (+) terminal of a battery (or other voltage source) to the negative (–) terminal. If you guess wrong about the direction of flow in a particular branch of the circuit, the current will have a negative value in the solution.

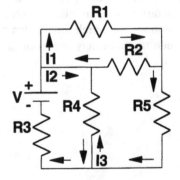

Figure 9.7. Current flow in a DC circuit with resistive branches.

3 Design an algorithm.

There is no need to design an algorithm for this problem, as it is a straightforward application of functions already written.

4 Convert the algorithm into a program.

There is also no need to write any new code to solve this problem. Simply create an appropriate data file in the same format as gauss.dat, as used by P-9.6, and run gauss.c.

5 Verify the operation of the program.

This is a problem that should not cause significant numerical difficulties. It is relatively easy to check the value for I_2 by noting that R_1 and R_2 are in parallel. Then, the resistance of this parallel combination plus R_5 is in parallel with R_4. Finally, this parallel combination is in series with R_3. If you do these calculations by hand, you should find that I_2 is approximately 14.4 mA.

9.6 Finding the Roots of Equations

Consider a function $y = f(x)$. A common problem in mathematics is finding the value(s) of x for which the equation $f(x) = 0$. As a simple example, consider the polynomial

$$f(x) = x^2 - 8x + 15$$

It is easy to determine the values of x for which this function equals zero because the polynomial can be factored by inspection:

$$f(x) = (x - 5)(x - 3)$$

The values $x = 5$ and $x = 3$ are called the roots of the function.

In general, it is not this easy to find the roots of a function. For example, although there are standard methods for finding the roots of a quadratic equation, there are no comparable methods for high-order polynomials. Consequently, numerical methods are often needed. In this section we will develop one intuitively simple numerical method. Often, it is of interest to find all real roots over a specified range, so that is how we will formulate the problem.

1 Define the problem.

Write a subprogram that will estimate the real roots for the equation $f(x) = 0$ over the range $[x_a, x_b]$.

2 Outline a solution.

The approach we will discuss is called the bisection method. How can we tell whether there are any roots in the range $[x_a, x_b]$? Suppose that the sign of $f(x_a)$ is different from the sign of $f(x_b)$. The obvious interpretation of this fact is that the function has crossed the x-axis at least once in the range $[x_a, x_b]$. It is also possible that the function crossed the x-axis more than once, in which case the total number of crossings must be odd. This means that $f(x)$ must have at least one real root in the range $[x_a, x_b]$.

A second possibility is that the sign of $f(x_a)$ is the same as the sign of $f(x_b)$. This means that there may be no roots or that the function has crossed the x-axis an even number of times, so that $f(x)$ must have either no roots or an even number of roots in the range $[x_a, x_b]$.

A third possibility, which is applicable in either of the above two situations, is that $f(x)$ just touches the x-axis without crossing it. This is true for the function

$$f(x) = x^2 - 6x + 9 = (x - 3)(x - 3)$$

This function, which never crosses the x-axis, has two identical real roots. Such possibilities complicate the search for a generally applicable root-finding algorithm. Figure 9.8 illustrates these three possibilities.

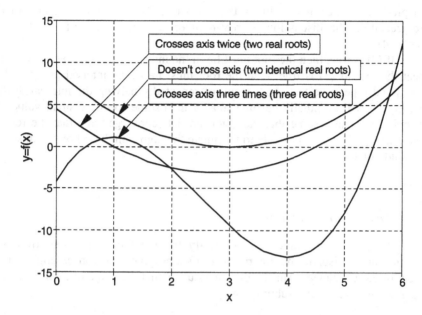

Figure 9.8. Polynomials with one or more real roots.

In any case, we will proceed on the assumption that roots can be found by identifying the places where a function crosses the x-axis. (That is, we will ignore the third possibility mentioned above.) Assume that the range $[x_a, x_b]$ is subdivided into intervals sufficiently small that each interval contains either one root or no roots. If the sign of f(x) at the left boundary x_L of the interval is different from the sign at the right boundary of the subinterval x_R, we will assume that the interval contains one real root. Otherwise, we will assume that the interval contains no roots. It is important to realize that this is just an assumption, and there is no way to guarantee whether the assumption is justified.

Now divide the interval $[x_L, x_R]$ in half. There are three possibilities, making use of the fact that if $f(x_L) \cdot f(x_R) < 0$, then the function crosses the x-axis somewhere in the interval $[x_L, x_R]$:

(1) $f(x_{mid}) = 0$
(2) $f(x_L) \cdot f(x_{mid}) < 0$
(3) $f(x_{mid}) \cdot f(x_R) < 0$

If (1) is true, then x_{mid} will be accepted as a root. It isn't quite accurate to say that x_{mid} is a root because of the limitations on real arithmetic. However, as a practical matter, we can usually assume that x_{mid} is sufficiently close to the real root. Also as a practical matter, it is unlikely that the value $f(x_{mid})$ will ever equal exactly zero (recalling the discussion of real-number arithmetic and $if...$ tests in Chapter 4).

If (2) is true, then the root must lie in the interval $[x_L, x_{mid}]$. Let $x_R = x_{mid}$ and repeat the test. If (3) is true, then the root must lie in the interval $[x_{mid}, x_R]$. Let $x_L = x_{mid}$ and repeat the test. As a result of repeatedly halving the interval in this way, $[x_L, x_R]$ will eventually become smaller than some specified small value. At that point, we can assume that the algorithm has converged and that the root is located at x_{mid}. It is also possible to terminate the algorithm based on the absolute magnitude of $f(x_{mid})$.

3

Design an algorithm.

As usual, it is important to specify the input to and output from the algorithm and to isolate the algorithm in a subprogram that can be applied in a variety of circumstances. This algorithm assumes that the name of a function will be passed as input to the subprogram.

SUBPROGRAM Bisect(IN: x_L, x_R, F; OUT: root, final_interval)
DEFINE (x_{mid}, hit (logical), epsilon_f, epsilon_x (values to test for
         convergence))
ASSIGN epsilon_f = ?
         epsilon_x = ?
         $x_{mid} = (x_R + x_L)/2$
         hit = false
LOOP (while $/x_R - x_L/ >$ epsilon_x and $/F(x_{mid})/ >$ epsilon_f and not hit)
      IF $F(x_{mid}) = 0$ *THEN* hit = true (found "exact" root)
      ELSE IF $F(x_L) \cdot F(x_{mid}) < 0$ *THEN* $x_R = x_{mid}$ (root in left half)
      ELSE $F(x_R) \cdot F(x_{mid}) < 0$ *THEN* $x_L = x_{mid}$ (root in right half)
      ASSIGN $x_{mid} = (x_L + x_R)/2$
END LOOP
ASSIGN root = $f(x_{mid})$
         final_interval = $/x_R - x_L/$

This algorithm assumes that the values against which convergence will be tested can be hard coded into the subprogram. You might instead wish to supply them as parameters. Note that *Bisect* returns the length of the final subinterval as well as the estimated root. This gives the calling (sub)program an additional chance to decide whether to accept the root.

Bisect will typically be called from another subprogram that divides the original range $[x_a, x_b]$ into a specified number of intervals and calls *Bisect* once for each such interval. The design of this subprogram is straightforward. The expectation is that some of these intervals will contain a root and some won't. One way to store the results is to create an array to hold a value for each of the specified intervals. When control is returned to the calling program, each element of this array will hold either a root or an initial value chosen such that it can't be mistaken for a root.

 Convert the algorithm into a program.

P-9.7 [bisect2.c]

```c
#include <stdio.h>
#include <math.h>
#define N_STEPS 10
#define LIMIT 1e-6

double f_of_x(double x);
int bisect(double left, double right,double (*f)(double),double
*root);

int main(void)
{
   double left,right,dx,x1,x2,root;
   int i,found;

   printf("Give left and right search limits: ");
   scanf("%lf %lf",&left,&right);
   dx=(right-left)/N_STEPS;
   for (i=1; i<=N_STEPS; i++) {
     x1=left+dx*(i-1);
     x2=left+dx*i;
     found=bisect(x1,x2,f_of_x,&root);
     if (found)
       printf("There is  a root between %8.2lf and %8.2lf: %lf\n",
              x1,x2,root);
     else
       printf("There is no root between %8.2lf and %8.2lf.\n",x1,x2);
   }
   return 0;
}

double f_of_x(double x)
{
   return x*x-2.0;
}

int bisect(double left, double right,double (*f)(double),
           double *root)
{

   double mid;
   int found;
```

```
if (f(left)*f(right) > 0.) /* No root in this interval. */
   found=0;
else {
   if (fabs(f(left)) < LIMIT) {
      *root=left;
      found=1;
   }
   else if (fabs(f(right)) < LIMIT) {
      *root=right;
      found=1;
   }
   else {
      mid=(left+right)/2.;
      if (fabs(f(mid)) < LIMIT) {
      *root=mid;
      found=1;
      }
      else if (f(left)*f(mid) < 0.)
      found=bisect(left,mid,f,root);
      else
      found=bisect(mid,right,f,root);
   }
}
return found;
}
```

Running P-9.7

```
Give left and right search limits: -4 4
There is no root between    -4.00 and   -3.20.
There is no root between    -3.20 and   -2.40.
There is no root between    -2.40 and   -1.60.
There is  a root between    -1.60 and   -0.80: -1.414214
There is no root between    -0.80 and    0.00.
There is no root between     0.00 and    0.80.
There is  a root between     0.80 and    1.60: 1.414214
There is no root between     1.60 and    2.40.
There is no root between     2.40 and    3.20.
There is no root between     3.20 and    4.00.
```

5 *Verify the operation of the program.*

The results from any root-finding algorithm can always be tested directly by substituting the estimated root back into the original function. In P-9.7, the function is tested with the simple function $x^2 - 2$, with obvious roots. The result should differ from zero by no more than some specified tolerance. As long as the function actually changes sign within a specified interval, the algorithm is guaranteed to converge as long as the specified tolerance is reasonable relative to the accuracy with which real arithmetic is performed; a tolerance of 10^{-15} is unreasonable when real arithmetic is performed only to seven or eight significant figures!

Once the bisection algorithm has converged, you should check values of the function in the vicinity of the root to examine its slope—essentially, its numerical derivative. If the derivative is very small, it means that the root returned by the algorithm will be very sensitive to the criteria you have chosen for terminating the bisection algorithm.

Although it is possible to test the roots returned by the bisection method, it is not so easy to guarantee that *all* the roots in the original range have been found. For any interval supplied to the parameter list, the bisection method will find one root. In the previous discussion of this method, we have *assumed* that when the original range of x values is divided into subintervals, which are then passed to `bisect`, each subinterval will contain either one root or no roots. However, it may be true that more than one root lies within an interval. As implemented, the algorithm searches for a sign change first in the left half of an interval. If the bisection algorithm finds one, it thereafter ignores the right half of the original interval. Therefore, a root that lies within the right half will not be found.

9.7 Numerical Solutions to Differential Equations

There are several numerical techniques for solving differential equations of various kinds. In general, the technique must be matched carefully with the problem. In this section, we will focus on a particular class of second-order differential equations that demonstrate clearly how mathematics can tie together apparently unrelated physical concepts. The equations we will discuss here all have analytic solutions, and we will give those solutions for the purpose of comparing them with the numerical calculations. However, you are not expected to be able to derive the solutions yourself unless you have had a course in differential equations. In general, the mathematical sophistication required to understand these results goes beyond that required in any other part of this text.

We will begin by presenting a particular problem. It may seem that this problem is more like a specific application than a general approach to solving a class of differential equations, but associating the results with a simple physical system will make the mathematics easier to follow. In addition, the solutions to this conceptually simple physical problem are broadly and directly applicable to other important problems in science and engineering.

9.7.1 Motion of a Damped Mass and Spring

Consider a mass hanging from the end of a massless spring. If this system is in static equilibrium—that is, if nothing is moving—the spring is stretched and the force due to gravity acting on the mass is counterbalanced by a restoring (upward) force provided by the spring. If the displacement in the spring is small, then according to Hooke's Law the restoring force provided by the spring is proportional to the displacement:

$$mg - kL = 0 \tag{1}$$

where k is a spring constant that can be determined experimentally by measuring the displacement resulting from hanging a known weight on the spring (mg = mass times the gravitational acceleration).

Now suppose that the mass is displaced from its equilibrium position in the downward (assumed positive) direction by an amount ℓ. As long as the total displacement $L + \ell$ is still small (i.e., as long as Hooke's Law still applies) the restoring force is still proportional to the displacement. If the mass is now released, it will vibrate around its equilibrium position. Ignoring damping forces, the equation of motion for the mass is

$$m d^2\ell/dt^2 = mg - k[L + \ell(t)] \tag{2}$$

Because mg = kL, this equation reduces to

$$m d^2\ell/dt^2 + k\ell(t) = 0 \tag{3}$$

The solution to this equation is a cosine-shaped curve with period T:

$$\ell(t) = A\cos(\omega_0 t) + B\sin(\omega_0 t) = R\cos(\omega_0 t - \delta) \tag{4}$$

where $T = 2\pi/\omega_0 = 2\pi\sqrt{m/k}$, $A = R\cos(\delta)$, $B = R\sin(\delta)$, $R = \sqrt{A^2 + B^2}$, and the phase angle $\delta = \tan^{-1}(B/A)$. The quadrant of δ must be determined from the signs of $\cos(\delta)$ and $\sin(\delta)$. The initial conditions for the system determine values for the constants. In a typical situation in which the mass is initially displaced downward (in the positive direction) by an amount L and released, A=L, the initial velocity equals 0, and B and δ are both equal to 0.

Because this motion is undamped, the amplitude of the oscillation does not decrease as a function of time. This is a physically unrealistic situation. Therefore, suppose that the motion is damped by having the spring move in a resisting medium. The resistance could be provided incidentally just by air or it could be an intentional part of the system, through the addition of a mechanical damping device (sometimes called a dashpot), for example. Such situations can be modelled by adding another term to the equation of motion, proportional to velocity:

$$md^2\ell/dt^2 + Dd\ell/dt + k\ell = 0 \qquad (5)$$

where D is a damping coefficient. For the interesting case of "small" damping, it can be shown that $D^2 - 4km$ must be less than 0. Then the general solution is

$$\ell(t) = e^{-Dt/2m}[A\cos(\mu t) + B\sin(\mu t)] \qquad (6)$$

where $\mu = \sqrt{4km - D^2}/2m$. It is at least qualitatively clear that this solution has the desired properties. The sine and cosine terms provide the oscillating component, and the exponential term guarantees that the amplitude of the oscillation will approach zero as time approaches infinity, no matter what its initial amplitude.

The presence of damping changes the period previously derived for undamped motion. This new quasiperiod T' still gives the time between successive maxima or minima of the function:

$$T' = 4\pi m/\sqrt{4km - D^2} \qquad (7)$$

which approaches the period for undamped motion as D approaches zero. This value is important when applying numerical methods because in order to characterize the behavior of the motion, it is of course necessary to use step sizes that are small compared to the period for undamped motion or to this quasiperiod for damped motion.

A standard technique for solving a second-order differential equation in the form of (5) is to rewrite it as a system of two first-order equations. For the mass and spring problem, the result is especially easy to understand because of the simple physical nature of the problem. Making use of the fact that velocity v is the time derivative of position ($v = dx/dt$) and that acceleration is the time derivative of velocity ($d^2\ell/dt^2 = dv/dt$),

$$d\ell/dt = v(t)$$
$$dv/dt = a(t) = -[Dv(t) + k\ell(t)]/m \qquad (8)$$

There are several numerical methods applicable to equations such as these, having the general form $dy/dx = f(x,y)$. They all involve, in some fashion, selecting a small interval Δx and estimating the value of y for this future value of x. (Again, this concept is easy to grasp when the independent variable is time, as is the case for the equations of motion we are discussing.) We will use the well-known Runge-Kutta method, which has the advantage that no higher order derivatives are required. In general,

$$
\begin{aligned}
\kappa_1 &= \Delta t \cdot f(x,y) \\
\kappa_2 &= \Delta t \cdot f(x+\Delta x/2, y+k_1/2) \\
\kappa_3 &= \Delta t \cdot f(x+\Delta x/2, y+k_2/2) \\
\kappa_4 &= \Delta t \cdot f(x+\Delta x, y+k_3) \\
y(x+\Delta x) &\approx y(x) + (\kappa_1 + 2\kappa_2 + 2\kappa_3 + \kappa_4)/6
\end{aligned}
\tag{9}
$$

For the equations of motion in (8):

$$
\begin{aligned}
\kappa_{1,\ell} &= \Delta t \cdot v(t) \\
\kappa_{2,\ell} &= \Delta t \cdot [v(t+\Delta t/2)] = \Delta t \cdot [v(t) + a(t)\Delta t/2] \\
\kappa_{3,\ell} &= \Delta t \cdot [v(t) + a(t)\Delta t/2] \\
\kappa_{4,\ell} &= \Delta t \cdot [v(t) + a(t)\Delta t]
\end{aligned}
\tag{10}
$$

$$
\begin{aligned}
\kappa_{1,v} &= -\Delta t \cdot [Dv(t) + k\ell(t)]/m \\
\kappa_{2,v} &= -\Delta t \cdot \{D[v(t) + \kappa_{1,y}/2] + k\ell(t+\Delta t/2)\}/M \\
&= -\Delta t \cdot \{D[v(t) + \kappa_{1,y}/2] + k[\ell(t)+v(t)\Delta t/2]\}/M \\
\kappa_{3,v} &= -\Delta t \cdot \{D[v(t) + \kappa_{2,y}/2] + k[\ell(t)+v(t)\Delta t/2]\}/M \\
\kappa_{4,v} &= -\Delta t \cdot \{D[v(t) + \kappa_{3,y}] + k[\ell(t)+v(t)\Delta t]\}/M
\end{aligned}
\tag{11}
$$

from which

$$
\begin{aligned}
\ell(t+\Delta t) &= \ell(t) + \kappa_{1,\ell} + 2\kappa_{2,\ell} + 2\kappa_{3,\ell} + \kappa_{4,\ell})/6 \\
v(t+\Delta t) &= v(t) + \kappa_{1,v} + 2\kappa_{2,v} + 2\kappa_{3,v} + \kappa_{4,v})/6
\end{aligned}
\tag{12}
$$

These kinds of numerical solutions suffer from several sources of error. Even if it can be assumed (which it can't) that there is no error due to the limitations of real arithmetic on computers, there remains an inherent *discretization error*. This is due to the fact that estimated values one step into the future are used as the initial conditions for the next step. However, these conditions are, by definition, estimates and not the true values. For each step, therefore, there is a local discretization error that propagates over the rest of the solution as accumulated discretization error. These errors can be analyzed—a topic that is beyond the scope of this text—but they are unavoidable whenever methods such as these are used. As always, therefore, it is necessary to be extremely cautious when applying numerical methods to real problems.

discretization error

9.7.2 Application: Current Flow in a Series LRC Circuit

As mentioned earlier in this section, the equations of motion used to describe the motion of a mass attached to a spring can also be used to describe other physical systems.

1 Define the problem.

An electrical circuit contains a resistor R (ohms) and an inductor L (henrys) in series with a source of constant (DC) voltage V (volts). A switch is initially opened and is then closed at time $t = 0$. What is the current flow in the circuit after the switch is closed? How does the addition of a capacitor C (farads) in series with the resistor and inductor change the current flow?

2 Outline a solution.

The generally applicable equation for this problem is

$$Ld^2q/dt^2 + Rdq/dt + q/C = V \tag{13}$$

where the current i is the time derivative of the charge q. This equation has the same form as the equation of motion for a damped mass and spring. The correspondence between the variables is:

$$
\begin{aligned}
m &\to L \\
D &\to R \\
k &\to 1/C \\
\ell &\to q \\
v &\to dq/dt = i \\
f(t) &\to V(t)
\end{aligned}
$$

The first part of the problem, with $1/C=0$ and V a constant, is a special case of the general problem. The second-order equation reduces immediately to a single first-order equation:

$$di/dt = (V - Ri)/L \tag{14}$$

The solution is

$$i(t) = V/R(1 - e^{-Rt/L}) \tag{15}$$

There is no oscillating component because there is no spring constant term (corresponding to parameter k). The solution satisfies the condition that i = 0 and di/dt = V/L at t = 0 and that i→V/R (from Ohm's Law) as t→∞.

For the second part of the problem, which adds capacitance to the circuit, assume that $4L/C - R^2 > 0$. Then the solution for charge q is

$$q(t) = CV\left[1 - e^{\frac{-Rt}{2L}}\cos\left(\frac{\sqrt{4L/C - R^2}\,t}{2L}\right)\right] \qquad (16)$$

This solution is a damped oscillation that exhibits the desired properties. At t = 0, q = 0. As t→∞, q→CV. It is also true that the current (i = dq/dt) approaches 0 as t→∞, as required by the fact that the voltage V is constant.

3 Design an algorithm.

One property of these calculations is that it is easier to calculate the Runge-Kutta coefficients in the context of a specific problem. It may not be worth the trouble required to write a general purpose Runge-Kutta integration routine. We will first design an algorithm that can be used to solve mass-and-spring type problems such as the one in this application.

SUBPROGRAM MassAndSpring(IN: D, K, M, F, dt; OUT x, v)
DEFINE k1_x, k2_x, k3_x, k4_x, k1_v, k2_v, k3_v, k4_v
(Calculate Runge-Kutta coefficients.)
    ASSIGN k1_x = v
            k2_x = v + AofT(x, v, D, K, M, F)•dt/2 (see **SUB.** AofT)
            k3_x = v + AofT(x, v, D, K, M, F)•dt/2
            k4_x = v + AofT(x, v, D, K, M, F)•dt
            k1_v = AofT(x, v, D, K, M, F)
            k2_v = AofT(x + v•dt/2, v + k1_v•dt/2, D, K, M, F)
            k3_v = AofT(x + v•dt/2, v + k2_v•dt/2, D, K, M, F)
            k4_v = AofT(x + v•dt, v + k3_v•dt, D, K, M, F)
(Propagate solution.)
        ASSIGN x = x + (k1_x + 2•k2_x + 2•k3_x + k4_x)•dt/6
                v = v + (k1_v + 2•k2_v + 2•k3_v + k4_v)•dt/6

Because of the way AofT is used, make a note in the algorithm that it should be implemented as a separate function:

SUBPROGRAM AofT(IN: x, v, D, K, M, F)
    ASSIGN AofT = -(-F + D•v + K•x)/M

Now design the algorithm for solving the first part of the problem: $Ldi/dt + Ri = V$.

WRITE *(prompt for input)*
READ *(V, L, R, t_final,n)*
INITIALIZE *i = 0*
           t = 0
ASSIGN *dt = t_final/n*
LOOP *(for j = 1 to n)*
(Calculate Runge-Kutta coefficients.)
        ASSIGN *k1_i = (V - R•i)/L*
            k2_i = [V - R•(i + k1_i•dt/2)]/L
            k3_i = [V - R•(i + k2_i•dt/2)]/L
            k4_i = [V - R•(i + k3_i•dt)]/L
(Propagate solution.)
        INCREMENT *i = i + (k1_i + 2*k2_i + 2*k3_i + k4_i)*dt/6*
            t = t + dt
        WRITE *(t, i, (V/R)•(1 – $e^{-Rt/L}$) (Include analytic solution.)*
END LOOP

Finally, solve the second part of the problem: $Ld^2q/dt^2 + Rdq/dt + q/C = V$. Include the analytic solution for q.

WRITE *(prompt for input)*
READ *(V, L, R, C, t_final, n*
INITIALIZE *q = 0*
             i = CVR/(2L)
          t=0
ASSIGN *dt=t_final/n*
LOOP *(for j = 1 to n)*
      CALL *MassAndSpring(q, i, R, 1/C, L, V, dt)*
      INCREMENT *t = t + dt*
      WRITE *(t, q, i, CV[1 – $e^{-Rt/(2L)}$cos((4L/C – $R^2)^{1/2}$•t/(2L))])*
END LOOP

Convert the algorithm into a program.

P-9.8 [circuit.c]

```c
#include <stdio.h>
#include <math.h>

double AofT(double x,double v,double D,double K,double M,double F)
{
  return -(-F+D*v+K*x)/M;
}
void MassAndSpring(double *x,double *v,double D,double K,
                double M,double F,double dt) {
  double k1_x,k2_x,k3_x,k4_x,k1_v,k2_v,k3_v,k4_v;

/* Runge-Kutta coefficients... */
    k1_x=*v;
    k2_x=*v+AofT(*x,*v,D,K,M,F)*dt/2.;
    k3_x=*v+AofT(*x,*v,D,K,M,F)*dt/2.;
    k4_x=*v+AofT(*x,*v,D,K,M,F)*dt;
    k1_v=AofT(*x,*v,D,K,M,F);
    k2_v=AofT(*x+(*v)*dt/2.,(*v)+k1_v*dt/2.,D,K,M,F);
    k3_v=AofT(*x+(*v)*dt/2.,(*v)+k2_v*dt/2.,D,K,M,F);
    k4_v=AofT(*x+(*v)*dt,(*v)+k3_v*dt,D,K,M,F);
/* Propagate solution... */
    *x=*x+(k1_x+2.*k2_x+2.*k3_x+k4_x)*dt/6.;
    *v=*v+(k1_v+2.*k2_v+2.*k3_v+k4_v)*dt/6.;
}
int main(void)
{
/* Use Runge-Kutta method to solve LRC circuit problems.
   Variable equivalences with mass-and-spring problem:
   V    => force F
   q    => displacement x
   i    => velocity v
   L    => mass m
   R    => damping constant D
   1/C  => spring constant K */
  double i,q,L,C,R,V,t,dt,t_final;
  double k1_i,k2_i,k3_i,k4_i;
  int j,n;
  char choice;
```

```
/* Choose circuit type... */
  printf("Specify [o]scillating or [n]o oscillating term...\n");
  scanf("%c",&choice);
  switch (choice) {
    case 'o':
    case 'O':
/* Ld^2q/dt^2+Rdq/dt+q/C=V */
      do {
        printf(" Give V, L, R, C (4L/C-R^2) > 0:\n");
        scanf("%lf %lf %lf %lf",&V,&L,&R,&C);
        printf("one period at t=%lf s\n",
               4.*3.14159*L/sqrt(4.*L/C-R*R));
        printf("Give t_final and number of points: ");
        scanf("%lf %i",&t_final,&n);
      } while ((4.*L/C-R*R) <= 0.);
      q=0.; i=C*V*R/2./L; t=0.; /* Initial values */
      dt=t_final/(double)n;
      printf("        time            q            i  analytic q\n");
      for (j=1; j<=n; j++) {
        MassAndSpring(&q,&i,R,1./C,L,V,dt);
        t=t+dt;
        printf("%12.6e %12.4e %12.4e %12.4e\n",
        t,q,i,C*V*(1.-exp(-R*t/2./L)*cos(sqrt(4.*L/C-R*R)*t/2./L)));
      }
      break;
    case 'n':
    case 'N':
/* Ldi/dt+Ri=V (no oscillating term)... */
      printf("Give V, L, R: ");
      scanf("%lf %lf %lf",&V,&L,&R);
      printf("time constant at t= %lf s\n",L/R);
      printf("Give t_final and number of points: \n");
      scanf("%lf %i",&t_final,&n);
      i=0.; t=0.; /* Initial values */
      dt=t_final/(double)n;
      printf("        time            i        analytic i\n");
      for (j=1; j<=n; j++) {
/* Runge-Kutta coefficients... */
        k1_i=(V-R*i              )/L;
        k2_i=(V-R*(i+k1_i*dt/2.))/L;
        k3_i=(V-R*(i+k2_i*dt/2.))/L;
        k4_i=(V-R*(i+k3_i*dt)    )/L;
/* Propagate solution... */
        i=i+(k1_i+2.*k2_i+2.*k3_i+k4_i)*dt/6.;
        t=t+dt;
        printf("%12.6e %12.4e %12.4e\n",t,i,V/R*(1.-exp(-R*t/L)));
      }
      break;
    default:
      printf("No such choice.  Try again...\n");
  }
  return 0;
}
```

Running P-9.8 (LR circuit)

```
    Specify [o]scillating or [n]o oscillating term...
n
  Give V, L, R:
100 .02 25
  time constant at t=   7.9999998E-04  s
  Give t_final and number of points:
.001 20
        time           i         analytic 1
  5.000000E-05  2.4235E-01  2.4235E-01
  1.000000E-04  4.7001E-01  4.7001E-01
  1.500000E-04  6.8388E-01  6.8388E-01
  2.000000E-04  8.8480E-01  8.8480E-01
  2.500000E-04  1.0735E+00  1.0735E+00
  3.000000E-04  1.2508E+00  1.2508E+00
  3.500000E-04  1.4174E+00  1.4174E+00
  4.000000E-04  1.5739E+00  1.5739E+00
  4.500000E-04  1.7209E+00  1.7209E+00
  5.000000E-04  1.8590E+00  1.8590E+00
  5.500000E-04  1.9887E+00  1.9887E+00
  6.000000E-04  2.1105E+00  2.1105E+00
  6.500001E-04  2.2250E+00  2.2250E+00
  7.000001E-04  2.3326E+00  2.3326E+00
  7.500001E-04  2.4336E+00  2.4336E+00
  8.000002E-04  2.5285E+00  2.5285E+00
  8.500002E-04  2.6176E+00  2.6176E+00
  9.000002E-04  2.7014E+00  2.7014E+00
  9.500002E-04  2.7801E+00  2.7801E+00
  1.000000E-03  2.8540E+00  2.8540E+00
```

Figure 9.9 shows more of the solution.

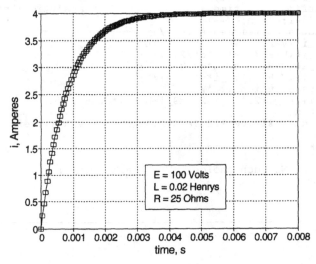

Figure 9.9.   Current in an LR circuit.

Running 9.8 (LRC circuit)

```
 Specify [o]scillating or [n]o oscillating term...
o
 Give V, L, R, C (4L/C-R^2) > 0:
100 .02 25 1e-6
 one period at t=  8.9206733E-04  s
 Give t_final and number of points:
.001 20
          time              q              i      analytic q
5.000000E-05   9.2773E-06   2.9723E-01   9.0252E-06
1.000000E-04   2.9345E-05   4.8089E-01   2.8413E-05
1.500000E-04   5.7054E-05   5.9355E-01   5.5211E-05
2.000000E-04   8.8488E-05   6.2533E-01   8.5756E-05
2.500000E-04   1.1950E-04   5.7706E-01   1.1616E-04
3.000000E-04   1.4623E-04   4.5952E-01   1.4278E-04
3.500000E-04   1.6560E-04   2.9151E-01   1.6266E-04
4.000000E-04   1.7562E-04   9.7026E-02   1.7382E-04
4.500000E-04   1.7559E-04  -9.8052E-02   1.7545E-04
5.000000E-04   1.6612E-04  -2.6931E-01   1.6794E-04
5.500000E-04   1.4894E-04  -3.9674E-01   1.5273E-04
6.000000E-04   1.2667E-04  -4.6702E-01   1.3212E-04
6.500001E-04   1.0238E-04  -4.7476E-01   1.0891E-04
7.000001E-04   7.9233E-05  -4.2269E-01   8.6037E-05
7.500001E-04   6.0056E-05  -3.2088E-01   6.6222E-05
8.000002E-04   4.7010E-05  -1.8499E-01   5.1659E-05
8.500002E-04   4.1362E-05  -3.4040E-02   4.3775E-05
9.000002E-04   4.3378E-05   1.1222E-01   4.3111E-05
9.500002E-04   5.2352E-05   2.3577E-01   4.9309E-05
1.000000E-03   6.6750E-05   3.2253E-01   6.1210E-05
```

Figure 9.10 shows more of this solution.

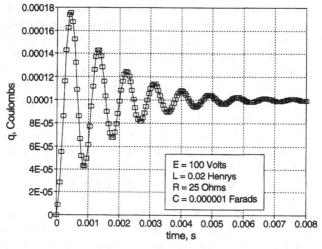

Figure 9.10. Charge in an LRC circuit.

5 *Verify the operation of the program.*

The code in P-9.8 includes the analytic solution, which can be compared side-by-side with the numerical solution. Even though this problem is identical to the mass-and-spring problem discussed earlier, it is important to test the program with physically reasonable values. It is easy to imagine a mass on the order of a few hundred grams or so bouncing up and down at the end of a spring, with a period on the order of a second. For LRC circuits in radio circuits, for example, the magnitudes of the quantities are much different. Millihenrys, microfarads or picofarads, kilo- or mega-ohms, and megahertz frequencies are typical working units for quantities in such circuits. When you select values for testing, make sure that the time step is appropriately chosen so that it is much less than one oscillating period; $\Delta t = t_{osc}/100$ would be reasonable.

For this problem, we can cheat in the sense that we know the analytic solution. In the code, the user is asked to input V, L, and R for the nonoscillating circuit, or V, L, R, and C for the oscillating circuit. In the former case, the program displays the time constant L/R to give an idea of the decay time. In the latter case, the program displays the oscillating period $t = 4\pi L/\sqrt{4L/C - R^2}$.

Problem Discussion

Of the numerical analysis problems presented in this chapter, solutions to differential equations pose the greatest difficulties. The Runge-Kutta algorithm has been chosen because it is a classic approach and is relatively simple to implement. However, it is in no sense a generally applicable technique or one that can always be depended upon to produce reliable results. Additional examination of this topic lies beyond the scope of this text. In contrast, Simpson's Rule integration as discussed earlier in this chapter will generally produce predictable and reliable results for functions without singularities and is therefore a reasonable working tool for evaluating many kinds of nonanalytic integrals.

For the LRC circuit treated in P-9.8 (and other oscillating systems), it is easy to pick values that don't work. If you don't have some idea of the oscillating period of the system, it is hard to pick time units and step sizes that will give a reasonable depiction of the motion. It is possible, for example, to pick a time step that produces what looks like the periodic motion of your system but which, in fact, is sampling from periodic motion taking place on a much smaller time scale. In other cases, your program will simply crash.

Incidentally, the Runge-Kutta algorithm can be implemented in a spreadsheet without much difficulty, and such an implementation was used to generate Figures 9.9 and 9.10. It is easy to try different values for the circuit and, of course, a spreadsheet has built-in graphics capabilities that make it easy to visualize the solutions.

9.8 Exercises

1. The "plus or minus three standard deviations" rule mentioned in Section 9.2.1 can also be applied to linear regression models.
(a) Modify P-9.1 so that it prints a report of all data values that fall more than three standard deviations above or below the regression line.
(b) Include an additional modification that replaces all such outlying data values with the modeled value. [outlyer.c]

2. Referring to the Problem Discussion following P-9.3 in Section 9.3.2, write a function Stirling_f that implements Stirling's formula for an analytic function whose derivative you know. Test this function with a driver program. [stir_f.c]

3. Refer to the application discussed in Section 9.3.2 and the measured distances and measured times (the ones generated with random errors) in Table 9.1. Assume that a functional relationship exists between time t and distance D: $D = at^2/2$ for constant acceleration a. Calculate the acceleration value that best fits the data by determining which value produces the smallest sum of squares of the differences between true and "measured" distances; a trial-and-error approach is okay. Determine the speed v at each measured time by taking the analytic derivative of your model: $v = dD/dt = at$. Are these values closer to the true values than the values obtained using Stirling's formula to estimate the speed? [fall2.c]

4. Write a function to implement Rectangular Rule integration. For a function whose integral is known, compare the results from Rectangular Rule integration with the results from Simpson's Rule integration as implemented in P-9.4 and Trapezoidal Rule integration as implemented in P-5.15 in Chapter 5. [rect.c]

5. Modify P-9.7 so that the convergence criteria are specified by the user and supplied to the subroutine. One possibility might be to specify the criterion for the size of the interval as a fraction of the original interval. [bisect3.c]

6. The Regula-Falsi method is a simple modification of the bisection method for finding roots which attempts to speed convergence to a root by making an informed guess about where the value x_{mid} that subdivides an interval should be. The bisection method puts this point in the middle of the current subinterval, but this is not the best place, in general. The Regula-Falsi method puts this point at the place where a straight line joining $f(x_L)$ and $f(x_R)$ crosses the x-axis. Modify P-9.7 to implement this modification. [regula.c]

7. Modify P-9.6 so that it calculates a residual vector $\mathbf{R} = \mathbf{AX} - \mathbf{C}$. It is necessary (but not necessarily sufficient) that the residual vector be small before the vector $\mathbf{X}$ can be considered a good solution for the system. [gauss2.c]

8. The bisection method of finding roots was discussed in Section 9.6. Its advantage is that an understanding of calculus is not required to understand and implement this

> A basic understanding of differential calculus is required.

method. Its disadvantage is that it is relatively inefficient and may be unreliable. Newton's method is an alternative that may work better in some cases. Its potential disadvantage is that both $f(x)$ and its derivative $f'(x)$ are required.

To implement Newton's method, guess a root and recalculate x_{root} using the two-step algorithm

$$x_{old} = x_{root}$$
$$x_{root} = x_{root} - f(x_{root})/f'(x_{root})$$

Continue to recalculate x_{root} until $|f(x_{root})|$ or $|x_{old} - x_{root}|$ is less than some specified value.

There are some situations in which this algorithm fails, for example, whenever $f'(x)$ equals zero for an initial guess or any subsequent estimate of a root. Therefore, it is a good idea to limit the maximum number of iterations. Note that, in contrast with the bisection method, a root found by Newton's algorithm may lie far from an initial guess and not necessarily within an initially specified range of x values. A function for which Newton's method will work well is $f(x) = e^x - 3x$, for which $f'(x) = e^x - 3$.

Hint: This algorithm can be implemented either iteratively or recursively. It would be good practice to do it both ways. [newton.c]

9. A manufacturer of laminated panels wishes to mold some ripple-shaped panels. The finished size of the sheet is 4' × 8', with the ripples running along the 8' side. Assume that

> A basic understanding of integral calculus is required.

the ripples are in the shape of a sine curve, with a specified amplitude ±b and length L, for example, ±0.5" and 3". (See Figure 9.11.) How long must the original sheet of material be to produce a finished panel with a length of 8'?

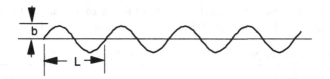

Figure 9.11. Parameters for a rippled panel.

The length of a segment ds along a curve formed by a function y(x) is

$$ds = \sqrt{dx^2 + dy^2} = \sqrt{1 + \left(\frac{dy}{dx}\right)^2}\, dx$$

For a sine curve of amplitude b and length L,

$$ds = \sqrt{1 + \left[\frac{2\pi b}{L}\cos\left(\frac{2\pi x}{L}\right)\right]^2}\, dx$$

The length of the material required to make L inches of panel is the integral of ds from 0 to L. This integral cannot be evaluated analytically. Use Simpson's Rule to evaluate the integral for user-specified values of b and L.

Extra Credit:
    If b << L, ds can be approximated by a series expansion, the terms of which can be integrated analytically. Use the first two terms in the binomial series for $(1 + x)^{1/2}$ to verify the results of Simpson's Rule integration as b approaches 0. [ripple.c]

10. This chapter has discussed the Gaussian elimination method for solving systems of linear equations. Another method (one of a class of so-called relaxation methods) is Gauss-Seidel iteration. To illustrate, consider a system of three equations:

$$x_1 a_{11} + x_2 a_{12} + x_3 a_{13} = c_1$$
$$x_1 a_{21} + x_2 a_{22} + x_3 a_{23} = c_2$$
$$x_1 a_{31} + x_2 a_{32} + x_3 a_{33} = c_3$$

Make an initial estimate for the unknowns (x_1, x_2, x_3); $(1, 1, 1)$ is a reasonable choice. Then solve the first equation for x_1 in terms of x_2 and x_3, the second for x_2 in terms of x_1 and x_3, and the third for x_3 in terms of x_1 and x_2:

$$x_1 = \frac{c_1 - a_{12}x_2 - a_{13}x_3}{a_{11}} \qquad x_2 = \frac{c_2 - a_{21}x_1 - a_{23}x_3}{a_{22}} \qquad x_3 = \frac{c_3 - a_{31}x_1 - a_{32}x_2}{a_{33}}$$

Repeat this process iteratively until convergence criteria are met. Note that the newest estimated value is always used in subsequent calculations. That is, the first iteration on x_2 uses the new estimate of x_1 and the original estimate of x_3, because a new estimate of x_3 isn't yet available.

Convergence can be either relative or absolute. If absolute convergence is required, for all values of x_i on the kth iteration:

$$\left| x_i^{\,k} - x_k^{\,k-1} \right| < \epsilon$$

If relative convergence is acceptable, for all values of x_i on the kth iteration:

$$\frac{\left| x_i^{\,k} - x_i^{\,k-1} \right|}{\left| x_i^{\,k} \right|} < \epsilon$$

where ϵ is some user-specified small number.

This method is trivial to generalize to larger systems, and it is relatively easy to program. However, for a variety of reasons that are beyond the scope of this text, the iteration will not converge for all systems of equations. (One obvious requirement is that all the diagonal coefficients must be nonzero.) Chances for convergence are good for diagonally dominant matrices of coefficients. Therefore, it is a good idea to arrange the equations so that, if possible, the diagonal terms are larger than all the others. It may also be helpful to normalize all the equations by dividing each equation by the diagonal coefficient so that the diagonal coefficients are all equal to 1. If the off-diagonal terms are all small compared to 1, then chances for convergence are good.

Because of possible convergence problems, your program should set a maximum number of iterations as one of the terminating conditions in the loop that controls the iterations.

Here is a system of equations for which Gauss-Seidel iteration will converge:

$$
\begin{aligned}
56x_1 + 22x_2 + 11x_3 - 18x_4 &= 34 \\
17x_1 + 66x_2 - 12x_3 + 7x_4 &= 82 \\
3x_1 - 5x_2 + 47x_3 + 20x_4 &= 18 \\
11x_1 + 16x_2 + 17x_3 + 10x_4 &= 26
\end{aligned}
$$

Note that the diagonal terms are largest in all but the last equation. [gaus_sei.c]

11. In the text (Section 9.5.1) it was stated that some matrices are ill-conditioned and resist attempts at solution with Gaussian elimination. One well-known example is the Hilbert matrix. Here is a 5×5 Hilbert matrix for $\mathbf{AX} = \mathbf{C}$.

$$\mathbf{A} = \begin{pmatrix} 1 & 1/2 & 1/3 & 1/4 & 1/5 \\ 1/2 & 1/3 & 1/4 & 1/5 & 1/6 \\ 1/3 & 1/4 & 1/5 & 1/6 & 1/7 \\ 1/4 & 1/5 & 1/6 & 1/7 & 1/8 \\ 1/5 & 1/6 & 1/7 & 1/8 & 1/9 \end{pmatrix} \quad \mathbf{C} = \begin{pmatrix} 1 \\ 0 \\ 0 \\ 0 \\ 0 \end{pmatrix}$$

Express the decimal fractions with seven significant digits (e.g., 0.3333333). What is the solution when you apply Gaussian elimination to this matrix? What is the solution if you express the decimal fractions with only four significant digits (e.g., 0.1667)?

12. Consider a radioactive particle inside a cube-shaped block. What is the probability, as a function of its original location, that the particle will exit the block on a particular side? Assuming that travel in all directions is equally probable, an answer to a simplified version of this question can be obtained by modeling the problem in two dimensions. Set up a grid of possible locations. Three rows of three locations each is sufficient:

```
┌─┬─┬─┐
─1─2─3─
─4─5─6─
─7─8─9─
└─┴─┴─┘
```

What is the probability that a particle will escape through a specified face of the grid? Suppose the bottom is chosen. The probability can be expressed as a system of equations in which P_n is the probability that a particle at position n will escape through the bottom of the grid. This probability is one-fourth the sum of the probabilities that a particle in the four locations surrounding n will escape through the bottom:

$P_1 = (0 + P_2 + P_4 + 0)/4$ $P_2 = (0 + P_3 + P_5 + P_1)/4$ $P_3 = (0 + 0 + P_6 + P_2)/4$

$P_4 = (P_1 + P_5 + P_7 + 0)/4$ $P_5 = (P_2 + P_6 + P_8 + P_4)/4$ $P_6 = (P_3 + 0 + P_9 + P_5)/4$

$P_7 = (P_4 + P_8 + 1 + 0)/4$ $P_8 = P_5 + P_9 + 1 + P_7)/4$ $P_9 = (P_6 + 0 + 1 + P_8)/4$

Rewrite these equations in the form $\mathbf{AP} = \mathbf{C}$ and solve for $\mathbf{P}$. Try both Gaussian elimination as described earlier in this chapter and Gauss-Seidel iteration as described in Exercise 10. For Gauss-Seidel iteration, are the results sensitive to the initial (reasonable) guesses for $\mathbf{P}$?

One test of your program's output is the fact that the probability of a particle initially in the center of the grid escaping through any specified side of the grid should be exactly 0.25. [escape.c]

13. Recall Exercise 15 in Chapter 4, in which, as one step in finding the angular position (true anomaly) of an orbiting object as a function of time, you were asked to solve Kepler's equation

$$M = E - e{\bullet}\sin E$$

for the eccentric anomaly E as a function of mean anomaly M. In that exercise, you were expected to use an iterative approach to find E for specified values of e and M.

Another way to solve Kepler's equation is to use the bisection method to find the root of

$$M - E + e{\bullet}\sin E = 0$$

Use a version of program P-9.7 with the necessary changes to the parameter list to solve this equation; you must pass both M (the independent variable) and e to the function. Be sure to read Exercise 15 in Chapter 4 before starting this program. If you already wrote the program for that exercise, you might wish to modify it to print out the value of E (which is an intermediate calculation required to find the true anomaly) so you can compare it with the result produced by the program you write for this exercise. Remember to use radians rather than degrees where appropriate.

14. An alternate method for solving sets of linear equations is called Cramer's rule. It involves the so-called determinant, a single numerical value derived in a specific way from the matrix containing the coefficients of the unknowns in a system of equations. It can be shown that if the determinant is not equal to zero then the system has a unique solution. The determinant is easy to calculate for sets of two or three equations but becomes cumbersome and computationally inefficient for systems with more unknowns.

Consider the linear system

$$a_{11}x + a_{12}y = c_1$$
$$a_{21}x + a_{22}y = c_2$$

for which the matrix of coefficients is

$$\begin{bmatrix} a_{11} & a_{12} \\ a_{21} & a_{22} \end{bmatrix}$$

The determinant D is

$$D = a_{11}a_{22} - a_{12}a_{21}$$

If $D \neq 0$, the solutions are N_1/D and N_2/D, where N_1 and N_2 are obtained by calculating the determinant of a matrix for which the indicated column in the coefficient matrix is replaced with the constant coefficients:

$$N_1 = c_1 a_{22} - c_2 a_{12}$$
$$N_2 = c_2 a_{11} - c_1 a_{21}$$

For the system

$$a_{11}x + a_{12}y + a_{13}z = c_1$$
$$a_{21}x + a_{22}y + a_{23}z = c_2$$
$$a_{31}x + a_{32}y + a_{33}z = c_3$$

the matrix of coefficients is

$$\begin{bmatrix} a_{11} & a_{12} & a_{13} \\ a_{21} & a_{22} & a_{23} \\ a_{31} & a_{32} & a_{33} \end{bmatrix}$$

and

$$D = a_{11}a_{22}a_{33} + a_{12}a_{23}a_{31} + a_{13}a_{21}a_{32} - a_{13}a_{22}a_{31} - a_{12}a_{21}a_{33} - a_{11}a_{23}a_{32}$$

If $D \neq 0$ then

$$N_1 = c_1 a_{22}a_{33} + a_{12}a_{23}c_3 + a_{13}c_2 a_{32} - a_{13}a_{22}c_3 - a_{12}c_2 a_{33} - c_1 a_{23}a_{32}$$
$$N_2 = a_{11}c_2 a_{33} + c_1 a_{23}a_{31} + a_{13}a_{21}c_3 - a_{13}c_2 a_{31} - c_1 a_{21}a_{33} - a_{11}a_{23}c_3$$
$$N_3 = a_{11}a_{22}c_3 + a_{12}c_2 a_{31} + c_1 a_{21}a_{32} - c_1 a_{22}a_{31} - a_{12}a_{21}c_3 - a_{11}c_2 a_{32}$$

Write a program that implements Cramer's rule for linear systems with two or three unknowns. Because of the multiple calculations of determinants with different sets of coefficients (which is why this method is inefficient for large systems of equations), your program should include a separate function to calculate the determinant. Try to implement the code in a general way with nested loops so the function will calculate the determinant regardless of whether there are two or three sets of coefficients, based on an input value—the number of equations—passed through the parameter list. That is, do not "hard code" the calculations for D for two or three equations. Test your program with equations for which the determinant is not zero. Store the coefficients and constants in an external data file in which the first line in the file contains the number of equations. [cramer.c]

15. A datalogger is used to capture measurements of UV-B radiation expressed in units of minimum erythemal dose per hour (MED/hr). (One MED is the amount of UV-B radiation, weighted by the skin's spectral response, that will produce a discernible color change in a light-skinned Caucasian who has not previously been exposed to significant amounts of UV-B radiation for the previous 30 days.) The datalogger averages 30 measurements taken at 1-minute intervals every half hour. A spreadsheet is used to produce an output file (aug96.txt) of these averaged measurements in the following format:

```
August 1, 1996
 -0.005 285
 -0.002 315
  0.009 345
  0.055 375
  0.113 405
  0.166 435
  0.337 465
  0.649 495
  0.698 525
  1.029 555
  1.039 585
  1.279 615
  1.463 645
  1.908 675
  1.817 705
  1.402 735
  2.332 765
  2.256 795
  2.431 825
  2.050 855
  1.814 885
  1.327 915
  1.008 945
  0.677 975
  0.424 1005
  0.253 1035
  0.128 1065
  0.052 1095
  0.014 1125
August 2, 1996
 -0.003 285
  0.003 315
```
(and so forth)

where the first value is the 30-minute average in units of MED/hr and the second is the time in minutes corresponding to the middle of each 30-minute interval.

Write a program that uses Trapezoidal Rule integration to calculate the cumulative UV-B radiation for each day in the file. (The file aug96.txt is incomplete for the month.) Assume that the MED/hr values preceding and following the first and last tabulated values for each day are equal to 0.

Although you may not assume that data for every day in the month will be included in the file, you *may* assume that each date present in the file is followed by 29 half-hourly averages. The first value is the 30-minute average over the times 4:30am–5:00am, and the last value is the 30-minute average over the times 6:30pm–7:00pm.

Because of drift in the UV-B detector's calibration, some of the averaged measurements at the beginning and end of the set of 29 may be small negative numbers. This is not physically reasonable, and your program should set such values to zero before using them to calculate the daily cumulative UV-B radiation. [uvb_1.c]

Binary Files, Random Access, and Dynamic Allocation

10.1 Binary and Random Access Files

10.1.1 Random Access File Concepts

In this section we will discuss a different kind of file that stores information in a **binary format** rather than as text. Recall from previous examples throughout this book that

| **binary format** |

data files were always text files in the sense that they could be created with a text editor or a word processor in a human-readable format. Even numerical information was stored in terms of readable characters—the digits 0–9 plus other appropriate characters such as a period serving as a decimal point. Through the use of appropriate conversion specifiers, the contents of this kind of file could be interpreted by a program either as text (characters) or as numerical information. We treated such files as sequential access files in which we always started reading information at the beginning of the file and proceeded sequentially from one value to the next. We stopped either when we found what we were looking for or, more typically, when we got to the end of the file.

Sequential access text files are simple to use, but they have some limitations that are especially obvious when you are faced with manipulating more information than can be stored in a statically allocated array while your program is running. One typical use of arrays is to store a list in a way that makes it efficient to look for things in the list. Once the list is stored in an array, you can sort the list and then use a binary search; the required algorithms were discussed in Chapter 8. However, you cannot perform a binary search on a sequential access file even if the information in the file is sorted in the desired order, and you cannot sort such a file. The inefficiency of using linear searches is most noticeable for large files—that is, just those files that may be too large to store in an array.

The solution to this kind of data management problem is to remove the restriction of sequential access. The easiest way to do this is to store data in records of fixed length. The problem with text files is that they do not lend themselves naturally to the imposition of a fixed record length. For example, consider these two lines (records) in a text file:

```
1001 17.77 313.5
999 3.3 2.1
```

This file is simply a string of characters, including blanks and end-of-line marks. We know that it can be interpreted in an appropriate way by using C intrinsic functions such as fscanf along with appropriate conversion specifiers. Thus it is easy to read the six values in this file, perhaps three at a time. However, the first line contains 16 characters and the second line contains only 11 characters. This is due simply to how the numerical information is represented in this form.

When a program stores the six values in this file in its internal binary format (that is, as a series of 1s and 0s), the space required in memory is independent of how the values are originally represented as text because the internal storage of numerical values depends *only* on the data type of the values and not on how they are expressed as characters. Thus, assuming the numbers 1001 and 999 are stored as integers, both values require the same number of bytes. Similarly, assuming the values 17.77, 313.5, 3.3, and 2.1 are all stored as real numbers, the memory requirements are identical for all four values. Internally then, each "record" of this file requires the same amount of storage space.

It is possible to copy the internal representation of values into a file and also to read such a file simply by reversing the process; that is, by copying the contents of the file directly into memory. Such a file, which preserves the internal binary format in which values are stored, is called a binary file. I/O operations are more efficient for binary files than for text files because it is no longer necessary to translate back and forth between internal and external (text-based) representations for numerical values. Most significantly, however, it is easy to implement random access to information in a binary file. This because each record in a binary file has the same length, based on the data types of the values stored in the record.

Finally, do not confuse the terms binary format or binary file in this discussion with terms such as binary search. The first two terms describe a way of storing data. The third term describes an algorithm.

10.1.2 Implementing Binary Files

To see how binary files work, we will return to a problem that first appeared as a file-processing example in Chapter 2. In Section 2.3, a programming problem was posed in which several remote instrument stations report measurements to a central data collection facility. The reports are then assembled into a data file for processing. A station can submit multiple reports, not necessarily sequentially, and it can submit up to eight measurements in a single report. A program was presented with the limited goal of counting the number of reports and the total number of measurements. Modifications of this problem presented as Exercise 1 in Chapters 6 and 7 used arrays or arrays of structs to keep track of the total number of reports and measurements for each station. If you did Exercise 1 in Chapter 7, your program should have used an array of structures whose index values 0 through 10 were obtained directly from the station IDs, assumed to be numbers in the range 1000 through 1010. (If you didn't do those exercises, it would be worthwhile to do them now.)

To see how binary files work, we will now present an alternative way of storing and manipulating the information in the original stations.dat text file. Symbolically, the file will be arranged in records that will look like this:

Now, however, the values in the file will be stored in their internal binary format and will no longer appear in a human-readable format. Obviously, some of the information appearing just once in the original text file is stored in more than one place in the new binary file; the station ID is stored with every measurement rather than just at the start of a particular station report. This allows every record to be identical in its format. We will assume that the extra file space required will have no significant negative consequences.

Suppose our objective is to write a program to sort the contents of the binary file by measurement, from smallest to largest. We will *not* store the data in an array. Instead—and this is the entire point of the example—we will actually move records in the file so they will be in sorted order. Initially, we will write a program that reads stations.dat and creates a binary file with the desired record format. Program 10.1 will also read the binary file, just to make sure everything is working properly. The rest of the problem is left as an end-of-chapter exercise.

P-10.1 [station4.c]

```
/* Read data from reporting stations and save in binary file. */
#include <stdio.h>
#define FILENAME "stations.dat"
#define FILEOUT  "stations.bin"
#define MAX_REPORTS 8

typedef struct {
  int ID;
  float measurement;
}
station_type;

int main(void)
{
  FILE *in, *bin;
  float m[MAX_REPORTS];
  int i, status, n_values, tot_values=0;
  station_type station;
  char *line_ptr, one_line[80];

  in=fopen(FILENAME, "r");
  bin=fopen(FILEOUT, "wb+");
```

```
/* Start main data processing loop. */
  while (1) {
    line_ptr=fgets(one_line,sizeof(one_line),in);
    if (line_ptr == NULL) break;
    status=sscanf(one_line,"%i %f %f %f %f %f %f %f %f",&station.ID,
            &m[0],&m[1],&m[2],&m[3],&m[4],&m[5],&m[6],&m[7]);
    n_values=status-1;
    for (i=0; i<n_values; i++) {
      station.measurement=m[i];
      tot_values++;
      printf("%5i %6.1f\n",station.ID,station.measurement);
      fwrite(&station,sizeof(station_type),1,bin);
    }
  }
  fclose(in);
  printf("Total values: %i\n",tot_values);
  rewind(bin);
  printf("Reading from binary file.\n");
  for (i=1; i<=tot_values; i++) {
    fread(&station,sizeof(station_type),1,bin);
    printf("%5i %6.1f\n",station.ID,station.measurement);
  }
  fclose(bin);
}
```

P-10.1 was written in two stages. First, code was written to read stations.dat and assign field values to a variable of type station_type. After this part was complete, the code printed in bold italics was added to create the binary file and verify its contents. This is a typical two-step strategy that you should follow when you create binary files. It is within the context of those few lines of new code that we will discuss C's implementation of binary files.

File Access Modes

Previously, we opened files as sequential access text files in either read-only ("r") or write-only ("w") mode. However, C supports several other file access modes for both text and binary files. For example, in P-10.1 we have used the mode "wb+", which is interpreted as, "Create a binary file in read/write mode."

Table 10.1 gives a complete list of file access modes. The choices include opening existing files in read or read/write mode and creating new files in write or read/write mode.

Table 10.1. File access modes

Mode	Interpretation
Text file modes	
"a"	Append to existing text file.
"a+"	Open existing text file in append mode for read/write.
"r"	Open existing text file for reading.
"r+"	Open existing text file for read/write.
"w"	Create text file for writing.
"w+"	Create text file for read/write.
Binary file modes	
"ab"	Append to existing binary file.
"ab+"	Open existing binary file for read/write.
"rb"	Open existing binary file for reading.
"rb+"	Open existing binary file for read/write.
"wb"	Create binary file for writing.
"wb+"	Create binary file for read/write.

The alert reader may notice that, according to Table 10.1, it appears possible to open text files in read/write mode as well as read-only or write-only. Even though this is, in fact, allowed as a matter of C syntax, we will not use read/write mode for text files. The basic problem is the implication that files with no fixed record structure can nonetheless be accessed randomly rather than sequentially. Consider the following text file that contains two numbers:

```
17.7 13.333□
▲
```

where the □ symbol represents an end-of-line mark and the ▲ symbol represents the initial position of a *file pointer* that is created when the file is opened. Suppose you wish to read   **file pointer** values in the file and then change them; this is certainly a reasonable thing to do with a file opened in read/write mode. You can think of read and write operations as moving the file pointer from place to place in the file. After reading the first number, 17.7, with an appropriate conversion specifier, the file pointer is positioned on the space just after the 7:

```
17.7 13.333□
     ▲
```

In order to replace the 17.7, you must move the file pointer backward to the 1 in the text representation of 17.7. How many characters must you move the pointer? In this case it's four. If you had just read the second number, 13.333, the file pointer would be positioned on the end-of-line mark, and you would have to move the pointer back six spaces to replace the 13.333.

This presents a problem because the positioning of the file pointer required for read/write operations depends unpredictably on the representation of the value and not just on the data type of the value. But that's not the only problem. What happens when you try to write a new number? Because this is a text file, you must supply a conversion format. Suppose you want to replace 17.7 with 187.345. There is not enough room to print this number in a character-based representation without overwriting some digits in the second value.

In principle, it is possible to overcome these problems. You could, for example, impose a uniform format on all values saved in a text file. However, read/write mode for text files really make sense only when their contents are being accessed one character at a time. This is usually not very practical for the kinds of problems addressed in this text, and it explains why we have used text files only in read-only or write-only mode. As we will see, binary files can be used to overcome these kinds of problems.

I/O for Binary Files

The I/O functions for binary files are fread and fwrite, with identical syntax:

```
int_variable=fread(address of first data object,
                   size of one data object,
                   number of data objects, pointer to file)
   or    (void)fread(...)
```

```
int_variable=fwrite(address of first data object,
                    size of one data object,
                    number of data objects, pointer to file)
   or    (void)fwrite(...)
```

The integer variable returned by fread is equal to the number of records successfully read and the variable returned by fwrite is equal to the number of records successfully written. Both functions are used in P-10.1. A notable feature of I/O operations on binary files is that when read and write operations are applied to records of structs, they operate on an *entire* record rather than one field at a time. Consider, for example, the statements

```
fread(&station,sizeof(station_type),1,bin);
fwrite(&station,sizeof(station_tpe),1,bin);
```

These read or write an entire record of type `station_type` from or to a file. To read or write the same information from or to a text file would require code something like this to read one value at a time:

```
fprintf(in,"%i %f\n",station.ID,station.measurement);
fscanf(in,"%i %f",&station.ID,&station.measurement);
```

The \n control character in the `fprintf` statement is optional, depending on whether you would like the text file to retain a line structure that will make it easier for humans to read. However, binary files aren't easily read by humans and end-of-line characters make no sense. Binary files consist just of a stream of bytes. There is no line structure and hence no end-of-line marks.

It is important to remember that the address-of operator is required for both read and write operations on binary files, because information is being copied either to or from an address in memory. That is, the first parameter of both `fread` and `fwrite` is the address of the data object being read or written and not its variable name. Hence `&station` is required in the `fwrite` function, rather than just `station`.

How is it possible to read an entire binary record at once? I/O on binary files works by copying groups of bytes directly back and forth between a file and computer memory, without any format conversion. The definition of `station_type` in P-10.1 tells your program, through the `sizeof` operation, how many bytes are required to hold a record of type `station_type`. In the above example, `fread` copies the appropriate number of bytes from the file into the address of the variable `station`. When a record is written to a file, the reverse happens: bytes are copied directly from memory into the file. Note, by the way, that the records in binary files don't have to be user-defined. They can also consist just of intrinsic data types whose size can still be determined for a particular C implementation with `sizeof`. However, every record in a binary file should hold the same kind of data object.

Because the number of bytes in a binary record is fixed by the data type of the field(s) in the record and not by the value(s) of the field(s), every binary record contains the same number of bytes. That is, they are fixed-length records. This makes random access easy to implement, as we shall see. For now, the code in P-10.1 accesses the records in the binary file sequentially, after using the `rewind` function to reset the file pointer to the beginning of the file:

```
void rewind(pointer to file)
```

Random Access to Binary Files

Previously, in P-10.1, we created the binary file stations.bin and read it sequentially from beginning to end. In P-10.2, we will show how to read this binary file in reverse order. Although this isn't a particularly significant programming achievement, the program is important because of the information it conveys about using binary files.

P-10.2 [station5.c]

```
/* Read data from stations.bin in reverse order. */
#include <stdio.h>
#define FILENAME  "stations.bin"

typedef struct {
  int ID;
  float measurement;
}
station_type;

int main(void)
{
  FILE *in;
  int n_recs,i;
  station_type station;

  in=fopen(FILENAME,"rb");
  fseek(in,0,SEEK_END);
  n_recs=ftell(in)/sizeof(station_type);
  for (i=n_recs-1; i>=0; i--) {
    fseek(in,i*sizeof(station_type),SEEK_SET);
    fread(&station,sizeof(station_type),1,in);
    printf("%5i %6.1f\n",station.ID,station.measurement);
  }
  fclose(in);
  return 0;
}
```

First of all, P-10.2 uses the binary file written previously by P-10.1. In order to use this file, it is essential to use a struct to create a data type identical to the one in P-10.1. The names of the fields don't have to be the same (although there is no reason why they shouldn't be), but the data types and the order in which they appear must be the same.

How will we control the reading of the file in a loop? If we were reading the file sequentially from beginning to end, we could use a conditional loop similar to what we have used previously for text files:

```
while (1) {
  status=fread(&station,sizeof(station),1,in);
  if (status == 0) break;
  ..
```

The only difference is that fread returns a 0 if no record is found, rather than EOF. This could also work for reading the file backward, using some syntax similar to that in P-10.2:

```
i=0;
while (1) {
   i++;
   fseek(in,i*sizeof(station_type),SEEK_END);
   status=fread(&station,sizeof(station_type),1,in);
   if (status == 0) break;
   printf("%5i %6.1f\n",station.ID,station.measurement);
}
```

However, P-10.2 illustrates another approach to determining ahead of time how many records the file contains. With this knowledge, we can use a count-controlled loop rather than a conditional loop. First we need a way to set the position of the file pointer. This is done with the fseek function, whose general syntax is

```
int variable = fseek(pointer to file, byte offset, origin)
   or      (void)fseek(...)

where origin is SEEK_SET, SEEK_CUR, or SEEK_END
```

Together, the *offset* and *origin* determine where to move the file pointer prior to a read or write operation. The *offset* value is in bytes and the *origin* has one of three predefined values—SEEK_SET (offset measured from the beginning of the file), SEEK_CUR (offset measured from the current position of the file pointer), or SEEK_END (offset measured from the end of the file)—which indicates the position from which the byte offset is to be measured. The fseek function returns an integer value of zero if the seek operation is successful, and nonzero otherwise. With properly written code, there is never any reason for fseek to be unsuccessful.

Next we use the ftell function to find the current position of the file pointer relative to the beginning of the file. Its general syntax is

```
int variable = ftell(pointer to file)
```

In P-10.2, the statements

```
fseek(in,0,SEEK_END);
n_recs=ftell(in)/sizeof(station_type);
```

first position the file pointer to the end of the file (that is, with an offset of 0 relative to the end of the file) and then determine the number of records in the file by dividing the return value from `ftell` by the size of the data object. This division is guaranteed to be a whole number because every record has length `station_type`.

A call to `fseek` is required whenever it is desired to read from or write to a file at some place other than the current file pointer position. In P-10.2, because we want to read the file in something other than sequential order from the beginning, we must use `fseek` to reposition the file pointer to `i*sizeof(stations_type)` bytes from the beginning of the file before every call to `fread`. The limits on the `for...` loop control variable in P-10.2 are `tot_values - 1` and 0, rather than `tot_values` and 1. To position the file pointer at the beginning of the last record in the file, the offset relative to the beginning of the file must be one less than the total number of records in the file. To position the file pointer at the beginning of the file, the offset must be zero.

10.2 Dynamic Allocation and Linked Lists

10.2.1 The Concept of Dynamic Allocation

In this section, we will consider some different ways to store and access data within a program. These new approaches are significantly different from how we have previously managed data, so we will devote considerable space to developing the concepts before applying them to specific programming problems.

Previously, we have stored information in an array holding either intrinsic or user-defined data types. As discussed in Chapter 6, space for arrays must be statically allocated at compile time and cannot be changed once your program is running.

An alternative is to allocate space for storing information *while* a program is running; that is, at runtime rather than at compile time. This is called *dynamic allocation*. Dynamic allocation takes place in an area of memory known as *heap space*, rather than in the area known as *stack space*. One potential advantage is that there may be more space available for dynamic allocation than there is for static allocation. An additional advantage is that dynamically allocated space can be "released" and reused while your program is running.

dynamic allocation
heap space
stack space

10.2.2 Dynamically Allocated Arrays

The simplest way to make use of dynamic allocation is to consider how to create arrays whose size is set at runtime rather than at compile time. Program P-10.3

shows a simple example of how to create an array of real numbers. In contrast to earlier programs, however, this program does *not* contain a static array declaration. Rather, the user is asked *after the program starts running* to specify how many elements the array should hold.

P-10.3 [calloc.c]

```
#include <stdio.h>
#include <stdlib.h>

void make_array(double *ptr,int n);

int main(void) {

    int i,n;
    double *ptr;

    printf("Give number of elements: ");
    scanf("%i",&n);
    ptr=(double *)calloc(n,sizeof(double));
    make_array(ptr,n);
    for (i=1; i<=n; i++) {
      printf("%lf\n",*ptr);
      ptr++;
    }

    return 0;
}
void make_array(double x[],int n) {
    int i;

    for (i=0; i<n; i++)
      x[i]=100.*rand()/RAND_MAX;
}
```

The critical statement in P-10.3, printed in bold italics, uses the `calloc` function, whose general syntax is

    pointer to data_type=(data_type *)calloc(n,sizeof(data_type))

where *data_type* is the data type of the elements of the "array" and *n* is the number of memory locations to be allocated. The word array is in quotation marks here because all `calloc` does is assign *n**`sizeof`(*data_type*) contiguous bytes in memory; it is up to the programmer to make use of this space in an array-like way. The return value from `calloc` is a pointer to the first of the allocated memory locations; this value is functionally equivalent to the name of a statically allocated array or the memory location &x[0] for the statically allocated array x. Note that it is required for the programmer to provide an explicit type cast for `calloc` in order for the pointer it returns to be bound to the appropriate data type.

In P-10.3, you can see two approaches to making use of dynamically allocated array space. For the function `make_array`, the function prototype includes a pointer to values of type `double`, but the function implementation uses array notation for this same parameter; we have already discussed the equivalence of such parameters in Chapter 6. In particular, we know that functions do not *reallocate* space for an array. Instead, they are passed the address of the first memory location associated with an array. After that, it is the programmer's responsibility to make sure that the program does not attempt to access memory locations beyond those that have been allocated.

The advantage of this arrangement is that, inside a function such as `make_array`, we are free to use a more natural index notation for generating and manipulating values stored in the array. In the context of dynamic allocation, the notational equivalence between a pointer and an array name followed by empty square brackets (e.g., `x[]`), may now make more sense: the bracket syntax is simply a notational device to tell the compiler that we will be using index notation to manipulate the contents of memory locations we have decided to treat as an array, instead of the pointer notation that C actually uses to access contiguous memory locations.

In the `main` function of P-10.3, we have not used array notation because there is no array declaration. However, it is still possible to access the elements that have been allocated (that is, the elements we wish to treat as an array) by incrementing the pointer. Again, this notation has been discussed in Chapter 6, although we typically have avoided using it with statically allocated arrays, in favor of index notation. As always, it is the programmer's responsibility to restrict access to only those memory locations that have been allocated.

Dynamically allocated arrays are not always reasonable replacements for statically declared arrays. In many of the problems in this text, starting with Chapter 6, we have depended on an array to hold values read from a file of unknown length. In that situation, we do not know how many memory locations we will need until we have read the complete file. This means that we are no more able to use `calloc` to allocate just the right amount of space while the program is running than we are able to statically allocate an array of just the right size. In the next section, we will examine another approach to dynamic allocation that will allow us to allocate memory locations on the fly, so our program will always have exactly the space it needs. If this sounds too good to be true, don't worry—the price we will pay is that we will no longer be able to apply an array-like model when manipulating these memory locations.

10.2.3 Dynamically Allocated Linked Lists

As mentioned at the end of the previous section, a typical programming problem involves processing data from an external file on the fly, without knowing ahead of time how much data there will be. The solution posed in Chapter 6, and extended to `structs` in Chapter 7, is to define a statically allocated array of sufficient size to store the maximum amount of data that might be encountered. At the time, we were willing to overlook the fact that this solution might waste memory if the actual amount of data was less than we had anticipated. In addition, this solution assumes that our programming environment is able to allocate the required amount of space, an assumption that can easily prove unwarranted.

An alternative is to use a dynamically allocated data structure called a **linked list** to store data. In a linked list, **data nodes** are created that contain, in addition to data fields for the information to be stored, at least one additional field—a pointer bound to the data type of the node. Each data node, which is roughly equivalent to an element in an array, is linked to at least one other node through its pointer field. Access to the linked list is provided by a separate pointer that points to the beginning of the list, where the definition of beginning depends on how the list is going to be used.

In a **linearly linked list**, the pointer to the beginning of the list points to the first node created. Information in the list can be accessed only from the begining and only in the forward direction from the oldest node (the first one created) to the newest node (the last one created). The pointer field in each node points to the next node in the list. The pointer field in the newest node has a value of NULL to mark the end of the list.

Because of the way C treats arrays, by storing a pointer to the first element in the array, a linked list is roughly equivalent to an array restricted to allow only sequential access to its elements. That is, once you have accessed element n, you can access element n + 1, but never element n − 1. This restriction is also similar to the restrictions placed on sequential access files, in which to access a value somewhere in the middle of the file, you must start at the beginning of the file and read through all records prior to the one of interest.

It is possible to relax the restriction of sequential access in only one direction by defining nodes with more than one pointer. In a data structure called a **doubly linked list**, each node has two pointers that can be interpreted as forward and backward or left and right pointers to adjacent nodes. In this case, two additional pointers must be saved, one to the oldest node and one to the newest node. It is also possible to provide direct access to nodes other than the first node just by saving pointers to these nodes.

Programs that use linked list structures have two basic components. First, there is the structure of the node itself as defined through a `struct`. For our purposes, every linked list contains nodes of `structs` because every node must contain at least one data record and one pointer to another node. Second, there are the algorithms required to manage the data in a linked list. It is important to keep these two components separate. The code for creating and accessing linked lists can (and should) be developed independently from the data contents of the nodes in the list. Thus, in our discussion of linked lists, we will think of each data node as a "black box" containing some data, along with a separate box for each pointer field. We are generally unconcerned about the contents of the data box except in a generic way, as in, "Store data in the node." As a result, the concept of a data record becomes more abstract than it has been in the past.

To begin our exploration of linked lists, here is a sketch of a linearly linked list.

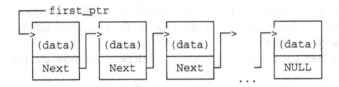

The list contains several nodes, each of which is linked by a pointer to the next node. The "handle" on the list is `first_ptr`, a pointer that points to the first node in the list. This handle is roughly equivalent to the name of an array. The end of the list is marked by the presence of a NULL pointer in the last node. It is a linearly linked list because the nodes can be accessed only from the beginning and only in the forward direction.

In order to use linearly linked lists, there are five essential operations that must be implemented:

1. Create a list.
2. Access all nodes in a list.
3. Append a new node to the end of a list.
4. Add a new node within a list.
5. Delete a node from a list.

The algorithms for these operations are not conceptually difficult, but their implementation requires a great deal of care because code involving pointers and dynamic allocation is notoriously difficult to debug. To help with algorithm development, we will invent a new pseudocode command,

NEW *(pointer)*

which creates a new node and associates a pointer with that node.

Here are algorithms for implementing each of the five required operations on linearly linked lists. Each algorithm is in the form of a subprogram.

1. Create a list.

SUBPROGRAM *Create_List(IN: source of data for nodes;*
                                            OUT: first_pointer)
DEFINE *current_pointer*

a. Create the first node in the list and save pointer to this node.

NEW *(current_pointer)*
ASSIGN *data fields in node*
ASSIGN *pointer field = NULL*
ASSIGN *first_pointer = current_pointer*

b. Create the remaining nodes.

LOOP *(as long as more nodes are needed)*
        NEW *(pointer field of current node)*
        ASSIGN *current node = pointer field of current node*
        ASSIGN *data fields in current node*
        ASSIGN *current pointer field = NULL*
END LOOP

2. Access all nodes in a list.

SUBPROGRAM *Access_List(IN: pointer to first data node (current_pointer))*
LOOP *(while current_pointer is not NULL)*
        WRITE *(data fields in current node)*
        ASSIGN *current_pointer = pointer field of current node*
END LOOP

3. Append a new node to the end of a list.

SUBPROGRAM *Append_List(IN: pointer to first data node (current_pointer))*
        (Move to end of current list.)
        LOOP *(while current_pointer is not NULL)*
                ASSIGN *current_pointer = pointer field of current node*
        END LOOP

> *(Add new node.)*
> **NEW** *(pointer field of current node)*
> **ASSIGN** *current_pointer = pointer field of current node*
> **ASSIGN** *data fields in current node*
> **ASSIGN** *pointer field of current node = NULL*

4. Add a new node within a list.

This code assumes that a new node will be inserted *after* a specified node. This code is relatively easy to write, but it may be more likely that you wish to insert a new node *before* a specified node. This code is left for an end-of-chapter exercise.

> **SUBPROGRAM** *Insert_Prior(IN: pointer to first data node (current_pointer),*
> *search_condition)*
> **DEFINE** *temp as pointer to node*
> **LOOP** *(while current_pointer is not NULL*
> *and search_condition is not met)*
> **ASSIGN** *current_ptr = pointer field of current node*
> **END LOOP**
> **IF** *(search_condition is met)* **THEN**
> **NEW** *(temp)*

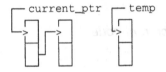

> **ASSIGN** *data fields in node to which temp points*
> **ASSIGN** *pointer field of temp = pointer field of current_pointer*

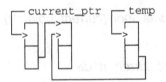

***ASSIGN** pointer field of current node = temp*

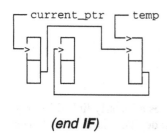

*(end **IF**)*

5. Delete a node from a list.

This code assumes that the node *after* a specified node will be deleted. This code is relatively easy to write, but it may be more likely that you would like to delete a specified node itself rather than the node following a specified node. Code to do this is left for an end-of-chapter exercise.

***SUBPROGRAM** Delete_After(IN: pointer to first data node (current_pointer),*
search_condition)
    ***DEFINE** temp as pointer to node*
    ***LOOP** (while current_pointer is not NULL*
             and search_condition is not met)
        ***ASSIGN** current_pointer = pointer field of current node*

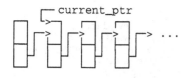

    END LOOP
    ***IF** (search_condition is met and pointer is not pointing at last node)*
    THEN
        ***ASSIGN** temp = pointer to pointer field of current node*
        (i.e., temp points to node to be deleted)
        ***ASSIGN** pointer field of current node =*
        pointer field of next node

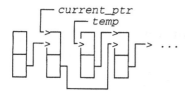

"Deassign" location to which temp points to free up space.

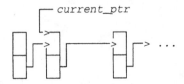

Program P-10.4 implements these algorithms. It creates a linearly linked list with 10 nodes and then displays the contents of each node. This is a "bare bones" program in which the *purpose* of the linked list is not addressed at all. Thus each node contains the bare minimum for the concept to make sense: one data field and one pointer field. We will examine each part of the program in detail.

P-10.4 [linklist.c]

```c
/* Demonstrate linked lists. */
#include <stdio.h>
#include <string.h>
struct data_type
{
  double data_field;
  struct data_type *next_ptr;
};
typedef struct data_type data_type;

data_type *create_list();
void access_list(data_type *first_ptr);
void append_end(data_type *first_ptr,data_type new_data);
void append_post(data_type *first_ptr,data_type what,
              data_type new_data,int (*compare)(data_type,data_type));
void delete_post(data_type *first_ptr,data_type what,
                int (*compare)(data_type,data_type));
int compare(data_type x,data_type y);

int main()
{
  data_type *first_ptr,new_data,what;

  first_ptr=create_list();
  access_list(first_ptr);
  new_data.data_field=9999.;
  append_end(first_ptr,new_data);
  printf("After append:\n");
  access_list(first_ptr);
  what.data_field=9999.;
  new_data.data_field=8888.;
  append_post(first_ptr,what,new_data,compare);
  printf("After insert:\n");
  access_list(first_ptr);
  what.data_field=8888.;
  delete_post(first_ptr,what,compare);
  printf("After delete:\n");
  access_list(first_ptr);
```

```c
    return 0;
}
int compare(data_type x,data_type y) {
  if (x.data_field > y.data_field)
    return 1;
  else if (x.data_field < y.data_field)
    return -1;
  else return 0;
}

void access_list(data_type *ptr)
{
  while (ptr != NULL)
  {
    printf("%lf\n",ptr->data_field);
    ptr=ptr->next_ptr;
  }
}
data_type *create_list()
{
  data_type *current_ptr, *first_ptr;
  int i;

  printf("Creating node 1\n");
  current_ptr=(data_type *)malloc(sizeof(data_type));
  current_ptr->data_field=100.0;
  current_ptr->next_ptr=NULL;
  first_ptr=current_ptr;
  for (i=2; i <= 10; i+=1)
  {
    printf("Creating node %i\n",i);
    current_ptr->next_ptr=(data_type *)malloc(sizeof(data_type));
    current_ptr=current_ptr->next_ptr;
    current_ptr->data_field=100.0*i;
    current_ptr->next_ptr=NULL;
  }
  return(first_ptr);
}
void append_end(data_type *ptr,data_type new_data) {
  while (ptr->next_ptr != NULL)
    ptr=ptr->next_ptr;
  ptr->next_ptr=(data_type *)malloc(sizeof(data_type));
  ptr=ptr->next_ptr;
  *ptr=new_data;
  ptr->next_ptr=NULL;
}
void append_post(data_type *ptr,data_type what,data_type new_data,
             int (*compare)(data_type,data_type)) {

  data_type *temp;

  while ( (ptr != NULL) && (compare(*ptr,what) != 0) )
    ptr=ptr->next_ptr;
  if (compare(*ptr,what) == 0) {
    temp=(data_type *)malloc(sizeof(data_type));
    *temp=new_data;
    temp->next_ptr=ptr->next_ptr;
    ptr->next_ptr=temp;
  }
}
```

```
void delete_post(data_type *ptr,data_type what,
                int (*compare)(data_type,data_type)) {
  data_type *temp;
  while ( (ptr != NULL) && (compare(*ptr,what) != 0) )
    ptr=ptr->next_ptr;
  if ( (ptr != NULL) && (ptr->next_ptr != NULL) ) {
    temp=ptr;
    ptr->next_ptr=ptr->next_ptr->next_ptr;
  }
}
```

Problem Discussion

First of all, P-10.4 contains some new syntax for accessing the fields in a struct through a pointer to that struct. The first instances of this syntax in access_list and create_list are printed in bold italics. In create_list, the statement

```
current_ptr->data_field=100.0;
```

is identical to the statement

```
(*current_ptr).data_field=100.0;
```

That is, current_ptr->data_field means "the contents of the data_field field in the data object to which current_ptr points." Either syntax form is acceptable, but the "->" notation is a little more compact and is preferred by many C programmers; we will use it extensively in the programs in this chapter.

Data Declarations

The data record for the nodes in P-10.4 is declared in a struct statement and consists of a numerical field that serves as a placeholder for data in a real problem, and a next-pointer field. The typedef statement allows the reference to struct data_type to be represented by the alias data_type in subsequent statements. Note, however, that the struct syntax used, which is different from what we preferred in Chapter 7, is required because the struct contains a reference to its own data type.

Function Prototypes

The create_list function requires no input in this example, but returns a pointer to the beginning of the list. Hence its declaration as

```
data_type *create_list();
```

In general, such a function needs to be data aware and, for example, would require as input the name of a file from which would come the data to be stored in the linked list.

The rest of the linked list manipulation functions are type void because they do not need to return a value.

Function main

The minimum local variable requirements for managing the list include a pointer to the head of the linked list of nodes of type data_type,

```
data_type *first_ptr;
```

and two nodes of type data_type, one containing new values to be added to a list and another containing one or more search criteria in its data fields.

Creating the List

The most critical part of the code in P-10.4 is creating the list. The implementation requires that new memory be allocated for each node as it is created. To do this, use the malloc function to allocate enough memory to store a single data node, as has been done in the statements printed in bold italics. The general syntax is

```
pointer to data_type=(data_type *)malloc(sizeof(data_type))
```

Compare this with the syntax of calloc in the previous section, which was used to allocate memory for a block of structs. As with calloc, the programmer must provide an appropriate explicit type cast for the pointer returned by malloc.

In create_list, the task of creating an entire list is divided into two parts. In the first part, the first node in the list is created using variable current_ptr. The data node is filled with a value, and the variable first_ptr is assigned the value current_ptr. Clearly, based on this example, it is okay to have more than one pointer pointing to the same node. The step of saving a pointer to the beginning of a list is critical. Without this pointer, the list will still occupy memory in heap space, but it will be useless because it can't be accessed by your program.

The second step uses a count-controlled loop to create the remaining nine nodes. If you were reading data from a file of unknown length, you would use a conditional loop instead. Inside this loop, the new node is created and assigned to the pointer field in the current node. Hence, the statement

```
current_ptr->next_ptr=(data_type *)malloc(sizeof(data_type));
```

After this assignment, the statement

```
current_ptr=current_ptr->next_ptr;
```

moves the current pointer to the new node. Finally, the statement

```
current_ptr->next_ptr=NULL;
```

terminates the list. The same statement in the code prior to the loop is merely a formality in this example, because you know ahead of time that there will be more nodes. However, it is good programming style to "terminate" every new node in a linked list as soon as you create it. If there are more nodes, then this NULL value will be overwritten with a new pointer.

In P-10.4, a single statement such as

```
current_ptr->data_field=100.0;
```

is responsible for assigning the single data field in a node. In a larger problem, such statements could be replaced with a call to a separate function.

Accessing Nodes in the List

The function access_list in P-10.4 receives as input a pointer to the beginning of the list. It then uses a conditional loop to step through the list one node at a time, looking for the node containing a NULL pointer in its next-pointer field. There is no need to define a local variable to hold the pointer, as it is passed by value to the function (that is, the function operates on a copy of the original pointer) so the value of the original pointer will be unchanged when control is returned to the calling function.

Adding and Deleting Nodes

In order to make the code for adding and deleting nodes as generic as possible, a separate function to compare data nodes is included in these functions' parameter lists. This is the same approach used to make searching and sorting code data-independent, as discussed in Chapter 8.

Because pointers in linearly linked lists always look ahead to the next node, the easiest place to add or remove a node is after the current node. This is not necessarily the best approach from a problem-solving point of view. As noted earlier, alternative approaches are left as end-of-chapter exercises.

For the purposes of appending a new node to the end of a list, the current code finds the end of the list by reading through all the existing nodes. It might be worthwhile to store a pointer to the node to the end of the list so your program can go immediately to this point. This code is left for an end-of-chapter exercise.

A minor modification of P-10.4 would be to include a so-called header node that contains no data. The header node would be created in the steps prior to the loop and would be useful if the linked list were being created from data stored in an external file. Suppose the external file is empty. You may still wish to have a linked list associated with this file, even though the list doesn't contain any data. In that case, the pointer field in the header node will be NULL and you can test for this value to determine if the list contains any real data.

Note that functions for accessing and manipulating the data fields in a linearly linked list are not aware of whether the list contains a header node. If the list includes a header node, the calling argument is the pointer field in the node to which `first_ptr` points (`first_ptr.next_ptr`) rather than `first_ptr` itself. In some cases, it may be possible to store useful information in the header node by using the existing data fields for some other purpose. For example, any integer data field could be used to store the total number of data nodes in the list.

Of course, there's nothing to prevent you from saving pointers to other nodes in the linked list so that, in principle, you can access the list from anywhere. However, you are still restricted to moving forward through the list from any starting point. One useful pointer you could save is a pointer to the last (and most recent) entry in the list. Then if you want to add a new record to the list, you can go directly to the end of the list rather than starting at the beginning and following the links through the list to the end.

It is *very* easy to become confused over the kind of code demonstrated in P-10.4. It is a good idea to write your own simple list-managing programs containing only the essentials, to serve as models for larger programming projects. Even though P-10.4 may seem complicated, it is actually very modest in its goals: to create a list, access its contents, and add or delete nodes. The actual purpose of the list is of no concern for this demonstration program, which therefore has no practical value.

10.3 Queues and Stacks

The linearly linked list has some important variants for managing different kinds of data. These data structures are defined in an abstract sense by the kinds of operations that can be performed on them.

    The first such structure we will discuss is called a *queue*. Its operation is analogous to a line (queue in British English usage) at a theater. Newcomers (new nodes) enter the line at the end farthest from the theater (the "tail" end), and people who have been waiting the longest (old nodes) get into the theater first (from the head end). That is, a queue implements a first-in/first-out data management model.

    The second structure we will discuss is called a *stack*. This is analogous to a stack of dinner plates. The old plates (old nodes) are buried at the bottom of the stack and the newest plate (newest node) added to the stack is also the first to be removed. That is, a stack implements a last-in/first-out data management model. Each of these structures must be supported by at least two basic operations: adding a node and deleting a node. These are sometimes called push and pop operations.

10.3.1 Implementing Queues

First consider a queue. Although it is linearly linked, two pointers are required because push operations happen at the opposite end of the queue from pop operations. We will call these two pointers the tail pointer and the head pointer. The head pointer is to the old end (the end at the theater door, to use that metaphor) and the tail pointer is to the new end (where arriving people join the line). The interior nodes of a queue are never available, by definition, so there is no need for code to search through all the nodes of a queue. Schematically, a queue looks like this:

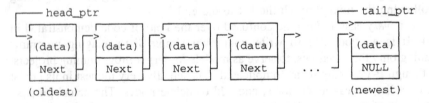

Program P-10.5 shows how to create a queue and implement push and pop operations.

P-10.5 [queue.c]

```c
/* Demonstrate queues.   QUEUE.C */
#include <stdio.h>
#include <string.h>

struct data_type{
  double data_field;
  struct data_type *next_ptr;
};
typedef struct data_type data_type;

void create_queue(data_type **head_ptr,data_type **tail_ptr);
void access_queue(data_type *head_ptr);
void push_queue(data_type **tail_ptr,data_type new_data);
void pop_queue(data_type **head_ptr);

int main(void){
  data_type *head_ptr,*tail_ptr,new_data;
  create_queue(&head_ptr,&tail_ptr);
  access_queue(head_ptr);
  new_data.data_field=9999.;
  push_queue(&tail_ptr,new_data);
  printf("After push:\n");
  access_queue(head_ptr);
  pop_queue(&head_ptr);
  printf("After pop:\n");
  access_queue(head_ptr);

  return(0);
}
void access_queue(data_type *ptr){
  while (ptr != NULL)   {
    printf("%lf\n",ptr->data_field);
    ptr=ptr->next_ptr;
  }
}
void create_queue(data_type **head_ptr,data_type **tail_ptr){
  data_type *current_ptr;
  int i;
  printf("Creating node 1\n");
  current_ptr=(data_type *)malloc(sizeof(data_type));
  current_ptr->data_field=100.0;
  current_ptr->next_ptr=NULL;
  *head_ptr=current_ptr;
  for (i=2; i <= 10; i+=1) {
    printf("Creating node %i\n",i);
    current_ptr->next_ptr=(data_type *)malloc(sizeof(data_type));

    current_ptr=current_ptr->next_ptr;
    current_ptr->data_field=100.0*i;
    current_ptr->next_ptr=NULL;
  }
  *tail_ptr=current_ptr;
}
```

```
void push_queue(data_type **tail_ptr,data_type new_data) {
    (*tail_ptr)->next_ptr=(data_type *)malloc(sizeof(data_type));
    (*tail_ptr)=(*tail_ptr)->next_ptr;
    **tail_ptr=new_data;
    (*tail_ptr)->next_ptr=NULL;
}
void pop_queue(data_type **head_ptr) {
    data_type *temp;
    temp=*head_ptr;
    (*head_ptr)=(*head_ptr)->next_ptr;
    free(temp);
}
```

Running 10.5

```
Creating node 1
Creating node 2
Creating node 3
Creating node 4
Creating node 5
Creating node 6
Creating node 7
Creating node 8
Creating node 9
Creating node 10
100.000000
200.000000
300.000000
400.000000
500.000000
600.000000
700.000000
800.000000
900.000000
1000.000000
After push:
100.000000
200.000000
300.000000
400.000000
500.000000
600.000000
700.000000
800.000000
900.000000
1000.000000
9999.000000
After pop:
200.000000
300.000000
400.000000
500.000000
600.000000
700.000000
800.000000
900.000000
1000.000000
9999.000000
```

The syntax in functions that return pointers through their parameter lists is relatively obscure, so these examples require careful study. However, the operations performed on queues are conceptually simpler than those for linearly linked lists because nodes can be added to and deleted *only* from one end or the other of the queue rather than to and from the interior of the queue; these restrictions are, in fact, what distinguish a queue from a linearly linked list. Finally, note that pop_queue will delete even the last node in a queue, leaving a pointer with a value of NULL.

A useful variant of a queue is a circularly linked queue, in which the tail of the queue is linked back to the head, rather than having a null pointer. In this way, it is easy to access both the newest and the oldest node in the queue without having to store two separate pointers. The implementation of such a data structure is left as an end-of-chapter exercise.

10.3.2 Implementing Stacks

In this special linked list, we need only a single pointer because push and pop operations both occur at the "top" of the stack. As with a queue, there is no need for code to search through a stack because, by definition, only the top node is available at any time. Thus, the code is once again conceptually simple; its implementation is left for an end-of-chapter exercise. Schematically, a stack looks like this:

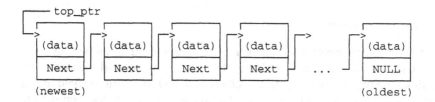

10.4 Application: Managing Data From Remote Instruments

In this application, we will apply dynamic allocation and linked lists to a problem addressed previously in Chapters 2 and 6.

1 *Define the problem.*

In Section 2.3, a programming problem was posed in which several remote instrument stations reported measurements to a central data collection facility. The reports were then assembled into a data file for processing. A station can submit multiple reports, not necessarily sequentially, and it can submit up to eight measurements in a single report. A program was presented with the limited goal of counting the number of reports and the total number of measurements. Modifications of this problem presented as Exercise 1 in Chapters 6 and 7 produced a program to keep track of the total number of reports and measurements for each station. If you did Exercise 1 in Chapter 7, your program should have used an array of structures whose index values 0 through 10 were obtained directly from the station IDs, assumed to be numbers in the range 1000 through 1010.

An additional reasonable program requirement is to save each individual report for future reference in the program. Also, we would like to remove the somewhat artificial restriction that each report can contain no more than eight measurements. The purpose of this exercise will be to write a program that will provide access to all measurements contained in the data file, by station, in the order in which the measurements were reported.

2 *Outline a solution.*

If you did Exercise 1 in Chapter 7, you should have defined an array whose elements are structures holding the station report and measurement summaries. One way to solve this new problem is to add an additional field to that structure—an array of real numbers to hold all the measurements for each station. (Remember that a structure can include an array as one of its fields.)

This approach has the advantage of making all measurements accessible in the form of a two-dimensional table provided by the array of structures. However, there is a potential disadvantage. Suppose that the number of reporting stations is large, even though most of them won't be included in any one data report. Furthermore, suppose that the number of measurements that can appear in a single report is no longer restricted to the maximum of eight as in the original problem specification, even though the typical number of measurements reported is much less than this maximum.

With statically allocated arrays, it is necessary to allocate enough memory space to hold the maximum possible amount of data even if it is likely that most of the space in the array will be wasted. Although this kind of potential inefficiency *may* have no practical consequences, it is certainly possible that the maximum space requirements for a statically allocated array will exceed the available space in your programming environment.

An alternative approach to this situation is to use linked lists, which will work whenever the total space required for data nodes does not exceed the available heap space for your C implementation. For this problem, every time a measurement is read from the data file, its station ID is noted and memory space for the measurement is allocated on the fly. We would like to implement a solution that will allow us to access all measurements through their station ID. That is, the user should be able to specify a station ID and the program should print all measurements reported from that station.

In order to meet this objective, we will use a series of linearly linked lists, one for each station ID. There will still be a statically allocated array in this solution, which will be used to manage access to the linked lists. Each element of the array of `struct`s will contain, in addition to the number of reports and total number of measurements for a station, pointers to the first and last measurements recorded for that station. Each data node includes the measurement itself and a pointer to the next measurement for that station. The last measurement reported for a station contains a NULL pointer. The linked lists are shown schematically in Figure 10.1 for the data originally given in Section 2.3 of Chapter 2.

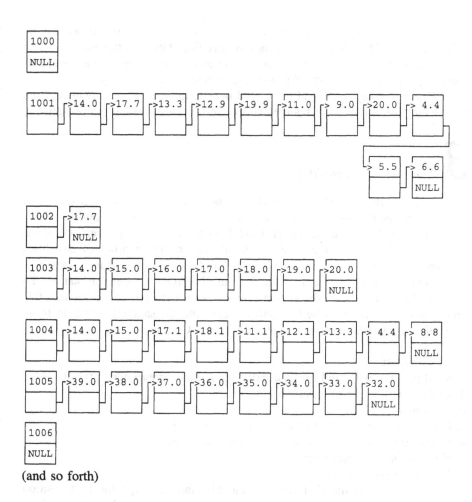

Figure 10.1. Representing station reports as a series of linearly linked lists.

In general, the advantage of maintaining a series of linearly linked lists is that memory is allocated for data storage—measurements from remote stations, in this case—only as it is needed. The advantage of this arrangement for the current problem is certainly not obvious, because space for a single measurement must now be augmented by the space required to store a pointer to the next data node. However, the advantages become more apparent if there are many data nodes and if each data node contains many pieces of information rather than just a single measurement. Then the space required for a statically allocated table of measurements in which most of the cells remain empty can quickly become excessive.

Once the data structure shown in Figure 10.1 is implemented, we will be able to access all the measurements for any specified station, in the order in which they were reported. Also, we should be able to add one or more measurements from any station as a result of processing another data file or by entering new reports from the keyboard, and we should be able to remove measurements from the list; implementing these features will be left as an end-of-chapter exercise.

3 *Design an algorithm.*

The critical part of the algorithm is the design of the loop that reads and processes measurements from the data file. We will first sketch an outline of this algorithm, which will require some careful thought (and probably several iterations with code). The array A referred to in the outline is an array of structures containing for each station the number of reports, the number of measurements, and pointers to nodes containing the first and last reports from that station. To simplify the code a little, the station IDs are defined so that the index into this array can be derived from the ID itself. For example, the station IDs start at 1000, so 1002 corresponds to an index value of 2 for a C array.

For each report:
1. Read the station ID and find the index for A that corresponds to the ID (A_{ID}).
2. Update the number of reports for A_{ID}.
Inside a loop:
3. Read the measurements in each report one at a time.
4. Update the measurement count for the station in A_{ID}.
5. If this is the first measurement in the report:
    (a) Create a new node.
    (b) If this is the first report from this station, assign the first-position pointer in A_{ID} to the new node. Otherwise, append the new node to the end of the current list, using the last-position pointer in A_{ID} as the reference.
  Otherwise,
    (a) Create a new node appended to the end of the current list, using the pointer to the current node as the reference.
    (b) Move the current pointer to point to the new node.
(end of loop)
6. After the termination of the loop that reads all measurements in a report, assign the last-position pointer field in A_{ID} to the current node.

The third step in this algorithm outline, "Read the measurements in each report one at a time," when the maximum number of measurements is unknown presents a programming challenge that we have addressed previously in program P-6.11 from an application in Chapter 6.

 Convert the algorithm into a program.

P-10.6 [station3.c]

```c
/* Read data from reporting stations. */
/* Includes individual station report summaries. */
#include <stdio.h>
#include <stdlib.h>
#define FILENAME "stations.dat"
#define N_STATIONS 11
#define MAX_REPORTS 8

struct data_type {
  float measurement;
  struct data_type *next;
};
typedef struct data_type data_type;

typedef struct {
  int reports,measurements;
  data_type *first, *last;
} summary_type;

void Initializations(summary_type A[],int n);
void StationDisplay(summary_type A[]);
void ProcessingLoop(char filename[],summary_type A[]);

int main(void)
{
/* Declare array to hold initial pointers and summary. */
  summary_type A[N_STATIONS];

  int i;

/* Initialize summary/pointer array. */
  Initializations(A,N_STATIONS);
  ProcessingLoop(FILENAME,A);
  for (i=0; i<N_STATIONS; i++)
    printf("%4i %2i %2i\n",i+1000,A[i].reports,A[i].measurements);
/* Search through array of stations. */
  StationDisplay(A);
  return 0;
}

void StationDisplay(summary_type A[])
{
  int i;
  data_type *current;

  for (i=0; i<N_STATIONS; i++)
    if (A[i].first != NULL) {
```

```
      printf("%4i ",i+1000);
      current=A[i].first;
      while (current != NULL) {
        printf("%5.1f",(*current).measurement);
        current=(*current).next;
      }
      printf("\n");
    }
}
void Initializations(summary_type A[],int n) {
  int i;

  for (i=0; i<n; i++) {
    A[i].reports=0; A[i].measurements=0.;A[i].first=NULL;
    A[i].last=NULL;
  }
}
void ProcessingLoop(char filename[],summary_type A[]) {
  FILE *in;
  int ID,status=0,n_lines=0,n_values=0,index,i,tot_values;
  double x;
  char *line_ptr;
  char one_line[80],seps[]=" \0";
  float m;
  data_type *new;

  in=fopen(FILENAME,"r");

/* Start main data processing loop. */
  tot_values=0;
  while (1) {
    line_ptr=fgets(one_line,sizeof(one_line),in);
    if (line_ptr == NULL) break;
    sscanf(line_ptr,"%i",&ID);
    line_ptr+=strspn(line_ptr,seps);
/* Update report summary fields. */
    index=ID%1000;
    A[index].reports+=1;
    n_lines++;
    n_values=0;
    while (1) {
      line_ptr+=strcspn(line_ptr,seps);
      if (*line_ptr == 0) break;
      sscanf(line_ptr,"%f",&m);
      line_ptr+=strspn(line_ptr,seps);
      A[index].measurements++;
      n_values++;
      tot_values++;
      if (n_values == 1) {
/* Allocate space for first data node. */
        new=malloc(sizeof(data_type));
        new->measurement=m;
        new->next=NULL;
/* If this is the first node for this station, assign first ptr. */
        if (A[index].first == NULL) {
          A[index].first=new;
        }
```

```
/* Otherwise, set current pointer to previous last pointer. */
      else
         A[index].last->next=new;
      }
/* Allocate more space as needed. */
      else {
      new->next=malloc(sizeof(data_type));
      new=new->next;
      new->measurement=m;
      new->next=NULL;
      }
   }
   A[index].last=new;
}
fclose(in);
printf("There are %i records and %i values.\n",
      n_lines,tot_values);

}
```

Running P-10.6

```
There are 7 records and 36 values.
1000  0  0
1001  2 11
1002  1  1
1003  1  7
1004  2  9
1005  1  8
1006  0  0
1007  0  0
1008  0  0
1009  0  0
1010  0  0
1001  14.0 17.7 13.3 12.9 19.9 11.0  9.0 20.0  4.4  5.5  6.6
1002  17.7
1003  14.0 15.0 16.0 17.0 18.0 19.0 20.0
1004  14.0 15.0 17.1 18.1 11.1 12.1 13.3  4.4  8.9
1005  39.0 38.0 37.0 36.0 35.0 34.0 33.0 32.0
```

5 *Verify the operation of the program.*

It is easy to write linked list code that doesn't work, and such code can be very difficult to debug. However, if P-10.6 correctly associates each of the measurements in the stations.dat file with the proper station, which can be verified by comparing the output against the contents of the file, it is reasonable to assume that the program will work for larger files, as well.

10.5 Exercises

1. Complete the problem discussed in Section 10.1.2, for which Program P-10.1 is a partial solution. That is, modify this program so that it sorts the records by measurement, from smallest to largest. Do *not* store the data in an array. To solve this problem, you can use the sorting algorithms discussed in Chapter 8, but you will have to modify the implementation of those algorithms to read and write records in a file rather than accessing elements of an array of records.

2. Modify the `create_list` function in P-10.4 so that it returns two pointers—one to the beginning of the list and one to the end. Then modify `append_list` so that its input/output parameter is a pointer to the end of the list rather than one to the beginning. This will make append operations more efficient because you will no longer need to search through the list from the beginning in order to append a new node.

   Remember that C passes output through a parameter list by referencing a pointer to the output quantity. In order to pass a pointer as output, the parameter list must include a pointer to a pointer. The new function prototype should look like this:

```
data_type *create_list(data_type **last_ptr);
```

with two levels of indirection indicated by the double asterisk. [`linklis2.c`]

3. Add a function to P-10.4 that will enable the program to delete a specified node in a linearly linked list rather than the node after a specified node. [`linklis2.c`]

4. Add a function to P-10.4 that will enable the program to insert a new node prior to a specified node in a linearly linked list rather than after a specified node. [`linklis2.c`]

5. Write a program similar to P-10.5 that implements stack operations as defined in Section 10.3.2. [`stack.c`]

6. Write a program that implements a doubly linked list. Such a data structure contains two pointer fields, one pointing to the left and one to the right. With such a structure, you must save two nodes, one each for the left and right ends of the list. You should be able to append/delete a node to/from either end of the list, search in either direction for a node in the list, and insert and delete nodes inside the list. [`dbl_link.c`]

7. Implement algorithms for a circularly linked queue as discussed briefly in Section 10.3.1 and as shown schematically in the sketch below. Your program should implement functions to add new nodes and remove old ones. In addition, your program should set the maximum number of nodes in the queue. That is, the queue should be thought of as defining a holding area (a buffer) of fixed size. When the buffer is full, a new node should replace the oldest node in the queue. This data management model is often used in dataloggers, for example.

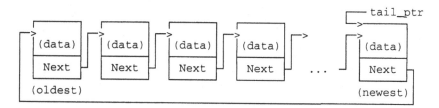

8. Recalling the station measurement problem, write a program that works like P-10.6, but which permanently stores the results in output files. Your program should produce one text file that stores the array created in P-10.6 and one binary file that stores the linked lists created when the program executes. In this case, however, the pointer fields are replaced with record indices in a binary file.

The advantage of this approach is that, unlike the linked lists that exist only while the program is executing, the binary file provides a permanent record of station measurements stored in a particular way. Suppose that tomorrow you wish to add some new reports. With the linked list approach, you must start all over again and create linked lists with all the original reports before you can add the new reports. With a file-based approach, you can open the previously created file and append new measurements.

Extra Credit:

Modify your program so it will append data from new reports to an existing set of files. [stationf.c]

Appendix 1: Table of ASCII Characters for Windows/DOS-Based PCs

Dec	Hex		Dec	Hex		Dec	Hex		Dec	Hex	
0	0		32	20		64	40	@	96	60	`
1	1	☺	33	21	!	65	41	A	97	61	a
2	2	●	34	22	"	66	42	B	98	62	b
3	3	♥	35	23	#	67	43	C	99	63	c
4	4	♦	36	24	$	68	44	D	100	64	d
5	5	♣	37	25	%	69	45	E	101	65	e
6	6	♠	38	26	&	70	46	F	102	66	f
7	7	•	39	27	'	71	47	G	103	67	g
8	8	◘	40	28	(	72	48	H	104	68	h
9	9	○	41	29	)	73	49	I	105	69	i
10	A	◙	42	2A	*	74	4A	J	106	6A	j
11	B	♂	43	2B	+	75	4B	K	107	6B	k
12	C	♀	44	2C	,	76	4C	L	108	6C	l
13	D	♪	45	2D	-	77	4D	M	109	6D	m
14	E	♫	46	2E	.	78	4E	N	110	6E	n
15	F	☼	47	2F	/	79	4F	O	111	6F	o
16	10	►	48	30	0	80	50	P	112	70	p
17	11	◄	49	31	1	81	51	Q	113	71	q
18	12	↕	50	32	2	82	52	R	114	72	r
19	13	‼	51	33	3	83	53	S	115	73	s
20	14	¶	52	34	4	84	54	T	116	74	t
21	15	§	53	35	5	85	55	U	117	75	u
22	16	▬	54	36	6	86	56	V	118	76	v
23	17	↨	55	37	7	87	57	W	119	77	w
24	18	↑	56	38	8	88	58	X	120	78	x
25	19	↓	57	39	9	89	59	Y	121	79	y
26	1A	→	58	3A	:	90	5A	Z	122	7A	z
27	1B	←	59	3B	;	91	5B	[	123	7B	{
28	1C	∟	60	3C	<	92	5C	\	124	7C	|
29	1D	↔	61	3D	=	93	5D	]	125	7D	}
30	1E	▲	62	3E	>	94	5E	^	126	7E	~
31	1F	▼	63	3F	?	95	5F	_	127	7F	△

Dec	Hex		Dec	Hex		Dec	Hex		Dec	Hex	
128	80	Ç	160	A0	á	192	C0	└	224	E0	α
129	81	ü	161	A1	í	193	C1	┴	225	E1	ß
130	82	é	162	A2	ó	194	C2	┬	226	E2	Γ
131	83	â	163	A3	ú	195	C3	├	227	E3	π
132	84	ä	164	A4	ñ	196	C4	─	228	E4	Σ
133	85	à	165	A5	Ñ	197	C5	┼	229	E5	σ
134	86	å	166	A6	ª	198	C6	╞	230	E6	μ
135	87	ç	167	A7	º	199	C7	╟	231	E7	τ
136	88	ê	168	A8	¿	200	C8	╚	232	E8	Φ
137	89	ë	169	A9	⌐	201	C9	╔	233	E9	θ
138	8A	è	170	AA	¬	202	CA	╩	234	EA	Ω
139	8B	ï	171	AB	½	203	CB	╦	235	EB	δ
140	8C	î	172	AC	¼	204	CC	╠	236	EC	∞
141	8D	ì	173	AD	¡	205	CD	=	237	ED	φ
142	8E	Ä	174	AE	«	206	CE	╬	238	EE	ε
143	8F	Å	175	AF	»	207	CF	╧	239	EF	∩
144	90	É	176	B0	░	208	D0	╨	240	F0	≡
145	91	æ	177	B1	▓	209	D1	╤	241	F1	±
146	92	Æ	178	B2	█	210	D2	╥	242	F2	≥
147	93	ô	179	B3	│	211	D3	╙	243	F3	≤
148	94	ö	180	B4	┤	212	D4	╘	244	F4	⌠
149	95	ò	181	B5	╡	213	D5	╒	245	F5	⌡
150	96	û	182	B6	╢	214	D6	╓	246	F6	÷
151	97	ù	183	B7	╖	215	D7	╫	247	F7	≈
152	98	ij	184	B8	╕	216	D8	╪	248	F8	°
153	99	Ö	185	B9	╣	217	D9	┘	249	F9	·
154	9A	Ü	186	BA	║	218	DA	┌	250	FA	˙
155	9B	¢	187	BB	╗	219	DB	█	251	FB	√
156	9C	£	188	BC	╝	220	DC	▄	252	FC	ⁿ
157	9D	¥	189	BD	╜	221	DD	▌	253	FD	²
158	9E	Pt	190	BE	╛	222	DE	▐	254	FE	■
159	9F	ƒ	191	BF	┐	223	DF	▀	255	FF	

Note: 0 is a null character, 32 is a space, obtained by pressing the space bar, and 255 is a blank.

Appendix 2: Program Listings by Chapter

This appendix lists every complete program appearing in the text, along with the names of data files if required. Program numbers marked with an asterisk are found in the Applications section of the chapter. The source code and data files for all listed programs are available on the Web site given in Section 6 of the Preface.

Chapter 1
(There are no programs in this chapter except for the "Hello, world!" program to type in for practice in using your computer system's C programming environment.)

Chapter 2

2.1	hello.c	Using the printf function
2.2	circle.c	Calculate area and circumference of a circle
2.3	oct.c	Demonstrate difference between %i and %d conversion specifiers
2.4	circle_f.c	Getting data from an external file (circle.dat)
2.5	filetest.c	Reading external data file using fscanf (structur.dat)
2.6	filetes2.c	Reading external data file using fgets and sscanf (structur.dat)
2.7	filetes3.c	Reading external data file with strings and numbers (structr2.dat)
2.8	stations.c	Reading external data file when each line contains a different number of values (stations.dat)
2.9	fileview.c	Reading external data file one character at a time (user-supplied file)
2.10*	beam.c	Deflection of a supported beam under a central load (beam.dat)
2.11*	rel_mass.c	Speed and relativistic mass of an accelerated electron (rel_mass.dat)

Data files for exercises: weather.96, track.dat.

Chapter 3

3.1	ranges.c	Information about range and precision of C data types
3.2	operator.c	Demonstrate use of various C operators
3.3	test_avg.c	Demonstrate effect of explicit type casting
3.4	math.c	Demonstrate various C intrinsic math functions
3.5	circlep1.c	Create simple user-defined functions with prototype
3.6	circlep2.c	Create simple user-defined functions without prototype

Chapter 9

Chapter 10

Appendix 3: Glossary

Term	Ch.	Definition
algorithm	1	A step-by-step solution to a computing problem.
alias	7	An alternate name for a data type in C.
ANSI-standard C	1	The standard that defines the language syntax and structure that all compliant C compilers must support.
arithmetic mean	9	The sum of n items divided by n.
argument list	3	A list of one or more values, variables, or expressions passed to a function when it is called. (See parameter list.)
arithmetic overflow	3	A condition in which a calculation that a program is asked to perform involves numbers larger than the program can support.
array	6	A data object that provides access to a number of related values through one or more indices.
array boundary violation	6	A condition, not tested by C during compilation or execution, in which a program attempts to access an array element that does not exist based on the declaration of that array.
array element	6	One value in an array, accessed through an array index.
array index	6	The integer value that identifies a particular array element. Multidimensional arrays require more than one index to identify an element.
ASCII character collating sequence	2	A code for representing characters, as defined by the American Standard Code for Information Exchange.
assignment statement	2	A statement that results in the value of an expression on the right side of an = sign being assigned to a variable on the left side of an = sign.
backsubstitution	9	A process of calculating roots starting from the last row in an upper triangular matrix.
batch mode	2	A program mode in which a program completes its task without human intervention during the time program is executing. (In contrast, see interactive mode.)
batch program	2	A program that runs in batch mode.
big O notation	8	A symbolic way to describe the dependence of a searching or sorting operation on the number of items to be searched or sorted.

Term	Ch.	Definition
binary file	1	Any file whose contents are not representations of characters.
binary format	10	A means of storing information that does not use character representations of numbers. (See binary file.)
binary operator	3	An operator that requires two operands, one appearing on the left of the operator and the other on the right. (In contrast, see unary operator.)
binary search	8	An algorithm that searches for an item in an ordered list by continuously dividing the list into partitions, ideally of equal size, one of which may contain the desired value and the other of which cannot contain that value.
boolean data type	3	A representation for variables that are restricted to the values true and false.
bug	2	A mistake in a computer program. (See debugging.)
calling argument	3	A value, variable, or expression passed to a function when it is called.
command-line interface	5	A text-based interface that allows a user to execute a program by typing commands at the keyboard.
compile	1	The conversion of source code into an executable program.
compile-time error	2	An error, usually a syntax error, that is detected during the compilation process. (In contrast, see run-time error.)
compiler	1	A program that converts source code into machine-level instruction.
component access operator	7	In C, the dot operator that gives a program access to a field defined in a struct.
conditional loop	4	A repetition (loop) structure in which the number of repetitions is determined while the loop is executing.
control character	2	Any of several characters that can be included as part of a character string or as part of the output format string associated with an output function such as printf. These characters provide access to such nonprintable characters as tab (\t)or new line (\n).
control structure	1	A program statement or statements defining or modifying the order in which other program statements are executed.

Term	Ch.	Definition
conversion specifier	2	A character string that tells C how an input function should interpret characters typed at the keyboard or read from an external text file.
correlation coefficient	9	A dimensionless value between 0 and 1 that is a measure of how well a regression line represents data.
count-controlled loop	4	A repetition (loop) structure in which the number of repetitions is specified prior to the start of the loop.
data abstraction	8	An approach to manipulating information in which the allowed operations on the data are defined independently of the nature of the data.
data-aware function	8	A function that operates on data objects of a specified data type, as opposed to a function that operates on a generic data type such as an array whose contents are specified elsewhere.
data declaration statement	2	A statement that associates variable names with a specific data type.
data field	7	A defined member of a `struct`.
data member	7	See data field.
data node	10	One in a group of data entities created with, for example, `malloc`, in which the relationship among entities is maintained through the use of pointers to one or more other entities of the same type.
data object	6	An abstract structure for manipulating information in which certain operations can be defined regardless of the nature of the information.
data type	1	Any of several representations, intrinsic or user-defined, for information used by a program.
debugging	2	The process of looking for and correcting errors (bugs) in a computer program.
dereferencing	5	Referring to the memory location to which a pointer points.
dereferencing operator	5	One use for the * symbol, which allows a program to reference the memory location to which a pointer points.
dimension	6	The storage space represented by one set of brackets in a C array declaration. Arrays can have more than one dimension.
discretization error	9	A typically cumulative error resulting from the fact that real number arithmetic is only an approximation.
dot operator	7	See component access operator.
doubly linked list	10	A series of data nodes in which pointers are maintained to both the next and previous node.

Term	Ch.	Definition
downward type cast	3	The process in which the value associated with an intrinsic data type is assigned to a variable of a lower data type, for example, float to integer, with a possible loss of information. (In contrast, see upward type cast.)
dynamic allocation	10	The process of allocating memory space while a program is executing, for example, with malloc. (In contrast, see static allocation.)
end-of-file (eof) mark	2	One or more characters that mark the end of a file and which can be detected by a program.
end-of-line (eol) mark	2	One or more characters that mark the end of a line in a text file and which can be detected by a program.
executable program file	1	A binary file containing instructions that can be interpreted and executed directly by a computer.
explicit type cast	3	An upward or downward type cast written explicitly into the source code. (In contrast, see implicit type cast.)
extent	6	The number of elements along a particular array dimension.
external data file	2	A file accessed by a program while it is executing.
file pointer	10	A pointer that keeps track of which location in a file is immediately accessible to a program.
floating-point number	2	A number that can include a decimal part, as opposed to an integer number.
format specifier	2	A character string that tells C how to display values as a result of calling an output function such as printf.
function	2	A C subprogram that, given appropriate input values, performs specified calculations and returns one or more specified values.
function implementation	3	The code that implements the calculations that a function is expected to perform.
function prototype	3	The code that defines the information interface for a function, specifically its input and output.
global constant	2	A constant value defined previous to the main function so that it is available to all functions in a program.
header file	2	A file that contains one or more function prototypes.
heap space	10	A part of computer memory that can be accessed by dynamic allocation functions such as malloc. (In contrast, see stack space.)

Term	Ch.	Definition
implicit type cast	3	An upward or downward type cast that takes place because of discrepancies between data types appearing to the left and right of an assignment operator. (In contrast, see implicit type cast.)
indirection operator	5	An operator that accesses the contents of the memory location to which a pointer points.
infinite loop	4	An unterminated count-controlled or conditional loop.
input stream	2	A series of bytes that can be interpreted as numerical and other values by a C program.
interactive mode	2	A program mode in which a user must provide input values while the program is executing, typically through the keyboard. (In contrast, see batch mode.)
interactive program	2	A program running in interactive mode.
internal read	2	A process in which a C program can extract values from a stored character string.
intrinsic function	1	Any of several functions for performing I/O, numerical, and other calculations that are supported by the C language standard. (In contrast, see user-defined function.)
language extension	1	A language feature that is supported by a particular C implementation but which is not supported by the ANSI C standard.
linear regression line	9	A statistically derived best fit line through a collection of data.
linear search	8	A searching algorithm that examines each item in a list, starting typically at the beginning of the list.
linearly linked list	10	A series of data nodes in which a pointer is maintained to the next node in the list.
link	1	The process whereby a compiled program is associated with previously compiled program elements, such as I/O and math libraries, which are required for the program to execute.
linked list	10	A series of data nodes in which one or more pointers maintain a relationship between nodes in the list. (See doubly linked list and linearly linked list.)
list	8	An abstract entity on which certain operations such as searching and sorting can be performed. An array is one example of a list implementation.
logical data type	3	See boolean data type.

Term	Ch.	Definition
loop counter	4	A value that keeps track of the number of times statements in a loop have been executed. As a matter of good programming style, loop counters in C should be integers.
loop structure	2	statements that provide the capability to execute one or more statements more than once.
machine language	1	The native language in which computer instructions are written, as opposed to a high-level language such as C.
main program	2	The group of statements that maintain overall control of the execution of a program, which typically includes several subprograms. In C, the main program is implemented as the `main` function.
member access operator	7	See component access operator.
modulus operator	3	The arithmetic operator (%) that returns the remainder from the division of two integers.
nonstandard function	1	A function supported by a particular implementation of C that is not supported by the ANSI C standard.
$O(\log_2 N)$ algorithm	8	An algorithm for which the number of operations to be performed on a list of size N is proportional to $\log_2 N$.
$O(N)$ algorithm	8	An algorithm for which the number of operations to be performed on a list of size N is directly proportional to N.
$O(N^2)$ algorithm	8	An algorithm for which the number of operations to be performed on a list of size N is proportional to N^2.
$O(N\log_2 N)$ algorithm	8	An algorithm for which the number of operations to be performed on a list of size N is proportional to $N\log_2 N$.
object code	5	Compiled source code before it is linked with other files to create an executable program.
operator	1	A symbol that is used to perform arithmetic, logical, and relational operations on one or more values.
operator precedence rules	3	The rules governing the order in which operators appearing in a statement are executed.
parallel arrays	6	Two or more arrays containing related information such that an element of one array is associated with the same element in the other arrays.
parameter list	3	A list of type-declared placeholders for variables appearing in a function prototype or implementation. (See argument list.)
partition	8	A subdivision of a list.

Term	Ch.	Definition
pass-by-reference	5	A means of passing information to a subprogram whereby the subprogram has direct access to the memory location(s) occupied by a calling argument.
pass-by-value	5	A means of passing information to a subprogram whereby the subprogram has access only to a copy of the contents of the memory location(s) occupied by a calling argument.
pivot value	8	The value used to separate a list into two partitions.
pointer	2	A variable whose value is an address in memory.
postfix operator	3	An increment/decrement operator in which the operator's action is applied to a variable after the variable is used in the expression.
post-test loop	4	A conditional loop in which the decision to terminate or continue the loop is made at the end of the loop rather than at the beginning.
prefix operator	3	An increment/decrement operator in which the operator's action is applied to a variable before the variable is used in the expression.
preprocessor directive	2	An instruction in source code to be carried out by a compiler prior to the actual compilation step.
pre-test loop	4	A conditional loop in which the decision to terminate or continue the loop is made at the beginning of the loop rather than at the end.
procedural language	1	Any programming language that supports procedural programming.
procedural programming	1	An approach to programming in which large tasks are subdivided into several smaller tasks and solutions to computing problems are implemented as a series of algorithms applied to user-supplied information.
pseudocode	1	A means of writing algorithms using generic representations of statements in a real programming language.
pseudocode command	1	A generic command that can be represented with real commands in a procedural language.
pseudorandom numbers	4	Algorithmically generated numbers that appear to be random and which therefore can be assumed to be random for a particular application.
queue	10	A linked list characterized by operations at the head and tail of the list. (In contrast, see stack.)
random number generator	4	An algorithm that generates pseudorandom numbers.

Term	Ch.	Definition
rank	6	The number of dimensions in an array.
recursive algorithm	5	An algorithm that calls itself.
run-time error	2	An error that occurs when a program is executing. (In contrast, see compile-time error.)
scalar data	6	Unrelated values, each of which is represented by a distinct variable name. (In contrast, see vector data.)
searching algorithm	8	An algorithm whose function is to locate one or more items in a list.
shape	6	An array property defined by its size and extent.
sorting algorithm	8	An algorithm whose function is to rearrange items in a list so they are in ascending or descending order.
source code file	1	A text file containing instructions written according to the syntax rules of a particular language.
stack	10	A linked list characterized by operations taking place only at the top of the list. (In contrast, see queue.)
stack space	10	A portion of computer memory available for declaring variables, including statically declared arrays. (In contrast, see heap space.)
standard deviation	9	A statistical measure of the variability of values in a collection of values. The square root of the variance.
standard error of estimate	9	A statistical measure of the extent to which a model represents values in a collection of data.
standard input/output (I/O) functions	2	Intrinsic functions that manage I/O operations in C.
static allocation	6	Allocation of memory space that cannot be changed while a program is executing. (In contrast, see dynamic allocation.)
strongly typed language	1	A language, such as C, that requires a programmer to provide explicit data types for every variable.
sum of squares of the residual	9	Typically, the sum of the squares of the differences between all individual values in a list minus the mean of all values in the list.
syntax error	2	An error that arises from violation of the syntax rules for a programming language.
syntax rules	2	The set of rules that determine how statements can be written in a programming language.
truth table	3	A table that specifies the outcome (true or false) of evaluating two logical expressions joined by a relational operator.

Term	Ch.	Definition
type casting	3	The act of reassigning a data type explicitly or implicitly as a result of executing an assignment statement that contains different data types on either side of the assignment operator.
unary operator	3	An operator that requires a single operand, appearing to the right of the operator.
UNIX	1	A popular operator system having an especially close association with the C language.
upper triangular matrix	9	A matrix in which all values below the left-to-right, top-to-bottom diagonal are zero.
upward type cast	3	An explicit or implicit type cast in which a value is promoted to a data type that can contain more information than the original data type; for example, `int` to `float`. (In contrast, see downward type cast.
user-defined function	3	A function whose prototype and implementation are provided by a programmer for use in a specific program or included in a programmer-written library. (In contrast, see intrinsic function.)
variable	1	A unit of information represented by a specified data type.
variable name	1	The symbolic name by which a variable is known within the source code for a program.
variance	9	See standard deviation.
vector data	6	Related values organized within a user-supplied data structure, typically an array. (In contrast, see scalar data.)

Index

All intrinsic functions are indexed under "functions." Conversion and format specifiers are listed under "specifiers" and are not individually indexed. Page references to glossary definitions are not indexed.